CARRY ME BACK

CARRY ME BACK

THE DOMESTIC SLAVE TRADE
IN AMERICAN LIFE

STEVEN DEYLE

OXFORD
UNIVERSITY PRESS

2005

OXFORD
UNIVERSITY PRESS

Oxford University Press, Inc., publishes works that further
Oxford University's objective of excellence
in research, scholarship, and education.

Oxford   New York
Auckland   Cape Town   Dar es Salaam   Hong Kong   Karachi
Kuala Lumpur   Madrid   Melbourne   Mexico City   Nairobi
New Delhi   Shanghai   Taipei   Toronto

With offices in
Argentina   Austria   Brazil   Chile   Czech Republic   France   Greece
Guatemala   Hungary   Italy   Japan   Poland   Portugal   Singapore
South Korea   Switzerland   Thailand   Turkey   Ukraine   Vietnam

Published by Oxford University Press, Inc.
198 Madison Avenue, New York, New York 10016

www.oup.com

Oxford is a registered trademark of Oxford University Press

Library of Congress Cataloging-in-Publication Data
Deyle, Steven.
Carry me back : the domestic slave trade in American life / Steven Deyle.
p. cm.
Includes bibliographical references and index.
ISBN-13 978-0-19-516040-6
ISBN 0-19-516040-1
1. Slavery—United States—History—19th century.
2. Slaves—United States—Social conditions—19th century. 3. Slave trade—
United States—History—19th century. 4. United States—Race relations. 5. United States—
Economic conditions—19th century. 6. Slave trade—Southern States—History—
19th century. 7. Southern States—Race relations. 8. Southern States—
Economic conditions—19th century. I. Title.
E449.D525 2005
381'.44'0973—dc22   2004056840

1 3 5 7 9 8 6 4 2

Printed in the United States of America
on acid-free paper

FOR MY PARENTS

CARRY ME BACK
TO OLD VIRGINNY
by James Bland
(1878)

Carry me back to old Virginny,
There's where the cotton and the corn and tatoes grow,
There's where the birds warble sweet in the springtime,
There's where this old darkey's heart am long'd to go,
There's where I labored so hard for old massa,
Day after day in the field of yellow corn,
No place on earth do I love more sincerely,
Than old Virginny, the state where I was born.

ACKNOWLEDGMENTS

A ny project that has been in the works as long as this one has far too many people to thank than can ever be fully expressed in a short acknowledgment like this. Still, a number of people do deserve special mention. This book began many years ago as a dissertation under the direction of Eric Foner at Columbia University. First and foremost, then, thanks need to be given to him for the excellent guidance that he has provided in encouraging and shaping this project. Only those of us who have had the privilege of working with him know how valuable his assistance can be. Thanks also to the late Jim Shenton and Eric McKitrick for their constructive criticisms of my work and to Alden Vaughan for his help in shaping my views on early American ideas about race.

I have also received incredible encouragement and support from several of my colleagues at Columbia. Most important are the debt and gratitude that I owe to Randy Bergstrom and David Mattern. Over the years, from our first seminar together to the present day, they have been consistent rocks of support and two of my closest friends. The same has proven true of Doron Ben-Atar, whose love of American history has been a real inspiration to me, and Tom Pearson, who offered me a place to stay on numerous trips to Boston. John Recchiuti has often believed more strongly in my work than I have, and Cheryl Greenberg provided important assistance in the early stages of this project. Bernadette McCauley has also become a good friend, and I thank her for allowing me to stay at her wonderful apartment in New York. Tim Gilfoyle and Cliff Hood likewise both deserve special thanks.

As with the publication of any book, numerous individuals have played major roles in bringing this project to fruition. The number of helpful archivists I've encountered are far too numerous to mention by name. Suffice it to say that their assistance has made my research on this book much more productive and enjoyable. Jon Pritchett not only shared his own research with me, but he also introduced me to several of the lesser known (and always wonderful) restaurants in New Orleans. Doug Egerton has likewise been a long-time supporter, and my work has benefited from his helpful suggestions. Over the past decade, one of my great pleasures has been participating in the Bay Area Seminar in Early American History and Culture. Special thanks to Dee Andrews and the late Jackie Reinier. Susan Ferber at Oxford University Press has been the best editor that a writer could want, and she has come to my aid in more ways than she could have ever imagined when she agreed to take on this project.

Over the years, I have also received much support from the University of California, Davis. I am especially grateful for all of the financial aid I have received for my research. The Davis Humanities Institute also provided financial support and generously allowed me to share my ideas in its seminar on premodern worlds. Steve Oerding at IET Mediaworks likewise deserves thanks for being such a wizard at compiling the visual images in this book. Most rewarding, however, have been all of my interactions with the students at UCD, both at the undergraduate and graduate levels. Little did they realize how many of my arguments were worked out in our seminars, "Slavery and the Old South" and "Slavery and American Society." I would especially like to thank all of the student research assistants who have worked on this project: R'lyeh Schanning, Kate Winchester, Kate Folker, Joe Alioto, Nicole Jones, Brady Price, Joe Sullivan, Mary Zahuta, Amy Takeuchi, and Renée Pyles. Courtney Goen provided valuable research assistance, and I also hope she realizes how much I have appreciated her encouragement and support over the years. Seth Rockman generously shared his own research and helped me to find my way through the various Maryland archives.

No writer could survive without the support of a warm network of friends. Foremost among these for me has been my companion, Betty Dessants. In addition to reading every word of this manuscript more times than she cares to remember, Betty has been my main pillar of support. Words can never express all of the gratitude I feel for having her play such an important part in my life. Another mainstay has been Bruce Berg. He is a true scholar, gentleman, and friend. Bill Carlson and Janet Morken have also been long-time friends and providers of aid in ways that they have probably never imagined. Thanks also to several other important people who have all provided support in their own way: Anne Bogert, Ross Stearn, the late Harold Abrahamsen, Jana Albert, Karen Dannewitz, Laurel Schmidt, Tara Kissane, and Bob and Gene Berkhofer. HCB and the BBC likewise played an important role in shaping my views today.

Finally, I would like to thank my parents, Henry and Shirley Deyle, as well as Gabe, Meghan, Janna, Rachel, Karissa, Daniel, Sarah, and especially Buddy. While they never read a word of this manuscript, nor even really understood what it is that I do, their presence in my life has made the writing of this book all the more enjoyable.

CONTENTS

CARRY ME BACK

Introduction

While on a tour of the United States in 1841, British abolitionist Joseph Sturge visited Hope Slatter, a slave trader in Baltimore. Like many foreigners, and most abolitionists, Sturge believed that he knew what type of man would become involved in the American slave trade, and in part, he was making the trip to lecture Slatter on the error of his ways. Ironically, it was the abolitionist who received the education that day. While the experience clearly distressed him, Sturge found the slave trader to be nothing like the monster he had imagined, and he walked away with a greater understanding of both the American slave trade and the institution of southern slavery. In a letter he wrote to Slatter following the visit, Sturge confided that their conversation had helped him to "realize the true nature of the system of slavery." He agreed with the slave trader that the man's "business was necessary to the system of slavery, and an essential part of it—and if slave-*holding* were to be justified at all, the slave-*trade* must be also." Furthermore, the visit had convinced Sturge that there was no moral distinction between a slave owner and a slave trader. Although he still disliked Slatter's occupation, Sturge concluded by saying that he felt "nothing but kindness and good will towards *thyself*."[1]

This British abolitionist's letter to a southern slave trader illustrates some of the misconceptions that most people have had over the years about the domestic slave trade and its place in American society. It reminds us of how essential the internal market in human commodities was for the smooth running of the southern slave system, and how the institution could not have survived without it. Moreover, as Joseph Sturge found out, a closer examination of the realities of that trade, and of the men who ran it, challenges many of our myths and stereotypes about this traffic in humans.

This is a study of the domestic slave trade, the buying and selling of American-born slaves, both informally and as an organized business. It is based on the belief that by exploring one aspect of the southern slave system, we can gain a greater understanding of not only the antebellum South but also of American society as a whole. In addition to broadening our knowledge of the day-to-day realities of chattel slavery, such a study helps us to comprehend the "true nature" of that system and what it meant to all involved. More important, it can help to explain many of the events that shaped the young nation, as well as shed new light on the central questions that the institution of slavery has raised for American society, from the first years of the republic down to the present.

In many respects, the story of the domestic slave trade is also the story of the early United States, and it is quite difficult to understand the growth of the latter without appreciating the significance of the former. While the buying and selling of human slaves had always been a part of American society, the nature of this traffic changed over time. In the seventeenth and eighteenth centuries, most slaves sold in British North America were imported from Africa or the West Indies, although by the mid-eighteenth century a small, locally based domestic trade had also developed. Following the American Revolution, this changed. The slave trade became an indigenous operation, annually transporting thousands of enslaved men and women from the Upper South to the Lower South and transferring an even greater number locally from one owner to another.[2] Some of the reasons for this transformation were ironic outgrowths of the Revolution itself, such as the closing of the African slave trade in 1808. Others, like the invention of the cotton gin in the 1790s, simply coincided with these events. What is important is that the emergence of this new trade went hand in hand with the birth of American liberty.[3]

The impact that this new traffic in human commodities had upon the southern states and on the early American economy cannot be overemphasized. For one thing, the magnitude of this trade made it a common form of commerce. Between 1790 and 1860, Americans transported from the Upper South to the Lower South more than 1 million African-American slaves, approximately two-thirds of whom arrived there as a result of sale. Twice as many individuals were sold locally. During this period, slave sales occurred in every southern city and village, and "coffles" of slaves (gangs held together in chains) could be found on every southern highway, waterway, and railroad. The domestic slave trade, in all of its components, was very much the lifeblood of the southern slave system, and without it, the institution would have ceased to exist.[4]

This important new trade proved essential for the creation of the Cotton Kingdom. Primarily, it transferred slave labor from those parts of the South where there was deemed to be "excess" to those areas where slaves were most in demand. Changes in agricultural production during the mid-eighteenth century meant that most southern slave owners, especially those in the Chesapeake, found themselves with a surplus of human property.[5] Not only did this lead to a drop in slave prices, but following the Revolution, it also made many in the Upper South question the future of the institution of slavery itself. By the early nineteenth century, this changed with the explosion in the international demand for cotton. As more and more land was opened up or turned over to the production of cotton, an almost insatiable demand for slaves developed in the new cotton states of the Old Southwest.[6] And, because the nation had closed off all outside sources of supply in 1808, this demand could only be met through a redistribution of the existing slave population. Recognizing that planters in the new cotton states were willing to pay hundreds of dollars more per slave than were owners in the older states, thousands of southern speculators transported hundreds of thousands of bondspeople from the Upper South and seaboard states to the markets of the Southwest.

In addition to fueling southern expansion, the domestic trade also solidified the region's commitment to the institution of chattel slavery. Because the demand for slaves was always greater in the Lower South than elsewhere, planters there drove up the price of slaves throughout the South. In other words, the market value of a slave in a place like Richmond was no longer dependent upon local demand, but upon what someone in New Orleans was willing to pay. While this rise in slave prices made it increasingly difficult for those who wished to purchase, it played a crucial role in the economy of the Upper South. What was formerly seen by those in Virginia, for example, as excess property now became a major source of capital that could be mortgaged to produce even more wealth. And it also became the Upper South's most infamous export. By linking the South's two main subregions in a common economic concern, the interregional trade raised the value of slave property for everyone who owned it and put to rest any doubts that white southerners in the Upper South may have had about the future of the institution. Even more important, it turned slave property into one of the most valuable forms of investment in the country, second only to land. This form of property became so valuable that, when threatened with its ultimate elimination in 1860, southern slave owners saw little alternative but to leave the Union.[7]

There were elements within the domestic trade itself that also led most slave-owning southerners to believe that they had to secede. Most troubling was the effect that the interregional trade had on escalating tensions among the various subregions within the South. While problems between the Upper South and Lower South had always been present, they neared the breaking point in the 1850s as the price of slaves soared to record highs. Elevated prices benefited all who held this type of property, but they also resulted in record sales and record numbers of slaves transported to the Lower South. This led many in the Deep South to wonder how the dwindling percentage of slaves in the border states would affect those states' commitment to the institution of slavery. In their eyes, places like Maryland and parts of Virginia looked increasingly like

Pennsylvania or Ohio, and less and less like Mississippi or Louisiana. While it seemed unlikely that the future of slavery was in any great danger of disappearing in the Upper South without the intervention of war, the intrasectional tensions caused by the interregional trade did contribute to the heightened sense of anxiety that characterized the South (especially the Deep South) in the late antebellum years that ultimately led to secession and to war. Because of their dependence on the export of slaves, Upper South states like Virginia realized that they too had little choice but to secede with their trading partners in the Deep South. Therefore, not only was the domestic slave trade responsible for the creation of the Cotton Kingdom and for bringing it great wealth, but in many respects, it also contributed to its eventual demise.

In addition to playing a leading role in bringing the nation to civil war, the emergence of the domestic slave trade in the early nineteenth century was part of a larger national development that has commonly been referred to as the *market revolution.* A series of economic revolutions—in transportation, communications, and industrialization—that modernized business practices, heightened consumerism, and made commercial activity a greater part of people's daily lives, the market revolution has been credited with bringing widespread cultural and political changes and leading to a complete transformation of American life.[8] Noticeably absent in the study of the market revolution, however, is any real discussion of one of the most important markets to develop during this time period: the traffic in human slaves. Likely this is because the majority of studies of the market revolution have tended to focus almost exclusively on the North.[9]

Yet, upon close examination, it becomes obvious that the South played a major role in the national market revolution and that this larger social transformation had an equally strong effect upon that section, albeit in a somewhat different form than in the North. And, most important, the domestic trade was not simply a consequence of this development but a central component in propelling it. For one thing, the creation of the Cotton Kingdom would have been impossible without the interregional trade, and the raw material that was produced there fueled the great textile mills of England and New England. In return, the revenues from this export were funneled back into the purchase of ever more land and ever more slaves to produce ever more cotton.

In addition, the domestic trade altered southern society in other significant ways. It helped to introduce many of the new business practices and principles that characterized the larger market revolution that was also transforming the North. Few in the South better personified these new practices and the values that they represented than the men (and they were almost all men) who operated this trade. Just like northern capitalists, they were acquisitive entrepreneurs engaged in a highly competitive business, who employed all of the latest marketing techniques and took advantage of the most recent forms of transportation and communication to increase their business. This was an occupation filled with risks, yet it could also pay tremendous financial rewards. While most men did not make fortunes, and many went bankrupt or lost their lives, a few were able to achieve incredible success and become some of the wealthiest individuals in the South. It is important to remember that southern slave traders were not forcing an unwanted product or ideology upon an unsuspecting public; they were providing a service that most white southerners desperately needed. And their actions also indirectly helped to make consumerism and market activity a greater part of everyday life in the South.

Important as these men were in promoting a market in human commodities, the overwhelming majority of southerners who bought and sold slaves were not professional slave traders but were white southerners who simply owned slaves. At one time or another, virtually every slave owner in the South participated in this trade. In addition, the southern courts actively engaged in this traffic. Some estimates claim that nearly half of all slave sales were court-ordered sales. As with so much about the domestic trade, this vast local trade is an aspect of the southern slave system that has all but disappeared from public remembrance and from most historical accounts, which focus almost exclusively on the long-distance trade. Unfortunately, the failure to account for the local trade misses the magnitude of the domestic slave trade and what a significant role it played in everyday life—not to mention that, essentially, every owner was a trader in slaves.[10]

Most antebellum white southerners would have disagreed with this characterization, however, that market forces (especially in relation to human property) had transformed their society. They liked to point out that their world was radically different from, not to mention far superior to, the increasingly modern, capitalistic society that was emerging in the North. They took pride in the fact that their region had remained a premodern society with traditional values, social arrangements, and labor relations. And it was to these traits that they attributed their section's prosperity and success. Yet these defenders of the southern way of life failed to notice one of the most important components underlying their region's undeniable wealth, that is, that their premodern society was propped up internally by a modern and market-driven domestic trade in slaves. Even if most owners did not regularly participate in this traffic, the increased capital gain that their slave force represented (which the interregional trade had produced) was frequently used to finance their operations and to provide economic security for their families.[11]

Despite the facts that the market revolution clearly affected all sections of the country and that the domestic trade was central to this development in the South, the effects of these changes were far different there than they were in the

North. The main reason for this was the long-term consequences of contrary decisions that the two sections made on the subject of slavery in the early years of the republic and the differing effect that the market revolution had on each as a result. Throughout the young nation, the ideals of the Revolution had forced many to question the presence of slavery in a country supposedly founded on the principles of freedom and equality. In the 1790s, a small number of southerners, primarily in the Chesapeake and Upper South, acted on these principles and emancipated their slaves. Yet such actions were quickly curtailed. The large slave populations found throughout the region made widespread emancipation too costly and, according to some, even dangerous. Yet, this somewhat hesitant decision not to abolish slavery in the postrevolutionary South was soon solidified by the new market changes, and whatever questions white southerners may have had about the future of the institution disappeared. In the white South, progress and regional identity became increasingly associated with cotton and slaves, and within a few years, the institution of slavery was no longer excused as a necessary evil but praised as a positive good.[12]

Developments in the North had a much different effect. Prior to the Revolution, slavery had been a national institution, but because of the much smaller slave populations in the northern states, it proved far easier for postrevolutionary people in that region to act on their principles. Following the Revolution, all of the northern states abolished the institution, either immediately or gradually. The result was that, as market developments began to transform northern society, that region became increasingly committed to the concepts of free labor and a market economy. Not only did this lead to widespread economic growth for the North, but it also increasingly meant that a majority of northerners began to see the South and its institution of slavery as backward and old-fashioned. And, over time, a growing number of them also started to perceive it as morally wrong. They were especially troubled by slavery's more cruel and inhumane features, the most disturbing of which was the buying and selling of humans as property.[13]

It is no coincidence, then, that when an abolitionist movement developed in the early 1830s, the movement's leaders quickly made the domestic trade a central component in their attack against slavery. The slave trade proved useful both as a tactical device to attract new supporters and as a focal point in their political argument for abolishing the institution. The abolitionists understood the effect that depictions of an auction block, a slave coffle, and the tearing apart of families had upon their audience. They also realized that these essential features of the southern slave system were public events and impossible to hide. Consequently, such images appeared repeatedly in their publications and speeches. Even more threatening for white southerners was the abolitionists' understanding of the role that the interregional trade played in sustaining the southern economy and the legal means by which Congress could abolish this trade. Over the years, the abolitionists employed a variety of strategies in their efforts to abolish slavery, but the domestic slave trade proved to be one of the movement's most unifying elements.

In many respects, the domestic trade always posed a problem for white southerners. On the one hand, it was essential for the smooth running of the slave system, as well as the foundation for the region's largest source of wealth. Yet the very nature of the business was offensive to many people, especially to those outside of the South. Somehow this traffic had to be preserved and, at the same time, be defended from the abolitionists' moralistic attacks.

The answer came in a multipronged, at times somewhat contradictory, defense of the institution. In Congress and in the courts, white southerners continually defended their right to trade in slaves, while at the same time arguing that few such sales ever took place, or at least that they only occurred on a marginal basis. They could make such claims because of paternalism, a belief that emerged in the early nineteenth century and soon formed a cornerstone of the southern way of life. As white southerners described it, slavery was based on a nonmarket relationship, radically different from that between a factory owner and his employees. Unlike the free-labor North, where the bond between an employer and employee was simply commercial and workers could be abandoned at will, they argued that in the South a special relationship existed between an owner and a slave, and the workers were supposedly taken care of for life. In the eyes of southern slave owners, this paternalistic relationship was at the heart of a system of hierarchies in which all people had their place and a set of duties and obligations to others. For self-proclaimed "masters," this meant looking after their charges, or their "people," as they liked to call them. Not only did they have to provide them with a lifetime of food and shelter, but they also cared for their personal lives. In return, the grateful slaves would perform whatever labor their beloved masters required. It is doubtful that the enslaved actually bought into this system, and the slave-owning class frequently did not live up to its responsibilities. Still, the theory of paternalism proved to be an effective means of defending the southern slave system from outside attack, and it allowed slave owners to claim that few masters ever sold their human property, despite the fact that thousands of such transactions occurred every year.[14]

Southern whites could not deny that some slave sales did occur, but the slave system contained within it an ideal scapegoat, a fantasized individual on whom all of those sales could be blamed. This was the stereotyped slave trader, a man who in the public imagination was the only aberration in an otherwise fine system. Compared to the paternalistic planter, who supposedly abhorred the thought of parting with his people, the imagined slave trader was the antithesis of this ideal. He was the one responsible for enticing individuals to part with their slaves against their will; he was the one who tore slave families apart and caused all of the other evils associated with the institution. The slave trader proved essential for the system. Not only did he provide a service that was absolutely crucial for the smooth running of southern slavery, but he also became the scapegoat for that system, absorbing both external and internal criticisms against it.[15]

Unfortunately, the southern slave system never ran as smoothly as its defenders would have liked everyone to believe. Dealing in humans as commodities raised questions that one simply did not have to confront when buying and selling other products. Some individuals found themselves caught between their region's two competing value systems: the commercial pursuit of economic gain at the expense of others and the paternalistic obligation to look after one's charges. Most southern slave owners had little trouble reconciling this apparent contradiction in their value systems and used both commercialism and paternalism to provide themselves with a wide range of justifications for their actions. Still, there is no denying that this dilemma clearly did cause anguish for some individuals and forced them to make business decisions that did not always coincide with their best economic interests.

Whatever uneasiness white southerners may have felt about the buying and selling of their people, however, paled in comparison to the anger and the pain felt by those black southerners who were being bought and sold like things. It is impossible to talk about the reality of the domestic slave trade and its long-term effects on American society without looking at the impact that it had on those who were the commodities in this trade. For these individuals, the domestic trade was not just an economic transaction nor an unpleasant necessity that needed to be defended as some abstract way of life. For the enslaved, each sale was an action with potentially devastating and lifelong consequences. Although not all black southerners were victims of this trade, it was an ever-present reality of life for most African Americans in the South. For most American slaves, little could be done to prevent the threat and actuality of sale. Yet many did resist. Even those who had never struck out against slavery before fought back when sale forced them to confront the reality of being torn away from family and loved ones. While most were unsuccessful in their attempts to prevent a sale, their collective efforts to resist the trade did make the system run less smoothly than slave owners would have liked. Even more important, they were also some of the most telling pieces of evidence, for anyone who wished to notice, that the fantasy that the slaveholders had created was all just one big lie.

The ramifications of that lie, and of the trade that sustained it, can still be felt in American society today.

. . .

In 1833, few Americans were more aware of the workings of the domestic slave trade and its implications for southern society than the future abolitionist and Liberty party presidential candidate James G. Birney. Having lived in both Kentucky and Alabama and having bought and sold slaves, Birney was in many respects a typical slave owner. Yet, by the early 1830s, he had begun to question the morality of the institution, and he also believed that he knew what would eventually bring it to an end. In an address that he wrote for the Kentucky Society for the Gradual Relief of the State from Slavery, Birney predicted: "We think it very probable, that the general movement, which is now going on, of the slaves, from the middle to the southern states, will be noted by the future historian as one of the prominent causes, which *hastened* the termination of slavery in the United States."[16] Birney's observation turned out to be true; the domestic slave trade *did* hasten the end of slavery in the United States. Yet, in one important respect, Birney erred in his projection. While there have been literally hundreds, if not thousands, of books written about American slavery, and even more on the coming of the Civil War, scant attention has been paid by historians to the domestic slave trade, and there has been almost nothing written on the role that it played in contributing to the institution's eventual demise.[17]

In part, this absence of historical scholarship is a result of the ambiguous place that slavery itself has held in American society since Emancipation and continuing to the present day. For many reasons, most Americans, black and white, continue to be uncomfortable talking about the subject of southern slavery and are divided over how it should be publicly remembered. While some believe that its victims should be commemorated and others contend that their descendants should be compensated, an even greater number would just as soon have this troubling part of their history forgotten. If most people today are uncomfortable discussing the institution as a whole, it is doubly true that they do not want to be reminded that earlier generations of Americans bought and sold their ancestors like cattle, or that some of their family fortunes were built upon this trade.

Despite the fact that the domestic slave trade was a constant presence in antebellum American society and that the lives of millions of men, women, and children were touched by this trade, since Emancipation this essential component of early American life has all but disappeared from public remembrance. In many respects this historical amnesia has been a consequence of the effort to reunite the country after the Civil War, when the abolitionist critiques of the Old South were muted, and white southerners were allowed to define what life had been like under their "peculiar institution," as they earlier had referred to their slave system. In books and in plays, the Old South was romanticized, and tales of the auction block and slave coffles fell by the wayside. Even today, such treatments continue, as seen by the persistent popularity of the film *Gone with the Wind* (1939). Despite its dated racial stereotypes, this film is consistently voted one of the nation's favorites, with its paternalistic planters, contented slaves, and complete absence of any reference to the buying and selling of slaves. This whitewashing of the past can also be seen on a visit to any of the restored antebellum plantations in the South. While it is true that a more realistic depiction of slavery has begun to appear at some of the more prominent homes, the guides at most plantations still try to avoid the subject of slavery entirely. When it does come up, the visitor will invariably be told that the family who lived there never sold any of its slaves, despite the fact that the family almost certainly participated in this trade.[18]

It is perhaps understandable why the American public has been reluctant to remember this painful part of its past, but the reasons behind the domestic trade's absence from most historical scholarship are somewhat more surprising, especially given the explosion of works on southern slavery. Yet the motivations behind this research have helped to lead historical scholarship in directions away from the domestic trade. As in post–Civil War popular culture, southerners controlled the early historical interpretation of slavery and the slave trade. Especially influential was the Georgia-born Ulrich B. Phillips, whose work in the early twentieth century dominated mainstream historians' views on slavery until the 1950s. In general, Phillips dismissed the domestic trade as inconsequential in magnitude and not out of line with traditional American values. As Phillips described it, "The long-distance slave trade was essentially a part of the westward movement," and "the slave market was in a sense the prototype of the more modern employment bureau."[19] These views were not challenged until 1931 with the pioneering work of Frederic Bancroft, whose *Slave Trading in the Old South* clearly showed how widespread this trade really was and how many people were involved in it. Yet it was not until the Civil Rights movement emerged that northern historians Kenneth Stampp and Stanley Elkins used Bancroft's work to challenge Phillips's paternalistic view of slavery. They argued that the system was far more harsh and cruel than most Americans had been led to believe and demonstrated that it had terrible consequences for those caught in its grasp, ultimately proving destructive to individual psyches, black family structure, and African-American culture.[20]

While the work of Stampp and Elkins was a much-needed corrective to the romanticized picture of slavery painted by Phillips, it also raised questions about the psychological and social impact that the institution had upon the enslaved. More than anything else, these questions fueled interest in historical studies about American slavery, especially during the 1970s, when some of the most prolific and original work was done. At the heart of these studies was the desire to prove that slavery had not simply destroyed the enslaved, as Stampp and Elkins had argued, but on the contrary, to show that black people in America had managed to create a rich and meaningful culture based upon loving and stable families in strong, supportive communities despite their enslavement. These works have added greatly to our understanding of southern slavery and African-American history, but by their very nature, they have neglected aspects of the institution that threatened the slave community, particularly the domestic trade. While Kenneth Stampp had an entire chapter on the domestic slave trade in *The Peculiar Institution* (1956), in most works of the 1970s and 1980s, it rarely, if ever, received more than passing notice. In one of the most seminal books of the period, Eugene Genovese's *Roll, Jordan, Roll* (1974), the domestic slave trade barely appeared at all.[21]

Another factor that contributed to the domestic trade's absence from most historical scholarship since the 1970s was the negative reaction from many in the profession to Robert Fogel and Stanley Engerman's much-publicized 1974 work, *Time on the Cross*. Using new, scientific methods of quantification, Fogel and Engerman made sweeping claims that supposedly overthrew much of the scholarship on American slavery. Especially contentious was their argument that the domestic trade was far smaller in size than previously thought and only affected a tiny percentage of enslaved families. Most historians dismissed this claim, noting the numerous weaknesses in Fogel and Engerman's methodology. Since then, economic historians have continued to argue over the extent and composition of the trade, often using the same type of elaborate mathematical formulas that appeared in *Time on the Cross*. But many traditional historians have remained skeptical of any work on this topic that employs the same controversial methodology as that of Fogel and Engerman.[22]

Of course, the domestic slave trade has not been totally absent from historical scholarship, and most works on southern slavery have at least touched on it somewhere in their accounts. Moreover, there are clear indications that this crucial topic is once again attracting the attention of scholars. Most notable has been Michael Tadman's important work, *Speculators and Slaves* (1989), which tried to bridge the gap between economic history and a more general audience. Tadman convincingly argued that the interstate trade was indeed extensive and that planters were not as reluctant to sell their slaves as had been previously thought. Also promising was Walter Johnson's book *Soul by Soul* (1999), which took a cultural approach to the New Orleans slave market and looked at what a sale meant to each of the parties involved. Finally, the recent work of

Robert Gudmestad has shown how white southerners' views on the slave trade changed over time.[23]

Yet, there still has been no overall account of what the domestic slave trade meant for American society, North and South, nor of the prominent role that it played in southerners' everyday lives. This study is an attempt to fill that void. The first part of the book begins with a look at the origins of this trade and how it ironically coincided with the birth of the nation. It then examines how this new trade led to the creation of the Cotton Kingdom and how it contributed to its eventual demise. It investigates the men who operated this trade and shows them to be a more diverse and modern group than the simple stereotypes of them have indicated. In addition to the long-distance interstate trade, this study explores the extensive local trade, including the role that the southern courts played in this business.

The book then examines some of the larger questions that the domestic slave trade raised for American society. It first looks at how the trade affected those outside of the South and how it contributed to their belief that the institution of southern slavery was wrong and, by implication, that something was wrong with the young nation itself. The slave trade had its biggest influence, however, upon those within the South. White southerners had to defend this seemingly indefensible part of their system from increasing outside attacks, and they had to do so by defending their right to trade in slaves while simultaneously arguing that few such sales ever occurred. But the trade's most life-altering impact was upon those individuals being bought and sold. Consequently, the book concludes with an examination of how these men and women attempted to mitigate this constant reality of life and what effect their actions had on the system as a whole.

Carry Me Back aims to restore the domestic slave trade to the prominent place that it rightfully deserves in early American history. It looks at the origins of this trade and describes how it became an essential part of the southern slave system. Moreover, it explores the long-term effects that the slave trade had on American society—North and South, black and white. The domestic slave trade is a painful part of the American past that has long been neglected, and it needs to be examined before we can truly understand southern slavery and antebellum American life.

ONE

The Irony of Liberty:
Origins of the Domestic Slave Trade

In 1798, a Delaware Quaker, Warner Mifflin, wrote a letter to President John Adams. The recent yellow fever epidemic in Philadelphia had caused Mifflin to ponder the reason for this disaster. After traveling from the Eastern Shore of Virginia to his home in Delaware, Mifflin believed that he had found the explanation for God's wrath. While passing through Maryland, he was struck by "the abominable Trade carried on through that part of the Country, by Negroe-Drovers, buying Drove after Drove of the poor afflicted Blacks, like droves of Cattel for Market; carrying them into the Southern States for Speculation; regardless of the separation of nearest Connections & natural ties." Not only did Mifflin believe that the yellow fever epidemic was God's punishment of the country for engaging in this trade in human slaves, but he also feared that "if the Practice continued, [it] was likely to produce punishment on the Government, Rulers, and those in Authority, who did not exert themselves for the suppression of this cruel Practice." Therefore, the Delaware Quaker had decided to write to Adams because he thought "that perhaps the President as prime Magistrate in the United States, may be entirely without the knowledge of this atrocious & abominable Crime."

One of the most disturbing aspects of this development for Mifflin was its occurrence "among a People who, by their Representatives a few Years back, declared to all the World, and (as I consider it) before the Majesty of Heaven, that 'it was self-evident all men were created equal; that they were endow'd by their Creator with certain unalienable Rights, among which are Life, Liberty, &c.'" As he thought about the nation's withholding "from so great a part of our fellow-men, the unalienable Right with which they are endow'd by their Creator," Mifflin wondered what "will be the Consequence to this Country, if the before mention'd barbarous Trade & Traffick is continued? I feel it at times almost sufficient to burst a human Heart; Then how will that God who is just & Merciful view those Actions?"[1]

Warner Mifflin's description of the nascent domestic slave trade could not have been more insightful or revealing. For one thing, Mifflin's suggestion that Adams did not know of the trade's existence indicates its relative newness. This was also made clear by Mifflin's shock at what he saw. His disgust and fear of God's retribution further signified a changing perception of both slave trading and slave traders. Finally, his questioning of how the domestic slave trade could be reconciled with the ideals of the American Revolution illustrates the conflict that many had with the presence of chattel slavery and especially one of its more distasteful aspects, the buying and selling of human beings, in the new republic.

Although slave trading had long been part of American society, its nature had changed over time. Before the Revolution, slave traders were wealthy and respected merchants who generally viewed their African and West Indian purchases as they did any other cargo. Despite the emergence of a small, locally based domestic trade in the mid-eighteenth century, most slaves sold in the colonial period were imported from Africa. By the nineteenth century, the slave trade had changed dramatically. It was no longer conducted in the North; most of the slaves traded had been born in America; and few slave traders were men of high social and political stature. For Americans, the slave trade had become an indigenous operation, transporting thousands of individuals from the Upper South to the Lower South each year.[2]

Taking the lead in the development of this traffic were those who had the most to gain from it, namely, white Virginians and their neighbors in the Upper South. Having the largest slave population in the nation, which was more human property than they needed or could safely employ, Virginians set about to relieve themselves of this burden, and the most effective means of doing so was through the interstate trade. While it is true that much of this traffic initially emerged on its own, very early on the Virginians did their best to promote it, primarily by preventing additional "supplies" from entering the market and by obtaining new territory in which to peddle their "goods." In addition, they used their extensive political power in the early republic to make sure that nothing ever interfered with its operation. Most amazingly, they managed to do all of this while maintaining an image of themselves as liberal and caring paternalists who wanted nothing more than the institution's demise.

The development of the domestic trade did provide the answer to many of the white South's needs, but it came at a price. While all segments of southern society felt its impact, the group most affected was composed of those who were the commodities in this new trade. Most important, it transformed the perception of American slaves, who were now seen not only as laborers but also as valuable investments in themselves. This proved especially true for enslaved women, who were increasingly appraised for their ability to reproduce. The emergence of the interstate trade also led to a rise in the frequency of slave sales and a greater separation of those who had been sold from their families and friends. Finally, all blacks in America were touched by this new trade as the profits that could be made from it triggered an outbreak in the kidnapping of free people of color and their transportation and sale into slavery in the Deep South.

One of the most noteworthy aspects of the domestic slave trade was that its birth coincided with that of the nation itself. The ideals of the Revolution led Warner Mifflin and many other Americans to question the place of chattel slavery in the land of the free. For northerners, this questioning resulted in their abolition of the institution and an end to their trade in human slaves. While these same principles led to a temporary questioning of slavery by some in the Upper South, by the early nineteenth century, such views had long since disappeared, and the southern states had become even more committed to their increasingly peculiar institution than they had been before the Revolution. And, unlike their northern counterparts, promoters of the domestic slave trade used the ideals of the American Revolution to justify this abominable new trade.[3]

I

The most important factor in the change that occurred in American slave trading was the closing of the African trade in 1808. Although occasional criticism had been voiced, real opposition to the trade did not develop until the struggle for American independence.[4] For many in prerevolutionary America, the rights of Africans became associated with those of the colonists. Americans often employed the same rhetoric when attacking the African trade that they used in their political struggle with Great Britain. Pamphleteers such as James Otis in his *Rights of the British Colonies* (1764) argued that the slave trade diminished "the inestimable value of liberty," while clergymen like the Reverend Levi Hart of Connecticut claimed the trade was "a flagrant violation of the law of nature, of the natural rights of mankind." Southern patriots also made these connections. In his 1774 pamphlet, *A Summary View of the Rights of British America*, Thomas Jefferson criticized the king for vetoing legislation prohibiting the African trade into the colonies, charging that "the rights of human nature [were] deeply wounded by this infamous practice."[5]

Although many opposed the African trade for religious or ideological reasons, others had more practical motives for wanting it closed. An oversupply in the American slave market had decreased the value of human property, and a halt in imports would stabilize prices. Also many equated an attack on the slave trade with economic retaliation against England since British merchants controlled the African trade into America. Finally, revolutionary fervor brought civil unrest and fears of slave revolt, especially in the South. The result was a concerted effort by the colonies during the 1760s and 1770s to ban slave imports, which came to fruition on October 20, 1774, when the First Continental Congress voted to "neither import nor purchase, any slave imported after the first day of December next." For all practical purposes, the African slave trade into America came to a halt.[6]

Following the Revolution, most Americans opposed reopening this trade. In addition to some opponents' humanitarian reasons, opposition to the international trade partially diverted Americans from the paradox of condoning slavery while professing liberty and equality for all. For many, it was easier to attack a problem whose source was distant and for which blame could be attributed to the British. There were also practical reasons, especially in the South. The Chesapeake already had more slaves than it needed, and outnumbered planters in parts of the Deep South feared possible slave revolts and deeper economic woes. Therefore, despite a reopening of the African trade in some states of the Lower South following independence, this form of traffic soon all but disappeared from North American shores. In 1786 North Carolina passed a prohibitive duty on all imported slaves, and South Carolina temporarily suspended the African trade early the next year. By the summer of 1787, only Georgia still openly imported slaves.[7]

The slave trade was a minor aspect of the Constitutional Convention with full debate on it lasting only two days. Many delegates saw the issue as a temporary problem that would eventually resolve itself. Although most thought the slave trade had no place in the new republic, South Carolina and Georgia obstinately refused to sign a constitution that abolished the African trade. A political bargain was struck whereby the South was guaranteed no interference in the slave trade for twenty years in exchange for trade regulations favorable to the North. There was some opposition to this clause by the antifederalists, especially in South Carolina and New Hampshire, but in no state did it become a major issue since most Americans anticipated the trade's eventual demise.[8]

At first glance, the actions of the South Carolinians at the Constitutional Convention might seem puzzling, considering that just a few months earlier, the state legislature had decided to prohibit slave imports into the state. Three of the four constitutional delegates had actually voted for the statewide ban. The explanation given at the time for this measure was the state's uncontrolled debt problem. Following the war, South Carolinians imported as many slaves as possible, often on credit from outside suppliers. Ending this wild speculation in slaves would help to stabilize prices and retain adequate specie in the state.[9]

The South Carolina ban was supposed to be temporary, but the 1791 slave revolt in Saint-Domingue terrified not just the Lower South but the entire United States. Now the trade was opposed on security as well as moral grounds. Petitions from across the country flooded Congress asking for a halt in the trade. In 1794 Congress made it illegal for U.S. citizens to participate in the foreign slave trade, a measure already enacted by most states. With the exception of the law's renewal in 1800, Congress took no other action.

Petitions were also sent to state legislatures. When the South Carolina ban on the slave trade was about to expire in 1795, a national abolitionist convention sent a petition to the state assembly asking for a "total prohibition of all traffic in Slaves," among other reasons because "of the dangers to which the Citizens of the United States are exposed." Numerous states passed anti-importation bills, banning both the domestic and foreign trade and especially slaves from the French West Indies. When Georgia finally prohibited the slave trade in 1798, it had already been officially abolished in every other state.[10]

In 1803 South Carolina shocked the country by reopening the African trade. This decision sparked concerns among the large slave owners in the state's lowcountry region. Most of these planters had more than enough laborers to meet their needs, and a new influx of Africans joining with the already large black population there only increased worries about a possible slave revolt. As state senator Robert Barnwell noted when arguing against the 1803 bill, those who already owned slaves would suffer, because "the value of this species of property would be considerably diminished." Despite this lowcountry opposition, changes in agriculture and demographics had caused an increased demand for slaves. A massive white migration to the upcountry brought with it an insatiable appetite for labor. The Louisiana Purchase provided another incentive for the reopening of the trade: Charleston slave traders now had an unlimited market for their goods. Many of the slaves imported by South Carolina went directly to the West, with ships just touching Charleston wharves on their way from Africa to New Orleans. The certainty of the African trade's closing in 1808 only gave traders an incentive to obtain as many slaves as possible while they still legally could. Between 1803 and 1808, South Carolina imported more than 39,000 slaves, almost twice as many as in any previous five-year period.[11]

Despite this burgeoning traffic, in 1807 there was little argument in the nation over whether African imports should be stopped. In Charleston, merchants petitioned for relief, and South Carolina congressmen were instructed "to exert with promptitude & zeal their utmost abilities to obtain such relaxation & alteration" as possible on the upcoming act. Yet most of the debate in Congress was over how to enforce the new ban. The two biggest questions were what to do with the captured Africans and how to punish offenders. After much contentious debate along sectional lines, the final bill left the first question up to each state, which meant that any illegally imported Africans confiscated in the South would still be sold as slaves, with the money going to the state in which they were imported rather than to the trader. The South also managed to get its way by limiting the punishment for this crime to a fine and a relatively short imprisonment of two to four years. The only other topic of debate was whether or not to regulate the coastal slave trade. Yet, once again after intense debate, the only action taken was a law requiring that slaves transferred between American ports by sea be registered and shipped in vessels larger than forty tons.[12]

On January 1, 1808, the United States officially abolished the African slave trade. Although this event caused much celebration, its effect was limited at first due to poor enforcement. Smuggling soon became a problem for customs officials from Georgia to New Orleans. According to one Georgia agent in 1818, "African and West India negroes are almost daily illicitly introduced into Georgia for sale or settlement, or passing through it to the Territories of the United States for similar purposes." The illegal importation of Africans continued to be a problem until 1820, when the slave trade was declared piracy and made punishable by death.[13]

On the one hand the movement to abolish the African trade did little to change slave trading in America. By 1800, whatever antislavery sentiment the Revolution had instilled in the Upper South had receded, and the region remained firm in its commitment to slavery. As to the Lower South, between 1790 and 1807 more slaves were imported into North America than during any twenty-year period in the colonial era, and the ban in 1808 proved ineffective in halting this process. Yet much had changed. Smuggling continued throughout the nineteenth century, but the numbers soon became so small that slave traders had to rely on domestic sources for their supply. Also, the country had committed itself to declaring that the African trade was wrong, and the implications of this were enormous. No longer was the buying and selling of Africans simply an economic concern; now it was branded as morally and legally unjust.[14]

II

If the ideals of the Revolution forced Americans to confront and eventually abolish the African trade, there were other significant consequences of the war as well. Most important was the eventual withdrawal of the British from territory east of the Mississippi River, which led to expulsion of the Indians and rapid westward expansion. Native Americans had always been an obstacle to white settlement, and the Revolution accelerated their elimination from the eastern United States. Most of the tribes had sided with the British during the war. That not only escalated hostility toward a perennial enemy but also defined the Indians as defeated nations, which resulted in a large loss of their land. The withdrawal of the British to far western posts likewise removed a check upon American expansion. The War of 1812 hastened this process of removal. While it was not until the 1830s that all of the Indian tribes were removed west of the Mississippi, by 1820 most of the present-day states of Kentucky, Tennessee, Alabama, Mississippi, and Louisiana were opened up for settlement.[15]

Following the Revolution, Americans streamed west to settle this new land. Within Virginia itself, movement into the Piedmont had already begun by the early eighteenth century, but with the cessation of hostilities, migrants poured into this region and into the state's southern and far western counties. In addition, settlers began leaving for land in Kentucky, Tennessee, and the Deep South. Between 1790 and 1820, nearly 250,000 whites from Maryland and Virginia migrated into this new territory.[16] The Carolinas also experienced massive migration. There was an enormous movement to the South Carolina backcountry (or uplands region) during the 1790s, and in the next decade approximately 47,000 whites left the state, most of them going to Georgia. North Carolinians likewise moved both west and south. One later migrant to Alabama reported to his father in Raleigh that "the whole country seems to be filled up by people from North Carolina. I have been no where that I did not meet with some of my acquaintances."[17]

Changes in southern agriculture further stimulated the economic opportunities that migrants saw in the West. In the Chesapeake, farmers shifted from tobacco to grain crops due to soil exhaustion and an increased demand for foodstuffs. While this process had begun before the Revolution, the war greatly accelerated it.[18] The greatest change in southern agriculture, however, had little to do with the Revolution but was a result of technical innovations in cotton processing. In 1790, the only cotton grown in the United States was on the coast and on islands off South Carolina and Georgia. The development of the cotton gin in 1793 made it economically feasible to plant and harvest a short staple variety that could be grown farther inland. This innovation led to a cotton boom throughout the South. In 1791, the United States exported only 889 bales of cotton. In 1795, this figure jumped to almost 28,000. By 1801, it reached nearly 92,000, and by 1820 exports reached close to a half million bales.[19]

Southerners rapidly moved west to grow this new money crop. Most initial settlers were poor whites, few of whom owned slaves. Yet some large planters, most frequently sons of large planters, migrated west and brought their slaves with them. Soon other settlers followed, bringing their "families," both black and white. Although white migration was higher than black, between 1790 and 1820 approximately 175,000 slaves from the Chesapeake moved west with their owners, most coming before 1810. And the numbers were just as great in the

Lower South. In 1760 less than one-tenth of all South Carolina slaves lived in the backcountry. By 1810 almost one-half did.[20]

Because cotton was a labor-intensive crop, slaves were usually the first item bought after land. With land easily available, the profitability of cotton was limited primarily by the number of toiling hands, and planters naturally wanted to increase their work force. Yet there was never enough labor available to satisfy the settlers' demands, despite all of the slaves being shipped west. As early as 1772, one Charleston slave trader claimed that "upwards of two-thirds that have been imported have gone backwards," or into the backcountry portion of the state. By 1800, almost all of the immigrants into this region were black slaves. Slave prices had always been higher in the backcountry due to shortage of supply, and it was this enormous demand, along with the extensive profits for traders, that led to South Carolina's reopening of the African trade in 1803.[21]

III

During the late eighteenth century, Charleston was the slave-trading center of North America. With the imminent closing of the African trade, however, a gradual shift began to occur. The inevitable curtailment of outside sources meant that slaves would now have to come from within the United States. Although Charleston continued to be a significant nineteenth-century trading site, its importance as a major supplier of slaves to the Southwest decreased, at least until midcentury, when local demand dropped.

The Chesapeake came to be the main source of slaves for the domestic trade. This was only natural since most American slaves lived there. In 1790 more than half of all blacks in the nation lived in Maryland and Virginia; 45 percent of all southern slaves resided in Virginia alone.[22] Also, the shift from tobacco, which necessitated year-round gang labor, to grain crops, which required specialized and seasonal work, resulted in a surplus of slaves. According to one traveler in the 1790s, "There is scarcely any estate but what is overstocked. This is a circumstance complained of by every planter." George Washington was typical in his frustrations at having "more working Negros by a full moiety, than can be employed to any advantage in the farming system."[23]

While some Chesapeake slave owners bemoaned their excessive charges, others fully realized the future role their region would play. These individuals understood that the only solution to their problem was to secure an outside market for their surplus slaves. Since the demand for labor clearly existed in the West, they set about establishing a means of transferring excess slaves from the Chesapeake to those areas where they were eagerly sought. Therefore, in the late eighteenth and early nineteenth centuries, many Virginia statesmen persistently advanced their interests through the development of the domestic slave trade.[24]

Foremost in their endeavors was the need to curtail the supply of new slaves entering the market. As early as the 1750s, Virginia led in the movement opposing the African slave trade. With a series of proposed import duties, Virginians tried to curtail the influx of African slaves, only to have their efforts vetoed by Great Britain. In the Continental Congress, Virginians promoted a national boycott of the trade, and in 1778, they prohibited the importation of Africans within the state.[25] At the Constitutional Convention, representatives from the Chesapeake spoke loudest against a continuation of this trade. Luther Martin of Maryland claimed the slave trade "was inconsistent with the principles of the Revolution and dishonorable to the American character," and Virginian George Mason adamantly argued in favor of closing the African trade, because "this nefarious traffic" would never stop on its own due to the strong western demand. Representatives from the northern states negotiated a compromise between those from the Deep South, who refused any restrictions on the African trade, and Virginians, who fought so hard for its prohibition.[26] When the twenty-year limitation was about to expire, it was representatives from Virginia, along with the strong support of a Virginia-born president, who urged Congress to quickly pass legislation to abolish it. Virginians even aided the effort to control smuggling, as can be seen in the 1816 and 1818 annual messages by Presidents Madison and Monroe. And another Virginian, Charles Fenton Mercer, wrote and pushed through both a law in 1819 that tightened up the enforcement loopholes against smuggling and the 1820 law that declared the African trade to be piracy and punishable by death.[27]

Meanwhile, Virginians were opportunistically promoting a market for their goods. They took the lead in encouraging westward expansion and fought hardest against any limit on the expansion of slavery into the territories. Thomas Jefferson and James Monroe greatly expanded the area available for settlement (and slavery) with the Louisiana and Florida purchases. A good indication of their motives can be found in the congressional debate over the Louisiana Ordinance of 1804. Some northerners wanted slavery prohibited in the region, while South Carolina and Georgia argued for allowing only those slaves who arrived with their migrating owners. But the Virginians, led by Jefferson, fought to permit to enter the territory any American-owned slave, including those brought there for the purpose of sale.[28] The Virginians were also willing to do whatever was necessary to protect their new form of trade. When some northerners sought to prohibit the interstate traffic in slaves during the 1807 congressional debates on closing the African trade, John Randolph took the lead in fighting against such restrictions, claiming it would "blow up the Constitution in ruins." In addition to promising civil disobedience, Randolph even threatened disunion if such a bill was passed. While little came of Randolph's threats, he did succeed in getting only minor restrictions enacted, and it does show how far the Virginians were willing to go to keep open their trade in human property.[29]

Obviously, Virginians were not the only Americans who advanced their own social and economic interests in relation to slavery. In 1798, South Caro-linian Robert Goodloe Harper helped Charleston slave traders by adding to the Mississippi Territory Bill an amendment prohibiting the foreign trade in the region.[30] Yet Virginians did more than any other Americans to promote the domestic slave trade. They had to because they believed that a surplus of slaves posed a threat to their social and economic existence. Their reasons for attack-ing the African trade were motivated in large part by a sincere hatred of slav-ery. Their dislike of the institution, however, stemmed more from the negative effects that slavery had on white society than from any humanitarian con-cern about African Americans. White Virginians feared the detrimental effects that slavery had on them: it impeded manufacturing and white migration; the large enslaved population always presented a threat of bloody revolt; and at times the institution forced them to take actions with which they clearly felt uncomfortable. Nevertheless, in a region where the largest form of wealth was in human chattel, curtailing the influx of slaves and providing an outlet for the surplus were necessary to maintain property values and economic security. Therefore, despite their misgivings about slavery, few Virginians wanted to give it up. It was just too valuable. So Virginians strengthened the institution while attempting to control its more harmful aspects. And the most effective means of doing so was through the interstate slave trade.[31]

Outsiders occasionally criticized Virginians for the selfish motives behind their actions. At the Constitutional Convention, Charles Pinckney of South Carolina pointed out, "As to Virginia she will gain by stopping the importa-tions. Her slaves will rise in value, & she has more than she wants." After the Virginians castigated South Carolina for reopening the African trade in 1803, the *Charleston Courier* retaliated by noting the reason why: "The Virginians well know that since our ports have been open for the admission of Negroes from Africa, few, if any, have been brought hither from that State. It is this which grieves them." Some northerners, however, saw through the hypocrisy of both the Virginians and the South Carolinians. During the 1804 Senate debate over the Louisiana Ordinance, William Plumer of New Hampshire expressed his disgust with all southerners, stating: "It is obvious that the zeal displayed by the Senate from the Slave States, to prohibit the foreign importation of Slaves into Louisiana, proceeds from the motive to raise the price of their own slaves in the markett—& to encrease the means of disposing of those who are most turbulent & dangerous to them."[32]

Despite these occasional complaints, Virginians successfully promoted the domestic slave trade while maintaining a veneer of self-respect. In large part this was accomplished by their ability to tie the development of the interregional trade to the ideals of the American Revolution. Using both expressions of freedom and a Lockean defense of property, the rhetoric of the Revolution helped to justify their cause.

The earliest example of this was evinced in the movement to abolish the African trade. Conflict with the Crown over control of the slave trade provided the image of a cruel Britain forcing the burden of slavery upon a defenseless American population. Thomas Jefferson helped to create this myth with his famous charge against King George III in the original draft of the Declaration of Independence. Jefferson called the slave trade a "cruel war against human nature itself, violating its most sacred rights of life and liberty" and claimed that the king perpetuated it because of his determination "to keep open a Markett where Men should be bought and sold." As leaders in the new nation, Virginia politicians continued to use libertarian sentiments in their efforts to abolish the trade. In *Federalist* number 42, James Madison argued that it was "a great point gained in favor of humanity" that the Constitution permitted the termination of this "unnatural traffic" after twenty years. In the opening session of the First Congress during debate over the nation's first tariff bill, Representative Josiah Parker of Virginia proposed a $10 tax on imported slaves. According to Parker, the African trade "was contrary to the Revolution principles," and he hoped such a duty "would prevent, in some degree, this irrational and inhuman traffic." Finally, in his 1806 message to Congress calling for a prohibition of the trade, more than one year before it could be constitutionally abolished, President Jefferson called on Congress to "withdraw the citizens of the United States from all further participation in those violations of human rights which have been so long continued on the unoffending inhabitants of Africa."[33]

Virginia's opposition to the African trade fit in perfectly with the antislavery spirit of the revolutionary era, and the state's position in leading the movement gave encouragement to abolitionists throughout the nation. Yet, unlike northerners who opposed slavery because of its effect on blacks, in Virginia the antislavery sentiment was based more on a concern for its effect on whites. Northerners, and even many southerners, failed to see this distinction, and Virginians were able to portray themselves as leaders of a humanitarian movement, despite any ulterior motives they might possess. It also helped to reaffirm the image many Americans had of Virginians as liberal, paternalistic slave owners who were trying to gradually eliminate the institution, unlike those from the Deep South who so openly fought for slavery's continuation and their own economic gain.[34]

Another example of Virginians invoking the spirit of the Revolution can be found in their justification for westward expansion and the spread of slavery into the territories. The opportunity that the West represented meshed perfectly with the revolutionary ideals of liberty and the pursuit of happiness. However, not only did Virginians use this connection when arguing that expansion was beneficial for whites, but they also extended that reasoning to include blacks. While Virginians always maintained that white settlers should be able to take their property into any territory and have that property protected by law, by the end of the century some also claimed that the extension of slavery was the best way to reform and then perhaps to eliminate it. Spreading or diffusing slavery over a wide area would help to decrease the dense concentration of slaves in the southern states. For proof, diffusionists pointed to the northern states, where, they maintained, slavery had been so easily abolished because slaves represented such a small proportion of the population. By lowering the ratio of slaves in the southern states, they believed that a similar result could be achieved. The argument was first expressed in 1798 by Virginians William Branch Giles and John Nicholas during the congressional debate over slavery in the Mississippi Territory. Prefacing his comments by noting that this would be the best means of "furthering the rights of man," Giles claimed that if slaves were allowed to enter the western territories, "there would be a greater probability of ameliorating their condition, which could never be done whilst they were crowded together as they now are in the Southern States." Some further argued that this process would also benefit blacks and make them happier by bringing them in closer contact with whites. Jefferson later summed up this theory most clearly when he asserted that "their diffusion over a greater surface would make them individually happier, and proportionally facilitate the accomplishment of their emancipation." In other words, white Virginians justified the sale and forced separation of their slaves to the Far West by contending that they were bringing a greater happiness and eventual freedom to those same slaves.[35]

While Virginia's liberal ideals and economic interests blended together smoothly on the abstract level, for many individuals reality was often less harmonious. This proved especially true in the revolutionary era when many Virginians found themselves both geographically and ideologically between the increasingly free-labor North and the slave-based Lower South. Virginia always remained committed to slavery, but the Revolution did force some individuals to question the morality of the institution. Numerous owners did free their slaves. Patrick Henry was more typical, however. He found the slave trade "repugnant to humanity" yet was incapable of freeing his own slaves due to "the general inconveniency of living without them."[36]

Although Virginia's economy was to be supplemented by the selling of surplus slaves, the actual prospect remained difficult for many owners. Sell-

ing excess slaves for profit not only challenged the planters' rationale for owning slave property but also indicated a failure to support their charges, which
affronted the humanitarian ideals of owners. While most were able to rational-
ize this dilemma, many had a difficult time justifying their actions. Paternalistic
planters constantly expressed their disgust at having to sell off family slaves,
even though economic necessity often forced them to do so. George Washington professed repeatedly to having a "great repugnance to encreasing my Slaves
by purchase" and to being "principled against this kind of traffic in the human
species." Yet Washington continued to buy and sell slaves when it was to his
advantage, although he constantly felt the need to defend his actions and assert
his displeasure whenever he did so.[37]

Patrick Henry and George Washington typified slave owners in the Upper
South in this most important way. Despite their stated repugnance for the
slave trade, each man continued to buy and sell human property. By the late
eighteenth century, the domestic slave trade had become the answer to many
of the Chesapeake's problems. But for numerous individuals—including
Henry and Washington—the conflict that resulted when moral ideals clashed
with economic necessity could only be resolved with self-deception on the
grandest of scales.[38]

IV

One consequence of the burgeoning domestic trade during the revolutionary
era was a shift in the perception of slave property. This proved especially true
in the Chesapeake and can be best seen in the changing attitudes toward black
women. In the colonial North, lack of demand and closer living conditions had
caused some owners to lament a slave woman's ability to reproduce. Often this
was cited as a reason for sale. In New York, one master offered a woman because
"she breeds too fast for her Owner to put up with such Inconvenience"; in Philadelphia, another woman was sold because her owner did not want "to have a
breeding Wench in the Family." The same was true for the urban South where
some buyers in Charleston also preferred that their house servants be "without
a Child."[39] In the rural South, however, there were few if any comments on
the subject. Colonial planters recognized the mixed blessings of childbearing.
Although it took away from valuable work time, it also helped to increase a
much-needed labor force.[40]

By the late eighteenth century, this perception of slave reproduction began
to change, albeit at first in two somewhat contradictory ways. The growing
number of slaves in the Upper South led some planters there to begin adopting
attitudes similar to those of colonial northerners. By the 1770s it was possible to

find advertisements in Virginia of healthy slave women for sale that mentioned "has never had a child" as a selling point. Also, the time lost during pregnancy annoyed some planters. Landon Carter best summarized this view in 1771 when he complained: "I hardly think my big bellyed are to be matched in Virginia. As soon as a wench is with child . . . they cannot work truely and not only fall behind, but come in, stay as long as they please, and care not ever to go out though close by their homes." Therefore, it is not surprising that a visitor to that state in 1791 reported that the owners he met there complained that their slaves "breed like sows."[41]

At the same time, however, an increasing number of slave owners in Virginia started to see the ability to reproduce as a valuable commodity and by the second half of the eighteenth century recognized the extra profits that the sale of slave offspring could bring. To help increase the value of their estates, some Virginia planters began stipulating in their wills that all leftover money should be "laid out in Negroe Wenches or Girls." Sale notices also started pointing out especially fecund women. One of the first advertisements mentioning "breeding" ability was in 1769, when "a fine breeding woman named Pat" was offered. While one reason for highlighting this trait could be because she was "lame on one side" and therefore unable to do much labor, soon announcements began to appear offering "likely young breeding NEGRO WOMEN" for sale. By the end of the eighteenth century, a woman's reproductive ability had clearly become part of her appraised value, and by the early nineteenth century, Thomas Jefferson regarded "a woman who brings a child every two years as more profitable than the best man of the farm"—a statement that would typify the Upper South for the entire antebellum period.[42]

While a slave woman's fecundity became especially important for owners in Virginia, planters in the Lower South also started showing a greater concern for this means of increasing their work force. As early as the 1760s, at least some South Carolinians were aware of the breeding potential of slave women. In a letter complaining that one British official thought that the price for a slave woman was too high, Henry Laurens, Charleston's largest slave trader, commented that "the Governor does not understand Plantation affairs so well as some of us Southern folks," explaining that in addition to being native-born and therefore more valuable, "Nanny is a breeding Woman & in ten Years time may have double her worth in her own Children." By the end of the century, one traveler noted that South Carolinians were "very attentive to this mode of enhancing the value of their estates," and another mentioned that pregnant slave women always brought more money at the auction block. This can also be seen in a Charleston advertisement in 1796 that offered "Fifty Prime Negroes" to be "sold on account of their present Owner's declining the Planting Business." The slaves had no fault and "were purchased for Stock, and breeding

Negroes, and to any Planter who particularly wanted them for that purpose, they are a very choice and desirable gang." Even in Louisiana, owners fostered reproduction in their chattels. One early nineteenth-century French traveler explained why planters encouraged their slave women to engage in numerous sexual encounters: "The masters favor these transitory unions which produce children for them, a source of their wealth."[43]

In addition to the shifting perception of slave women and their offspring, changes occurring in postrevolutionary America affected African Americans in other important ways. One of the most tragic was the increased kidnapping of free blacks and their sale into slavery in the Deep South. Slave stealing had always been present, but the concern that owners expressed over the return of their property had kept this crime to a minimum. Free blacks were another matter. Few whites noticed their loss, and most even thought their absence to be desirable. In the late eighteenth and early nineteenth centuries, a large free black population developed in the North and Upper South, and with it came the increased kidnapping and sale of many of these newly freed individuals once again into a life of slavery. Almost every state in the region passed laws against such action, some with heavy penalties. Virginia's law of 1788 even called for the death penalty without benefit of clergy, although in 1819 the punishment was changed to imprisonment. Delaware's 1793 law declared that anyone convicted of kidnapping would "be publicly whipped on his or her back with thirty-nine lashes well laid on, and shall stand in the pillory for the space of one hour, with both of his or her ears nailed thereto, and at the expiration of the hour, shall have the soft part of both of his or her ears cut off." Nevertheless, despite these harsh penalties (which were seldom fully enforced), the security of free blacks remained in jeopardy, simply because they were so little protected and the demand for slave labor in the South had become so great.[44]

Furthermore, many northern owners evaded emancipation laws and sold their soon-to-be-freed slaves south. Most northern states passed laws prohibiting the sale of slaves out of state, and abolitionist societies exerted much of their efforts trying to prevent violations of these laws, as well as the illegal kidnapping and sale south of free blacks. Some groups, such as the Pennsylvania Abolition Society, did have limited success in curbing these practices. Yet unlawful sales still continued. In 1807, eight years after the state's gradual emancipation law was passed, the New York Manumission Society reported that "the illegal Transportation of Slaves is now carried on to an alarming extent from this [state] to the Southward, particularly to New Orleans." Groups in neighboring Pennsylvania and New Jersey made similar complaints as late as the 1820s. Owners employed an endless variety of schemes to avoid their states' manumission and sale restriction laws, including carrying pregnant women across

Free black woman and child being kidnapped into slavery. This was a constant danger for free black people in the northern states and the Upper South. From Torrey, *Portraiture of Domestic Slavery.*

state lines so their children would not be born free, manumitting their slaves under long indentures and then selling them to out-of-state buyers, "renting" their slaves to southerners on long-term leases, selling slave children as "apprentices" to interstate buyers, and prosecuting their slaves for spurious reasons so that they could get permission from a judge to sell them south. These practices proved especially troublesome in areas with stronger commitments to slavery, such as New York, New Jersey, and Pennsylvania, although the dumping of human property occurred in every northern state, particularly before prohibitory laws were passed. Already by the early 1770s, traders were in Boston looking for unlimited quantities of young, healthy slaves for the domestic trade. Between October 1772 and April 1773, an advertisement appeared sixteen times in the *Boston Gazette* seeking "Any Persons who have healthy Slaves to dispose of, Male or Female, that have been some Years in the Country, of 20 Years of Age or under." (For three issues in December, the age was raised to twenty-five.) While it is uncertain if these slaves were sent south, it is quite probable since this advertisement had not run previously in Boston newspapers and was similar to those soon to appear in the Upper South.[45]

Freedom for blacks in postrevolutionary America, therefore, came at a price. In one of the many ironies of the period, the ideals of the Revolution helped thousands of men and women to obtain their freedom, yet the increased demand for American-born slaves, which was also in part caused by the Revolution, made the growing free black population of the North and Upper South an easy target for unscrupulous traders. Unfortunately, we will probably never know the exact number of Americans who were kidnapped or sold illegally. What is known, however, is that these practices were a significant problem and presented a constant threat to almost every free person of color in the early republic.

V

Equally disconcerting for enslaved African Americans was the increased frequency of sale that occurred in the late eighteenth century. The selling of humans from one colonist to another had always taken place, but in the early eighteenth century these sales usually involved either entire estates or the occasional individual sold to settle debts and balance accounts. By the second half of the century this had changed as more and more slaves, especially in Virginia, found themselves being sold to new owners for a multitude of reasons. One example of this trend can be seen in the growing use of slave sales as a form of labor management. The early eighteenth-century planter William Byrd II employed a variety of chastisements when correcting his slaves, yet he never threatened them with sale. This sharply contrasts with later Virginians such as Landon Carter, George Washington, and Thomas Jefferson, who often used sale to punish runaways and other "unruly" slaves.[46]

Another indication of the increased frequency of sale can be found in Virginia runaway-slave advertisements, public notices that often mentioned previous owners or prior sale. Examining these advertisements over time reveals how the percentage of slaves who had experienced domestic sale rose over the course of the eighteenth century, although using this source for measuring the percentage of slaves sold does present certain limitations. Frequently, slaves ran away precisely because of sale; numerous advertisements included phrases like "was purchased but a few days before he went off" in their descriptions. Also, individuals who ran away were often deemed to be more "unruly" than other slaves and therefore were more likely to be sold. Yet, the possibility of overrepresenting slaves with a history of sale is easily outweighed by the even greater probability of underrecording prior sales. Runaway-slave advertisements only mentioned previous owners or sale if the advertiser thought it would help in finding his property. Advertisements usually listed the probable destination of the slave. Sometimes this was a previous owner, but in many cases it was not. This proved especially true during the war years when numerous slaves left to join the British army or to seek their freedom elsewhere. Also, many advertisers gave no indication where they thought their property had gone. Therefore, while runaway-slave advertisements might be slightly biased by individuals who were more prone toward sale, this limitation is more than offset by the number of advertisements for slaves who had previously been sold but which for a variety of reasons did not mention a prior owner.[47]

Given these limitations, when one looks at the percentages over time, a clear pattern emerges. In the first half of the eighteenth century, the number of runaway-slave advertisements in Virginia that mentioned a previous owner barely reached 10 percent. By the second half of the century, the percentage of these advertisements increased considerably, to over 28 percent by the 1780s (table 1.1). This trend becomes easily noticeable when one examines the two decades encompassing the American Revolution. In the 1770s and 1780s the percentage of runaway slaves who definitely had a previous owner, or whose listed destination indicated a high probability of having experienced a prior sale, doubled from that of the preceding four decades (table 1.2). After the Revolution, the percentage rose even more. By the end of the 1780s, more than one-third of all advertised runaway slaves in Virginia had been sold at least once, and nearly one out of every two had a high probability of having been sold (table 1.3). Again, it is important to remember that these figures are most likely underrepresented and the percentage of slaves who had experienced prior domestic sale was probably greater.

Finally, the high frequency of sale in the late eighteenth century is corroborated by the testimony of the enslaved themselves. Although most slave narratives involve individuals from the antebellum period, enough from the eighteenth century are available to argue that the widespread selling of human property occurred at that time. Virtually every slave autobiography from the late eighteenth century mentions at least one sale (often at an early age), and most record numerous owners over a lifetime. The most famous narrative from that period belongs to Charles Ball, a slave born in Maryland who was sold at a young age in 1785 along with his mother and all of his brothers and sisters, each to a different owner. His father soon met the same fate. Ball had several more owners before being sold to a Georgia trader around 1805. The same pattern proved true for those in Virginia. William Grimes was born in 1784 and as a small boy was sold from the Tidewater into the Piedmont region of the state. Over the next thirty years, he had ten different owners. A Virginian named Dick was born in the mid-eighteenth century and sold a number of times throughout his life. He even claimed to have been sold twelve times in one year during the Revolution.[48]

TABLE 1.1. Runaway Slaves Listed in Virginia Newspapers,
1730–1789, Who Had Previously Been Sold Domestically at Least Once
and Who Had Probably Been Sold Domestically at Least Once

Decade	Number of Advertised Runaway Slaves Sampled[a]	Number and Percentage of Slaves Previously Sold[b]	Number of Slaves Returning to Relations[c]	Number of Slaves Returning to Previous Home[d]	Total Number and Percentage of Slaves Previously Sold Plus Those Probably Sold[e]
1730–1739	42	1 (2.4%)		1	2 (4.8%)
1740–1749	36	4 (11.1%)		2	6 (16.7%)
1750–1759	65	7 (10.8%)	1	3	11 (16.9%)
1760–1769	166	30 (18.1%)	1	8	39 (23.5%)
1770–1779	183	50 (27.3%)	6	6	62 (33.9%)
1780–1789	185	52 (28.1%)	9	12	73 (39.5%)

Source: Windley, ed., Runaway Slave Advertisements, 1:1–244, 389–410.
[a]Williamsburg newspapers consulted include Virginia Gazette, 1736–1750; Virginia Gazette, 1751–1778; and Virginia Gazette, 1779–1780; and in Richmond, Virginia Gazette and Weekly Advertiser, 1781–1789; and Virginia Independent Chronicle, 1786–1789. For 1730–1759 all available newspapers were used. For 1760–1789 only select newspapers were sampled. For the 1760s and 1780s, all runaway-slave advertisements in the select papers were examined. Due to the large number of entries for the 1770s, a random sampling of every third entry was used.
[b]For inclusion in this category, a former owner from the mainland colonies or an actual domestic sale had to be mentioned.
[c]For inclusion in this category, only blood relations were counted. Since husbands and wives often lived on different plantations, slaves heading toward spouses were excluded from this category because there is no indication that the runaway slave had previously been sold.
[d]For inclusion in this category, another mainland colony or county where the slave had been born, bred, raised, previously lived, or came from had to be listed.
[e]This column includes those runaway slaves who had definitely been sold domestically at least once in their lives in addition to those from categories 2 and 3 who had a high probability of having been sold domestically at least once.

In addition to the increased probability of sale, westward expansion meant that many slaves were being carried a greater distance from home after sale. Earlier in the century when slaves were sold, most at least stayed in the same locale. Later sale frequently meant separation forever from family and friends. Many owners tried to keep families together; this not only appealed to their paternalistic sensibilities but was also a good form of labor control. Nevertheless, when forced to choose, economic considerations usually prevailed. And there were plenty of owners, such as the planter who offered to sell a man "and his wife also, if required," who cared little about black family connections unless it benefited them.[49] All family members faced the possibility of sale, but children were normally sold first. The reason for this was simple. As the Virginian Peter Randolph explained to William Byrd III when recommending such a sale: "The only objection to this scheme is, that it will be cruel to part them from

TABLE 1.2. Runaway Slaves Listed in Virginia Newspapers
Who Had Previously Been Sold Domestically at Least Once
and Who Had Probably Been Sold Domestically at Least Once

Years	Number of Advertised Runaway Slaves Sampled	Number and Percentage of Slaves Previously Sold	Number of Slaves Returning to Relations	Number of Slaves Returning to Previous Home	Total Number and Percentage of Slaves Previously Sold Plus Those Probably Sold
1730–1769	302	42 (13.6%)	2	14	58 (18.8%)
1770–1789	368	102 (27.7%)	15	18	135 (36.7%)

Source: Windley, ed., *Runaway Slave Advertisements*, 1:1–244, 389–410.

their parents, but what can be done. They alone can be sold without great loss to you, and at present they are a charge."[50]

While the selling of children and the splitting of families might have benefited some white Americans, the historical record in the late eighteenth century is filled with accounts of the disastrous effect this had on slave family life and the grief that African Americans suffered because of it. More than one runaway slave was thought to have gone "after a parcel of Negroes lately purchased." The destruction of a family and the attempt to regain its scattered members can be witnessed in the advertisement for a slave couple believed to be heading for their offspring: "They have had several children, who are sold and dispersed through *Culpeper, Frederick,* and *Augusta* counties, to one of which, if they are not in *Lancaster,* I suspect they are gone." In his autobiography, William Grimes lamented that "it is not uncommon to hear mothers say, that they have half a dozen children, but the Lord only knows where they are." The old Virginian Dick remarked in reference to the dozen children of his who had been sold

TABLE 1.3. Runaway Slaves Listed in Virginia Newspapers
1786–1789, Who Had Previously Been Sold Domestically at Least Once
and Who Had Probably Been Sold Domestically at Least Once

Years	Number of Advertised Runaway Slaves Sampled	Number and Percentage of Slaves Previously Sold	Number of Slaves Returning to Relations	Number of Slaves Returning to Previous Home	Total Number and Percentage of Slaves Previously Sold Plus Those Probably Sold
1786–1789	92	32 (34.8%)	4	8	44 (47.8%)

Source: Windley, ed., *Runaway Slave Advertisements*, 1:1–244, 389–410.

away: "It was a hard trial to part with my little ones, for I loved them like a father; but there was no help for it, and it was the case of thousands besides myself." By 1805 it was not unusual to find an advertisement like one in Virginia which stated that a sixteen-year-old girl in the Powhatan County jail claimed that she "was raised by Wm. Gathright, of the county of Henrico, who sold her to Mr. Fulcher, the butcher, of Richmond, and by him sold to one Williamson, who sold her to one Webster, of Buckingham, who sold her to a Mr. John Cambell, of King & Queen county, who left her at Lewis Fortine's, a free Negro of this county; from which last place she eloped."[51]

VI

There were many reasons for the increased domestic sale of slaves by the end of the eighteenth century. Changes in demographics and southern labor supply obviously played a large role. As the Tidewater region became overstocked with slaves, many were sold west. Perhaps even more important by the middle of the century was the growth of a native-born slave population, which provided an easily procurable source of labor and expanded the number of acculturated (and therefore more desirable) creole slaves available for sale. Also, in a society where slaves were often used in lieu of cash, as more and more planters found themselves going into debt, the number of slaves sold to pay off loans and settle accounts naturally grew.[52]

While most of these factors had little to do with the American Revolution, the growing frequency of sale at that time coincided perfectly with the social and demographic changes caused by that event. The Revolution also had a direct impact on the number of slaves sold. During the war, thousands of slaves were captured and sold either locally or after being carried to other states.[53] Also, the abolition of primogeniture and entail forced the breakup of large plantations, increasing the number of slaves sold when estates were divided. While primogeniture and entail were never well established in America, their use had increased by the late colonial period as the availability of land had declined. However widespread, after the Revolution these practices were eliminated, and a more equitable division of estates was employed in the late eighteenth century. Although an overstatement, James Madison later remarked that it was the abolition of primogeniture and entail that was responsible for the breakup of large slaveholdings following the war. Interestingly, Madison cited this as an example of how the treatment of slaves had improved in Virginia since the Revolution, which not only shows how little white Virginians understood (or were willing to admit) of their charges' concerns but also illustrates another of the many ironies of this period. The dismantling of large estates was seen as a democratic improvement by white Americans, yet it produced drastically different results for American blacks.[54]

Most of the individuals sold went to other planters, and it was not until the nineteenth century that professional slave traders came to dominate the market. Nevertheless, by the 1780s, buyers were regularly coming into Virginia and Maryland to purchase slaves for South Carolina, Georgia, and the West. As early as 1780, one Williamsburg man commented on the many Carolina and Kentucky slave traders who "are dayle coming from all parts to purchase them, at most enormos prices." During that decade, advertisements from traders looking for slaves to buy also began appearing in the Virginia newspapers. In 1787 Moses Austin of Richmond offered "a good price" for 100 young blacks regardless of character for sale out of state: "Harty and well made is all that is necessary."[55] At the same time, notices for runaway "Virginia born" slaves greatly increased in Georgia. Although still only a scant proportion of the total, in the five years from 1785 to 1789 the number of runaway-slave advertisements in Georgia listing individuals born in the Chesapeake more than doubled over that of the previous twenty-five years, and the percentage of such notices multiplied by six and one-half times (table 1.4). Unlike the advertisements before 1785 that never noted how long a Chesapeake-born slave had been in the state, many of those later in the decade mentioned that the runaway was "not more than a few days in Savannah when he went off." Once again, the total number of slaves involved remained small. But by the second half of the 1780s, a clear jump occurred in the number of Chesapeake-born slaves appearing in Georgia runaway-slave advertisements. Since many of these individuals were "imported a few months ago" and did not enter with migrating planters, most undoubtedly arrived as a result of the developing interstate trade.[56]

TABLE 1.4. Runaway Slaves Listed in Georgia Newspapers Who Were Born in Delaware, Maryland, or Virginia

Years	Number of Advertised Runaway Slaves Sampled	Number of Slaves Born in Delaware, Maryland, or Virginia	Percentage of Runaway Slaves in Georgia Originally from the Chesapeake
1760–1784	961	6	.6%
1785–1789	330	13	3.9%

Source: Windley, ed., *Runaway Slave Advertisements*, 4:1–173.
[a]Newspapers consulted, all published in Savannah, include *Georgia Gazette*, 1763–1776; *Royal Georgia Gazette*, 1779–1782; *Gazette of the State of Georgia*, 1783–1788; and *Georgia Gazette*, 1788–1789. All available newspapers were used.

☞ *WANTED,*
ONE HUNDRED
NEGROES,
From 12 to 30 years old, for which a good price will be given.

THEY are to be fent out of the ftate, therefore we fhall not be particular refpecting the character of any of them—Hearty and well made is all that is neceffary.

Mofes Auftin & Co.

Richmond, Dec. 15, 1787.

Early interstate slave trade advertisement that appeared in the Richmond *Virginia Independent Chronicle*, December 26, 1787, just months after the signing of the new U.S. Constitution. Courtesy of the Library of Virginia.

Over the next decade, this activity only increased. The separation of black families had become so frequent that by 1792 Virginia governor Henry Lee blamed "the practice of severing husband, wife and children in sales" for an attempted slave revolt in two Tidewater counties. By that same year, notices featuring "Virginia-born" slaves were appearing in western newspapers, such as the advertisement in a Knoxville, Tennessee, paper featuring "a few young, likely Virginia born Negroes" for sale. Many Virginia counties had resident slave traders, and by 1795, at least one western trader was "Carrying on the Business, Extensively."[57] Most slave narratives of the period also mentioned out-of-state traders. Georgia buyers bought the Virginians William Grimes and Dick, and every member of Charles Ball's Maryland family ended up being purchased by traders from South Carolina or Georgia.[58]

By the turn of the century, Virginia had clearly become a major slave-trading region. The presence of out-of-state buyers in Alexandria was so common that in 1802 a grand jury presented "as a grievance, the practice of persons coming from distant parts of the United States into this District for the purpose of purchasing slaves." Advertisements seeking slaves for sale regularly appeared in Richmond and Fredericksburg newspapers, and travelers noted that "the Carolina slave dealers get frequent supplies from this state."[59] Thomas Jefferson supported this observation when in 1803 he noted that there were "generally negro purchasers from Georgia passing about the state." Virginia-born slaves had also established a reputation in the Deep South, as can be seen in an 1810 notice that appeared in the Natchez, Mississippi, *Weekly Chronicle*, which featured "twenty likely Virginia born slaves . . . for sale cheaper than has been sold here in years." Although not all were going with professional slave traders, in 1804 former Virginia governor James Wood estimated that between 8,000 and 10,000 slaves were exported annually from the state.[60]

Up until the War of 1812, the majority of Chesapeake slaves forced west went with migrating planters; however, after that date, the numbers brought by professional slave traders rapidly increased. One historian has estimated that 45,000 blacks went by this means during the 1810s alone; by that time, most Chesapeake slaves were no longer going to Kentucky but more than 60 percent went to Alabama, Mississippi, Louisiana, and the western territories. Yet, while the majority of slaves transported west prior to 1810 most likely went with migrating planters, there can be little doubt that by the end of the eighteenth century an organized interregional traffic in Chesapeake-born slaves was in operation. This trade had begun as early as the 1780s and by the nineteenth century had become a major factor in American life. By 1810 most Virginia and Maryland towns had professional slave traders who served both the local and interstate markets, and by 1820 the region had evolved into the predominant source of slaves for southern expansion. As one Maryland newspaper described it the year before, "The selling of slaves has become an almost universal resource to raise money."[61]

VII

In 1818, Estwick Evans, a New Hampshire native, traveled throughout the western states and later wrote of his experiences. Dismayed by the coarseness of western life, Evans was especially shocked by the magnitude of the traffic in human slaves that he found in Natchez, Mississippi. According to Evans, "They are a subject of continual speculation, and are daily brought, together with other live stock, from Kentucky and other places to the Natches and New-Orleans market." Like the Delaware Quaker Warner Mifflin before him, Evans also wondered what effect this trade would have upon the young nation: "How deplorable is the condition of our country!—So many bullocks, so many swine, and so many human beings in our market!"[62]

Estwick Evans's comments about the Natchez slave market illustrate the great change that had occurred in American slave trading in the late eighteenth and early nineteenth centuries. No longer were the majority of slaves sold in America imported from Africa; a domestic trade had developed, with increased sales between local owners and thousands of men and women forcibly transported from the Upper South to the Lower South each year. In many respects, this traffic evolved naturally, but it was also helped along by Virginia politicians who recognized that a large-scale export of their enslaved population was the solution to many of their state's growing concerns. Through their efforts, an interregional trade developed that transferred slaves from an area that had a surplus to a region where they were needed to satisfy the frontier planters' insatiable demand for labor. Beginning slowly in the 1780s, by the turn of the century it had become the answer to many of the Upper South's problems. Over the next forty years, this traffic in American-born slaves continued to mushroom, both in magnitude and importance, and the buying and selling of human property became an ever-present aspect of southern life.

Yet, while this new internal slave trade brought many benefits for southern whites, it had far different consequences for those who were the commodities within this trade. This proved especially true for enslaved women and children, who were increasingly valued for their breeding abilities and their utility as a quick source of cash. The emergence of the domestic slave trade likewise meant a greater probability of sale and transportation farther away from family and friends after such a transaction. Finally, the conjunction of the interstate trade, along with the abolition of slavery in the northern states, placed all black people in America at risk for kidnapping and sale into servitude in the Deep South.

There were many reasons for this transformation in American slave trading, but much of the responsibility lies with the American Revolution. The ideals of the Revolution helped lead to the eventual closing of the African trade, which meant that thereafter most slaves had to be obtained internally. The removal of the British from the trans-Appalachian West following the war resulted in rampant westward expansion fueled by land hunger and changes in agriculture. The promoters of this traffic frequently used the rhetoric of the Revolution to justify their actions, be it the closing of the African trade or the promotion of a new market for their goods. Not all of these changes were related to the Revolution, and some, such as the invention of the cotton gin, just happened to coincide at that time. Yet it is impossible to imagine the interregional slave trade developing without the American Revolution and the forces which that event unleashed. Not only did they lead to the abolition of slavery in the North, but they also resulted in a solidification of that institution in the South, primarily through the workings of the interstate trade. In many respects, the birth of American liberty also gave rise to this abominable new trade.

TWO

A Most Important Form of Commerce: The Rise of the Cotton Kingdom

In the first two weeks of January 1832, an extraordinary debate over the future of slavery took place in the Virginia state legislature. Held in response to the Nat Turner rebellion of the previous August, this was the first and only time in the nineteenth century that a southern state openly considered abolishing the institution of chattel slavery. For many white Virginians, this most successful of all North American slave insurrections shook their confidence in the slave system and its presumption that their "people" were happy with their lot. Yet, slavery had been a part of their society for more than 200 years, and it defined their very way of life. This debate carried ramifications for the rest of the South as well, since Virginia was not only the oldest slave state but also the largest. In the end, the slaveholders in the state managed to thwart this challenge to their identity and their livelihood, but just barely, as the legislature came within fifteen votes of abolishing the institution.[1]

The domestic slave trade played a major role in forcing the Virginia state legislature to reach this portentous decision. Among the many defenders of slavery in that body was a thirty-three-year-old delegate from Brunswick county named James Gholson. While not the most prominent speaker in this debate, in many respects, he raised the most important issue, as well as the most fateful. Gholson reminded white Virginians that no matter how much they might fear another slave revolt, they no longer had any real choice in the matter. Their state had become too economically dependent upon the institution of slavery to ever give it up, especially through some form of emancipation. He noted that "our slaves constitute the largest portion of our wealth, and by their value, regulate the price of nearly all the property we possess." Moreover, he understood how this wealth was contingent upon the interstate trade. As he told his colleagues, the value of their slave property was "regulated by the demand for it, in the western markets; and any measures which should close those markets against us, would essentially impair our wealth and prosperity." Therefore, not only would it be suicidal for them to eliminate their state's largest form of wealth, but they also had to be careful not to do anything that might threaten its source, namely, the domestic trade. If they did, it would "diminish the value of the existing slave property of this State, by the amount of twenty-five millions of dollars."[2]

Just barely a decade after its full implementation, the domestic slave trade had transformed southern society, making human chattels the most valuable form of property in the South. What James Gholson understood to be true about Virginia in 1832 also applied to the South as a whole: slave property had become so valuable that it was no longer possible for any southern state to eliminate it. The main reason for this was the steady escalation in slave prices resulting from the interregional trade. Furthermore, by serving as security for countless other investments, the vast capital in slaves propelled the southern economy and brought the region great wealth.

Most important, the domestic trade proved indispensable to the development of the Cotton Kingdom, an economic system based on the production of cotton through the use of slave labor. One of the most defining characteristics of the Cotton Kingdom was its constant expansion to the south and the west, fueled by the interstate trade in slaves. As thousands of enslaved African Americans were transferred from the Upper South to the Lower South each year, each subregion benefited, and this further strengthened their commitment to the institution of chattel slavery. This trade enriched all involved except the commodities themselves, yet it also brought troubling problems to the region. For one thing, both the Upper South and the Lower South performed actions that the other resented, and they increasingly viewed one another with mistrust. They sought to remedy this situation through legislation, but usually to no avail. Nevertheless, despite these occasional difficulties, both the Upper South and the Lower South recognized that they each needed the other for their continued economic success. So as the South expanded toward the Southwest, the interregional slave trade held together the various states within it in a mutually dependent relationship.

The domestic slave trade was also part of a larger economic transformation, commonly referred to as the market revolution, taking place in America in the first half of the nineteenth century. This was a period of immense economic growth that made commercial activity a greater part of people's daily lives. Moreover, it led to the creation of a national market, in which the South played a major role. The cotton grown there fueled the large textile mills emerging in the Northeast, and the products produced in those mills, and others like them, were shipped back into the South for consumption. Yet, while the South was certainly a part of this larger economic transformation, the effects were different there than elsewhere in the nation. This was because of the region's commitment to, and reliance upon, slave labor. And, as the slave trade made white southerners ever more firmly committed to the institution of chattel slavery, they were increasingly at odds with northerners whose response to the market revolution had been an embracing of free labor and a radically different way of life.

Therefore, while the domestic slave trade was responsible for bringing great wealth to some white southerners and solidifying the region's commitment to chattel slavery by making slave property too valuable to ever give up, it also helped to lead to the institution's demise. The social and ideological conflict between the North and the South eventually forced the majority of southern states to leave the Union, an action that ultimately led to a devastating war and a legal end to slavery. Yet, despite these drastic consequences, at the time most slave owners believed that they had little choice but to secede. By 1860, the rise in slave prices had made slave property so valuable and such a major part of the southern economy that few could accept its possible elimination.

I

Like other Americans in the early nineteenth century, southerners were constantly on the move, heading both south and west. And as they migrated, the South itself continually changed. Not only was its population moving and its borders ever expanding, but over time it also developed numerous subregions, each with its own interests and needs. Nothing illustrates these changes in the Old South better than the domestic slave trade, which both fueled southern expansion and helped to shape the complex variations within it. The factors that led to the development of an interregional slave trade by 1820 continued over the next forty years, and the constant southwestern movement of its people, especially its black population, was one of the defining characteristics of southern society.

One graphic illustration of this movement can be found in the changing demographic composition of the South. In 1790, 45 percent of all southern slaves lived in Virginia. By 1820 this figure dropped to 28 percent, and by 1860 it had sunk to 12 percent. In 1790 Virginia was the geographic center of the black population. By 1860 this location had shifted to western Georgia, and four other states had nearly as large a slave population. While Virginia continued to have the largest total number of slaves, between 1820, when its slave population was more than 425,000, and 1860, it had increased by only 66,000, or 15 percent. In contrast, the slave population of the states in the Deep South soared.

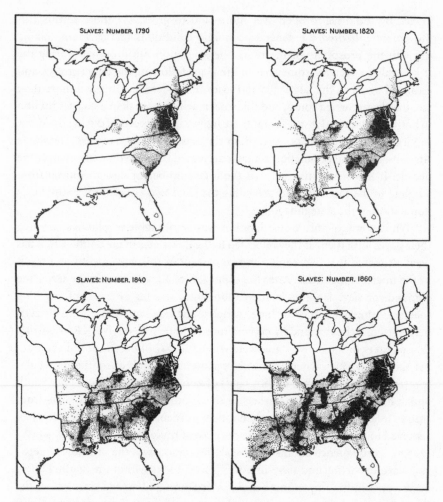

The spread of the slave population across the South, 1790–1860. Each dot represents 200 slaves. From Gray, *History of Agriculture*, 652–55.

Between the same years, the slave population of Alabama grew by more than 393,000. The growth in Mississippi was even more spectacular. In 1820 there were fewer than 33,000 slaves in the state; by 1860 the number had swelled to nearly 437,000. Even Louisiana, which had a sizable slave population in 1820, saw a growth of almost 263,000 during these years.[3]

In all, between 1820 and 1860, more than 875,000 American slaves were transported from the Upper South to the Lower South in what historian Herbert Gutman has called "one of the great forced migrations in world history."

Fueled by the drive to open ever more land to grow ever more cotton, this movement mirrored the general economic conditions of the South. Taking off with the prosperity of the 1820s, the migration mushroomed during the 1830s, only to decrease somewhat in the 1840s following the Panic of 1837, and escalated again in the late 1840s and 1850s. Each decade witnessed more than 150,000 slaves carried south, and this total reached more than a quarter million in both the 1830s and 1850s. To put these figures in perspective, during the 1830s, in Virginia alone, one out of every four slaves was forcibly removed. The state's African-American population actually decreased by more than 18,000 over the decade. It has been estimated that the total number of slaves removed from Virginia in the three decades preceding the Civil War equaled the entire black population of the state in 1790.[4]

While some of this vast migration was attributable to planters carrying their slaves with them as they relocated to the new states in the Southwest, it has been estimated that between 60 and 70 percent of this movement was a result of the interregional trade. After the explosion of King Cotton in the 1820s, the demand for slave laborers in the cotton states was far in excess of anything that migrating planters could have carried with them (and they eventually even helped to fuel the demand by craving more laborers themselves). Recognizing that planters in these new states were willing to pay hundreds of dollars more per slave than were owners in the older states, thousands of southern speculators transported hundreds of thousands of bondspeople from the Upper South and seaboard states to the markets of the Southwest. In the forty years from 1820 to 1860, more than a half million men, women, and children were forcibly removed to the cotton states for the purpose of trade alone.[5]

One consequence of this large-scale migration was the creation of separate slave-exporting and slave-importing subregions within the South. Differences between the Upper South and Lower South had existed since before the Revolution, but by the early nineteenth century, those distinctions increasingly turned upon whether a state was a net exporter or a net importer of slaves. As the South expanded and changed, so did these two major subregions within it. By the late eighteenth century, the states along the Chesapeake Bay (Delaware, Maryland, and Virginia, along with the District of Columbia) had already become net slave-exporting states and would remain so until the abolition of slavery. Initially the slave-importing states included Kentucky, Tennessee, North Carolina, South Carolina, and Georgia. By the early nineteenth century, the slave-exporting and slave-importing regions had already begun shifting to the southwest. North Carolina had become a net slave-exporting state, and by 1820, Kentucky and South Carolina had done so as well. In addition, by this date, Alabama, Mississippi, Louisiana, Florida, Missouri, and Arkansas had been added to the list of slave-importing states. The gradual southwestward drift of the slave-exporting and slave-importing regions continued through the nineteenth century as Texas became a major slave-importing state in the 1840s, and by 1850, Georgia and Tennessee had shifted to become net slave-exporting states.

This transformation in Georgia is a good indication of how far the slave-exporting and slave-importing regions had spread over the nineteenth century. At the beginning of the century, residents in the Chesapeake indiscriminately used the term "Georgia men" to refer to traders seeking slaves for the interstate trade; fifty years later, Georgia itself had become a net source of supply for the trade. These generalizations about slave-exporting and slave-importing states refer to net figures, and in many states, especially in transitional areas such as Georgia and Tennessee, there were always pockets of both slave-importing and slave-exporting subregions. This can perhaps be best seen in Missouri, which remained a net slave-importing state in the 1850s, in large part because of the strong demand for slave labor along the Missouri River in the northwestern portion of the state, even though, at the same time, the area along the Mississippi River in the southeastern portion of the state had become a major slave-exporting region.[6]

By serving as the economic conduit between the slave-exporting and slave-importing states, the interregional slave trade not only linked together the two main subregions within the South, but it also provided numerous benefits for both and subsequently strengthened the institution as a whole. The demand for slave labor in the Southwest gave owners in the Upper South an outlet for their surplus or "troublesome" slaves and furnished the region with much-needed revenue, albeit by placing an economic strain upon the Lower South. One indication of the magnitude of this economic exchange can be found in the 1837 report of a citizens' committee in Mobile, Alabama, which determined that their state's current financial hardship was due to purchasing $10 million worth of out-of-state slaves in each of the previous four years.[7] Moreover, limited supplies and added transportation costs forced planters in the Lower South to pay inflated costs for their laborers. Still, the region did benefit from the domestic trade. Planters no longer had to depend upon foreign sources for their slaves, and they were guaranteed a steady supply of native-born, acculturated bondspeople for their plantations. But, even more important, the interregional slave trade made the South's two main subregions economically dependent upon each other and strengthened the overall region's commitment to the institution.

In addition, the creation of a regionwide slave market provided a relative stabilization of slave prices and an escalation of property values across the South. While prices continued to vary from state to state, and slaves were still often sold for several hundred dollars less in the Upper South than in the Lower South, the high prices in the cotton states influenced the rates offered throughout the region. Because interregional traders paid for their purchases based on the amount that slaves would bring in New Orleans and other Deep South markets, this affected the price paid for similar individuals in Richmond, Charleston, or St. Louis, which in turn determined property values in even the remotest southern village or hamlet. Of course, there were always minor exceptions to this rule. But in general, the strong demand for labor in the Southwest drove up slave prices throughout the South. As one Virginia writer noted when complaining of the thousands of slaves that traders had carried from his state: "We cannot even enter into competition with them for their purchase. . . . Their price here is not regulated by our profits, but by the profits of their labor in other states."[8]

Therefore, by linking the South's two main subregions into a common economic concern, and making the entire slaveholding class wealthier as a result, the creation of a regionwide slave market became an indispensable component in the southern slave system. While this rise in slave prices often made it difficult for individuals who wished to purchase, it certainly proved beneficial for the region as a whole. Most important, it increased the monetary value of human property for everyone who owned it.

II

While the domestic slave trade certainly led to the creation of the Cotton Kingdom and brought great wealth to many southern whites, it also had its drawbacks and seldom ran trouble-free. For one thing, the interstate trade was often a source of tension among the various subregions within the South. Almost from its beginning, at times both the slave-exporting and slave-importing states had difficulty accepting their role in the regionwide slave market. Many in the Upper South cringed at the charges that they supposedly "bred" slaves for sale, while those in the Deep South resented the exorbitant prices they had to pay, as well as the quality of the individuals they were forced to buy. Therefore, the subregions frequently saw each other as more of an adversary than a partner in this trade and often took actions that benefited their section at the expense of the other.

Most troubling for whites in the Upper South was the accusation that they deliberately bred their slaves for export. This proved especially difficult to deny since, in fact, their region did receive a sizable economic gain from the export of its slaves to the Lower South, and some owners went out of their way to encourage this additional source of profit. As one Virginia man explained to his brother, "I would rather sell such negroes as brought the highest price, and keep women who will breed and increase our stock." Still, the implications behind such charges were offensive to many, and they tried to repudiate them whenever possible. As residents of the largest state in the South and as some of the most self-deceptive slave owners in the country when it came to their perception of themselves as "humane" masters, it is not surprising that Virginians in particular bristled at the allegation that they mated and sold their slaves as they did their barnyard livestock. In an 1859 article in *DeBow's Review*, the prominent Virginia agriculturalist and journalist Edmund Ruffin made this point most emphatically when he argued: "It is an old calumny, often repeated in England and by Northern abolitionists, that negroes are bred and reared in these older Southern States for sale, and that the surplus individuals were annually selected for market, precisely in the same manner as a grazier selects his beasts for sale." According to Ruffin, such charges were "entirely false."[9]

There is some truth to the denials of Ruffin and other Upper South defenders of slavery; to this day, no records have been found of "stud farms" or planters who deliberately bred their human property in the same way as their horses, cows, or pigs. This is not to say that Upper South slave owners were not aware of the reproductive capabilities of their slave women. They certainly were, and some did everything in their power to encourage procreation among their enslaved work force. But slave owners all across the South recognized this easy source of capital gain and did the same thing. Moreover, unlike livestock, which could be bred and the offspring sold within a year or two, to reach the same maximum return for a slave required a time lag between birth and sale of at least fifteen to twenty years. Therefore, it made little economic sense to invest in slaves with the sole purpose of breeding them.

While Upper South slave owners may not have deliberately bred their slaves exclusively for sale, they certainly were aware of their economic value and did sell off more of their human property than did their Lower South counterparts. They also knew that much of their slaves' market value was based not on what people in their region were willing to pay but on what those in the Lower South would pay. All of this was stated most clearly by a northern newspaper editor living in Washington, DC. In *The Progress of Slavery in the United States* (1857), George Weston acknowledged that "the citizens of Virginia indignantly deny that they breed and rear slaves for the purpose of selling them. Not only do those who interpose this denial, do so, in the vast majority of cases, with a consciousness of truth; but, perhaps, in no single instance can it be truly affirmed, that any individual slave is raised for the purpose of being sold." That being said, however, Weston then went on to argue that there still was some validity to this accusation:

> The fallacy of the denial interposed by the people of Virginia, consists in this, that although no one slave may be raised with a special view to his sale, yet the entire business of raising slaves is carried on with reference

to the price of slaves, and solely in consequence of the price of slaves; and this price depends, as they well know, solely upon the domestic slave trade.[10]

Understandably, white Virginians did not appreciate such sentiments coming from outsiders, and Edmund Ruffin's earlier comments make it clear that many southerners blamed northern abolitionists for the public perception of the Upper South as a region engaged in deliberate slave breeding. Some recent historians have also attributed this negative image of the Upper South to "a long abolitionist tradition." While it is true that the abolitionists frequently made use of this accusation and sometimes even carried it to ridiculous extremes, these Upper South defenders of slavery failed to recognize that the abolitionists were not the only ones who believed that the Upper South made much of its profits from slave sales.[11] There are also clear indications that a majority of southerners, including several prominent Virginians and border state politicians, considered the Upper South a slave-breeding region well before the abolitionist movement even became an organized force. As early as 1829, in a speech before the Kentucky Colonization Society, Henry Clay maintained that nowhere in the Upper South "would slave labor be generally employed, if the proprietors were not tempted to raise slaves by the high price of the Southern markets, which keeps it up in their own." Moreover, James Gholson made this same argument in the debates over slavery in the Virginia state legislature in 1832. And in a widely reprinted pamphlet that analyzed these debates, Professor Thomas Dew of William and Mary College also acknowledged, "Virginia is in fact a *negro* raising state for other states," and "it is one of their greatest sources of profit." Finally, an indication of how widespread such views were can be seen in an article that appeared two years later in the *Farmers' Register*, a Virginia journal edited by Edmund Ruffin. In this piece, the writer (quite likely Ruffin himself) admitted that "the rearing of slaves in Lower Virginia has so generally been considered a source of profit to their owners that it has scarcely been questioned or doubted."[12]

Such sentiments also continued to be held all the way up to the Civil War. Some Virginians even openly bragged about this source of their wealth. While traveling through the state in the late 1850s, the New York journalist and later architect and landscape designer Frederick Law Olmsted met a planter who boasted that his slave "women were uncommonly good breeders; he did not suppose that there was a lot of women anywhere that bred faster than his." He then added that "every one of them, in his estimation, was worth two hundred dollars, as negroes were selling now, the moment it drew breath."[13]

Southerners from the Deep South likewise believed that much of the Upper South's income derived from slave selling, although most of them did not see this as a source of pride. On his way back to New York, Olmsted's steamboat companion was a gentleman from Mississippi who "sneered at the Virginians." According to this Mississippian, the Virginians did not keep slaves to make crops, "they kept them to breed and raise young ones. It was folly to pretend that they did not." He also ridiculed the argument that the Virginians only sold slaves when forced to do so by financial difficulties, or that they only sold those who had committed some type of offense. As this man put it, there were few Virginians "who did not sell their niggers off, some of them, every year or two; whenever they wanted money. Some pretended they only sold the rascals, but the rascals they sold were generally likely boys, just the thing for cotton pickers, and would bring more money than the slow men and the women whom they kept."[14]

While some in the Upper South may have been uneasy about their region's reputation, this did not prevent them from recognizing the value of their property and knowing how to get the most for their merchandise. Buyers from the Deep South continually complained about the Upper South owners and their refusal to part with their slaves at anything less than top-dollar prices. As one Louisiana sugar planter on a slave-buying trip to Virginia noted to his factor back in New Orleans, "The farmers is aware of the prices, and will hold on. It is only after the harvest that people may be got cheaper, and not certain at that, then." After being offered some slaves who turned out to be "deseased," this Louisiana planter further added that "there is a cunning sett of people in this country and gentlemen to, or considered as such."[15]

But Virginians were not the only ones who knew how to get the most for their human property, as one man in Delaware found out when he tried to buy some slaves for his brother-in-law in New Orleans. This individual visited the house of a recently deceased man hoping to purchase some slaves at a discount before the estate was offered at auction, only to find "a man there before me on the same business." To make things worse, not only was he informed "that there had been several before me to purchase them," but the administrator "said he did not intend to sell before fall." As this disappointed buyer crudely realized, "by that time there will be enough purchasers to eat the negroes, fethers guts & all."[16]

In addition to the high prices they had to pay, whites in the Lower South also complained about the types of individuals sent to their states for sale. Primarily, they believed that the Upper South used them as a dumping ground for all of their enslaved criminals and other "undesirables." After finding out that a man offered for sale in Atlanta had previously been sold in Richmond under legal orders that he had to be taken out of the state, one Georgia newspaper asked, "Is it fair that Georgia and the other Southern States should be made the receptacle for all the vicious and unruly negroes of Virginia, Maryland, and

North Carolina?" Some in the Deep South blamed the slave traders for this practice. According to one Mississippian, "the sole purpose of a sale" for these businessmen was "profit," and the best way to increase their profits was "by purchasing the cheapest slaves, which would always be the most wicked and dangerous." These "insurgents and malefactors" were then "sold in a distant state at the highest price, to those who would be ignorant of their dangerous character." Needless to say, this man was sick of his state being "inundated" with "the sweeping[s] of the jails of other states."[17]

Others chastised unscrupulous owners in the Upper South. After an enslaved man was burned alive for killing his owner in Alabama, a Georgia newspaper reported that on a previous occasion, this same individual had "murdered his then owner in Kentucky, and that *he was run from that State, and afterward sold in Alabama.*" The paper then explained what it saw as the source of its region's problems and where that blame lay:

> These words that we have italicised contain the key to much of the arsons, rapes and murders perpetrated by our slaves. The sordid love of money rising superior to indignation for outrageous villany and foul murder, has been the means of escape of many a guilty negro from the gallows. The owner preferred to assist his escape, in order to save his value in dollars and cents.

Indignation over this "unfortunately too common practice" even reached into Texas, where one newspaper demanded: "It should be made a penal offence in every State where slavery exists for a person to carry a negro into another community than that where the crime was committed and offer him for sale."[18]

While the overwhelming majority of slaves sent south through the interstate slave trade were not criminals nor were they sold for any reason besides want of money by their owner, enough individuals were transferred as a form of punishment to give some credibility to these concerns. For one thing, several Upper South states openly exported slaves convicted of a crime. Leading the way in this practice was the state of Virginia, which between 1785 and 1865 transported nearly 1,000 convicted slaves outside of its borders in lieu of execution or imprisonment. While most of these exiled convicts were supposed to be shipped outside of the United States, a sizable number of them were undoubtedly smuggled into the Deep South. Maryland and Delaware also passed laws, in 1818 and 1828, respectively, allowing for the transport for sale of convicted slaves. As in Virginia, not only did this reimburse owners for executed or imprisoned slaves, but it also saved the states money in jailing costs. And it had another important benefit, as can be seen in the petition of one Maryland owner. After his enslaved man was sentenced to the penitentiary for stealing, this individual successfully requested "an opportunity of immediately transporting him out of this State into Louisiana; after which he apprehends this State will never be troubled with him again."[19]

In addition to the state-sanctioned transport of convicts, thousands of individual owners in the Upper South routinely sold off their "troublesome" slaves. Ironically, as the slave-exporting and slave-importing regions gradually shifted to the southwest, some states that had initially complained about the dumping of "undesirable" slaves within their borders eventually engaged in the same practice themselves. In the early 1800s, when South Carolina was a major slave-importing state, its newspaper editors dismissed attacks by other southern states on the state's reopening of the African trade by noting that "it prevents them from smuggling their own villains into our state, and selling among us those vicious negroes whom the laws of their state, or their own safety obliged them to get rid of." But, by the early 1830s, when South Carolina had become a slave-exporting state, a judge there admitted that the residents of his state engaged in the same practice, pointing out that "the owners of slaves frequently send them off from amongst their kindred and associates as a punishment, . . . separating a vicious negro from amongst others exposed to be influenced and corrupted by his example."[20]

III

Given the intraregional tensions created by the domestic trade, it is not surprising, then, that there were those in the South who worried about the consequences of this trade and argued that something should be done to bring it under control. One of the most vocal early critics of the slave trade was the Baltimore editor Hezekiah Niles. In his influential *Weekly Register*, Niles exposed the harmful effects this trade had on the Upper South, such as the increased kidnapping of free blacks, as well as the dangers it posed for the importing states, foremost of which was the importation of so many troublesome slaves. In one 1825 editorial that was reprinted throughout the Deep South, Niles pointed out that nearly 200 slaves had been shipped from Baltimore to New Orleans over a period of only a few months. He then asked: "Is it not time for the people of Louisiana to begin a-looking to the end of these things? The worst of the bad are those that are sent to them." As Niles made clear in this and numerous other articles, something needed to be done to regulate this trade.[21]

The type of remedy that Niles had in mind was a statewide ban on the importation of slaves for sale, an action that in 1825 had already been taken by a majority of the southern states, and something that Louisiana would likewise do the next year. By the Civil War, at one time or another, all of the southern states except Missouri, Arkansas, Florida, and Texas had passed such laws (and even these four states passed laws against the importation of criminals). Some of these state bans were of long duration; others proved to be only temporary; and some states opened and closed their borders with confusing frequency. For the most part, states in the Upper South banned the import of slaves for sale early in their histories and kept these bans well into the nineteenth century, while states in the Deep South and frontier Southwest were more erratic in their prohibitions, if they had them at all. The majority of these bans only tried to stop the importation of slaves brought by professional traders and did nothing to prevent residents from purchasing slaves out of state and bringing them in for their own use. The only state to enact such a prohibition against its own citizens was Kentucky, which did so in 1833. Yet, the severity of this act, along with wide-scale violations of it, led to its repeal in 1849.[22]

A couple of states in the Upper South also took the radical step of banning the export of their slaves for sale. Foremost in this regard was Delaware. As early as 1787, that state's legislature outlawed both the import and export of slaves for sale. Over the next several years, these prohibitions were strengthened, and, except for the 1828 law allowing the export of criminals, they remained in effect until the end of the Civil War. The only other state to have a modified version of this type of ban was Maryland. In 1817, that state criminalized the sale or transport out of state of slaves who had been promised their freedom after a term of years.[23]

While the restrictions on slave exports, led by Quakers and other antislavery groups, derived from genuine humanitarian concerns, none of the prohibitions placed on slave imports had compassion or abolition as their primary motivation. True, those individuals in the South who sympathized with the enslaved and who sincerely desired to halt the interstate trade in slaves rallied behind these laws. But humanitarian sentiment does not appear to have played a major role in their passage. This is even true for those bills that were ostensibly designed to protect the enslaved, such as those that prohibited the sale of small children away from their mothers. At one time or another, four southern states had such laws. The most sweeping was Louisiana's act of 1829. Based on the old French *Code Noir*, this law forbade the sale of children under the age of ten without their mothers, and it also outlawed bringing into the state any such child whose mother was still alive. In addition, Alabama passed a law in 1852 that prohibited the sale of children under the age of five without their mothers (if alive), and later that decade, Mississippi and Georgia exempted the sale of small children without their mothers from certain court-ordered sales. At first glance, these laws appear to have been motivated by the desire to protect enslaved families, but the simple fact is that at that age, such young children were more of a liability than an asset (especially in the Deep South), and they were worth more with their mothers than without them. While Louisiana's prohibition against the importation of such children does seem to have had some effect in curtailing this practice, most interstate slave traders had little use for this type of merchandise since they were difficult to transport and even harder to sell. Furthermore, these laws had no effect in the Upper South, where most of the family divisions took place. This meant that the majority of the children affected had already been made "orphans" by their owners well before the slave traders got hold of them. Therefore, the most significant aspect of these laws is their reminder of just how frequently slaveholders throughout the South must have divided their enslaved families, since legislators in some states thought that such laws were necessary.[24]

Practical motivations also governed the passage of the various bans on slave importations. The prohibitions in the Upper South were easy to understand considering their slave surplus; the last thing they wanted was to add even more to their already flooded market. Other considerations triggered those in the importing states. One fear was that slave populations were growing too rapidly and that disastrous consequences were inevitable. This can be seen in a Mississippi man's call for a ban on the importation of any more of "these pests" into his state. As he saw it, "The great increase of the slaves, together with those that are imported, will, in a short time, cause an overflow, which might give rise to an insurrection, and be the means of the shedding of much blood." Another concern was the loss of so much money from the region. According to a grand jury in Alabama: "Perry County has suffered much from the introduction of that species of property among us, by persons who live in other states, who have no interest in common with ours, who drain us of our money and leave us a superabundance of laborers." Others saw these laws as a form of revenge. After Louisiana passed an anti-importation bill in 1832, local planter T. S. Johnston believed that his state's slumping economy would improve: "We have been every year drained of the whole profit of our Capital for the purchase of more negroes. They will now be brought by actual settlers & our money returned to the country." But equally important for Johnston was knowing who would suffer the most from this act: "Virginia now begins to see & feel the difference between selling her slaves for money & having them carried away by her own people. The effect will be as beneficial to us as it will be injurious to her."[25]

Yet the most frequently cited factor for halting this trade in the importing states was the fear of whites over the type of individuals who they thought were being imported into their state. This was the biggest complaint that slave owners in the Deep South had against their counterparts in the Upper South, and more than anything else, it motivated them to pass laws prohibiting importation and to keep them in place once they had them. This can be seen as early as 1821, when Georgia considered removing the ban on slave imports that had been in place in that state since 1817. If the ban were lifted, one angry letter to the editor of a local newspaper complained: "Every man knows that speculators would constantly introduce into the state the dregs of the colored population of the states north of us; that the jails of North and South Carolina, Maryland and Virginia, would be disgorged upon this deluded state." It was also the reason that Alabama, Mississippi, and Louisiana all passed restrictions against slave imports immediately after Nat Turner's 1831 revolt in Virginia. One Mississippi lawyer later explained his state's ban at that time by noting, "The Southampton insurrection had just occurred, and negro traders had brought large numbers of the slaves concerned . . . into the state, and it was thought that the prohibition would prevent a recurrence of similar evils."[26]

Because most of these prohibitions in the importing states were based on temporary fears of revolt or the drainage of capital, that also helps to explain why so many of them were quickly repealed. However much slave owners in the Lower South may have worried over the quality of the people they were importing, or the flow of their money into the pocketbooks of slave owners in Virginia, the simple fact is that most of them could not get enough slaves to satisfy their needs and were willing to pay almost any price to get them. For that reason, the laws that were passed in the Deep South that banned slave imports were seldom of long duration. Some states, such as Louisiana and Mississippi, tried to compensate for this by requiring certificates of good character for all imported slaves. This meant that the trader had to provide an affidavit vouching for the individual's "good moral character" from two freeholders in the county where the person had previously lived. Several states also tried to regulate the trade by periodically raising and lowering the tax imposed on slaves imported for sale. But, in general, most slave owners in the importing states found these bans and restrictions inconvenient and of little value in alleviating the problems they were intended to prevent. As one planter in Mississippi noted when demanding a repeal of his state's ban: "This law is a barrier in the way of our people's buying negroes at a reasonable price. It does not keep bad negroes out of the state at all. It may keep honest traders out of our state, but it will not keep a dishonest trader from getting the necessary certificate of good quality &c of the worst negro that ever lived."[27]

As this man's complaint makes clear, probably the most important reason that these prohibitions, in all of the southern states, were eventually repealed was because they were almost impossible to enforce. This point was stated most bluntly by the South Carolina General Assembly's Judiciary Committee in the fall of 1821. Responding to the governor's call for a ban on slaves imported into the state, this committee agreed with the governor's sentiments but decided not to enact such a bill, stating that "it would be extremely difficult to effect this object. It is easy to pass laws highly penal, but in themselves they would be ineffectual to arrest a trade so lucrative between states whose territories are continuous & between which no officers are stationed to prevent illicit commerce."[28]

Slave traders and planters determined to buy easily found ways to skirt these restrictions. One common practice was for traders to set up camp just outside the boundaries of a state that had such a ban and let buyers cross into that prohibition-free state and sign their titles there. Georgia had one of the longest bans against slave imports in the Lower South, yet, as the *Savannah Republican* complained in 1849, that did not prevent "hundreds of negroes" from being "annually introduced and sold." According to the *Republican*, "It is a practice among these speculators, after having agreed with their several purchasers upon the prices to be paid, to take the Rail-Road or stage to the nearest point in Alabama or South Carolina, and there make out and sign their bills of sale." Also, these laws could not prevent interstate slave traders from transporting their merchandise on public roads, railroads, or waterways. Thus, while Tennessee had a ban on importations for sale that lasted from 1812 to 1855, given its crucial location between the Upper South and Deep South, it is impossible to know for certain how many thousands of slaves were driven along that state's roads, or how many were sold secretly to Tennessee planters for cash.[29]

Therefore, while the majority of southern states passed laws against the introduction of slaves for sale during the early decades of the nineteenth century, by 1850 all such bans had been repealed in the importing states, and by the time of the Civil War they had disappeared from every state except Delaware. Even there, they were unenforceable, as can be seen in the 1859 comments of a Virginia planter, who suggested, "Negroes are too high in our Market, so we will have to go or send to Delaware for our Supply." Most white southerners at one time or another thought that some type of restriction should be placed on the interstate slave trade, but in the end, such laws proved too inconvenient and ineffectual. For one thing, almost all southern states had pockets of both slave-importing and slave-exporting sections within them and, consequently, had difficulty speaking with a united voice on this issue. Also, the only effective way of regulating this trade would have been by coordinating efforts on the federal level, which was something that southerners would never have accepted. But the biggest problem with these restrictions was that southerners in the Deep South were simply too determined to buy slaves at any cost. While this had always been the case, it became especially true as the country rapidly expanded into the West and the price of slave property soared to record highs.[30]

IV

Over the course of the nineteenth century, southern slave prices more than tripled. The rate for a prime male field hand in New Orleans began at around $500 in 1800 and rose to more than $1,800 by the time of the Civil War. This was not the average price given for a southern slave; in the slave market, the term "prime" only referred to the best male and female workers, those who were young, healthy, and strong. According to sales records, the average bondsperson sold for roughly half the price of a prime male hand and prime women for slightly less than prime men. Moreover, prime hands often sold in New Orleans for as much as $300 more than in other parts of the South. Nevertheless, the price paid for a prime hand is still the most useful for understanding the dimensions of the trade, especially when assessing long-term trends in the market. It was the figure most frequently used by both slave traders and planters alike, and the rate for prime hands in New Orleans determined the prices offered elsewhere throughout the South.[31]

It should also be pointed out that southern slave prices did not rise at a smooth and even pace. Just as the overall forced migration mirrored the general economic conditions in the South, so did the long-term price of slaves. Following a steady rise through the 1820s, prices peaked in the spring of 1837, when they suddenly went into a tailspin, bottoming out in the mid-1840s, only to climb to new highs again in the last decade before the Civil War. Many factors determined the price of slaves, including the market rate of most southern staples. But over the course of the antebellum period, the price of slaves generally followed the price of cotton. As the *Richmond Enquirer* explained it: "The price of cotton as is well known, pretty much regulates the price of slaves in the South, and a bale of cotton and a 'likely nigger' are about well-balanced in the scale of pecuniary appreciation." This close connection between the South's two main commodities can also be found in a comparison of the two markets following the Panic of 1837, when the price of cotton plummeted from seventeen cents a pound down to six cents, and the rate for prime male hands in New Orleans dropped from $1,300 to $700.[32]

The price of southern slaves also fluctuated over the course of the year. The interregional trade was very much a seasonal business. The same person could sell for varying amounts from month to month with maximum prices offered during the height of the slave-trading season. In this trade, the majority of slaves were bought in the Upper South during the fall and were brought to the Lower South for sale in the winter and early spring. There were several reasons for this, the most simple being that sellers in the Upper South were more willing to part with their bondspeople after harvesting their crops, and buyers in the Lower South were more inclined to purchase after they had sold theirs and had extra cash. As one trader in Alabama noted, "Negros are [a] dull sale now. They have bin but little cotton soled yet." Moreover, there were also health concerns, as many in the Deep South feared buying freshly imported, or "unseasoned," individuals during the "sickly" summer months. Writing in early August 1847, a commission merchant in New Orleans advised a client in Missouri to wait a few months before bringing his slaves to the city for sale. A yellow fever epidemic was raging and "it is hard to say at this season of the year what negroes are worth, for they will not bring their value. Fall winter and Early spring is the proper time to bring them here." He added that "during the proper season of the year they would bring from 50 to 150 and in some instances $200 more." One study has found that, in the New Orleans market, slaves sold during the month of January brought prices 10.8 percent higher than those sold in September.[33]

Other factors temporarily influenced the price of slaves as well. International events, such as the threat of war, often dampened prices. As one slave dealer in Savannah complained, "Nothing doing on account of the decline of cotton and prospect of war in Europe." Local conditions also affected prices. In addition to the usual economic determinants, like the number of slaves in a particular market and the availability of money or easy credit, sometimes specific events could curb prices. Shortly after the threatened Denmark Vesey slave revolt in 1822, a South Carolina man noted that the price of field hands had risen considerably, "yet servants had not; owing I believe, to the bad conduct of great numbers of that description, at the time of the intended revolt in Charleston." In addition, according to one slave trader in Mississippi, "politicks Runs So high [it] keeps trade Back. After the Election I have no doubt Business will improve." Finally, another trader in Louisiana explained to his partner back in North Carolina that he "Could of Sold all the negros that I broght very Soon had it not of been for the Cholera."[34]

The most influential factor, however, on slave prices was the regular fluctuations in the price of cotton. More than anything, the price of this staple affected planters' willingness to purchase slaves. According to one Mississippi trader, "Sales have become a little dull since the decline in the price of Cotton." Conversely, a speculator in Georgia noted that "it is a uphill buisness here to do anything though cottin is looking up some in the last few days."[35] Even the slightest change in the cotton market could have an effect on slave prices, and many a trader saw his profits disappear after purchasing at the wrong time. As one Georgia resident observed in 1851, "The negro traders from Va are having a hard time of it as negros have gone down with the decline of cotton." Apparently they had "bought in Richmond when cotton was up and paid prices accordingly" and were now "sick of the prospect" of making any sales. Therefore, most slave traders followed the price of cotton religiously, in both good times and bad, and were constantly speculating on which direction they thought the market was heading. One good example of this can be found during the prosperous but volatile mid-1830s. In the fall of 1833, one North Carolina trader was fearful of buying any more slaves at such "strong prices since cotton has declined so rappidly," although two seasons later, another trader from South Carolina believed that "if cotton keeps up, and it is now on the rise, negroes will be very high in the spring and may be sold for almost any price on extended credit."[36]

This close connection between the South's two main commodities naturally led to a great deal of speculation, both monetarily and verbally. As one visitor noted, "The topic most frequently discussed is cotton and 'niggers,'" and throughout the South, people from all walks of life endlessly debated which direction they thought the two markets were heading. Attention became particularly intense during periods of high prices. This proved especially true during the mid-1830s, when slave prices reached record heights, and many questioned how long they could sustain their current levels. According to a woman in Missouri, "Negroes at this time are selling astonishingly high," while a buyer in Virginia observed that "even the negro traders are surprised at the prices demanded."[37] Of course, these supposed experts also differed in their opinions about the future of this market. In August 1836, one trader in Richmond wanted to buy even more slaves, "for I believe that some money can be made on them at present prices, and as I see no prospect of prices coming down." Another dealer in Tennessee, however, feared that "our country must under go a great change before Long as we cant stand things as they now are." Probably the most sensible assessment came from a doctor in Alabama, who noted the speculative nature of this market and ridiculed those who thought they could predict its future direction, commenting, "It is all guessed worke and . . . in truth none of them know anything about it."[38]

The financial panic that struck the nation in the spring of 1837 resulted in a slashing of prices of all types of commodities across the South. According to one man in Natchez, Mississippi, every type of property had fallen, including slaves who were now valued "at half the price of three months ago." By the following fall, normally a time of heavy selling in the slave-exporting states, a North Carolina resident noted that "no sales of negroes of consequence have taken place within my knowledge since the pressure," and a few years later, a Georgia newspaper reported that at least one coffle of slaves from North Carolina "were marched back for want of bidders."[39] Still, in many parts of the South, the demand for slave labor persisted, especially in the slave-importing states. In 1840 a Tennessee man informed his brother-in-law in Washington, DC, "Negroes sell very high here, partickularly on credit. It is really astonishing, why people will give such prices when the price of no article of produce will justify it, nor is the prospect ahead any thing but gloomy." The following year, an Alabama man echoed this sentiment when he noted, "They all cry out hard times here but when a likely negro is put mony will come."[40]

When the economy turned around in the late 1840s and cotton prices began to pick up, it is no surprise that the demand for slaves increased as well, and slave prices skyrocketed to new heights. In the fifteen years preceding the Civil War, the cost of human property more than doubled—and studies have indicated that this increase occurred in both the slave-exporting and slave-importing states. In Richmond, the price for prime men nearly tripled during this period; in western North Carolina, during the 1850s alone, the price of slaves rose by 108 percent; and in Texas, despite an increase in the slave population of more than 200 percent, the cost of slaves nearly doubled over the same decade and rose by 122 percent between 1845 and 1860.[41]

The spectacular rise in prices resulting from the interregional trade made human property one of the most costly, and therefore most valuable, forms of investment in the country. By 1860, the average price for a prime male hand in New Orleans had reached more than $1,800, an amount equal to more than $30,000 today.[42] By anyone's definition, a prime male hand was certainly a major purchase. Even more significant is the monetary value of all slave property when taken as a whole. According to economic historians, the total value of all slave property across the South in 1860 was at least $3 billion. This figure assumes an average price of only $750 per slave, which most recent studies have indicated is probably too low. (Many contemporary assessments also placed the total value of slave property much higher, usually at $4 billion.)[43]

Even at the conservative estimate of $3 billion, the value of the southern slave population was still enormous when placed in a comparative perspec-

TABLE 2.1. Estimated Value of U.S. Wealth and Expenditures in 1860

Slave population	$3,000,000,000
Capital invested in manufacturing	$1,050,000,000
Capital invested in railroads	$1,166,422,729
Capital invested in banks	$421,890,095
Currency in circulation	$442,102,000
Livestock	$1,107,490,216
Farm implements and machinery	$247,027,496
U.S. cotton crop	$250,291,000
Expenditures of U.S. federal government	$63,131,000
Assessed value of real estate	
Free states	$4,562,104,152
Slaveholding states	$2,411,001,897
Total	$6,973,106,049

Sources: U.S. Census, *Preliminary Report on the Census,* 190, 193–94, 197, 199, 231; U.S. Census, *Historical Statistics,* 647, 711; Bruchey, ed., *Cotton and the Growth of the American Economy,* table 3-A.

tive. It was roughly three times greater than the total amount of all capital, North and South combined, invested in manufacturing, almost three times the amount invested in railroads, and seven times the amount invested in banks. It was also equal to about seven times the total value of all currency in circulation in the country, three times the value of the entire livestock population, twelve times the value of all American farm implements and machinery, twelve times the value of the entire U.S. cotton crop, and forty-eight times the total expenditures of the U.S. federal government that year. Needless to say, the domestic slave trade had made human property one of the most prominent forms of investment in the country, second only to land. In fact, by 1860, slave property had even surpassed the assessed value of real estate within the slaveholding states (table 2.1).[44]

V

Given the enormous economic wealth in human property that the slave trade had brought to the region, both as capital gains and as collateral for other investments, it is easy to see how the slave-owning class believed that it had little choice but to secede and form its own confederacy when it realized that its predominant form of capital investment was seriously in danger of being eliminated. While there were obviously many factors involved in the decision to secede, the domestic trade had made slave property so valuable and such a critical part of the southern economy that it was impossible to conceive of southern society without it. Slave owners had to risk it all with secession or face certain economic collapse. For that reason, it is no surprise that the order in which the southern states seceded was in almost direct correlation to the percentage of their population that was enslaved, with those states most committed to the institution going first and those with the least involvement remaining in the Union (table 2.2).[45]

Most Americans at the time were aware of the immense value of slave property. As early as 1822, one South Carolina newspaper reported that the number of slaves in the United States was 1.5 million, and calculated at a cost of $300 each, they "would amount to four hundred and fifty millions dollars!" Forty years later, southerners were even more boastful about the economic worth of their slave property. In a story that was reprinted throughout the South, the *St. Louis Herald* gave an account of the value of Missouri's slave population on the eve of the Civil War. Estimating the average price of each slave at $800, the paper reported that the slaves in that state "would amount to the enormous sum of $82,969,000."[46]

TABLE 2.2. Order of Secession and Percentage
of Population Enslaved

First Wave (December 1860–February 1861)

South Carolina 57%	Georgia 44%
Mississippi 55%	Louisiana 47%
Florida 44%	Texas 30%
Alabama 45%	

Second Wave (April–June 1861)

Virginia 31%	North Carolina 33%
Arkansas 26%	Tennessee 25%

Border States (did not secede)

Delaware 2%	Maryland 13%
District of Columbia 4%	Missouri 10%
Kentucky 19%	

Source: U.S. Census, *Preliminary Report on the Census*, 131;
McPherson, *Battle Cry of Freedom*, 236.

Southerners openly worried about the loss of this huge investment with a Republican administration and frequently cited it as a reason for secession. In one of the more widely circulated pro-secession pamphlets, *The Doom of Slavery in the Union: Its Safety Out of It* (1860), South Carolinian John Townsend warned that the election of Abraham Lincoln would result in the loss of $9 billion to southern whites: $4 billion in slaves and another $5 billion in related property that would become worthless with the abolition of slavery. This same fear was likewise echoed by the secession commissioners sent out by the states in the Deep South and in the secession conventions themselves. In his letter to the governor of Kentucky, Alabama commissioner Stephen Hale tried to persuade that border state to join their cause by pointing out that slavery "constitutes the most valuable species of their property, worth, according to recent estimates, not less than $4,000,000,000." In its "Declaration of Immediate Causes" explaining why it had no choice but to secede, Mississippi's secession convention concluded, "We must either submit to degradation and to the loss of property worth four billions of money, or we must secede from the Union."[47]

Northerners were also aware of the tremendous value of this form of property and of the crucial role that the domestic trade played in creating it. Moreover, they understood that this vast wealth would force southerners to do whatever was necessary to protect it. In a story that analyzed the census data from 1850, the *New-York Tribune* determined that between 1840 and 1850 nearly 170,000 slaves were exported out of Virginia, Maryland, and North Carolina

via the internal slave trade. Using an average of $500 per slave, the *Tribune* esti-
mated that during this decade these three states received "$8,429,450 yearly for
their staple article of export. We see, therefore, these States have strong reasons
for clinging to slavery besides the one usually assigned to it, to wit: 'Northern
Agitation.'"[48]

While stories of this nature regularly appeared in the abolitionist press, perhaps the most telling account of how ordinary northerners perceived the real
reason behind the South's decision to secede can be found in the words of a
Union soldier stationed in Louisiana in late 1862. In a letter back to his mother
in New York, this young man wrote: "I tell you, a man that owns ten, twenty,
or thirty thousand dollars in *slaves, will not* give them up without a struggle to
maintain their (so-called) rights."[49]

THREE

A Most Fateful Form of Commerce:
The Fall of the Cotton Kingdom

In late November 1860, a short article entitled "A Tall Price for a Negro" appeared in the *Charleston Courier*. It told of a local estate sale where one enslaved man, a carpenter named George, "brought the enormous sum of thirty-five hundred dollars!" The report noted that George "was purchased by Rev. J. P. Boyce" and "that Mr. Boyce was afterwards offered four thousand dollars for him!" Its author added that "judging from the present price of negros, we should say that the 'peculiar institution' was far from being unpopular. We don't wonder that some men are in favor of re-opening the slave trade." At first glance, this remark calling for a reopening of the transatlantic trade might seem surprising, since the trade in Africans had been outlawed for more than fifty years. But this writer believed that the astonishingly high price of slaves made it impossible to prevent their importation, legally or not, and concluded by predicting: "One of the two things, we think must occur—the price of negros must fall, or the slave trade will be re-opened. The country may take either horn of the dilemma."[1]

In the end, neither of these things occurred, at least not in the way that this author intended, but the article does accurately convey some of the troubling issues that the domestic trade had raised for slaveholders on the eve of the Civil War. By the late 1850s, the escalation in the price of slaves had not only made this type of property too valuable to ever give up, but it also presented other serious problems. Most important, it had increased tensions between the slave-exporting and slave-importing states and heightened the anxieties of all slave owners over the future of their institution. For one thing, many white southerners had started to worry that their slave market was spiraling out of control and being driven by wild speculation. Not only did this cause some to fear that their economic bubble would soon burst, but the rising prices also made it increasingly difficult to purchase this form of property. Thus, slave ownership was becoming concentrated in fewer and fewer hands, and some worried that the growing number of nonslaveholding whites might lose their commitment to the slave system. Even more troubling, however, by the late 1850s disagreements between the Upper South and the Lower South over the perceived long-term consequences of the domestic trade threatened to tear the region apart.

As with the disintegrating relationship with the North, much of the South's internal breakdown over the slave trade had its origins in the nation's expansion into the West. While conflicts between the Upper South and Lower South over the interregional trade had always been present, in the early decades of the nineteenth century the economic benefits that this traffic produced allowed each subregion to overlook these differences. Yet by the late 1830s tensions between the Upper South and Lower South began to escalate as external forces increasingly threatened the slaveholding regime. In addition to the growing abolitionist movement, the Panic of 1837 had a devastating impact on the South, slashing the value of slave property in half. Consequently, by the early 1840s, white southerners had begun to see the expansion of slavery and an increase in the slave trade as the best means of alleviating their concerns. They believed that annexing Texas and opening up other new lands in the West would not only increase their political power in the federal government (by adding more slave states), but they also reasoned that all of the new settlers in this region would stimulate the demand for slaves from the current slave states. Hence, this increased demand would drive the value of slave property back up to its predepression levels.

By the early 1850s, expansion had fulfilled many of the white South's expectations, albeit at a heavy price. Simply put, expansion forced slave owners into an impossible bind. On the one hand, they believed that they needed new territories in the West for political parity and what they perceived as their economic survival. But at the same time, the acquisition of this land, which was largely achieved in the 1840s, unleashed forces concerning the slave trade that threatened to bring about the institution's demise.

As projected, the acquisition of new territory in the West did help to stimulate the interregional trade and bring about a subsequent rise in the market value of slaves. Yet the price of human property did more than return to earlier levels; by the 1850s, it had soared to record heights. For many, the high price of slaves became a subject of endless fascination, and stories of ever more spectacular sales filled the southern press. As one North Carolina editor put it: "It really seems that there is to be no stop to the rise."[2]

But with this escalation in slave prices came a heightened sense of anxiety for many white southerners. Most troubled were those in the Deep South, who not only feared possible economic collapse and a smaller concentration of slave ownership, but they also agonized over the unprecedented number of slaves imported into their region from the Upper South and the effect that was having on their trading partners' commitment to the institution of chattel slavery. While the drain of slaves from the Upper South through the interregional trade never seriously threatened the institution of slavery in most of the states in that subregion, many in the Deep South came to believe that it did. And, as is often the case in politics, the perception of reality is often more influential than reality itself.

For many in the Lower South, the answer to their problems could be found in reopening the African slave trade, and from the early 1850s on, efforts were made to accomplish this goal. While this endeavor attracted far more supporters than most Americans today like to believe, it was not successful, in large part because the movement to reopen the African trade only further divided the South. Most important, it outraged those in the Upper South who saw this as an attempt to flood their market with additional slaves, which would subsequently decrease their slave exports and slash the value of their slave property. Therefore, instead of unifying the South in the face of increasing outside attacks, as many in the Deep South had hoped, the effort to reopen the African trade only heightened the anxiety and mistrust within the region and led many to wonder how much longer their slaveholding empire would last.

Much of this debate about the long-term consequences inherent in the domestic slave trade was carried out in public arenas, such as legislative bodies and commercial conventions. But nowhere were opinions more freely exchanged than in the region's press. As the predominant communications medium, southern newspapers offered the most widespread vehicle for expressing public concerns about this topic. In the 1850s, editorials, letters, and stories about the internal trade and the pros and cons of reopening the African trade filled their pages. It is of course impossible to accurately measure the influence that this form of debate had on the southern public. But if the frequency with which such items appeared in the southern press is any indication of the importance that this topic held for readers, then the long-term implications of the domestic slave trade were certainly an issue that concerned many white southerners.

While the motivations behind the decision to secede were certainly multifaceted and encompassed a variety of factors, one important contributor to this action was the long-term consequences inherent in the domestic slave trade. While the expectations of those in the slave-exporting and slave-importing states were often at odds over the trade, as long as each subregion recognized that it had more to gain by maintaining this economic relationship, it was able to overlook these relatively minor tensions. But when those tensions became compounded by increasing outside pressures, slaveholding southerners were forced to acknowledge what they perceived as the inevitable outcome of this trade, and their relationship began to fall apart. As it did, many in the South, especially in the Deep South, increasingly came to believe that the only way to maintain their peculiar institution was through drastic action. Therefore, in addition to a desire to protect their predominant form of property, there were other forces associated with the domestic trade that led many white southern- ers to conclude that they had little choice but to secede. They feared that if they did not act soon, the domestic slave trade would bring an end to their fortunes and their cherished way of life.[3]

I

While it is generally acknowledged that the question of slavery in the western territories first became a serious concern in American politics in 1844 with the debate over the annexation of Texas, less known is the dispute that also began to occur at that time among southerners over the long-term consequences of the domestic slave trade. At the forefront of both of these debates was Sena- tor Robert Walker, a Democrat from Mississippi. Born in Pennsylvania, Walker relocated to Mississippi as a young man and, like many of his new neighbors, became a large slaveholder. While he had no moral qualms about slavery and saw it as the best way to control the supposedly unruly black population, he did believe that the institution posed impending economic problems that threat- ened the South. Consequently, he became an ardent expansionist because he saw that as the best way to rid the country of both slavery and blacks.

Walker explained his views in a lengthy public letter advocating the imme- diate annexation of Texas. Ostensibly addressed to the people of Carroll County, Kentucky, the letter was clearly intended for a larger audience, espe- cially the undecided voters of the North. For years, the majority of northerners had opposed annexation because they saw it as primarily an effort to expand and strengthen the institution of slavery. As early as 1829, seven years before Texas even declared its independence, the British minister to the United States claimed that most northerners opposed Texas coming into the Union, because adding so much new territory would "afford an immense opening of the domestic slave trade." Therefore, one of Walker's most important tasks in this letter was to convince people in the North that their fears had been misplaced and that annexation was really in their best interests.[4]

At the heart of Walker's letter was his argument that, contrary to popu- lar belief, the addition of Texas would not extend the boundaries of slavery, but would actually help to bring about slavery's gradual elimination from the United States. It would do so by accelerating forces already in motion—namely, the movement of slaves from the Upper South and East to the Lower Southwest via the interstate slave trade. Walker pointed out that, since the purchase of Louisiana and Florida, more than a half million slaves had already left Delaware, Maryland, Virginia, and Kentucky. With the annexation of Texas, he predicted, the institution would disappear from Delaware within ten years and from Maryland in twenty and would greatly decrease in the other two states. As Walker saw it, as "slavery advances in Texas, it must recede to the *same extent* from the more northern of the slaveholding States" and soon disappear from them entirely. Moreover, as the lands in Texas eventually became worn out as they had in the East, slavery would continue to drift farther southward into a climate supposedly more congenial "for the African race." Therefore, according to Walker, annexation would result in a relocation of slavery, and Texas would prove to be a great "safety-valve, into and through which slavery will slowly and gradually recede, and finally disappear into the boundless regions of Mexico, and Central and Southern America."[5]

Walker's letter proved to be a big success and was credited with helping to win the presidential election that fall for the Democratic ticket of James K. Polk and George Dallas, who had campaigned for annexation, while their Whig opponents had opposed it. His letter first appeared in the Washington *Globe* on February 3, 1844, but by the following fall, it had been reprinted in countless newspapers across the country and had come out in five pamphlet editions. According to John L. O'Sullivan, editor of the *Democratic Review* and a well-known advocate of manifest destiny, by the end of the year, this letter had been "circulated by millions throughout the Union" and had served as the "text-book" for the Democratic party during the recent elections. Even those who opposed annexation had to agree with this assessment, admitting that Walker's letter presented "in a condensed form, all the arguments in favor of this measure."[6]

As could be expected, Walker's letter came under sharp criticism in the North and was hotly debated among politicians, newspaper editors, and the public at large. Even some northern Democrats found Walker's arguments far-fetched. One of the earliest and most formidable critics was Theodore Sedgwick, an antislavery Democrat from New York. In his public letter, which was also reprinted as a pamphlet, Sedgwick called Walker's argument "almost ludicrous" and asked: "How in the nature of things can the addition of slaveholding States diminish the extent or influence of that institution? ... Is the addition of a great mart for the sale and consumption of slaves likely to diminish the supply of the article?" Some northerners, including several prominent Democratic politicians, did come to Walker's defense. Both the secretary of war, William Wilkins, and the chairman of the House Foreign Affairs Committee, Charles Ingersoll, repeated Walker's claim that the annexation of Texas would quickly lead to the abolition of slavery in the Upper South and eventually in the entire United States. While Walker's letter may not have convinced every northern voter, his argument was certainly discussed by them, and it provided northern Democrats with a justification for supporting annexation.[7]

Robert Walker's letter also circulated in southern newspapers, where it raised far less controversy. In fact, there was hardly any public debate on it, in large part because of the widespread support for annexation in the South already. Not only were the cheap farmlands of Texas attractive to most southerners, but so too was the prospect of more slaveholding members of Congress for this large territory. So, fewer southerners needed to be convinced of the benefits of annexation, and most of those who did lived in the Upper South. For many of these individuals, Walker's argument struck a responsive chord. People could still be found in the Upper South who hoped that slavery might one day disappear from their states, and by the early 1840s their numbers had risen with the grim economic conditions of the time. Walker gave them a reason to believe that their wishes could come true, however unrealistic they may have been. Walker's thesis was also not that different from Thomas Jefferson's old ideas about "diffusion," a term Walker employed when describing how slavery would vanish from the South. As a result, at least some southerners who had previously opposed annexation must have found his letter appealing and changed their minds because of it.[8]

Still, Walker did have his critics in the South, although most of them were more troubled by his projected outcome than they were by his logic. While never totaling many in numbers, the arguments of these dissenters were nevertheless significant, as they foreshadowed the debates that would tear the slaveholding South apart over the next fifteen years. Notably, two of the most vocal opponents of annexation were Whigs from the Deep South. Living in states with high percentages of slaves, they had no desire to see slavery disappear from the Upper South and opposed annexation for precisely the same reason Robert Walker endorsed it. The first of these men was Senator Alexander Barrow of Louisiana. In a letter published in the Washington *National Intelligencer*, Barrow noted that Maryland, Virginia, Kentucky, and Tennessee were all turning their backs on slavery, and if Texas were annexed, "some, if not all of these States, will be drained of their slaves." He then asked, "What, then, becomes of this bugbear of the balance of political power, should all or the most of these States join themselves, as in the course of time they would probably do, to the non-slaveholding States?"[9]

Even more encompassing in his attack on annexation was Representative Waddy Thompson of South Carolina. In a letter to the *Intelligencer* published a little more than a month after Barrow's, Thompson also proclaimed his opposition to annexation, which surprised many in the South since he had once been a leading advocate for Texas and was even the first member of Congress to call for its recognition. After reading Walker's letter, as well as those by William Wilkins and Charles Ingersoll, Thompson fully accepted their argument that "the certain and inevitable tendencies of the annexation of Texas are to promote the abolition of slavery." He, however, did not see this as a desirable outcome. For him, slavery was not an evil but a blessing, and its removal would be "absolutely ruinous to the South."[10]

Few white southerners paid much heed to Barrow's and Thompson's warnings in 1844, for the same reason that they said little or nothing about Walker's argument: they needed to regain the market value of their slaves. In 1844, the country was still mired in the depths of a major depression that had begun with the Panic of 1837. The majority of slave owners supported annexation because they knew that expansion into Texas and the rest of the West would create an increased demand for their slaves and a rebound in their price. This can be seen most clearly in the words of James Gholson, the Virginia state legislator who back in 1832 had warned his colleagues about the importance of the domestic slave trade to their state's economy. In 1844 he supported annexation because he believed that "the acquisition of Texas would raise the price of slaves fifty per cent at least." It is also why so many slave traders came out in favor of James K. Polk that year; they knew that his election would increase their business. The *New-York Tribune* reported that "nearly every slave-trader in the Union zealously support[ed] him and the 'Polk and Dallas' flag" could be seen "streaming from the great slave-dealer's pen in Washington."[11] It really did not matter to the majority of white southerners at that time whether or not they actually believed that Walker's prediction would ever come true. The one thing that they did know, and that they did truly care about, was that the addition of new territory for slavery would increase the demand for their human property and bolster the capital value of all American slaves in the process.[12]

In many respects, the events of the next fifteen years proved these southerners to be correct. As ever more settlers moved into Texas, the demand for slaves from the older states increased, and so did their price, which stimulated the call for even more new territory and even more slaves. Coupled with this was the rise in the price of cotton as the country slowly came out of its long economic depression. The impact of all of this on the southern economy was astonishing. Following the annexation of the Lone Star state in 1845, the price of slaves began to pick up and by 1860 it had risen by more than 150 percent. Whatever doubts that some individuals may have had about the profitability of slavery in the mid-1840s disappeared as the market value of their slaves climbed to record highs. Politicians all across the South demanded that slavery continue to expand. While much of this effort was obviously motivated by politics, there is no denying that many people understood the economic benefits that expansion could bring. When running for governor of Virginia in 1855, Henry Wise was reported to have said that if slavery were permitted in California, slaves would sell for $5,000 apiece.[13]

II

The rapid rise in slave prices during the 1850s naturally led to a great deal of excitement among the southern public. As one slave trader in South Carolina described it: "Every body is in high Spirits about the high prices of negros." Recognizing the interests of their readers, newspaper editors across the South started publishing accounts of noteworthy sales. Featuring headings such as "ENORMOUS PRICES FOR SLAVES" and "BIGGEST SALE YET,"[14] stories frequently concluded with assessments like "this is the most remarkable sale of negroes we have ever known take place in Georgia," "we doubt if ever such prices were paid for negroes in Mississippi," or "such a sale we venture to say has never been equalled in the State of Louisiana."[15] Not only did they publicize the record prices in their own or neighboring states, they also reprinted stories from more-distant locations, especially in the Southwest. A newspaper in Nashville told of the "PRICES OF NEGROES IN TEXAS," while another in Savannah cited the "HIGH PRICES OF SLAVES IN NATCHITOCHES," Louisiana. Finally, stories of unbelievable bargains appeared, such as the report in an Austin, Texas, paper that claimed, "A tip-top Negro blacksmith was sold in this city yesterday for the sum of $2000, and the purchaser was offered shortly after, $500 [more] for his bargain."[16]

Historian Gavin Wright tried to explain this phenomenon by comparing southerners' fascination with the slave market in the 1850s to home ownership today. He noted that "most families buy one house to live in and do not frequently buy and sell in response to fluctuations in price; yet these households maintain an active and sometimes intense interest in the value of their homes." Wright's analogy is not perfect as most southern slave owners bought and sold their slaves much more frequently than modern home owners buy houses, and the price of a prime southern slave, roughly $30,000 in today's dollars, was actually closer to an expensive automobile than a house. Nevertheless, the analogy is useful in illustrating how those who never regularly buy and sell a valuable form of property, or even own it for that matter, still maintain an interest in the market fluctuations of that property, especially during periods of rapid escalation.[17]

By the late 1850s, runaway inflation had caused drastic changes in the southern slave market. Not only were slave prices at dizzying heights, but most important, they had broken away from their long-standing connection to cotton. No longer was the price of human property tied to the fortunes of the region's most dominant crop or to any other staple; insatiable demand and rampant speculation had become the sole determinants of slave prices, which seemed to increase daily. Planters in the Deep South began buying slaves at an almost frantic pace, driven by the fear that if they did not buy now, prices would go even higher in the future. As one Louisiana man explained it, "They are bought up as fast as they get here and at the present time there is not a single A no 1 man on the market." Still, this planter was going to "purchase eight or ten men even at these prices, for I feel perfectly satisfied that negro men will bring next winter from $1700 to $1800, and there is no telling what point they will finally reach."[18]

There are also indications that by the late antebellum period, the interregional slave trade was transforming from a seasonal business into a full-time affair. As the editor of the Richmond *Dispatch* noted in July 1856, "There has been a greater demand for negroes in this city during the months of May, June and July, than ever known before and they have commanded better prices during that time. This latter is an unusual thing, as the summer months are generally the dullest in the year for that description of property." He added that "a large number of negroes are bought on speculation, and probably there is not less than $2,000,000 in town now seeking investure in such property." This conversion to a full-time business can also be seen in the Deep South, where by the late 1850s, several prominent slave dealers in New Orleans advertised that their services would now be available all year long. In July 1860, Charles Hatcher announced a new "Summer Arrangement" that allowed him to keep his Gravier Street depot "open Winter and Summer."[19]

While most white southerners initially saw the rise in slave prices as a positive development, by the late 1850s, many began voicing their concern, especially in the Deep South. After reporting the "ENORMOUS PRICES" of the slaves sold at an estate sale in central Louisiana, the *New Orleans Bee* noted that it was "difficult to conceive how slave labor can be profitably applied at such exorbitant prices. If an adult field-hand is worth over twenty-three hundred dollars, what would a first-rate negro mechanic bring on the auction table?" This sentiment was echoed by a Tennessee resident who complained, "Negroes are out of all question. A negro man sold about a month ago for $1800 & nothing but a field hand at that." Having experienced the consequences of the economic boom of the mid-1830s, many in the region agreed with the Mississippi planter who worried that "a crash must soon come upon the country."[20]

Articles in the Deep South's newspapers tried to counter this fear. The *New Orleans Crescent* argued that it did not matter if slave prices had surpassed the price of cotton because that old relationship no longer accounted "for the present aspect of the slave market." Therefore, according to the *Crescent*, "the great demand for slaves in the Southwest will keep up the prices of negroes as it caused their advance in the first place." The Tallahassee *Floridian and Journal* agreed and also argued that the "extraordinary advance in the price of slaves" only worked to strengthen the South: "In fact, it is impossible to avoid the conclusion that slavery has never had more of the appearance of permanency than at the present time. Never before have the Southern States presented such a firm, united, unflinching front for its defense."[21]

Most editors, however, were not so optimistic and warned of the economic consequences of buying so many slaves at such high prices. The New Orleans *Picayune* reminded its readers that "the present value of slaves is not without a precedent," and "in 1835, the demand for slaves at the South commenced palpably to increase" only to be cut in half during the following crash. The *Mobile Register* worried that the overproduction of cotton would lead to a drop in the price of that staple, and "a decline of a few cents in cotton would produce a reaction that must, necessarily seriously embarrass the planting interest." In Athens, Georgia, the *Southern Banner* warned that "everybody except the owners of slaves must feel and know that the price of slave labor and slave property at the South is at present too high when compared with the prices of everything else. There must ere long be a change." Another Georgia paper, the Milledgeville *Federal Union*, was even more blunt, stating: "There is a perfect fever raging in Georgia now on the subject of buying negroes. . . . Men are demented upon the subject. A reverse will surely come."[22]

Even more troubling than a potential crash in the southern economy, many of the Deep South's newspapers also started worrying about the dangerous impact of the high price of slaves on the institution of slavery as a whole. One major concern was the effect that rising prices had on the percentage of white southerners who could afford to own slaves. In 1854 the *Charleston Mercury* took the lead in voicing this fear, warning that "there was danger to the institution itself arising out of the high price of slaves, by tending to concentrate them in the hands of the few." In the following years, the *Mercury* ran numerous editorials and letters that touched upon this topic and included, among other things, census data that proved that the percentage of southern whites who owned slaves, and therefore had a stake in the system, was shrinking.[23]

Similar stories appeared in newspapers, large and small, all across the Deep South. According to one paper in Macon, Georgia, there was "no chance for poor men to get African laborers at such a price," while another in Tuskegee, Alabama, feared that "Negro property is getting to be a monopoly—the high price of it makes it so." Other editors let their readers know what would happen to the South and its cherished way of life if things did not change soon. After noting that "the present price of negroes is exorbitant and ruinous. The rich only are able to possess them," the *Ouachita Register*, a paper in rural Louisiana, warned, "Let things go on as they are now tending, and the days of this peculiar institution of the South are necessarily few. The present tendency of supply and demand is to concentrate all the slaves in the hands of the few, and thus excite the envy rather than cultivate the sympathy of the people." Another small-town editorial reprinted in the *New Orleans Crescent* left no doubt as to what would happen next: "That minute you put it out of the power of common farmers to purchase a negro man or woman to help him in his farm, or his wife in the house, you make him an abolitionist at once."[24]

Added to this fear of decreasing white ownership of slave property was the staggering number of slaves entering the Deep South from the exporting states. By the late 1850s, stories appeared in newspapers all across the Lower South commenting on the large shipments of slaves bound for their region. Most of these pieces focused on the removal of slaves from the border states and were enhanced with corroborating articles reprinted from papers in the Upper South. In February 1859, the Austin, Texas, *State Gazette* published an item from the Petersburg, Virginia, *Express* claiming that "an almost endless outgoing of slaves from Virginia to the South has continued for more than two weeks past," and the next month, the *Savannah Republican* noted that "the Weldon (N.C.) Patriot says that two thousand negroes passed through that place during the month of January, and not less than fifty thousand, it is informed, went into the cotton regions during the last year." In one of the more widely quoted editorials on this subject, the Montgomery *Confederation* not only warned of the flow of slaves from the border states but also suggested that slaves from South Carolina and Georgia were part of this exodus as well. After relaying a report from the Portsmouth, Virginia, *Transcript* that claimed "heavy shipments of negroes for the far South are made almost every day by the Seaboard and Roanoke Railroad," the *Confederation* then estimated that during the previous two months "the daily shipments by the railroads from Augusta, south and west alone, have not averaged less than some two hundred, . . . and they are still coming at that, if not a greater ratio. There has never been anything like it before."[25]

The main reason that whites in the Deep South were so troubled by this flood of slaves entering their region was the negative effect that this process was bound to have on the Upper South and its commitment to the institution of slavery. For years, whites in the Lower South had expressed concern over the large numbers of slaves brought into their states for sale, but in the past, most of this anxiety had been related to the quality of the individuals imported and to fears of slave revolts. By the 1850s, however, this changed, in large part because of the intensifying attacks on their slave system by the North. Also, in many respects, what white southerners feared in the 1850s was the same process that Robert Walker had advocated fifteen years earlier, which so few southerners at the time had paid any heed. Therefore, as the price of slaves skyrocketed and the sectional crisis with the North escalated, a growing number of southerners, especially in the Deep South, became increasingly worried about the long-term implications of the steady drain of slaves from the states in the Upper South.

One of the earliest papers to address this issue was the *Savannah Republican*, which began a series of articles on the topic in January 1849. According to the *Republican*, "The acquisition of Texas, by affording a new outlet to the surplus negro population of the old States, has given a wonderful impetus to the slave trade. Thousands are brought South or carried West every season." However, "so great has this traffic become, that it will effectually drain Maryland and Virginia in a few years, if it is not arrested." The paper placed a major portion of the blame for this dilemma on planters in its own region when it noted that "we are actually offering them inducements to become free States by allowing them to bring their slaves amongst us and paying them large prices for them."[26] These sentiments appeared again and again in papers across the Lower South over the next ten years. In 1859, the Jackson *Mississippian* summed up the fears of many when it wrote:

> The great demand for slave-labor in the South, and its precarious tenure
> in the border States, is causing them to send us their slave population
> in unprecedented numbers and we are buying it at marvelous prices.
> What is to be the effect of this upon the border States? Free labor will
> necessarily take the place of slave labor, and when it preponderates—as
> it soon must—they will become anti-slavery States.[27]

To prove to their readers that this was happening, newspapers in the Deep South ran countless articles during the 1850s demonstrating that the states in the Upper South were losing their slave populations and, with them, their commitment to slavery. One state that drew particular attention was Virginia, in large part because of its historical importance as the originator of American slavery and the fact that it was the largest supplier of slaves for the interstate trade. Headlines such as "A VIRGINIA COUNTY WITHOUT A SLAVE" (Aberdeen, Mississippi, *Sunny South*) and "A FREESOIL CANDIDATE FOR CONGRESS IN VIRGINIA" (*Charleston Mercury*) attracted much concern.[28]

Another state that received its share of attention was Missouri, primarily because of the political inroads that the Free Soil movement had made into that state. As growing numbers of slave owners in Missouri sold their slaves to avoid losing them, this process was sensationalized in stories like "WHAT THE HIGH PRICE OF SLAVES IS DOING FOR US" (*Mobile Register*). This piece quoted from a report in a St. Louis paper that "upwards of four hundred" slaves were leaving that city every week for the Deep South. Not surprisingly, when the *New Orleans Crescent* looked at census data and asked in an 1857 article, "IS SLAVERY DECLINING IN MISSOURI? " the answer was a resounding yes.[29]

To make matters worse for those in the Deep South, reports from newspapers in the Upper South increasingly reaffirmed their worst fears. Under the heading "INLAND TRAFFIC IN BLACKS," the *St. Louis Democrat* sent shivers down the spines of whites in the Lower South with statements like:

> We have no intention of concealing our satisfaction at the rapidly increasing importance of the commerce in blacks between Missouri and the South. There is no true friend of the State who will not be gratified by the fact that the slaves of Missouri are rapidly finding purchasers who take them out of the State, and leave in their stead thousands of good dollars. . . . The South is doing good work for Missouri.

While never quite as blunt, newspapers in Virginia voiced similar views. One paper that especially drew the ire of editors in the Deep South was the *Richmond Enquirer*, particularly in articles like "SENSIBLE," that reprinted a piece from a Missouri paper explaining how that state did not need to legally abolish slavery, because "the negro population will be driven out by commercial causes, most surely."[30]

Several papers in the Upper South tried to warn their readers about the dangers of removing so many laborers from their states. According to the Norfolk, Virginia, *Southern Argus*: "We see frequent notices in the papers of the sales of slaves, and the high prices which they bring, as if it were a mark of the prosperity of our State. But this is a great mistake. Every slave that is sold, to go out of the State, diminishes the amount of production in the State. We need all the labor we now have and more."[31]

There were also papers in the Lower South that thought the question of a border state slave drain had been blown all out of proportion. Foremost in this regard was the New Orleans *Picayune*, which pointed out that fifteen years earlier in the debate over Texas, most of the South believed that the domestic slave trade needed to be expanded to save the institution, and now many of these same people were worried that this trade had gone too far and was converting much of the Upper South into free states. Therefore, the *Picayune* saw no need for concern and concluded that the "subject of supply and demand will regulate itself."[32]

Still, by the late 1850s, voices like those in the New Orleans *Picayune* had become increasingly isolated as ever-growing alarmist publications came to dominate the southern press. This proved especially true in the Deep South, which saw the rising price of slaves and the steady stream of them leaving the Upper South as detrimental to both themselves and the institution of slavery.

As a result, more and more papers in that region began echoing the comments found in the *New Orleans Crescent* in April 1857. After arguing that the domestic trade was rapidly depriving the state of Missouri of its slaves, the *Crescent* added:

> The same fact applies with equal force to the States of Kentucky, Maryland and Virginia, and the drain of slaves Southward, which has continued for full fifteen years, if not checked by State legislation, or the introduction of some other description of labor, will, in two decades, place those States more completely in the power of Emancipationists than Missouri bids fair to be in three or four years.

Obviously, according to the *Crescent* and numerous other papers in the Deep South, something needed to be done to stop this ominous state of affairs.[33]

III

Throughout the 1850s, southern writers and politicians proposed a variety of remedies to counteract the skyrocketing price of slaves and its dangerous consequences. For some, the solution was the passage of laws to exempt slaves from seizure for payments of debts and other legal action. According to its proponents, exemption would guarantee that those who currently held slaves would continue to do so, while those who did not would still have the opportunity of becoming slave owners themselves. Thus, not only would exemption help to prevent the percentage of whites who owned slaves from dwindling, but it would also allow for this percentage to grow. Advocates of this policy could be found throughout the South. In Tennessee, the *Memphis Eagle and Enquirer* believed that "the laws of the South must encourage every citizen to not only become, but remain, a slaveholder"; in the Upper South, the *Richmond Whig* thought that exemption would do exactly that, and "instead of only three hundred thousand actual slaveholders, we should soon have as a slaveholder every head of a family in the Southern States." Southern politicians also promoted this measure, such as when the governor of South Carolina recommended passage of an exemption law for his state, noting that "as you multiply the number who acquire the property, so you will widen and deepen the determination to sustain the institution."[34]

Despite frequent endorsement, little action was taken on these measures, in large part because the logic of exemption did not hold up under close scrutiny. In a series of articles calling such laws "short-sighted, impracticable and absurd," the *New Orleans Crescent* summed up their main weakness. Arguing that such a bill would "produce exactly opposite results to those contemplated by its authors," the *Crescent* noted that by limiting the number of slaves available on the market, exemption would only make their price that much higher and "inevitably, tend to diminish the number of slaveholders instead of adding to the number." Therefore, while exemption laws seemed like an easy solution to some, serious discussion of their feasibility never really materialized.[35]

Far more compelling, and controversial, were proposals to ban the interregional trade in slaves. As shown earlier, statewide prohibitions against the importation of slaves for sale dated back to the Revolution, and the majority of southern states had enacted them at one time or another. Yet, prior to the 1850s, the catalyst behind virtually all of these laws was local concerns. In the Upper South, states had more slaves than they needed and the last thing they wanted was to add even more commodities to their already flooded market. In the Lower South, similar bans usually appeared after short-lived outbreaks of alarm, such as fears over the exportation of too much capital, the importation of too many "undesirables," or slave revolt.[36]

By the 1850s, however, this had changed, as more and more whites in the Deep South began calling for a ban on the interregional trade in slaves from the border states in order to protect the institution of slavery itself. One of the earliest publications to reflect this was the *Savannah Republican*. In an 1849 series of articles lamenting the fact that, through the domestic trade, planters in the Deep South were "virtually *paying* Virginia, Maryland and Kentucky for *emancipating* their slaves," the *Republican* argued that "by passing stringent prohibitory laws on the subject we will force them to keep their slaves, as well as make it their interest to protect the institution." The two papers that later came to be most identified with this issue were the *New Orleans Crescent* and the *New Orleans Delta*. The *Crescent* repeatedly called for the states below Virginia, Maryland, Kentucky, and Missouri "to prohibit, exclusively and unqualifiedly, any further emigration of slaves southward for at least ten years," while the *Delta* advocated a similar ban "until all fear of emancipation shall have been dispelled."[37]

Citizens' groups and politicians in the Deep South also called for such action. In 1849 the residents of Hancock County, Mississippi, petitioned for an extra session of their state legislature "for the purpose of enacting laws prohibiting the further ingress of slaves from the border States of the South." When similar petitions reached the South Carolina state assembly two years later, the Committee on the Colored Population rejected such a law as unenforceable. A minority of the committee issued a report, claiming that a ban was necessary, as

> many of the Border States, and particularly Maryland and Virginia are endeavouring rapidly to rid themselves of their Slave population, ...

and that unless this rush of emigration into the cotton growing States be arrested, South Carolina is destined, at no great length of time, to become a Border State, with Maryland, Virginia and even North Carolina hostile to our peculiar institution.[38]

Yet, as with the call for exemption laws, not much came of these public outcries for banning the further importation of slaves from the border states. In fact, during the 1850s, most of the prohibitions that were in place actually disappeared, and by the time of the Civil War, they had been repealed in every state except for Delaware. The main reason that no new laws were passed was because, as the South Carolina state assembly noted, these bans were almost impossible to enforce. This had been true for decades, and few people believed that they would work now. Moreover, by the 1850s, southerners in the Deep South were simply determined to buy as many slaves as possible and were willing to pay almost any price to get them.[39]

In addition to these practical concerns, there was an even graver problem with any regionwide ban issued by the Deep South, and that was the effect it would have on the South as a whole. Not surprisingly, newspapers in the Upper South expressed outrage over such proposals. But even some papers in the Lower South opposed these measures, most notably, the *Charleston Mercury*. In a lengthy article attacking the editorials of both the *New Orleans Crescent* and the New Orleans *Delta*, the *Mercury* argued that such a ban would have a disastrous effect upon Virginia, slashing the price of its slaves and flooding the state with black paupers. Furthermore, it would increase the price of slaves in the Deep South and, by decreasing the number of slaves available, cut off expansion into the Southwest. Most troubling, such an action would further splinter the already shaky unity of the South and possibly drive the border states into an alliance with the North. As the *Mercury* described it, more than a year before Abraham Lincoln made this metaphor famous, "If any division or policy of separation is to take place, let it be between the North and the South—and not between the different parts of the South. 'A house divided against itself must fall.'"[40]

IV

The policy that the *Charleston Mercury* and many others in the Lower South came to advocate instead was a reopening of the African slave trade. While isolated calls for a repeal of the federal ban on African imports had been made for years, the movement did not really take off until 1853, when a young South Carolina editor named Leonidas Spratt bought the Charleston *Southern Stan-*

dard and turned it into a mouthpiece for promoting this issue. More than any other individual, Spratt helped to turn this cause into a prominent topic of debate in the southern press, politics, churches, and commercial conventions. In large part because of his efforts, the following year the *Mercury* came out in favor of reopening the African trade, and two South Carolina districts, Richland and Williamsburg, issued resolutions calling for it as well. According to the one from Williamsburg, renewing this trade would be "a blessing to the American people, and a benefit to the African himself." Two years later, in November 1856, Governor James Adams of South Carolina recommended that the state legislature repudiate the federal ban suppressing the African slave trade. The following year, the legislative committee that had been appointed to respond to Adams's message agreed, declaring that "*the South at large does need a re-opening of the African slave trade.*" By 1856 the movement had also clearly spread beyond South Carolina, as the Louisiana editor James D. B. DeBow came out in favor of this policy in his influential publication, *DeBow's Review*. By the time of the Civil War, this issue had become one of the most prevalent, and divisive, topics in southern society.[41]

For Leonidas Spratt and numerous other supporters of the African slave trade, reopening this traffic promised to answer many of the problems that they believed threatened southern society in the mid-1850s. First, it would provide additional slaves for expansion into the West. It would also enhance the political power of the South by augmenting the southern population and adding more slave states. It would relieve the southern labor shortage and strengthen the southern economy by lowering the costs of production and increasing profits. Finally, reopening the African trade would cut the price of slaves and expand the number of slaveholders in the South. As Spratt contended in his Charleston paper, "The foreign slave trade will bring slaves enough for all, and at prices which poorer men may purchase. . . . It will thus render it possible for all to become slave owners." The importance of this was made clear in a letter to the Augusta *Dispatch* that noted: "Remove the restrictions upon the Slave Trade, and where is there a poor man in the South who could not soon become a slaveholder—who could not thus become more and more identified with slavery, and more and more ready to defend the institution?"[42]

In addition to economic and social benefits, reopening the African trade also promised to improve the increasingly strained relationship between the slave-exporting and slave-importing states and thereby strengthen the institution of slavery throughout the entire region. Most important, it would provide an endless supply of laborers to those areas most in need of them and allow those states that were losing their slaves to retain them. In other words, it would stop the drain of slaves from the border states, preventing their eventual transformation into free states, which would benefit the entire South. Furthermore, the African trade would also provide advantages for each subregion. According to the Jackson *Mississippian*, "It would prevent this rapid conversion of past friends into future enemies, and at the same time stop the present enormous drain of money from the cotton States to the border States." In the Upper South, the *Richmond Whig* believed that reopening the African trade would "constitute a sovereign and almost instantaneous panacea for all abolition troubles." Leonidas Spratt could also not help adding that there was probably "no place in the Union where 100,000 slaves could be so profitably planted as upon the soil of the brave old State of Virginia."[43]

As might be expected, not all white southerners agreed with these arguments, and many thought that even bringing them up was reckless, if not downright absurd. After Governor Adams of South Carolina called for a reopening of the African trade, the New Orleans *Picayune* described that possibility as "the wildest of hallucinations," while the *Savannah Republican* claimed that this was another "symptom of the political distemper with which South Carolina politicians have been afflicted for the past twenty years." For most whites in the Upper South, however, the movement to reopen the African trade was not simply foolhardy but dangerous, as it threatened to eliminate their most important export commodity and slash the capital value of their largest form of property.[44]

Consequently, the majority of newspapers in the Upper South came out against it. As the *Lynchburg Virginian* put it: "We have a paramount interest in maintaining the integrity of the law which prohibits the reopening of the Slave Trade. If the restrictions upon this 'execrable commerce' were removed, we should witness a depreciation in the price and value of this property in Virginia that would tell seriously upon the destinies of the State." As a warning to the Lower South, the *Richmond Enquirer* further made clear that the effort to revive this trade had "sown the seeds of distrust between the slave producing and slave buying States—a distrust, which, if perpetuated, may eventuate in worse consequences to the entire South."[45]

While most of the support for reopening the African slave trade came from the Lower South, it is also important to note that there were a number of individuals in that subregion who opposed this measure. For one thing, they too worried about the consequences of cutting the price of slaves. According to a minority report issued by the South Carolina legislature opposed to removing the federal ban, if the African trade were reopened, the value of slaves would drop by one-half, meaning that the loss to South Carolina alone would be as much as $140 million. Not only would this affect those wanting to sell, but it would also have an impact on "all those cases where the exchangeable value of slaves is taken into consideration, as in the payments of debts, distributions of estates, &c." Governor Henry Foote of Mississippi likewise worried that "if the price of slaves comes down, then the permanency of the institution comes down. Why? Because every man values his property in proportion to its actual intrinsic worth." To emphasize his point, Foote then asked, "Would you be willing to fight for them and risk your domestic peace and happiness if your slaves were only worth five dollars apiece? Why, every man sees that that is an absurdity. *Therefore, the permanence of the system depends on keeping the prices high.*"[46]

Others in the Lower South voiced other concerns against reopening this controversial trade. Unionists knew that northerners would never support such a policy and pushing it would only lead to secession. And, as in other parts of the nation, there were those like William Gregg of South Carolina who had moral objections to the African trade and considered it a "horrible traffic" that would "bring upon us the censure of the Christian world." But most important, many people understood that this issue would only further divide the South and, according to some, would even hasten the process of eliminating slavery in the Upper South. As the *Charleston Courier* explained, "The revival of the slave trade would speedily abolitionize the border Southern States, by rendering slaves of no value, and the institution an incubus among them."[47]

Still, despite these objections, proponents of the African trade defended their position and countered most of these claims, including the charge that the introduction of so many cheap laborers would lower the worth of those slaves already in America. Leonidas Spratt pointed out that "the slave trade shall reduce the price of slaves without reducing the value of their labor, and if slave-owners shall be able to buy two instead of one, and thus be able to double the profits on their investment," they would benefit from the "tide of wealth that . . . will overspread the country." He also added that there would be other capital gains that made up for whatever reductions might occur in the market value of slaves, such as a rise in the cost of land. As a result, he predicted that for "slave owners as a class there will be a gain of one hundred dollars for every one that will be lost."[48]

Others, like the *Charleston Mercury*, noted that the high price of slaves was not, in fact, helpful to most slaveholders, and "it is only when he becomes a seller, that he really benefits by the advance in price; while in the more permanent characters of owner, employer, and purchaser, he would derive the amplest advantages from their cheapness." Therefore, in the minds of many whites in the Deep South, the only people who really profited from keeping up the price of slaves were those who routinely sold them, namely, slave owners in the Upper South. For that reason, in their report, the South Carolina special legislative committee that recommended repealing the ban on the African trade claimed that "the *true* question" was "not whether the 163,000 owners of slaves in the five slave exporting States would have their interests a little impaired, . . . but, whether the monopoly they now hold is just and proper." It then asked "whether the value of their slaves should continue to be augmented at the expense of the country, . . . and whether the interests of *ten millions* of people in the Southern States . . . should not be paramount to that of the few." Not surprisingly, the committee concluded that "the answer to this is evident."⁴⁹

Even more disturbing for many white southerners was the way that the proponents of the African trade forced them to rethink their interpretation of this traffic and, with it, the institution of chattel slavery. They acknowledged that most Americans regarded the African trade as cruel and un-Christian, but that was only because they had been "so bedevilled with clap-trap" into thinking that way by old prejudices and by the northerners who controlled the federal government. As long as Americans continued to think of the African trade as wrong, by implication, slavery itself would always be tainted as wrong and something that had to be eliminated. Or, as they saw it, as long as the nation treated the African trade as piracy, slavery could never be recognized as the ideal way of life. Instead it was branded a crime and their slaves only plunder. Therefore, the slave-trade advocates wanted the white South to follow up on the full meaning of the proslavery argument and realize that if slavery truly was a blessing to people of African descent, then there could be nothing wrong with the African trade, and in fact, it should expand that benefit to even more Africans. As the *Charleston Mercury* explained it, "If slavery is *right*, the Slave Trade is right also, and the South must come to this point sooner or later."⁵⁰

Advocates of the African trade also challenged the hypocrisy of those who condemned the traffic in slaves from Africa but had no trouble with a similar trade in American slaves. The New Orleans *Delta* was one of many newspapers in the Deep South to address this contradiction, asking, "As a merely moral question, where is the difference in buying a negro in Virginia or in Africa?" Former South Carolina governor James Adams also made this comparison when he noted, "Virginia and Maryland, without shock to our moral sensibilities, enjoy the humane privilege of breeding and rearing christianized slaves for the Southern market, just as the Kentuckians do mules and hogs. . . . Some charity should be manifested toward those who think there is no more wrong in going to Africa to buy a slave than to Virginia or Maryland." In many people's eyes, the only difference between buying a slave from Virginia and buying one from Africa was the price. Not surprisingly, this led papers like the *Sunny South* of Aberdeen, Mississippi, to ask: "What authority has Congress to force Southern planters to pay the negro-breeder of Virginia $1400 for a negro man, when the same can be purchased in Ludamar for $150?"⁵¹

Finally, in their attacks upon this double standard, writers in the Lower South continually made the point that those who seemed to complain the loudest about the inhumanity of the African trade were those who profited the most from the American version. After reprinting a piece from the *Richmond*

Enquirer that denounced the African trade as an "infamous traffic," the *New Orleans Crescent* observed "that if one kind of slave trade is 'infamous,' all other kinds are necessarily 'infamous,' and that, if such be the case, a Virginia journal is the last which should presume to stigmatize the business, for the good and sufficient reason that the domestic slave trade of Virginia exceeds that of any half dozen Southern States combined!" The paper then added, "If the theory of the Enquirer be true, Virginia is the most 'infamous' State in Christendom."[52]

The proponents of the African trade also made a claim that made many uncomfortable, namely, that the foreign slave trade was more humane. Relying upon the logic of the proslavery argument, one writer in the *Charleston Mercury* asked, "If it be cruel to bring the savage negro from Africa and improve his condition in this country, how much worse it must be to sell to the Western planter the more than half-civilized negro from our plantations, where they have been brought up with all the associations of home!" Leonidas Spratt also expressed this view, noting that as long as there was a demand, there would always be a trade in slaves to the Southwest. He then asked, "At present, they are torn from homes in Maryland, Virginia, and North and South Carolina, and the question is, should they not rather be brought from Africa? From hence they can be brought with less inhumanity than a laboring population can ever be taken from one country to another, and infinitely less than characterizes the trade between the States." According to Spratt, not only would the African trade benefit the African people, but it would also be more humane than the countless separations that currently took place every year between American slaves and their families and friends. Therefore, the African trade would make life better for slaves in America because it would eliminate the need for the interstate trade.[53]

While the campaign to reopen the African slave trade has frequently been ignored or belittled by historians, the movement had an influence that far exceeded its political accomplishments. For one thing, it forced white southerners to rethink their understanding of chattel slavery and the role that both it and the domestic slave trade played in American life. It also had considerable support. As the Tallahassee *Floridian and Journal* crudely reported in early 1859: "Advocates for the re-opening of the trade in 'Wool' are increasing"; *DeBow's Review* concurred, claiming "no cause has ever grown with greater rapidity than has that of the advocates of the slave trade." Many of these supporters firmly believed with the *Tuskegee* (Alabama) *Republican* that "the very existence of the South depends upon the re-opening of the African Slave Trade."[54]

The majority of white southerners never supported this measure, but the historian W. E. B. Du Bois was probably correct when he wrote, more than a century ago, that "there certainly was a large and influential minority, including perhaps a majority of citizens of the Gulf States, who favored the project."

Moreover, the African trade's supporters were not crackpots or social misfits, but some of the wealthiest, most prominent, and successful politicians and professional men in the South. In some states, such as South Carolina, they were also the largest slave owners. In addition, the movement had the support of much of the region's press. Virtually every city of any size in the Lower South had at least one newspaper that came out in favor of reopening the trade. In 1859, the *Liberator* reported that, in Mississippi alone, "twenty leading Democratic papers" had endorsed it. And, while most of the press in the Upper South came out against the trade, at least three Virginia papers, the *Richmond Examiner*, *Richmond Whig*, and *Petersburg Intelligencer*, published editorials supporting the measure.[55]

The advocates of the African trade also failed to achieve legislative success, but the main reason for this had little to do with lack of support. A far more convincing explanation lies in the fears that many people in the Deep South had of the effect such actions would have had upon the region as a whole. By the late 1850s, it had become obvious to all that the slave-exporting states would never support a reopening of the African trade, and any effort to do so would only heighten their distrust and possibly drive them into an alliance with the North. It was for this reason that the *Charleston Courier* finally came out against the African trade in 1858. According to the *Courier*, "The very agitation of the question is calculated to distract and divide the South, the harmony and unity of which is especially necessary in these disjointed and distempered times." It was also why in 1859 the *Charleston Mercury*, one of the earliest and staunchest supporters of reopening the trade, decided to no longer promote it, explaining that "whilst having these great issues with the North, we should make no side issues amongst ourselves. . . . To agitate it in the South, and to divide the South by parties to it, it appears to us, is sheer madness."[56]

Therefore, once again, no action was taken, despite the fact that the measure had wide support in the Deep South and was debated by every state legislature in that subregion. Although it was no longer openly advanced by some of its earlier advocates, the issue persisted, but in the end, the movement to reopen this traffic had exactly the opposite effect intended by its proponents. While the African trade was meant to unify and strengthen the southern states, it only heightened their anxiety and tore them even further apart.

V

The magnitude of the division between the Upper South and the Lower South can be seen in the changing nature of the various southern commercial conventions that were held in the late 1840s and 1850s. Ostensibly designed to improve the material and political interests of the southern states, these gatherings became increasingly more political as Leonidas Spratt and other Deep South advocates of the African trade forced this issue onto their agendas. A resolution recommending such a measure first appeared at the 1855 meeting in New Orleans, where it was quickly dropped. But each year the African trade attracted more and more supporters until it was finally endorsed by the Vicksburg convention in 1859. The main reason for the measure's passage at this meeting was because the states of Delaware, Maryland, Virginia, Kentucky, Missouri, and North Carolina had refused to attend. The debates over the African trade the previous year at the Montgomery convention had been so tumultuous, and Virginia's loyalty to slavery and the South had come under such attack, that politicians from the border states no longer felt that anything productive could come from sending delegates to another session. If nothing else, this meeting at Montgomery exposed how far apart the two main subregions of the South had drifted by the spring of 1858. As a correspondent for the New Orleans *Delta* explained: "This Convention has done either a great good or a great evil; for it has shown that there are, instead of two, three sections in the Union. It has shown that the true division of interests is now, not those of North and South, but of Cotton States, Tobacco States and Wheat States."[57]

There were other indications that by this time whites in the Lower South clearly saw the Upper South as a region distinct from their own. Most notably, they began referring to the states in the Upper South as the "frontier" states. They of course did not coin this term; it had a long history in America as a word to describe contested areas of settlement in the West. By 1849, however, the *Savannah Republican* expanded that definition to include residents in the Upper South as well when it warned how "the people of the frontier States" were seeking to emancipate their slaves through the domestic trade. Other newspaper editors continued to use this label to describe that subregion all the way up to the Civil War.[58]

While the Upper South had long been known as the border states, it is significant that the Lower South now began thinking of them as the frontier. Even more than the word "border," "frontier" implies an area that fronts another country, which says a lot about the way that many whites in the South had come to view the North by this time. But there is more to a frontier than a physical place; it is also an area with a different mindset and a way of life often less absolute than that of the dominant society. Those in the Deep South meant these inferences when referring to the Upper South, especially in regard to those states' commitment to chattel slavery. As the *Charleston Mercury* warned in the summer of 1857: "This institution in the frontier Southern States is weaker than it has been." Therefore, just as mainstream American society had always felt uneasy about what was happening along the more well known western frontier, those in the Lower South believed that whites in the Upper South needed to be monitored to make sure that they did not slip over to the other side. Or, as the New Orleans *Delta* put it, it was their responsibility "to look to the permanency of the institution along the frontier."[59]

For many in the Lower South, however, it was already too late for, at least in their eyes, slavery had virtually disappeared from some of the frontier states. As early as 1850, in a speech before the state assembly, the governor of South Carolina claimed that "one-half of Virginia is now almost as alien to us as Pennsylvania," and as to its neighbor, "Maryland is hopeless." Leonidas Spratt likewise expressed this sentiment at the Montgomery convention, when he lamented that "the States of Delaware and Maryland have so few slaves that it is only by courtesy they can be called slave States." The best assessment of this situation, though, came a month later when the *New Orleans Crescent* pointed out: "We have now, nominally, fifteen Slave States. But, Delaware has gone from us to all intents and purposes. Missouri is going, and Maryland is not much better off. Really, we have only twelve Slave States we can count upon with certainty, taking doubtful Kentucky into the calculation." The paper then asked, "We *now* complain of abolition outrage and abuse. What sort of chances will we have when three of our own States desert us, and five or six new Freesoil States are created in the Northwest?"[60]

The *New Orleans Crescent* and other newspapers and their readers in the Deep South had a real reason for being concerned, as slavery truly was losing its importance in some of the frontier states. By 1860, there were fewer than 2,000 slaves in all of Delaware, and only half of the black population in Maryland was still enslaved. In fact, by 1860, that state had 18,000 fewer slaves than at the beginning of the century.[61]

The future of the institution also seemed doubtful in Missouri. With free states surrounding that state on all but one side, it was relatively easy for any slave who wanted to run away. As one owner in St. Charles noted to his brother in Mississippi, he was bringing a young man to that state for sale, explaining: "The sole object in disposing of him is the danger of loosing him here. We are on the edge of the state of Illinois, and they can make their escape across that state to Canada. And do do it every day." While always a nuisance, this problem became much worse in the 1850s with the controversy over slavery in neighboring Kansas. As a result, numerous owners in Missouri decided to sell their slaves south rather than lose their valuable property to flight.[62]

Added to this insecurity, by the 1850s, several antislavery strongholds could be found throughout Missouri. This proved especially true in the area around St. Louis, which had experienced heavy foreign immigration in recent years. Antislavery sentiment became so strong that in 1856 the city elected a Republican, Francis Blair, Jr., to Congress, and the next year, the party easily carried the municipal elections, giving the city its first Free Soil mayor. Soon Republicans controlled other cities as well, including the state capital of Jefferson City. Needless to say, none of this was lost on whites in the Deep South. Newspapers in that region reported these events and warned of their results, often by including articles from papers in Missouri. After reprinting such a story in the summer of 1858, the *New Orleans Crescent* told its readers: "We had thought it would take ten years to bring about the abolition of slavery in Missouri, but the St. Louis Democrat is of the confident belief that it can be accomplished 'within two or three years.'"[63]

Nothing disturbed slave owners in the Deep South more than the events taking place in Virginia. For years, this state had held a special place in the southern imagination. As the home to American presidents and the largest slave population in the nation, Virginia was crucial for southern identity. It was also the primary source of slaves for westward expansion and, as such, was seen by many as the matriarch of the slaveholding domain. According to the *New Orleans Crescent*, Virginia was "the mother of the slaveholding States of the West and Southwest. With the exception of the Carolinas, all the slaveholding commonwealths sprang from her prolific loins."[64]

Yet, as in Delaware, Maryland, and Missouri, slavery was coming under attack in this historic state, or so it seemed to many in the Lower South. Especially troubling was the effort by a Republican congressman from Massachusetts named Eli Thayer to colonize Virginia and convert it into a free-labor state. Thayer had earlier been a founder of the New England Emigrant Aid Company, which had sent antislavery settlers to Kansas, and he now wanted to do the same in Virginia. In early 1857, he established the American Emigrant Aid and Homestead Company and advertised his plan to buy up large tracts of land in Virginia at low, slave-state prices and then distribute it to free-labor immigrants. He believed that his colony would stimulate the local economy, thereby attracting more antislavery settlers and hastening the process of abolition that was slowly occurring in that state through the interstate trade.[65]

When Eli Thayer first announced his plans in the *New York Herald*, he received a mixed reaction from the Virginia press. Some papers from economically depressed areas, such as the *Wheeling Intelligencer*, *Norfolk Herald*, and *Norfolk Argus*, welcomed his arrival as a means to stimulate their economy. Others dismissed the threat. Under the sarcastic heading "The Vandal Invasion of Virginia," the *Richmond Examiner* called the whole scheme "preposterous." But many of the Virginia papers denounced the plan and even advocated violence if Thayer tried to carry out his venture. If he did so, the *Richmond Whig* threatened to make "the carcasses of those colonists adorn the trees of our forests."[66]

Despite this hostility, papers in the Deep South were outraged that the Virginians did not take Thayer and "his band of nasal-twanging emigrants" more seriously. Leading the way in this regard was the New Orleans *Delta*, which argued, "Virginia is not as fully awake as she should be to the great question of Southern interests." The paper repeatedly tried to warn the Virginians of the dangers that Thayer and his movement represented, but the Richmond papers only "cracked jokes . . . and treated the whole subject with ill-timed irony." Even worse, they accused the *Delta* of "meddling with business which did not concern [it]" and went so far as to label its editors "Down South Yankees." Yet, according to the *Delta*, it was "to the interest of the whole South, that not a single organized Thayer band shall ever be permitted to cross that frontier." When Thayer established his first colony, Ceredo, in the summer of 1857, the *Delta* was livid, claiming that "the citadel of Virginia Slavery is endangered and the watchmen upon its walls are asleep. There is not even a journalistic goose among our revilers that will cackle to save Rome."[67]

For many in the Deep South, the Thayer movement represented all that was wrong with their region, and they even adopted the terms "Thayerism" and "Thayerized" to describe what was happening to slavery throughout the frontier states. As they saw it, this invasion of northerners was proof that whites in the Upper South were losing their commitment to slavery. It was also the inevitable consequence of the interregional slave trade and the inflation of slave prices due to the labor shortage. According to the *Charleston Mercury*, it was the steady drain of slaves which "encouraged the Thayers of the North to look upon Virginia as already ripe for their Abolition designs." As another writer in that paper made clear, this situation "must be remedied if we do not wish to see our border Southern States *Thayerized*."[68]

Whites in the Upper South saw this situation differently, and, as was made clear in their responses to the admonitions from the New Orleans *Delta*, they did not appreciate having their loyalty to the South or its peculiar institution questioned. After such a reproach from the *Delta*, the *Lynchburg Virginian* lashed out: "One thing is certain, that we shall exercise our own volition and be controlled by our own judgment and interests, and slavery in Virginia will not be perpetuated one day to promote the single interest of any other State." The Richmond *South* likewise responded to a similar challenge, asking, "How is it ascertained that the 'border States' are deficient in devotion to the rights of the South? In what emergency have they betrayed a want of spirit or of patriotism?" The paper then added, "We throw out these inquiries in the spirit of defiance; for we are well aware that it is not in the power of any man to detract from the well-earned reputation of the Old Dominion, or to impair her position as the foremost State of the South."[69]

The most outspoken publication, however, when it came to defending the reputation and stance of Virginia in relation to slavery was the *Richmond Enquirer*. As with other papers in the state, the *Enquirer* railed against those from the Deep South who regarded "Virginia as a mere colonial dependency of 'King Cotton.'" And it continually argued that "if the extreme Southern States shall decide to dissolve this Union *because they cannot open the African slave-trade*, Virginia will have no part nor lot in such dissolution."[70]

The *Enquirer* really unleashed the wrath of the Deep South in its response to the Montgomery convention of 1858, with that meeting's efforts to reopen the African trade and its attacks upon Virginia for opposing it. In an editorial of May 25, 1858, the paper asked what the South hoped to accomplish by advocating "a measure that would destroy the value of her now largest interest." It then laid out what it thought best for the state: "If a dissolution of the Union is to be followed by the revival of the slave trade, Virginia had better consider whether the South of the Northern confederacy would not be far more preferable for her than the North of a Southern confederacy." As the paper explained, "In the Northern confederacy Virginia would derive a large amount from the sale of her slaves to the South, and gain the increased value of her lands from Northern emigration—while in the Southern confederacy, with the African slave trade revived, she would lose two-thirds of the value of her slave property, and derive no additional increase to the value of her lands."[71]

Not surprisingly, newspaper editors throughout the Lower South expressed outrage over such a threat. In Columbia, South Carolina, the *Southern Guardian* complained that "the Union-adoring 'Enquirer' values the Virginia slave market more than it does the independence of the South," while a writer in the *Charleston Mercury* declared: "Better, far better, that the institution shall at once know its friends and foes. If the grand 'Old Dominion' decides to be Thayerized, the sooner we know it the better." After the *Enquirer* repeated its desire that Virginia should go with the North if promised "State equality," the New Orleans *Delta* could only proclaim, "Why, thou Judas Iscariot! go and hang thyself, after a declaration so damnable as this!"[72]

Some Virginia papers (and a few in the Lower South as well) went to great lengths to reassure the rest of the South that the *Enquirer* did not speak for the majority of the state. Foremost in this regard was the Richmond *South*, which made it clear that "the cotton States are mistaken in supposing that Virginia desires the continuance of the Union for the purpose of keeping up the value of slave property," and "she will never be seduced into being the South of a Northern Confederacy by mere pecuniary considerations." Therefore, according to the *South*, "the cotton States may yet rest assured that . . . we will not estimate our alliance with the slave States by its value in dollars." Many people in the importing states viewed such statements with skepticism, but at least some papers in the region, such as the *New Orleans Crescent*, tried to convince their readers that "the course of the Enquirer was severely criticised in Virginia by the press of that State."[73]

Still, the comments of the *Enquirer* and other Virginia papers left many whites in the Deep South concerned. While antislavery sentiment had always been present in the western portion of Virginia, by the fall of 1857, the New Orleans *Delta* noted that two former Democratic papers in the Shenandoah Valley had also taken such a stance. Consequently, despite all claims to the contrary, the *Delta* could only conclude that "the Virginia Democracy is being Abolitionized, and that the great wave of Northern fanaticism has rolled over the border into the center of Virginia." Such fears reverberated across the Deep South, as many wondered what role, if any, Virginia would play in the future of the region. But one thing was certain, as the *Charleston Mercury* made clear, "Virginia, amongst the Cotton States, is not now considered as 'the foremost State of the South.'"[74]

VI

While the drain of slaves from the Upper South never truly endangered the institution of slavery in the majority of those states, at least not by 1860, the important point is that many people in the Lower South believed that it did and behaved as if this was actually taking place. By the late 1850s, the majority of whites in the Deep South were convinced that the states in the Upper South were losing their slaves through the interstate trade. They understood that the demand for slaves in the Southwest had driven up their price to such record levels that owners in the Upper South had little choice but to sell, as was apparent from the large numbers of slaves being shipped out of those states. It was this belief that had made reopening the African trade so appealing to many people in the Lower South and why they increasingly viewed those in the Upper South as distinctly different from themselves when slaveholders in those states refused to endorse the proposal. Moreover, it was why they began to think of the Upper South as the "frontier" states and why they thought that Thayerism posed such a serious threat.

Whites in the Deep South were not the only ones who believed this scenario; northerners likewise saw this rupture occurring within the South and were not afraid to exploit it, much to the Deep South's dismay. After the fiery debates in Congress over the Kansas issue, the *Memphis Appeal* reprinted an article from the *New York Herald* entitled "SOUTHERN TREACHERY." According to the *Herald*, this debate had shown "that the traitors to the South are chiefly from the border States—Maryland, Kentucky, North Carolina, Tennessee and Virginia." The paper then gloated that "there is a vein of treachery to the institutions of the South running all through those States, like a fissure in a solid rock. The South is no longer a solid rock, and will suffer more from this insidious undermining of enemies in its own camp than from all the assaults of its open and avowed enemies."[75]

Equally disturbing was a piece that the *New Orleans Crescent* reprinted from the *New York Express*, whose main argument was that "the high price of Negroes is abolishing slavery in the State of Virginia—as fast as such a process can well go on—and 'Southern cotton' is thus rapidly effecting what Northern 'wool' for twenty years has been at work for, in vain." While less than egalitarian in its views of society, this New York paper made clear that the strong demand to grow staple crops in the Deep South had driven up the price of slaves in the border states, resulting in their departure through the interregional trade. Consequently, the *Express* found it ironic that "cotton, rice and sugar are greater abolitionists by far than Garrison, Greeley, Giddings, or Gerritt Smith."[76]

Therefore, it is hardly surprising that the states in the Lower South decided to secede after Abraham Lincoln's election in the fall of 1860. Not only did they fear what the Republican president might do to their most valuable form of property, but they also worried about how much longer their slaveholding coalition might last. Whether or not the interregional trade was actually turning the Upper South into free states, many in the nation—and especially in the Deep South—believed that this was true. While there were numerous reasons behind the decision to secede, the long-term consequences of the domestic slave trade certainly escalated the tensions and anxieties that permeated the region at that time. As a result, after Lincoln's election, many believed that if they did not act soon, it would be too late.

Several of the Deep South's newspapers expressed this concern, as well as their confidence that the frontier states would join them in their new confederacy. Even before the presidential election, the *New Orleans Crescent* recognized that "under the present Union the border States must all in a short time be lost to us. [But] were that Union at an end the South would become at once a *unit*, and continue such for perhaps a century." One of the reasons that the *Crescent* and others believed that the southern states would remain united was because of the large black populations in all of their states. As the New Orleans *Delta* made clear, emancipation was thus out of the question, and "common danger and common interest would compel Maryland, Virginia, Kentucky, and even Missouri, to keep up a permanent alliance with the Carolinas, Tennessee, Arkansas, Georgia and the Gulf States."[77]

The *Crescent* best understood why the Upper South needed its connection with the rest of the slaveholding states: "The slave property of those States, including Virginia, is worth fully $500,000,000. The people thereof will experience no lack of attachment for the 'institution' as long as they are so deeply interested, and will cling to it and fight for it to the last before they will submit to ruinous despoliation." Careful not to offend their Upper South readers, the

Crescent then added: "This is human nature, and is, therefore, no disparage-
ment to the inhabitants of the States named. We are all alike when the 'pocket-
nerve' is touched."[78]

To make sure that the "pocket-nerve" of slave owners in the Upper South
would indeed be touched, politicians from the seceding states had no qualms
about using economic pressure to force their laggard compatriots into joining
their cause. Not long after seceding, the governor of South Carolina recommended passage of a law prohibiting "the introduction of slaves from States
not members of the Southern Confederacy, and particularly the border States."
If those states refused to enter into the new slaveholding republic, "let them
keep their slave property in their own borders, and, as the only alternative left
them, let them emancipate them by their own acts, or the action of their Confederacy." Soon thereafter, the governor of Mississippi recommended passage
of a similar bill in his state.[79]

The Montgomery convention of February 1861 that established the new
Confederate government also took aggressive action. Recognizing that they
needed to make some concessions to convince those wavering states from
the Upper South to join their new nation, the representatives at this gathering inserted a clause into their constitution prohibiting the African trade from
the Confederate States of America. But, along with this bribe came a threat.
Their constitution also contained a clause giving the Confederate Congress the
"power to prohibit the introduction of slaves from any State not a member
of, or Territory not belonging to, this Confederacy." William Yancey of Alabama made the meeting's intentions clear when he explained that the border
states could either "join the South and keep their slaves, or sell them, as they
choose," or they could "join the North, and lose their slaves by abolition." To
make sure that the Virginians understood that they were in earnest, the state
of Georgia sent a commissioner to tell the delegates at the Virginia secession
convention, "If you do not join us but join the North, that provision would be
put in force."[80]

As could be expected, many in the Upper South did not appreciate such
hardball tactics coming from their supposed southern friends. Especially outraged was the Charlottesville, North Carolina, *Observer*, which exclaimed: "And
this is the *friendship* which the 'Border States' are to experience from the 'Cotton
States!' . . . Preserve us from such '*friends*' who openly tell us that they intend
to force us to join them or to emancipate our slaves." Others, such as the *National
Intelligencer*, cut through all the niceties and described what was really happening to the region: "The policy of this prohibition, as proposed to be laid by
Southern friends on the inter-State slave trade, is . . . plainly designed to 'coerce'
the action of the Border States by extorting at their hands a willing or unwilling
acquiescence in the projects of the South Carolina leaders."[81]

Despite this blatant extortion, others in the Upper South realized that they had little choice but to comply. Interestingly, one of the more pragmatic voices in this regard was the *Richmond Enquirer*, the old advocate of autonomy for the South's largest slaveholding state. After the *Richmond Whig* lashed out against the Deep South, claiming that "we do not believe that Virginia is the slave of the Gulf States, or can be made the slave of those States, under any circumstances," the *Enquirer* chided its neighbor, noting, "This is all very well to tickle State pride. But is it true? Can Virginia take such an independent course, and separate her destiny from the Cotton States?" Although the paper believed "that there is not one man in Virginia that desires the dissolution of this Union," it also understood that "hitched as she is to the Southern States, she will be dragged into a common destiny with them, no matter what may be the desire of the people." If not,

> her condition would, in five years be more pitiable than that of St. Domingo. The Gulf States having dissolved their connection with the Federal Union, would, as foreign nations, prevent the importation of Virginia negroes, and here would begin the financial ruin that would soon culminate in a desolating and bloody servile war. Such would be the price of Virginia's boasted independence of the cotton States.

Therefore, no matter how much white Virginians may or may not have wanted to stay within the Union, in the end, their dependence on the domestic slave trade gave them little alternative but to secede. Virginia's entire economy was based upon the institution of chattel slavery and, most notably, on the export of human slaves to other states. This trade had brought great wealth to Virginia by turning a previously "excess" population into the largest form of capital investment in the state. But it also meant that Virginia would have to keep up this traffic, or the value of that property would collapse. The *Richmond Enquirer* understood this, and as much as the paper may have wanted Virginia's independence from the rest of the South, it realized that "the institution of slavery binds all the States wherein it exists so intimately, that a common destiny awaits alike the planting and the farming States."[82]

FOUR

"CASH FOR NEGROES": Slave Traders and the Market Revolution in the South

On October 27, 1855, a notice appeared in the *Memphis Eagle and Enquirer* offering not only slaves for sale, but also advice for planters on how to get ahead in life. Placed by the slave-trading firm of Bolton, Dickens & Co., this advertisement began like many others of its kind, noting that the company had just "completed one of the best prisons in the State" and that it was "now receiving daily large supplies of Fresh negroes from the buying markets." The slave traders invited "the planting community to call on us before making other purchases, as we flatter ourselves that we can furnish you negroes as cheap as you can buy them." But Bolton, Dickens & Co. did more than just make known what it had to offer and that it would beat any price. The company also advised planters to "call and buy before the present stock is picked over, as some is of the opinion that the first show at a fresh lot is one hundred dollars the advantage." Furthermore, it urged them to "call and make your purchases to gather your crop—and then call quick again and buy to make another crop. By those means if you will keep up your purchases for ten years there is no telling how much you may be worth." According to these savvy merchants, "This is the true Road to wealth and if you neglect the present offer of becoming wealthy its your fa[u]lt and not ours as the Road is laid out plainly."[1]

Advertisements like this had made Bolton, Dickens & Co. one of the most successful business firms in the antebellum South. Consisting of Isaac, Jefferson, Wade, and Washington Bolton and Isaac's son-in-law Thomas Dickens, the company was centered in Memphis, had branch offices in Lexington, St. Louis, and Vicksburg, and employed agents throughout the South. While some of the Boltons had been involved in the slave trade since at least the 1830s, the firm was not founded until the late 1840s. In many ways, its rise mirrored the growing commercial importance of Memphis. The Boltons also benefited from the city's ideal location as a halfway point between the slave-exporting states of the Upper South and the slave-importing states of the Deep South. As such, they could both import slaves to sell in the local market and buy slaves to export to the states farther south.[2]

Yet there was much more to this slave-trading firm's success than a fortuitous location; the owners also understood the importance of modern business practices, including innovative advertising, which they regularly employed in newspapers and city directories. This can already be seen in their earliest notices, which began appearing in the summer of 1849. With crops still in the ground, many planters lacked money, so Bolton, Dickens & Co. catered to their needs (and acquired merchandise for the southern trade) with an advertisement that read: "Cash for Negroes. ONE HUNDRED NEGROES WANTED." By the fall, as their customers' wants changed, so did their message. Planters now had money in their pockets, so the firm's new advertisement announced, "NEGROES! NEGROES!! FOR SALE," adding that "we have two buyers now in the buying market—which will keep our stock monthly replenished until the season closes in the spring." In addition to customizing their messages to their customers' seasonal needs, the owners of Bolton, Dickens & Co. also sought to ease whatever fears potential clients may have had about unfamiliar businessmen, especially in this uncertain form of property. They reassured readers that "we have the right kind of negroes—and always deal in such" and ended another early notice with the catchy slogan "Our motto is, quick sales and short profits."[3] Such shrewd advertising played a major role in helping the firm to become a huge financial success. Within a few years it was placing announcements in newspapers as far away as Lexington and St. Louis, offering to buy as many as 1,000 slaves, and then selling them in Memphis and the Lower Mississippi River Valley. By their peak in 1858, one Tennessee newspaper reported that the Boltons were worth nearly $1 million.[4]

Therefore, not only did the development of the domestic slave trade lead to the creation of the Cotton Kingdom, and play a role in bringing about its eventual demise, but as the example of Bolton, Dickens & Co. makes clear, it also made some of the men who operated this trade quite rich. These men likewise introduced many of the elements of the nation's emerging market economy into southern society. While the market revolution that transformed American life in the first half of the nineteenth century had a far different outcome in the South than it did in the North, in large part because of that region's ownership of its primary labor force, it still had an impact there. And one of the most important engines driving this development was the new interregional trade in slaves. In addition to bringing great wealth, as with the market revolution in the North, this traffic, and the men who operated it, helped to encourage consumerism and make market activity (and the speculation in commodities) a greater part of people's everyday lives.

Few southerners better personified the new business practices associated with the market revolution, and the values that they represented, than the men who operated this trade. While most southern slave traders probably never saw themselves in this light, in many respects, they were the agents of the emerging market world. In addition to taking advantage of all of the new innovations in transportation and communications, these men also introduced many of the new business practices that were revolutionizing American society at the time. These included developing complex (and often urban-based) company organizations, improving accounting techniques for recording profits, and standardizing commodities for easier purchasing and retail. Moreover, they stimulated sales through their creative marketing practices and customer service. Most important, their effective use of advertising not only sold thousands of men, women, and children, but it also helped to increase the desire for, and dependence upon, cash in southern society. And the quick profits that could be made in this business enticed even more southerners to speculate in this valuable commodity. Therefore, as with many of the new economic opportunities in the North, for those willing to take the risks and work hard, the domestic slave trade offered lucrative financial rewards.

This image of modern, entrepreneurial businessmen is not the one that comes to mind when most people today think of southern slave traders. The common stereotype is that of the fictional trader Dan Haley in Harriet Beecher Stowe's *Uncle Tom's Cabin* (1852). As Stowe portrayed him, Haley was an uncouth and unprincipled man who, according to one character, would "sell his own mother at a good per centage—not wishing the old woman any harm either." This caricature of slave traders as marginal, unscrupulous monsters began in both the antebellum North and South. The main reason for this is the deplorable nature of this business, which has influenced our view of the men who worked in it. Yet it is important to look at these individuals for who they really were, in all their variety and on their own terms, no matter how distasteful they may appear to modern eyes. That is the only way to fully appreciate the diversity of people who engaged in this trade and to comprehend the important role that they played in southern society.[5]

Simply put, there was no such thing as a typical slave trader. Also known as dealers, brokers, and speculators, these men came from all parts of the South (only a small percentage had been born outside the region) and all types of backgrounds. Some fit parts of the slave-trader stereotype, while others could not have been more dissimilar. They also performed different functions and engaged in the business over varying lengths of time. The one thing they all had in common was the drive to get ahead as quickly as possible. They understood that the surest way to do so was by entering the new market economy and by speculating in their region's most important commodity.[6]

In the end, southern slave traders proved less influential in modernizing their region than their mercantile counterparts in the North—although neither group saw that as their ultimate goal. One reason for this was the fact that the commodities they chose to deal in were not textiles or shoes, but enslaved human beings. Moreover, increased market development threatened the dominance of the large slaveholders, who used their vast economic and political power to prevent such a transformation from taking place. Nevertheless, southern slave traders still introduced many of the nation's new market values into their region. It is just that when they did so they met with drastically different results than did merchants in the North. Instead of creating a more diversified, free-labor economy, their trade in men, women, and children only further entrenched the southern slave system.

I

One major reason for the many misconceptions about southern slave traders and the role they played in American society has been the difficulty of determining who these men actually were. Few occupations have been harder to define than that of slave trader. Even if one only looks at the interregional trade and at those who engaged in the business on a regular basis, many different types of individuals fit this label. Moreover, the vast majority of southerners who made an income off this trade, for a multitude of reasons, never identified themselves in this way. Many only participated in the slave trade seasonally, or for a limited number of years. They saw themselves primarily as farmers, planters, or merchants who supplemented their income by trading in slaves. Others, such as commission brokers and auctioneers who specialized in this type of property, usually referred to themselves by their general occupation. The same was true for all of those people who worked as agents, clerks, and other salaried personnel. Finally, much of the domestic trade was financed by outside investors, who, while not directly involved in the buying and selling of slaves themselves, certainly profited from these actions by others. Therefore, to fully appreciate the importance of this trade and the number of southerners who made their living from it, one needs to look at all of the individuals involved, and not just focus on those men who fit a limited definition of "slave trader" or who publicly identified themselves as such.

The most well known and in many respects the most important type of slave trader was the individual who bought slaves in the exporting states, transported them to the importing states, and sold them for a profit. In the formative years of the domestic trade, during the late eighteenth and early nineteenth centuries, the majority of southern slave traders fit this mold. Most were small-time operators from Georgia and other southern and western states who roamed the countryside looking for bondspeople to buy and sell. When purchasing in the Chesapeake, some advertised in newspapers, but most just checked the local sales and jails and let it be known that they were looking for slaves. As one Virginian noted, "There was a Gentleman from Georgia now in Bath County who sent him word that he wanted 15 or 20 thousand dollars worth of Negroes in families for which he would give liberal prices." After acquiring enough slaves to form a "lot," the trader then led them overland on foot in a coffle, or gang held together in chains. Upon reaching their destination, most were sold informally, usually in the area near the trader's place of origin, or wherever a buyer could be found. Typical of these early traders was a Mr. M'Giffin, the man who purchased the former slave Charles Ball in 1805. M'Giffin bought a total of fifty-two bondspeople in Maryland before setting out for his home state of Georgia. But like many other early traders, his destination was not set in stone. Along the way, he sold a few slaves and then decided on the advice of an acquaintance to sell the remainder, including Ball, at auction in Columbia, South Carolina.[7]

By the 1820s, the domestic trade started to change, as innovative traders expanded their operations and made them more profitable. Like many of their mercantile counterparts in the North, the more successful slave traders began capitalizing on the new modes of transportation available in the first half of the nineteenth century. In addition, they started centralizing their offices in urban areas and forming complex business relationships (although still often along family lines).

Taking the lead in this development was Austin Woolfolk of Augusta, Georgia. Woolfolk first began advertising for slaves in Maryland in 1815. Like many other early traders, he operated out of a well-known tavern on the Eastern Shore of that state. After purchasing his lot, he then transported them by coffle to Augusta where his uncle John Woolfolk helped him to sell his human property to local farmers. By 1819, however, Woolfolk had moved his operation to Baltimore, in large part to take advantage of that city's rapidly growing port. He realized that as the nation expanded westward following the War of 1812, the demand for slaves in the new Southwest would be even greater than that in Georgia. Therefore, instead of carrying his slaves overland in coffles, or floating them down rivers on flatboats as many western traders had done, Woolfolk became one of the first traders to extensively use ocean-going vessels to transport large cargoes of slaves from the Chesapeake to New Orleans.[8]

While shipping slaves by water was slightly more expensive than other methods of transportation (roughly $2 more per slave than overland coffle), it provided traders with several important advantages.[9] For one thing, it greatly cut the time required for transit. Even with good roads and weather, coffles could cover only twenty to twenty-five miles a day. That meant that it would take seven to eight weeks to travel from the Chesapeake to Natchez, Mississippi (a common destination for many coffles), and even longer to get to New Orleans. Vessels in the coastal trade could make it to the Crescent City in less than three weeks. Consequently, by drastically curtailing the turnaround time from purchase to resale, traders lowered their maintenance costs. Shipping was also safer. There was less chance for escape at sea, and the quick trip and protection from the elements proved healthier for their human cargo as well. Finally, the coastal trade allowed traders to transport more slaves each season. While some coffles had well over 100 bondspeople in them, most contained only 30 or 40. The larger sailing vessels could ship more than 200 individuals at one time. Moreover, the trader did not have to accompany his property during transit, which gave him more time to purchase additional slaves for shipment.[10]

Austin Woolfolk transformed his business in other important ways as well. In 1823, he purchased a residence and office on Pratt Street in Baltimore, which gave him a fixed base to work from and made him a permanent member of the community. No longer was he an itinerant outsider; now, area slaveholders knew where to find him, and they thought of him as one of their own. Subsequently, they felt more comfortable bringing him their business. In addition, Woolfolk maintained his own slave jail, or "pen," behind his residence. Prior to this, most traders either stayed with their purchases or housed them with a local sheriff for a small fee. By having his own jail, Woolfolk cut his housing costs prior to shipping.

Finally, to conduct a business of this size, Woolfolk needed additional partners and agents to operate it. Luckily, he had numerous relatives who stepped in to help. His brother Joseph Woolfolk set up a permanent office in Easton, Maryland, on that state's slave-saturated Eastern Shore. Another relative, Richard Woolfolk, also worked the area in that capacity, as did numerous other agents who purchased slaves for Austin on commission. All of these men let it be known that they were looking for large numbers of slaves to purchase at "liberal prices." As the former slave Frederick Douglass recalled, Woolfolk's "agents were sent into every town and county in Maryland, announcing their arrival, through the papers, and on flaming 'hand-bills', headed CASH FOR NEGROES." In New Orleans, relatives John and Samuel Woolfolk and occasionally even Austin's father, Austin Woolfolk, Sr., received the slaves and saw to their resale from their office on Chartres Street. Like their relatives in Maryland who understood the importance of advertising, both John and Samuel announced the arrival of their slaves in the New Orleans newspapers. The result was that by the mid-1820s, Austin Woolfolk and his family had come to domi-nate the interregional trade.[11]

Yet, the Woolfolk family's success was soon eclipsed by that of another Chesapeake-area firm whose entrepreneurial innovations helped it to become arguably the most successful slave-trading company in America. Isaac Franklin and John Armfield formed their partnership in February 1828, and by the time that Franklin retired in 1835, their company and its affiliates had become one of the largest business operations of any kind in the South. Franklin and his brothers had long been involved in the slave trade, shipping bondspeople and other goods down the Mississippi River from their native Tennessee to Natchez and New Orleans as early as 1810. He was therefore well acquainted with the western trade when he met Armfield, a successful trader out of North Carolina, mostly likely in Natchez in the early 1820s. The two men soon realized, how-ever, that there was more money to be made through the coastal trade. Conse-quently, when they formed their partnership, they moved their headquarters to Alexandria, which at that time was still in the District of Columbia. Armfield, the junior partner, controlled their purchasing from that city, while Franklin did the selling in New Orleans and Natchez, the two most important slave-trad-ing centers in the Southwest. The two men also made their partnership a family affair when, in 1831, Armfield married Franklin's niece.[12]

Three months after forming their partnership, Franklin & Armfield leased a three-story brick house for their office on Duke Street in Alexandria. While such establishments were becoming common with the larger slave-trading firms, this facility was more elaborate than most. In addition to the main build-ing, there was a large yard of about 300 square feet surrounded by several out-buildings and a high, neatly whitewashed wooden fence. There were separate covered yards and two-story buildings for the men and the women, a kitchen, a hospital, and a tailor shop where the enslaved each received two new sets of clothing—although these were not to be worn until they had reached their final market.[13]

Franklin & Armfield's most important business innovation, however, involved purchasing and operating its own vessels in the coastal trade. From its beginning, the company provided shipping service on boats under its com-mand. While it is not known for certain what its connection was with some of its earlier vessels, the firm eventually owned at least three brigs: the *Tribune*, the *Uncas*, and the self-titled *Isaac Franklin*, which it had constructed "expressly for this trade." Eliminating the middlemen not only cut the partners' charges for shipping, but it also gave them an advantage in the buying market. The money that was saved on transportation allowed Franklin & Armfield to offer more for its purchases than did its competitors and still make a profit. In addition, these vessels carried goods like sugar, molasses, whiskey, and cotton to eastern ports

Painting of Isaac Franklin, leading slave trader in New Orleans and Natchez during the early 1830s and partner of John Armfield. He was reported to have made more than $1 million in the slave trade. Courtesy of the Manuscripts Division, Tennessee State Library and Archives.

Photograph of John Armfield, leading slave trader in Alexandria during the early 1830s and partner of Isaac Franklin. He later used the money he made from the slave trade to help bankroll the founding of the University of the South at Sewanee. Courtesy of the Manuscripts Division, Tennessee State Library and Archives.

Photograph of the front entrance to the slave pen on Duke Street in Alexandria, which was originally established by Franklin & Armfield in 1828. This building is now listed as a National Historic Landmark. Courtesy of the Alexandria Library, Special Collections.

on their return trips. Finally, the company also increased its revenue by offering empty space aboard its ships to other traders. While the absence of complete records makes it impossible to know for certain what percentage of the business this entailed, extant manifests indicate that a sizable number of bondspeople on each voyage were owned by someone else.[14]

One big reason for Franklin & Armfield's success was its adaptation of a shipping innovation that was transforming business in the North; the firm offered the relatively new service of "packet lines." Unlike the method of previous vessels, which did not sail until they had a full cargo, a packet line was guaranteed to sail at a specified date, whether it was full or not. Naturally, this led to some cut in profits since few of the company's boats sailed full. Although the *Tribune* was capable of holding up to 180 slaves (100 men and 80 women), most of the firm's ships left port with only 75–100 on board. Rarely did the cargo exceed 150, although on one occasion Armfield shipped 254 bondspeople aboard the *Isaac Franklin*. Still, the partners more than made up for this loss in revenue by attracting more customers with their reliable shipping schedules.[15]

Franklin & Armfield actively sought customers for its packets. The company's running advertisements noted that in addition to landing in New Orleans, its ships would "at all times go up the Mississippi by steam" to Natchez. The advertisements reassured customers that its boats were "all vessels of the first class, commanded by experienced and accommodating officers," and every effort would be "used to promote the interest of shippers and comfort of passengers." The firm also offered its jail facilities for anyone who needed them. According to its notices, "Servants that are intended to be shipped, will at any time be received for safe keeping at 25 cents per day." The success of Franklin & Armfield's packet service can be seen not only in the rapid growth of its fleet, but also in the increased frequency with which the ships sailed. In 1833, its advertisements stated that its boats would leave Alexandria "every thirty days throughout the shipping season," which began in October and lasted until April. Two years later, the partners moved their schedule to start service on September 1 and announced that one of their "*Alexandria and New Orleans Packets*" would "leave this port on the 1st and 15th of each month throughout the season."[16]

Franklin and Armfield further expanded their operation by sending a large number of their slaves to the Southwest by land. Every summer, Armfield led a coffle of several hundred bondspeople from Alexandria to Natchez. This allowed the firm to move slaves west earlier than they could by sea. Few traders transported slaves by water during the summer months because of the lack of demand and fear that the drastic climate change would prove deadly to their property. This change was far more gradual on the overland route and less threatening to the slaves' health. And, by leaving in mid- to late summer, by the time the coffle arrived in Natchez, the selling season would be just getting

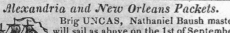

Alexandria and New Orleans Packets.
Brig UNCAS, Nathaniel Baush master, will sail as above on the 1st of September; brig TRIBUNE, Samuel C. Baush master, on the 15th of September ; brig ISAAC FRANKLIN, William Smith master, on the 1st of October.
They will continue to leave this port on the 1st and 15th of each month throughout the season. They are all vessels of the first class, commanded by experienced and accommodating officers, will at all times go up the Mississippi by steam, and every exertion used to promote the interest of shippers and comfort of passengers.
Shippers may prevent a disappointment by having their bills of lading ready the day previous to sailing, as they will go promptly at the time.
Servants that are intended to be shipped, will at any time be received for safe keeping at 25 cents per day.
JOHN ARMFIELD,
july 15—d&ctf   Alexandria.

Advertisement for Franklin & Armfield's innovative packet lines that transformed the shipment of slaves from the Chesapeake to the Deep South by sea. *National Intelligencer* (Washington, DC), August 19, 1835. Courtesy of the Virginia Historical Society.

under way. It should be noted that this summer trip and its large holding facilities also allowed the company to purchase slaves even during the off-season. Consequently, unlike most of its competitors, from the very beginning, Franklin & Armfield ran newspaper advertisements year-round.[17]

Finally, the two partners created a series of complex business relationships to help run their extensive enterprise. Isaac Franklin's nephew James Franklin was brought in to assist his uncle in the two main selling markets. At the other end, Armfield supervised a wide network of purchasing agents. In addition to several part-time buyers, by 1833 the company had set up permanent agents in Richmond, Warrenton, and Fredericksburg, Virginia; and in Frederick, Baltimore, Annapolis, Easton, and Port Tobacco, Maryland (the firm's agent in Baltimore was another of Franklin's nephews, James Purvis).[18] Most of these buyers worked on commission. Other traders in the area sometimes sold their slaves through the firm on consignment, and it is likely that at least one supposed competitor actually worked for the company as an unnamed agent.[19] To further increase its purchasing ability, in 1831 Franklin & Armfield formed a subsidiary-like company with one of its agents, Rice Ballard. This new company was a branch of the larger firm, in which Ballard purchased slaves in Richmond (employing agents of his own) and then sold them through Franklin in the Southwest under the name of Franklin, Ballard & Co. After Franklin's retirement in 1835, the firm reorganized with Ballard moving to Natchez to take on the selling responsibilities until the company eventually dissolved in 1841.[20]

All of these business innovations and entrepreneurial skills helped to make Franklin & Armfield the dominant slave-trading firm during the boom years of the mid-1830s, easily surpassing Austin Woolfolk in importance. By 1831, Woolfolk's business had dropped off dramatically, and the following year Armfield confided that "we have gott all the Jailors and some of his agents in our employ." In New Orleans, Samuel Woolfolk later served as one of Isaac Franklin's agents.[21] By 1835, a resident of Natchez claimed that, for the past fifteen years, Isaac Franklin had "supplied this country with two-thirds of the slaves brought into it." Franklin had concurred with this assessment two years earlier when he bragged that he had "sold more negros than all the Traders together." Visitors to its Alexandria office were told that the company sent at least 1,000 to 1,200 slaves of its own each year to the Southwest. Most likely, the total was far greater since in 1834 the firm held $400,000 in accounts receivable, an especially high figure considering that most slave traders liked to sell for cash or easily convertible paper.[22]

By the 1830s, large-scale, urban-based interregional dealers in slaves, like Austin Woolfolk and Franklin & Armfield, had become an important part of the domestic trade. Most urban markets in the Chesapeake (including Baltimore, Washington, Alexandria, Richmond, and Norfolk) had such firms. As the number of slave-exporting states expanded to the west and south, they started appearing in towns such as Lexington, Louisville, St. Louis, and Charleston. Most of these larger firms continued to funnel their slaves into the two main selling centers of Natchez and New Orleans, although a number of sizable markets developed in places like Mobile and Montgomery, Alabama. By the late 1850s, regular trading routes had developed within the Deep South itself. In 1859, the firm of Mosely & Spragins announced that it had established a permanent slave depot in Alexandria, Louisiana, where Spragins would remain "always ready to wait upon purchasers," while Mosely would send "additional supplies from time to time" from his base in northern Alabama.[23]

Furthermore, by the 1850s, important intermediary markets located between the selling states and the buying states, such as Memphis, Tennessee, had also emerged. Bolton, Dickens & Co. had obtained great wealth by capitalizing on this geographical advantage, and after that company's demise in the mid-1850s, its operation was most likely surpassed by the former itinerant trader Nathan Bedford Forrest, who put together one of the largest slave-trading enterprises in

Prewar photograph of Nathan Bedford Forrest, leading slave trader in Memphis during the late 1850s. His annual profits from selling slaves exceeded $50,000 and most likely reached $100,000 in his best years. During the Civil War he achieved notoriety when Confederate troops under his command massacred U.S. Colored Troops after they had surrendered at Fort Pillow. Following the war, he was also the first grand wizard of the Ku Klux Klan. Courtesy of the Memphis Pink Palace Museum.

the country. Running huge block advertisements in newspapers as far away as Charleston, Forrest announced that he wanted to purchase "500 NEGROES . . . suited to the New Orleans market." Also, in these same notices, he informed readers that he had slaves imported from states as widespread as Missouri, Kentucky, Virginia, North Carolina, South Carolina, and Georgia for purchase in his "Negro Mart" in Memphis, which, he added, was "capable of containing Three Hundred, and for comfort, neatness and safety, is the best arranged of any in the Union."[24]

While large-scale, urban-based interregional dealers in slaves were only a tiny fraction of the number of people who made their living from the domestic trade, they always remained the industry's leaders. This proved true not only in the number of slaves they handled each year, but also in their introduction into the trade of modern business practices. Like their mercantile counterparts in the North, they understood how changes in transportation and company organization could increase their profits.

II

As in most businesses, the vast majority of interregional slave traders were not large entrepreneurs, but midrange and small-scale operators who dealt in dozens of slaves instead of hundreds. While there was obviously some similarity between the larger firms and their smaller counterparts, there was also much that made the occupations of these two types of traders different from one another. For one thing, many of the smaller speculators continued to engage in the same daily work pattern as that of the early slave traders. Some employed agents of their own, but most went in search of slaves wherever they could find them and then carried them south themselves, usually by coffle. Also, unlike the large dealers who based themselves in the urban markets, most interregional traders worked in what one of them called "the country trade."[25] In other words, they traversed the countryside, selling slaves wherever they could find a buyer, and only used the urban markets as a last resort. Nevertheless, these small businessmen also participated in the new market world. While they may not have had the same kind of influence as their larger colleagues, they too helped to bring its practices and values into southern life.

One big difference between the majority of interregional slave traders and the handful of larger firms that dominated the trade can be seen in the way that they purchased their slaves. Most had to go out and solicit their own business. Some had regular territories that they worked when purchasing, usually the area within a county or two of their homes. This gave them certain advantages, such as familiarity with their customers and knowledge of all the local sales. According to one trader working out of Winchester, Virginia, he got "the refusal of all the negroes that are offered near here, and they are generally the likelyest in the world." Others went from town to town, checking the jails and court sales for possible purchases. These itinerant traders also advertised for slaves, although not in the same way as those traders with a more permanent address, whose inserts in the newspapers often ran for months. Instead, they put out advance notices in the towns they intended to visit, stating when they would arrive, where they could be found, and how long they intended to stay in the area. Finally, there were those traders who simply went door to door looking for slaves. As the former slave John Brown recalled, the trader who bought him, Sterling Finney, just "made his way up to our plantation, prospecting for negroes."[26]

Lacking the resources of the more established firms, the majority of smaller traders also employed less efficient methods when housing their slaves before shipment and transporting them to the importing states for sale. Only a handful owned their own jails. One such man was the early Kentucky trader Edward Stone, who had several iron-barred cellars under his house. Most, however, had to board their slaves wherever they could, be it on their own farms, with a local sheriff, or in the pen of a larger dealer. Many itinerant traders simply never left their new purchases, or kept them under the watchful eye of one of their assistants. Their journeys south were also often quite modest. Like a lot of early western traders, Stone just floated the men and women he bought down the Ohio and Mississippi rivers on flatboats (sometimes shipping more than seventy-five at one time). Most of the others led their human property overland in coffles, spending their nights in taverns, in barns, or encamped under the stars. As one trader described another in Alabama: "He lives in his tents."[27]

The smaller traders also differed from their larger urban counterparts in that many of them had no set destination when transporting their slaves. While it is true that some midrange traders had a partner located in one of the selling states, or they had made arrangements to sell their slaves through one of the resident dealers in the Deep South, most country traders just set out with their human merchandise looking for purchasers. Some headed where they had heard that prices were good. On the night before departing with his coffle, one North Carolina trader wrote to his brother: "I have not determined where I shall go but I think to Alabama. I understand negro men are selling in that state from $900 to $1000 and all others in proportion." Others had assistants who helped them to determine the best place to go. Such was the case with another North Carolina trader, Allan Gunn, who set off on foot with his slaves about the same time that one of his associates, a Dr. McCadin, left by stage. While they too had determined to head toward Alabama, McCadin's job was to "traverse the country in order to find a market."[28]

Only known photograph
of an itinerant slave
trader, Elias Ferguson,
who was based out of
North Carolina during
the 1850s. Courtesy of
North Carolina State
Archives in Raleigh.

Most country traders peddled their human commodities wherever they
could find a buyer. Many sold or swapped slaves on their way to the importing states. According to the previously mentioned John Brown, his trip from
Virginia to Georgia "lasted six weeks, as we made a good many stoppages by
the way, to enable the speculator, Finney, to buy up, and change away, and
dispose of his slaves." Once they arrived in Georgia, Finney took "out his slaves
every day, to try and sell them, bringing those back whom he failed to dispose
of." Some traders attended the various county court sales hoping to find purchasers. As one speculator in Alabama noted, a colleague was "following the
counties Round attending courts." Others just moved from town to town and
plantation to plantation. According to one former Texas slave, "There used
to be nigger traders who came through the country with the herd of niggers,
just like cattlemen with the herd of cattle. They fixed camp and the pen on the
ridge outside of town and people who wanted to buy more slaves went there."
The daughter of a prominent Georgia planter also recalled that every year

traders brought a gang of slaves to her home; they camped in a grove of trees near the highway.[29]

These men remained constantly on the move and felt little hesitation in leaving a dull market for potentially greener pastures. As one trader in Alabama informed his partner in Virginia, "If I dont make some sales soon I shall cut out from here but dont know where now." After running out of buyers in South Carolina, a North Carolina man, Obadiah Fields, informed his wife that he now planned on leaving that state "to hunt a market for the ballance of the negros I have on hand." Perhaps the best description of the selling activities of these men came from an Alabama chief justice, who wrote that "a slave merchant or trader may engage in this business without being located in any particular county. He is often migratory with his slaves."[30]

The country traders also sometimes brought their slaves to the major urban markets of the Deep South. Unlike the larger firms, which used these as their primary base of operations, many of the smaller traders only went there as a last resort, mainly because of the higher expenses involved in trading there. Nevertheless, they occasionally did so when sales were poor and word had reached them of greater possibilities in one of the bigger markets. Such was the case of a trader in rural Alabama who found "the market very dull" and informed his wife that he was thinking "of going to New Orleans." More frequently, they went to these larger centers to get rid of their hard-to-sell slaves, or to sell out so they could head back home, or to return to the selling states to engage in another venture. Once again, this is what happened to John Brown. After "Finney disposed of a good many of his drove, ... he became anxious to sell the rest, for he wanted to take another journey into Virginia, on a fresh speculation." So, Finney took Brown and the other remaining slaves to the state capital at Milledgeville, where he put them up at auction and took whatever he could get for them. Obviously, such sales were often not the most profitable, and most traders tried to avoid them. Still, they were better than no sales at all, especially when a trader was anxious to get back home. As one frustrated trader in Alabama put it, he intended to "go to Mobile next week and sell out" so that he could "be at home shortly."[31]

Despite the day-to-day differences from their more influential counterparts, these small businessmen also embraced and profited from the practices of the new market economy. For one thing, they sometimes formed business associations. Many traders worked together with family members or collaborated informally, but a number of unrelated country traders also entered into legal partnerships with one another. Most of these agreements only lasted for a season or two, but some survived for several years. Their articles of partnership usually called for an equal contribution of capital and a sharing of expenses and profits. Some partners performed their duties interchangeably, while others divided the jobs of buying and selling. Not only did these arrangements allow men of modest wealth to pool their resources and expand their operations, but it also permitted them to spend less time away from home and only engage in those aspects of the business with which they felt most comfortable. This proved true for George Kephart, a former agent for Franklin & Armfield, who purchased his employers' Alexandria pen after their retirement. When establishing his own firm, Kephart sought a partner in the Deep South because he thought "it would be unpleasant . . . to be in the selling market." Not surprisingly, many of these men found these partnerships advantageous and sought to extend them whenever possible. As one trader in Mississippi informed his associate back in North Carolina: "I shall be willing to go into any arrangement with you that you may think proper the next season." Another in South Carolina stated simply, "do let us Spur up once more."[32]

Many of the smaller and midsized traders also employed agents to help them with the purchasing and transporting of slaves to the selling markets. One such case was the firm of Isaac Jarratt and Tyre Glen, which operated out of western North Carolina during the early 1830s. While each man bought and sold slaves, they also employed an agent who purchased others for them on commission. In addition to this regular employee, they hired part-time workers to help them drive their coffles to Alabama—although the terms of service for these individuals could be quite short. Glen hired one man, Baldy Kerr, "with the privilege of dismissing him at any time." Interestingly, it was in this lowermost, and often most dangerous, part of the domestic trade that one of the few women who worked in this business could be found. For this same trip with Kerr, Glen also hired a woman named Jenny to assist them. According to a colleague who saw the coffle depart, "Jumping Jinny . . . carries up the rear armed and equiped in a style that renders it quite a certainty that if life lasts you will see her in montgomery."[33]

Many small and midsized traders also took advantage of all of the new shipping innovations brought by the transportation revolution. Although they did not possess their own ships, some of those working near the port cities of the Chesapeake found it more convenient to ship their slaves on ocean-going vessels owned by others in the coastal trade. For traders in the West, the most important development was the arrival of steamboats during the 1820s. Most large traders in that region, such as John White from Missouri, used these vessels to transport the hundreds of Missouri, Kentucky, and Virginia slaves that they and their agents bought each year to Louisiana and other states in the Deep South. But numerous small-scale traders also made their journeys on steamboats, often stopping in riverbank towns along the way to sell their human goods.

Some small traders even made steamboat travel an important part of their business. This was certainly the case with a Mr. Walker, a Missouri trader who hired the slave William Wells Brown as his assistant for a year. On one buying trip, Walker took a steamboat up the Missouri River to Jefferson City, where he then took a stage and began purchasing slaves at "different farms and villages." After acquiring some twenty individuals, Walker drove them overland to his farm near St. Louis, where he placed them in "a kind of domestic jail" that he had specially built on his property. After his gang was completed, he then shipped them down the Mississippi River by steamboat, stopping in places like Rodney, Vicksburg, and Natchez, Mississippi, before arriving in New Orleans. After selling out his lot, Walker made the return trip to St. Louis by steamboat and began the process anew.[34]

By the 1840s and 1850s, many speculators had also begun transporting their slaves on the region's emerging railroad lines. This advance in technology proved a real boon to slave traders, as it cut both costs and travel time. On southern trains, slaves rode for half price (the same as children), and most trains carried a "nigger car," which often doubled as the freight or baggage car. One indication of the effect that railroads had on slashing shipping times can be found in the message a trader in southern Virginia sent to his partner in Alabama. Despite having to travel to Richmond first, Philip Thomas could still expect that "in 8 days after I leave home I will be in Montgomery with a fresh lot of negroes." This was almost one-third the time it took via the coastal trade and at least six weeks faster than overland coffle. One month later, Thomas noted that he had made the return trip home from Montgomery to Richmond in just fifty-five hours.[35]

Not surprisingly, railroads quickly became an important part of the slave-trading business for traders large and small. As early as 1841, the former slave Solomon Northup reported that the trader James Birch had transported him from Washington to Richmond in part by "the cars." By 1848 the large Baltimore dealer Hope Slatter was shipping slaves to the Georgia market by rail, and, not long after, most other traders were doing so as well. According to one Virginia trader, a competing firm, Smith & Edmonson, had "shipped all their negroes this Season by the Jackson & New Orleans Rail Road," adding to his partner that he was sorry that "we did not know it before." Others routinely used the rails when looking for slaves to purchase or when sending new purchases to their associates in nearby markets. Having gotten used to this form of transportation, when forced to drive a coffle of twenty-three slaves overland to Georgia, the Virginia trader Zachary Finney even complained that he "found it quite a task to travel with negroes in this mode."[36] The railroads also proved an excellent place to conduct business. In Virginia, J. J. Toler "bought a man on the cars for $1400," while in South Carolina, A. J. McElveen noted that he "met with a man on the cars yesterday that is likely to buy the Seamstress." Even partnerships were proposed. After meeting another trader on a train in Alabama, J. P. Pool wrote to his new friend that he would "like to carray out the conversation we had on the Cars relative to trade."[37]

Finally, slave traders of all size capitalized on the latest developments in communication, especially the telegraph after its invention in 1844. One of the biggest problems for American businesses before this advancement was the delay in conveying information to associates in other locations. Companies had to depend upon the speed and reliability of the mails or personal couriers, which could often take days, if not weeks, to relay important information. This proved especially troublesome for businesses like the slave trade where profits depended upon knowing the latest prices in both the buying and selling markets. As a result, interregional traders continually corresponded with one another to obtain this information and complained when it was not provided to them on time. As one North Carolina trader admonished his partner in New Orleans: "Write often as the times is Criticle & it depends on the prices you get to Govern me in buying." Another in Virginia protested, "It has been so long since I have heard from you that I know nothing about the market in any way." Even large dealers like John Armfield suffered from this problem, and he ended one letter to Rice Ballard with the plea, "Write, write, write, how many have you on hand."[38]

As telegraph lines spread across the South, slave traders jumped at the opportunity to use this invention to confirm the receipt of letters or money, to inform their partners of their whereabouts, and to decide whether or not to buy another lot and at what price. It even allowed them to assess the profitability of specific purchases. After informing his partner in Alabama of some field hands for sale, one Virginia trader wanted to know if they would turn a profit at their asking price, adding, if so "Telegraph me and I will buy them, if not do not Telegraph and I will understand not to buy." While the availability of the telegraph was limited to those areas with telegraph offices, which naturally benefited the larger urban firms, all traders made use of it whenever possible.[39]

Therefore, small and midsized traders likewise took advantage of the latest commercial innovations to better increase their profits. Of course, this was less true for those at the bottom end of the business than it was for those who were well on their way to becoming large traders themselves. And most of the country traders would have agreed with the Virginian who admitted that he was "only a small drop in the Bucket compared with the Orleans Traders." Still, like their larger counterparts, these small businessmen played a major role in ushering the new market world into southern society.[40]

III

While long-distance speculators, both large and small, were certainly the most well known type of southern slave trader, there were just as many other men, if not more, who also made at least part of their living from the interregional trade. These individuals worked as commission brokers, dealers, auctioneers, financiers, and various types of agents and auxiliary personnel. Some historians of the domestic trade have not considered these men as traders proper. Yet, the failure to see them in this way has only obscured our understanding of the total number of people who were actually involved in this business. Part of the problem stems from the fact that most of these men did not identify themselves as slave traders. Although they did often engage in other business activities besides selling slaves, many of them still made a significant portion of their income from this trade, and their services proved essential for making it run as smoothly as it did. Therefore, to fully appreciate the range of people involved in this business, it is important to recognize that all of these men were slave traders as well.[41]

Foremost among this group were those individuals who bought and sold slaves on commission. Located mostly in urban areas, these brokers played an important role in the transfer of human property from one owner to another. They purchased slaves on order and got a good price for those who wanted to sell. Like most other brokers in the new market economy, who often dealt in a variety of goods, almost all bought and sold a number of commodities besides slaves. Some only sold a handful of men and women each year, while others specialized in this trade and sold hundreds. They had their own depots where they housed the slaves that they had for sale and provided boarding services for others. A few also held their own slave auctions. And many partook in the interregional trade: forming associations with long-distance traders, making purchases for clients in other states, and even agreeing to sell slaves for dealers from other cities who could not get a good local price.

One of the more successful of these traders was Ziba B. Oakes of Charleston, South Carolina. Like most of his broker colleagues, Oakes had a diversified business, including dealings in real estate, mortgages, insurance, and all types of stocks. But the vast majority of his business came from the buying and selling of slaves. He purchased them extensively on his own, through his agents, and from dealers in other cities. He then sold these men and women to his numerous clients, either on order or to walk-in customers at his own depot. By the end of the 1850s, he also sold increasing numbers of bondspeople by auction and even bought the slave mart complex on Chalmers Street. While much of his business was local, Oakes's reputation was such that he also sold slaves to planters as far away as Texas and Louisiana. As one Tennessee man noted when placing his order, "I would rather risk your purchases than those of any Agent I could send there." In addition, Oakes had dealings with traders all over the South. Not only did he frequently collaborate with brokers in other South Carolina and Georgia cities, but he also conducted business with dealers in such major markets as Richmond, Montgomery, and New Orleans. Most important, he supplied a number of western traders (from a variety of states) with their human stock. Some came into his depot to pick out their goods, while others just allowed Oakes to purchase for them. Such was the case with the trader who informed Oakes that he had made arrangements with his bankers to send him "$10,000 the first of December to invest in negroes." While men like Z. B. Oakes were locally based commission brokers who bought and sold other goods, they played an important role in the interregional slave trade.[42]

Every southern city of any size also had resident traders who made the boarding of slaves at their depots an important part of their business. Brokers like Oakes likewise provided this service, but not to the same extent as others, who prominently featured it in their advertisements. According to one such dealer in Lexington, Kentucky, his was "the largest and most secure jail in the State," while a competitor in that same city claimed that he owned "the largest and best constructed building for a jail in the West." The main reason that owners might take advantage of this service can be seen in another notice by that same trader, who offered to "keep negroes by the day or week, for any one wishing to confine them in Jail for sale or any other purpose."[43] The usual charge for boarding a slave was twenty-five cents a day, although Bernard Lynch in St. Louis asked thirty-seven-and-a-half cents, and John Sydnor in Galveston, Texas, got forty. This service proved quite a savings for those individuals with large numbers of slaves to confine, such as long-distance traders. According to a visitor to one of these depots in Washington, DC, the fee of twenty-five cents a day was nine cents cheaper than that charged by the city-owned jail.[44]

In addition to boarding slaves, these dealers also provided other valuable services. Most sought out enslaved men and women to buy, usually for resale in their depots. They also sold slaves for others on commission, normally collecting a 2.5 percent fee on all sales, including those made by other traders boarding slaves in their jails. Some, such as the Nashville firm of James & Harrison, even had "regular Auction Sales of Negroes every Saturday morning at 10 o'clock." Somewhat more typical were Blakey & McAfee of St. Louis, which offered to "pay the highest CASH prices for all description of Negroes." This firm's notice also claimed that it would "attend to the sale of Negroes on commission, having a cheap, safe, and comfortable place for boarding them" and that "persons visiting St. Louis with negroes for sale would do well to call on us." Like most of these dealers, they had "Negroes for sale at all times."[45]

While depot-owning traders drew much of their business from local customers, most also participated in the interregional trade. Dealers in the Upper
South frequently purchased large numbers of slaves for export to the importing
states. In St. Louis, Corbin Thompson offered to "pay the highest cash prices"
for "THREE HUNDRED NEGROES," as well as "board, buy and sell on commission as low as any other dealer in the State of Missouri." Resident traders in
this part of the South also made much of their income from traveling speculators, who frequented their depots to purchase slaves to fill out their lots and to
confine their recent purchases until they were ready for shipment south. Not
surprisingly, some, such as R. H. Thompson of Lexington, advertised for their
business, noting that he would "take care of the negroes of Traders and others,
who may desire them kept safely on liberal terms."[46]

Nowhere in the Upper South, however, did these resident dealers play a
more important role than in the largest market, Richmond. One significant
branch of the domestic trade was those speculators who purchased slaves in
the Chesapeake states and then brought them to Richmond for resale to traders who worked the Deep South. Some Richmond firms, like Silas and R. F.
Omohundro, had their own depots from which to make these sales. But many
others did not and had to conduct the majority of their business through
the city's auction houses. Consequently, these individuals, as well as all those
interregional buyers, needed someplace to board their human property while
in the city.[47]

As in all successful markets, a few enterprising dealers set up special boarding houses and jails to cater to the needs of these itinerant traders. In the early
1830s, Bacon Tait erected several "commodious buildings . . . for the accommodation of all persons who may wish their NEGROES safely and comfortably
taken care of." Tait understood that his customers might have concerns about
the health dangers posed by such a facility, so he reassured them that their new
purchases would be provided with "general cleanliness, moderate exercise, and
recreation within the yards during good weather, and good substantial food at
all times." It was his intention, he added, "that confinement shall be rendered
merely nominal, and the health of the Negroes so promoted, that they will be
well prepared to encounter a change of climate when removed to the South."[48]

Two decades later, the most important complex of this type belonged to
Robert Lumpkin. One visitor to his facility in 1850 referred to it as "a kind of
hotel or boarding house for negro traders and their slaves." Lumpkin's Jail, as it
was known, consisted of four brick buildings on about a half acre of fenced-in
land. One building served as Lumpkin's office and residence, another as housing for out-of-town traders and buyers, another as a kitchen and barroom, and
the fourth as a two-story jail for boarding those who had been recently purchased or were about to be sold (men on the bottom floor, women on the top).

While Lumpkin himself also bought and sold slaves for the long-distance trade (as did Bacon Tait before him), much of his income came from this prosperous jail, which filled a vital need in the Richmond market.[49]

The Lower South likewise had a number of resident traders who also served an important function in the interstate trade. In addition to boarding slaves for local owners and buying and selling on commission, these dealers provided a place in the larger urban markets for interregional traders without their own depots. Some itinerant speculators found these depots useful for selling off the remainder of their stock, while others brought their lots there and stayed the entire season. They had to pay an extra expense for this service (board, commission, and city taxes), but the higher prices they usually obtained and assistance in sales from the dealer and his staff made it worthwhile for many smaller traders.[50]

As the largest and most important market in the importing states, New Orleans naturally had the greatest number of depot-owning brokers in the Lower South. Not surprisingly, most made an effort to appeal to out-of-town sellers, even going so far as to advertise in distant cities for their business. In his notice in one northern Louisiana newspaper, Thomas Frisby highlighted his depot on Baronne Street, saying he was "prepared to accommodate Transient Traders and their Slaves on as reasonable terms as can be obtained in the city, having accommodations for between two and three hundred Negroes, and the advantage of a large yard." Charles Hatcher made similar claims "To Traders and Slave Owners" in his announcement in the Nashville *Republican Banner*. In addition to "building a very commodious SHOW ROOM, and otherwise improving the premises" of his depot on Gravier Street, Hatcher likewise could "accommodate from 200 to 300 NEGROES for sale," adding that "owners can also be furnished with comfortable rooms and board on reasonable rates."[51]

No dealer prospered more in this market niche than Thomas Foster. In 1853, Foster advertised that he had acquired "the large, commodious brick house" next to his depot at the corner of Baronne and Common streets and was now "able to accommodate 300 negroes for those who may import from Virginia, North or South Carolina, Missouri or Kentucky." Three years later, Foster had "converted the family part of the large three-story building to the use of slaves" and "made it the best depot in the city," claiming it was "well furnished for the comfort of the slaves." By 1858, he had expanded to "three extensive yards" and was now "prepared to accommodate FIVE HUNDRED SLAVES." In this enlarged facility, he provided "every accommodation for Traders, both for Boarding and Lodging, with servants in attendance." One reason for Foster's success was his "carefully selected stock of slaves, calculated to please the purchaser let his wants be what they may." But, even more important, unlike most of his colleagues, who also bought and sold slaves on their own accounts, by 1858 he had "strictly confined" his business to selling on commission, "giv-ing thereby each and every trader an equal opportunity in the disposal of his negroes." By gaining the confidence of his customers in this manner, Foster could claim that his "stock of Slaves" was "equal if not superior to any offered in this market."[52]

In addition to commission brokers and depot-owning traders, most major markets also had auctioneers who specialized in the selling of slaves. Like brokers, almost all of these men dealt in a number of goods besides slaves. In Mobile, John Geyer had a "PUBLIC AUCTION every day at 11 o'clock A.M., for the sale of Negroes, Houses, Horses and Carriages, Buggies, Furniture, &c." Every city, however, always had some auctioneers who made the sale of human property the primary focus of their business, and they supplied large numbers of bondspeople for the interregional trade. Like the brokers who specialized in this trade, these auctioneers had depots and yards of their own for boarding the slaves of local sellers and itinerant traders prior to sale. They also did apprais-als, arranged for transportation, ran the advertising, and helped to prepare the men, women, and children for sale. For this they usually received a fee of 2–2.5 percent on all sales, although some, especially those doing court-ordered sales for the state, received slightly less. Some had their own auction rooms, while others used public facilities or open spaces, such as "the North side of the Cus-tom-House in Charleston." In Memphis, one auctioneer advertised the sale of several slaves "in front of the Post Office," adding that "persons wishing to add to the list will please call and see me previous to Monday next."[53]

Once again, these auctioneers played their biggest role in the markets of Richmond and New Orleans. In the Virginia capital, four or five firms con-ducted a prosperous business transferring slaves from local owners and traders to buyers for the Deep South market. During certain times of the year, they sold dozens, and even hundreds, of slaves a day from their own auction rooms or from public facilities like the Odd Fellows Hall on Franklin Street. To attract business, most of the major companies had their own depots. As Edward Stokes informed the public in his notice, he was "prepared to board persons engaged in the trade, and also their servants, having ample accommodations for both." In fact, several of these facilities were quite extensive. In 1857 a local editor reported that the three largest firms employed nineteen people and had depots assessed at more than $25,000.[54]

Many of the Richmond auctioneers also participated in the interregional trade by providing funds for other traders or by buying and selling slaves on their own account. They employed agents to purchase slaves for them, whom they then auctioned off to southern buyers, collecting both a commission fee and their share of the profits. Not all, however, thought this personal stake in the trade was good for business, and these auctioneers tried to capitalize on their supposed impartiality to attract customers. In its company letterhead, Pulliam & Co. described itself as "Auctioneers for the Sale of Negroes" but made it clear that it had "no connection with the Negro Trade" and that it sold "ONLY ON COMMISSION."[55]

Slave auctioneers in the Crescent City likewise performed a vital, albeit somewhat different, function in the domestic trade. Unlike Richmond, where large numbers of interregional slave sales passed through the hands of auctioneers, in New Orleans and most other southern cities, estate and other court-ordered sales made up the bulk of their business. Quite simply, long-distance speculators in New Orleans got better prices by selling out of their own (or someone else's) showrooms than they could by selling at auction. Nevertheless, the city's auctioneers still played an important role in the interregional trade. Depot sales often took time, so for those who wanted to sell out quickly or who had difficult slaves to sell, the city's auction rooms were a valuable resource. As William Wells Brown noted when describing the selling practices of the slave trader he worked for, "After the best of the stock was sold at private sale at the pen, the balance were taken to the Exchange Coffee House Auction Rooms, kept by Isaac L. McCoy, and sold at public auction."[56]

Some New Orleans auctioneers did much of their business in this trade. The majority of slaves Benjamin Kendig sold were single men and women in their teens and twenties who had been born out of state. Others sold large lots from the exporting states. Julian Neville offered "SEVENTY VALUABLE SLAVES . . . all from one cotton plantation in Georgia," stating that if they were "not sold at private sale previous to the 1st Jan., they will then be offered at public auction." Such heavy involvement in the domestic trade meant that most of these auctioneers also had their own depots. Joseph Beard claimed to have "ample accommodations for quartering 250 slaves." Although, once again, some tried to distance themselves from any conflict of interest that this might suggest. According to one potential client, the auctioneer N. Vignie refused to open his own yard, "offering as a reason that if he seemed to be connected in any way in interest, that he could not have that confidence of the buyers that he now has."[57]

In addition to brokers, dealers, and auctioneers, there were also southerners who speculated in the slave-trading abilities of others. Often serving as silent partners, these individuals engaged in the trade by bankrolling the ventures of others. Interregional traders constantly needed large sums of cash to make their purchases. As one trader lamented, "It requires a considerable Amount of Cash Capital to do business to advantage." Most large and midsized firms got this money from banks and other sources at a nominal rate of interest. But many smaller traders lacked the credit for such loans and were therefore willing to give up a share of their profits to outside investors. This could amount to as much as half of all the proceeds after expenses, although there were always arrangements, such as the one that Henry Badgett and John Glass made with Levi Holbrook, where they simply agreed "to refund the said five thousand dollars with such profits as may be fair and just." Whatever the terms, these slave-trading financiers usually received a healthy return on their investments.[58]

Typical of these men was the famous North Carolina jurist Thomas Ruffin. In the early 1820s, Ruffin entered into a partnership with Benjamin Chambers to buy slaves in North Carolina and transport them to Alabama for sale. According to their agreement, Ruffin supplied the initial $4,000 to purchase the human property, while Chambers did all of the actual buying and selling. Over a three-year period, the two men made more than $6,000 in profit. In addition to receiving his share of this money, Ruffin also had his pick of all of the men and women they bought for his own plantations. This profitable slave-trading partnership lasted five years and only ended with Chambers's death in 1826.[59]

Finally, there were all those individuals who worked as agents, supervisors, overseers, and clerks. These men performed the supporting jobs that made the business of slave trading happen—they bought and sold slaves for others, ran the depots and pens, and kept the books. Some worked on commission, while others were salaried personnel. Many who transported the coffles across the southern countryside only received a one-time fee, usually around $50 to take a gang from Virginia to New Orleans. But, as one slave dealer in that city testified, "Men may be had for all prices, some would do it merely for their passage money when they are anxious to come out in the fall." A large number of these auxiliary personnel only lasted a year or two, but there were also those who spent a lifetime in the trade. And there were many, like Benjamin Thorn, who testified that he had "been engaged in the business of taking slaves south, off and on, for twenty years," adding that "when I can't do that I do something else." While not actually risking their own money in the speculation of human property, these individuals derived the majority of their income from this trade and were certainly seen as slave traders in the eyes of many, including the enslaved themselves.[60]

Just as various brokers, dealers, auctioneers, financiers, and supporting personnel proliferated in northern industries in the new market economy, the same was true for the most important trade in the South. Not only did this business financially support those men directly engaged in it, but it also provided a livelihood to a vast secondary work force. Traditionally, these other men have not been viewed as slave traders, but they were among the large number of people who made a living from this trade, and they played a crucial role in promoting economic development in the South.

IV

Uniting all of these various slave traders was their acquisitive desire to get rich quick, or at least more quickly than they could in most other walks of life. As with northern capitalists, southern slave traders were willing to take risks for the enormous profits that could be obtained in this trade. And some men truly did obtain great wealth, often in a short period of time. The Washington trader William H. Williams boasted of making $30,000 in just a few months. While such claims may have been exaggerated, the large traders routinely made more than that in a single year. Isaac Franklin and John Armfield certainly bettered that amount. By 1834, Armfield was said to have made $500,000, and contemporaries referred to Franklin as a millionaire, which he may have been. At the time of his death, in the economically depressed mid-1840s, Franklin's estate was appraised at $750,000, most of it acquired through the slave trade. During the boom years of the 1850s, the most successful traders raked in huge earnings. In Memphis, Nathan Bedford Forrest's annual profits exceeded $50,000 and most likely reached $100,000 in his best years. Auctioneers who specialized in the selling of slaves could also make that kind of money. The Richmond firm of Dickinson, Hill & Co. was reported to have sold $2 million worth of slaves in 1856. At 2.5 percent commission, that meant $50,000 in gross sales.[61]

The possibility of such wealth attracted many white southerners into this trade. As one visitor to the South explained, "The gain is considerable, and the inducement in proportion." Sometimes, larger traders played upon this hope when attempting to attract potential agents. In his notices, Austin Woolfolk promised that "liberal commissions will be paid to those who will aid in purchasing for the subscriber." Another Maryland trader was even more direct, stating, "Persons desirous of engaging in this business as agents, either in town or country, can procure employment and obtain liberal commissions."[62] Most traders, however, did not need to resort to such appeals, as potential agents and even auctioneers contacted them. In his letter to a Richmond trader, one eager Virginia man offered "to purchase for you all the year."[63]

There was also no lack of individuals willing to pursue slave trading on their own. According to one North Carolinian, it seemed that "every man that can get Credit in the Bank and his Situation will let him leave home is a negro trader." Obviously, this was an overstatement, but it does indicate the trade's attractiveness for many people. Some were like the Alabama man who thought this the best way "to make a fortune here as soon as possible." Others just saw the slave trade as an easy way to earn some needed cash. A Tennessee man and his brother-in-law were typical in this respect. They agreed to enter the trade and use their profits to buy a plantation and the slaves to work it. As this man put it: "This course has seemed best to me, for the reason that it would be a more speedy way of adding to our capital than planting. Make the trade in negroes merely subservient to a future planting operation."[64]

Of course, the overwhelming majority of men involved in the slave trade failed to achieve the kind of wealth enjoyed by Franklin, Armfield, and Forrest. As in any speculative endeavor, the business was filled with risks, any one of which could wipe out a season's profits, lead to bankruptcy, or worse. The close quarters and unsanitary conditions of many of the slave pens meant that disease was always a possibility, especially in the Deep South, where outbreaks of yellow fever, smallpox, and cholera were routine. In 1832, after losing nine adult slaves and seven children within two weeks to a cholera epidemic, Isaac Franklin lamented that "it has been the most Trying times that ever sailed in my high seas." But the following year proved even worse, prompting Franklin's nephew James to fear that "the damned cholera . . . will take off all of our profits." Three months later, all of the "sickness and Deaths" led Isaac to conclude, "I would not see another such a season for all the money in the world."[65]

The business had other potential pitfalls that could bring economic disaster to even the most careful trader. Agents sometimes ran off with their boss's money. After one such man swindled the Richmond auctioneer Hector Davis out of more than $10,000, another trader in that city warned, "Bad agents will ruin Anyone." Accidents were likewise a possibility, especially in the coastal trade. In 1831 one brig was forced to abandon 164 slaves (most belonging to Franklin & Armfield) after it struck rocks on the Bahama Banks; four years later, weather drove another ship carrying 75 slaves (valued at $40,000) to Bermuda, where the cargo were all set free.[66] The commodities themselves could also cut into a trader's profits. At one time or another, almost every slave trader had at least a couple of individuals who successfully made their escape. While such losses could be written off by the larger firms as a cost of doing business, the high price of slaves meant that even one runaway could wipe out all of the profits of a smaller operation. Moreover, the business was filled with danger, and dozens of slave traders lost their lives at the hands of the men and women they were hoping to sell. Finally, the greed that drove these men also sometimes led to their undoing. Probably the most costly example in this regard was in 1840, when William H. Williams got caught trying to smuggle twenty-seven Virginia slaves condemned for crimes to be sold out of the country into New Orleans. Not only was Williams forced to forfeit the slaves, but with his fines and legal fees, this failed venture ended up costing him an estimated $48,000.[67]

Still, despite the risks, the majority of men working in the slave trade managed to make a decent living. Economic historians have found that, on average, slave traders made profits of 20–30 percent a year, which is high by antebellum standards. This was roughly equal to the profit rates of southern industrial firms. And for those individuals, such as Williams, who were willing to stretch the law, this rate could go even higher. One of the most infamous traders in New Orleans in the 1850s was Bernard Kendig, who routinely bought slaves with known faults and then sold them to unsuspecting buyers as sound. On his legitimate sales, Kendig earned an average profit of 25 percent, but on his fraudulent sales, this rate climbed to 37 percent.[68]

Even without resorting to such tactics, however, the slave trade offered to men of ambition in the South an opportunity to make more money than they could earn in most other occupations available to them. At a time when a southern bank president's annual salary was $5,000 or less, even moderately successful slave traders could easily make twice that much, if not considerably more. And the larger firms outperformed the wealthiest cotton planters. The same was true for those at the lower end of the economic spectrum. A good annual income for southern yeomen farmers was $300, while overseers made $100–200 a year, and white laborers were paid even less. Even those just starting out as assistants in the slave trade could make that much, and those with experience made $600 or more per year. The reason for this disparity is that it was harder to get southern whites to work in this trade. Unlike an overseer, who was given room and board and could stay in one place with his family all year, slave traders and their assistants often spent months away from home, trudging across the country and living outdoors in all types of weather. Moreover, as one experienced slave-trading agent explained, "It is a laborious business and there is a great deal of risk to be run, and danger to be encountered." But, for those willing to take these risks and work hard, the payoff could be rewarding.[69]

Therefore, for many industrious white southerners, the slave trade was seen as a reasonable way to get ahead in life. While several large traders, such as the South Carolinians Thomas Gadsden, Louis DeSaussure, and John Springs III, came from prominent southern families and used the slave trade to enhance their personal wealth, hundreds of other men from more humble origins entered the trade hoping to make their fortunes. And there were plenty of examples of those who had done just that. Two other of South Carolina's leading slave dealers, Ziba Oakes and John Riggs, came from more modest backgrounds. Oakes was the son of a grocer, and Riggs was an Irish-born immigrant whose father was a harness maker. Yet, by 1860, the slave trade had made their sons two of the wealthiest men in Charleston. Most important, some of the largest slave traders in the South owed their financial success almost entirely to this trade. Both Isaac Franklin and Nathan Bedford Forrest grew up under rugged conditions along the southwestern frontier, and John Armfield came from simple North Carolina stock. The vast majority of slave traders who started out with nothing failed to achieve the kind of wealth acquired by these men. One did need a certain amount of capital or influence to obtain the financing necessary for large-scale success. Nevertheless, for those who worked hard and lived frugally, the slave trade proved to be one of the quickest and surest routes for making money in the Old South.[70]

V

Like their northern counterparts, the various southern slave traders all embraced the hard-nosed and hypermasculine ethos of the emerging world of commerce. Any business that promised such huge financial rewards naturally led to a great deal of competition among its practitioners. Traders constantly complained about the number of rivals at market. As the Richmond dealer Bacon Tait grumbled when trying to buy slaves for the Deep South, "It is with Buyers as it is with crows, kill one & two comes to bury him." Conversely, traders in New Orleans moaned at how "no one looks at our negroes any more, preferring the latest arrivals."[71] Subsequently, many would have agreed with the Richmond auctioneer who noted that "there was rather a bitter feeling in the market this morning" or with the trader in Mobile who believed it was "evry man for his Self in this place."[72]

To get ahead, traders frequently tried to outsmart their competition through deception. Because so much of the success of this business depended upon knowledge of the various market conditions, speculators sought to keep the information they had hidden from others. As one trader warned his partners, "You all must keep dark on this subject partickularly as the old saying is he that does well must keep his business to himself." Others deliberately planted false information to deceive their rivals. One such trader was Joseph Meek of Nashville, who sent a letter erroneously announcing the falling price of cotton to his partner, Samuel Logan, in Virginia. Logan, who had earlier been informed of the plan, then let the letter fall into the hands of other buyers, who subsequently lowered their prices and thus allowed Logan to outbid his competitors. As Meek explained when describing this scheme, "The way to purchase negroes to advantage is to work head work as well as Body and monie."[73]

Some traders even resorted to sabotage to hinder their rivals. One tactic was running up the price at auction sales to prevent others from purchasing at profitable rates. After engaging in such antics against a competitor, the North Carolina trader Tyre Glen gleefully noted that the man "finaly bought 3 at prices that would not afound a profit sufficient to Justify the value." It was also common to circulate false information about the business practices of other speculators, or the qualities of the men and women they offered for sale. In 1828, a New Orleans trader was forced to defend himself in the newspapers after a report appeared claiming that the slaves he had for sale were from Kentucky, not Virginia as he had advertised. In his notice, this man made known that "all the negroes which I have on hand, and shall hereafter keep for sale are and will be Virginia born negroes, of good character; [and] that the person who has stated to the contrary, with the view of injuring me, I call upon in this public manner to come forward and support this charge if he can, or hereafter hold his peace."[74]

For many speculators, competition with their rivals became personal. One South Carolina trader thought a competitor "one of the poriest apoleges for a man I Ever Saw," while a resident of Memphis even described some local traders as being "at war with each other." It also proved the case for the Lynchburg dealer Seth Woodroof. In a letter to his friend, the Richmond auctioneer Richard Dickinson, Woodroof noted how several agents for the Richmond firm of Pulliam & Davis were "determined to Give me and you Hell & Rub it in." Woodroof assured his friend not to worry, however, as he was "laying low & giving it to them when ever I can get to them." He also added, "If I only had my health good I feal confident I would Eventually kill the Hole Party, & I will Bother them a great deal as it is."[75]

Not surprisingly, many traders came to see their occupation as a "game," in the same way that countless other American businessmen would later colloquially refer to their line of work (e.g., "I am in the insurance game"). Or, they saw themselves and their competition as engaged in a constant struggle for survival. No speculators better expressed this lingo than Isaac Franklin and his associates, the slave traders who arguably achieved the greatest success. Franklin, his nephew James, and John Armfield all spoke of their business as "the game."[76] Moreover, they referred to themselves as "Old robbers" who could always "Robb for more." And they routinely dismissed their competitors as "land pirates," as when James Franklin complained of "alsorts of little Pirats in market."[77] Like other ruthless businessmen, they took pleasure in destroying their competition. In a letter to Rice Ballard, Isaac informed his Richmond-based colleague that he had "assisted in Scining [skinning] your friend [the Richmond trader Lewis] Collier," and subsequently, he should "not Trouble you much this season." After ruining Collier's credit relationship with his bankers, Franklin crowed that "he looks as much like a thief as any man I have ever seen in my life."[78]

One needed a great deal of self-confidence to survive (much less prosper) in this rough-and-tumble, cutthroat environment. Most successful traders certainly exhibited this trait, frequently bragging about their accomplishments. As one Virginia speculator boasted of the men and women whom he had recently purchased, "I have nailed Christ to the † on them." The same proved true when assessing their selling abilities. One trader in New Orleans believed that he could "sell almost any kind of Negroes in this Market," while another in Alabama stated simply, "I flatter myself that I can beat any living man selling negroes at this place."[79] Part of this self-confidence also implied a certain contempt for one's customers. Lamenting all of the hard-to-sell slaves who were left over at the end of the selling season, James Franklin employed a nineteenth-century slang term for penis ("one-eyed man," which implied a meaning more equivalent to the modern word "dick") and hoped that "all the fools are not yet dead & some one eyed man will buy us out yet." Moreover, when a buyer threatened to return a supposedly unhealthy purchase, Franklin's response was to "tell him to go to *Hell*."[80]

It also took a great deal of hard work to be successful, and many traders took pride in their strong work ethic. Isaac Franklin liked to brag that he had "been seeking and ranging up and down the Mississippi untill I hardly know my self," while his nephew James thought himself "the busiest man you ever saw & have seen & expect to see." Savannah dealer William Parker likewise had periods of nonstop work, such as the day he "left the office at 12 oclock at Night. I have not been at home since before 5 a.m." Parker even worked on holidays, noting one Christmas Eve that it was a "rather dull Christmas with me I guess as I am full of Business. Been in the office all day until late at night."[81]

Their hard work and financial success also came at a personal cost for many speculators. For some, it was the normal strains of business. Joseph Meek made it clear that worrying about credit problems had taken their toll when he lamented, "my god I did not sleep I dont think one hour last night. I thought the night 20 hours long." Another trader in Georgia also found the late 1840s "the dam est hard is times I ever saw to sell negroes. . . . to lay out all the winter and take all kind of wither and make no money, I had rather be doing any thing else."[82] And customer relations could always be trying. According to one speculator, "It requires a man of a deal of patience to trade in negro property," and many a trader lacked that personal trait. Trouble with a disgruntled purchaser even made one Georgia trader "so mad I could not See and felt like I could hav got under the ground for a while." Finally, the months on the road became tedious for a number of speculators. Not only would many country traders have agreed with the North Carolinian who was "sick and tired of Alabama," but even the major markets could become tiresome. Writing from Natchez, James Franklin complained that he "never wanted to leave any place so bad as I do want to leave this damned hole."[83]

This devotion to their business took its greatest toll on slave traders' home lives. This proved especially true for interregional traders, who often felt the strain of being absent for months from their loved ones. Some missed their parents, such as the young North Carolina trader who asked his father, "Tell Mar that I want to see her very bad & that I will come home as soon as I can." But most missed their wives and children. Typical was the North Carolinian Obadiah Fields, who addressed his letters home to his "Dir Loveing wife" and signed them "husband of Jane M Fields till time shall be no more." Fields also wanted her to "kiss my dear little children and tell them thar Pap will soon come home."[84]

The demands of the job were why so many traders remained single or married later in life after they had ended their slave-trading careers. Isaac Franklin did not marry until the age of fifty, well after he had retired from "the game." The conflict between marriage and slave trading became evident for the North Carolinian Isaac Jarratt, who was active in the business for several years prior to marrying a woman named Harriet in 1834. Almost immediately, Harriet began sending Isaac what she would later call "silly letters" complaining of her loneliness during his absences and wishing that he could soon come home. As she made clear in one telling letter: "I am affraid my Dear Husband that you and your friend Carson will keep up negro trading as long as you can get a negro to trade on." And she could not help adding, "but one good thing Mr. Carson has no wife to leave behind when he is gone." Isaac got the message and promised his wife that he would "engage in something else by which I can accumulate a little and remain with my family." Following the 1835–1836 season, Jarratt kept his word, and, except for a few return trips south to collect debts, retired from the business.[85]

Yet, many unencumbered southern men jumped at the opportunity that the slave trade provided for adventure and seeing the country. A friend of Isaac Jarratt's envied his occupation, with all of the "interesting scenes" that were "constantly presenting themselves to your view." Another young man on a slave-trading trip to Alabama informed his parents back in North Carolina that he was "verry fond of travelling. I like my trip verry well." When presented with the chance to take an enslaved man to New Orleans for sale, a Tennessee youth explained to his family that "having nothing particularly to do and feeling an inclination to see New Orleans, [I] concluded to take him to that place which I accordingly did, travelling on a steam boat from Memphis down the Mississippi River."[86]

The slave trade also provided these men with plenty of other opportunities that were not possible at home, but for which places like New Orleans were well known. Given the large sums of money associated with this business, most of them had the resources to act on their indulgences, if they so desired. Consequently, many a trader lost all of his profits at the card tables or by treating his friends to drinks. As one colleague described the New Orleans trader Thomas Coote, he was "very fond of gambling" and "in the habit of drinking spirituous liquors to a great excess, and he was always very liberal in his liquor and treating his friends and acquaintances."[87]

But the most infamous excitement for many of these young men was the unhindered access to sex. In addition to all of the prostitutes and other white women who might be drawn to men flashing large wads of cash, southern slave traders were notorious for raping the young enslaved women under their control. As abhorrent as this practice was, it did have a certain appeal to many of these sexually charged young men. It was also something common to all levels of traders. Not only did Isaac Franklin and several of his associates keep enslaved concubines, but their correspondence is peppered with sexual innuendoes, especially from Franklin's young nephew James. In addition, Isaac himself even once suggested setting up a whore house in Richmond "for the Exclusive benefit of the consern & thure agents." Yet, as with excessive drinking and gambling, this practice did have its perils, especially with the prevalence of sexually transmitted diseases. After the North Carolinian Tyre Glen contracted such a virus and was forced to wear a catheter, a friend reported that "his penis was as stiff and as hard as it was when the fair dame of Greensborough imparted to him the cause of his great calamity."[88]

Despite all of their aggressive competition and cutthroat practices, the masculine lifestyle of the trade led many speculators to develop deep and sincere friendships with one another. As Isaac Franklin made known about his partner, John Armfield, "I have a most Exalted friendship for him and if he was to Die I would have but little inducement to Live." While such feelings among partners were perhaps understandable, numerous other traders developed meaningful relationships with their colleagues. In large part, this was due to the work culture of slave trading and the lifestyle they shared with one another as men of business. Slave traders frequently lived together on the road and stayed in the same boarding houses. They also experienced a certain camaraderie and male bonding as they boasted, cursed, drank, gambled, and shared women together. It is not surprising, then, that many of them also honeymooned together, named their children after one another, celebrated Christmases together, and eventually served as one another's executors. As a result, not only did the domestic slave trade provide these men with lucrative economic rewards, but it also gave them great personal satisfaction.[89]

VI

Most slave traders were sharp businessmen who thought of themselves and their activities as such. That is why one visitor to New Orleans described the speculators there as "live business men"; a trader in that city referred to his partner as "a very active business man"; and an agent informed his Richmond employers that he was "highly pleased with you as men of buisiness." Moreover, when Rice Ballard questioned Isaac Franklin's efforts in selling his slaves, Franklin responded by noting that Ballard was "too Good a judge of business to believe that any salesman could have done better."[90]

Slave traders likewise understood all of the important maxims of the new market world. For one thing, they knew that the only way to make money was to invest money. After chastising a colleague for being too "Scearry" during the boom market of the late 1850s, a Virginia trader remarked that the man "mit make som money" if he did not keep his "money lying perfectly ded." In addition, a trader in South Carolina recognized that the best "way to get a good price is to ask a good price," although another speculator in that state also realized that "to Push Sales a man must come down in prices that is ceartain." One resident dealer in Savannah expressed his knowledge of how to cultivate new customers. After visiting slaveholders in several nearby counties, William Parker thought that he "may have planted an Acorn that will probably germinate in the course of time and bring fourth fruit." Yet, Parker also had doubts about the marketing abilities of his neighbors, adding that he did "not think the farmers understand this business."[91]

The most obvious way that southern slave traders acted like modern businessmen was in their obsession with profits. To be successful, they had to buy wisely and hope that their final sales would exceed their expenses and leave them with a healthy return for their efforts. Consequently, one North Carolina trader reminded his brother to "get as many good bargins as posable," while another in Alabama cautioned his partner to "be sure not to buy any except good saleable young negroes. The market is slow here & scrub stock wont sell atall."[92] Isaac Franklin also understood this rule, first counseling that "a few negroes well purchased will always make more clear money than the many badly purchased" and later adding that "if the negroes are likely & sailable, we will get Back our Capital [in]vested and some profit." Interstate traders generally accepted as a fair return on their investment a $100 to $150 net on each slave sold, although they sometimes made more, and often accepted less, especially when market conditions made sales difficult. Then their profit rates could decrease considerably. Typical was the Virginia trader who "would actually take $25 net profit on the head if I could not do any better." And there were also those like the speculator in Alabama who just hoped "to sell the balance for proffit enough to pay expenses." If so, he vowed to "jump up and crack my heels together and make the sovreigns a low bow wishing them great luck until next fall."[93]

In addition to thinking about profits and losses, slave traders employed modern accounting practices to record all of their transactions. Unlike the majority of planters, who just kept lists of local debts and credits, many slave traders adopted the relatively new method of double-entry bookkeeping for the most accurate accounts. While this technique had been around for centuries, it gained wide acceptance among American men of business during the early nineteenth century, and southern speculators proved no exception. In fact, they often paid careful attention to these records. The Savannah dealer William Parker once complained that he had "Been Busy all day looking after 2 cents in the Balance of my Ledger." They also made sure their employees followed suit, and more than one agent had to promise his boss that he would "keep a strict account of all your loosses & Proffitts."[94]

Southern slave traders likewise made frequent use of the financial instruments of the new market economy. Most important, they constantly sought funding from banks to finance their operations and extended their own network of credit to customers. Most speculators preferred to sell their slaves for cash, in part to pay off their own loans but also to avoid the difficulties of collection. Typical was the trader in Mississippi who did "not expect to be able to collect more than ⅓ or ½" of his notes. Yet, by necessity, they were often forced to accept promissory notes if they wanted to make sufficient sales. As one Alabama trader advised, "A good note with interest ought not to be refused." During the cholera-ravaged year of 1832, Isaac Franklin was "compelled to sell almost alltogether on Time." Some traders even capitalized on this practice. Bernard Kendig of New Orleans became quite successful through his liberal credit policies, as did Walter Campbell, another dealer in that city, who began his early advertisements under the heading "Long Credit Sale of Negroes." Speculators then used the cash and commercial paper that they received to pay off their own loans and to obtain more credit to acquire the cash to purchase more slaves.[95]

Furthermore, slave traders had to have a good understanding of the nation's money markets. At a time when the country's main form of currency consisted of discounted bank notes, they had to keep track of the comparative value of the various drafts, in order to deal in those with the greatest acceptability. For that reason, whenever possible, they favored paper from major northern banks, which generally held its value better nationally than did that from local southern banks. As one Nashville trader remarked after sending his partner some sight drafts on a New York bank, "They are the best funds and safe to Remit." To be successful, then, southern slave traders needed to follow not only the price of cotton but all of the nation's financial markets also. So it is not surprising that a Memphis newspaper noted that one local trader did not speak much about his personal life, but became "very animated on the subjects of dollars, negroes and cotton."[96]

Many southern speculators also sought to protect themselves against unexpected losses by taking out insurance policies on the men and women they were shipping to the Deep South for sale. As early as 1822, the Louisiana Insurance Company issued a policy to William Kenner & Co. of New Orleans on 100 slaves being transported to the firm aboard the brig *Fame*. For a 0.25 percent premium on $40,000 worth of coverage, this policy insured against the risks

of the sea, men of war, fire, enemies, pirates, rovers, thieves, jettison, letters of mart and counter-mart, surprisals, taking at sea, arrests, restraints
and detainments of all kings, princes or people of what nation, condition or quality soever, barratry of the master and mariners, and all other
perils, losses and misfortunes that have or shall come to the hurt, detri-
ment or damage of the said goods or merchandize, or any part thereof.

Not all losses, however, were covered under such policies. In 1841, after the
slaves aboard the *Creole* mutinied and sailed the ship to the Bahamas, one
trader noted that "the negroes were all Insured but I do not think they have any
chance to get their Money for it is the Custom to write there policy Mutiny and
Elopements excepted."[97]

Traders likewise took out policies on slaves being shipped down American
rivers. In 1850, Calvin Rutherford paid premiums of between $8.75 and $12.38
per person for $8,400 worth of life insurance on eight men and eight women
whom he had recently purchased in Kentucky. While this policy from the
Mutual Benefit Life and Fire Insurance Company of New Orleans did not cover
deaths resulting from suicide, flight, insurrection, criminal activity, maltreat-
ment, or kidnapping, it did cover most other losses and granted Rutherford
permission "to take the said negroes to New Orleans, on board the Alexander
Scott, or any other Steam Boat & to hold them for sale in that city, during the
term of this Policy."[98]

A number of traders also covered themselves against losses caused by sickness and disease. After noting that it was "very sickly here among negroes, 1 or 2
dies every day," the Richmond trader Philip Thomas informed his partner that
he was "having all I by [buy] insured." Some traders even used this protection
as a selling point. After announcing his arrival in Natchez with 100 slaves from
Virginia and Tennessee, R. H. Elam added that "there is also a Life Insurance
on them for twelve months, with policies transferable." Many traders had the
slaves they purchased vaccinated, especially those being shipped to unhealthy
environments where contagious diseases were frequently present. Writing from
New Orleans, Isaac Franklin reminded Rice Ballard to "be sure never to ship a
negroe that has not been vacinated." Another trader in that city was even more
emphatic, instructing a new partner in Savannah that "whenever you buy a
negro have it *vaccinated at once. It does not matter if they have been vaccinated
before, do it again.*"[99]

Finally, as participants in a long-distance commodity market whose profits were dependent upon prices in divergent parts of the South, speculators
needed a way to communicate with their colleagues about the state of one
another's markets. Like other brokers, slave traders had to categorize their
human merchandise so that they could accurately compare their information.

Usually this was done by sorting people into classes, such as first-, second-, or third-rate men and women, with boys and girls normally divided according to age or height. One Richmond firm, D. M. Pulliam & Co., even broke the market into twenty different categories, with everything from "No. 1 MEN, Extra" down to "Scrubs," a term that traders frequently used to refer to the elderly, diseased, physically handicapped, or other hard-to-sell individuals. Much of this information was provided by the larger Richmond auctioneers, who sent out printed circulars to their regular customers (and anyone who asked for them), describing the current state of their market, along with advice, like "now is the time to buy good ones & bring them in," or "Fancy girls would sell exceedingly well just now. Hoping to see or hear from you soon."[100]

This depersonalizing of humans into objects of trade was an ever-present reality of the domestic trade, where enslaved men and women were seen as commodities and almost always spoken of in market terms. In Savannah, William Parker lamented that "the Stock cant be had to supply the demand," while another trader in Alabama remarked that he was "retailing them fast." Like Parker, most traders referred to their slaves as their "stock," and they counted them as so many "head." As these terms suggest, it is not surprising that many speculators used animal-like images to describe the men and women they were selling, such as the trader who characterized a man as "Black & slick as a mole," or the one who found a little girl named Hester "as peart as a crickit." And there were always those like the speculator in Alabama, who spoke of his "stock of darkees," or James Franklin in Natchez, who made the depersonalization complete when he bragged of his "fancy stock of wool & ivory." These attitudes were part and parcel of the domestic slave trade, where skillful businessmen trafficked in people as goods and consequently thought of them as such.[101]

VII

The most significant way in which southern speculators resembled northern businessmen was in their use of extensive advertising to purchase and market their human commodities. One reason for the slave traders' success in the exporting states was their heavy reliance upon cash when acquiring their merchandise. In a world where most business transactions were conducted on credit, slave traders were one of the few groups in the South who dealt primarily in cash. Consequently, that became their main selling point. Throughout the Upper South, traders filled the newspapers with long-running, bold-type advertisements that blared this point home. "CASH FOR NEGROES" or "NEGROES WANTED" were the most common headings, but the more innovative dealers grabbed readers' attention with phrases like "WHO WANTS CASH!"

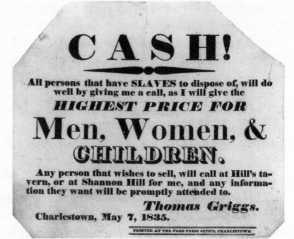

CASH!

All persons that have SLAVES to dispose of, will do well by giving me a call, as I will give the

HIGHEST PRICE FOR

Men, Women, &

CHILDREN.

Any person that wishes to sell, will call at Hill's tavern, or at Shannon Hill for me, and any information they want will be promptly attended to.

Thomas Griggs.

Charlestown, May 7, 1835.

PRINTED AT THE FARM PRESS OFFICE, CHARLESTOWN.

Handbill found in the slave-exporting states of the Upper South. Courtesy of the Library of Congress.

"☞HIGHEST CASH PRICE!☜" or simply "CASH! CASH!! CASH!!!" Not only did slave traders introduce much-needed currency into a cash-strapped society, but by doing so, they also helped to promote consumerism.[102]

While all traders stressed the promise of cash when advertising for slaves, they also needed to be creative to make their notices stand out from their competitors. One dealer on the Eastern Shore of Maryland emphasized his reliability by assuring customers that he was "permanently settled in this market, and at all times will give the highest cash prices." Another buyer in that same region made it clear that he was willing to purchase any type of enslaved person, no questions asked, when he offered to "give the highest cash prices, with or without competition" and added that "no certificates of character will be required."[103] Virtually all traders claimed to offer the highest prices. As Franklin & Armfield phrased it in its long-standing notices: "Persons wishing to sell would do well to give us a call, as we are determined to give higher prices for slaves than any purchaser who is now or may be hereafter in this market." At least one St. Louis dealer, Thomas Dickens, played upon these assertions, warning potential sellers to "test the market by giving every buyer a *chance*, and not rely upon advertisements that profess to pay more than others. We *know* that we *can* and *will* pay as high prices as any other person or persons." The majority of traders likewise pledged responses to all inquiries, with some guaranteeing immediate service. Working on the Eastern Shore of Virginia, John Bull promised that a letter sent to him would meet with a personal visit "in two days from the time it arrives at Drummond Town [present-day Accomac]." In Missouri, the St. Louis firm of Blakey & McAfee was even "prepared to visit persons wanting to sell in any part of the State."[104]

No trader relied upon creative advertising more than Austin Woolfolk, especially after he started losing business to Franklin & Armfield in the early 1830s. In an attempt to regain customers, Woolfolk employed humor in his advertisements. He first sought "to inform the owners of Negroes in Maryland, Virginia, and N. Carolina, that he *is not dead*, as has been artfully represented by his opponents, but that he still lives, to give them CASH and the HIGHEST PRICES for their NEGROES." After that notice had run its course, he then announced to slaveholders "that their friend still lives," and added that if they visited his office on Pratt Street, "they shall see the justly celebrated AUSTIN WOOLFOLK, free of charge." He concluded this last advertisement with a play on words, noting that "his CHECKS are such as usually *pass*, and will convince the holders thereof that *'there's nothing broke!'*" It is unknown what readers thought of these notices, but they apparently failed to achieve the desired result, as Woolfolk was soon out of the business.[105]

Speculators also caught readers' attention by making it appear that they wanted to purchase an endless number of enslaved men and women. In the early years of the trade, many of the notices called for a reasonable number of slaves. In his 1816 advertisement, Edward Stone of Kentucky wished "TO PURCHASE TWENTY NEGROES." Yet, most traders soon started publicizing in bold headlines that they were looking for hundreds of slaves to purchase. By the 1850s, Thomas Dickens of St. Louis even advertised that he wanted "One Thousand Negroes," only to be outdone by John Denning in Baltimore, who offered to "pay the highest prices, *in cash*, for 5,000 NEGROES." As the numbers asked for became impossibly high, however, many just stopped giving actual figures. After calling for 100, then 150, then 200 slaves, Franklin & Armfield eventually just advertised for "any number of Likely Negroes," as did R. W. Lucas of Lexington, who stated simply: "A LARGE NUMBER OF NEGROES WANTED!"[106]

While calls for an endless number of slaves may have attracted attention, in the text of their notices interregional traders were much more specific about the types of men and women they wanted to purchase. As Bernard Lynch in St. Louis made clear, he and most others were looking "for all descriptions of negroes suited to the Southern markets." By this, they meant what one dealer in Lexington called "good young, merchantable NEGROES." Therefore, most advertised for "likely" slaves of both sexes between the ages of twelve and twenty-five, although it was not uncommon to see notices asking for children as young as eight, or even six. In Missouri, William Selby even advertised for "likely negroes from 5–25." Some traders were also quite firm in restricting their purchases to only younger individuals. According to one Maryland speculator, he sought "a number of likely Negroes, none to be over 35 years old."[107]

The main reason that they wanted enslaved men and women of this type was because they were the ones most in demand in the buying states. As one early trader in South Carolina put it: "It is hard to sell old negrows at any price." Moreover, young, healthy, unattached men and women were the safest to transport (they could most readily survive the climatic changes) and the easiest to market, and they brought the highest profits. Therefore, when interregional traders spoke of slaves "suited to the Southern markets," everyone knew what type of individuals they desired.[108]

While "the Southern markets" were the most commonly advertised destination for their purchases, many speculators listed more specific markets in their notices. Some historians have argued that there was something unusual, or "specialized," about one of these markets, namely New Orleans, and that the traders who operated there supposedly desired slaves who were different from those purchased by other interregional traders. This claim, however, seems exaggerated. While a number of speculators, especially those operating out of the Chesapeake region, did advertise for slaves "for the New Orleans market," their main reason for doing so was because that city was the most common terminus for the coastal trade and the South's largest slave market. Most of the dealers who operated there, like Franklin & Armfield, advertised for the same type of individuals to be sold out of New Orleans as out of other markets, like Natchez. Moreover, there were just as many other traders who advertised that they were looking for slaves to sell in other specific locations, such as "for the Louisiana and Mississippi markets," "the Memphis and Louisiana market," and "the Texas market." More often than not, these destinations, like New Orleans, simply reflected where the greatest demand for slaves was at that time in the South's westward expansion, and they all sought the same types of individuals.[109]

Upon their arrival, interregional traders also employed creative advertising when selling their slaves. Almost all began their notices with bold-type headings, such as "SLAVES FOR SALE" or "NEW ARRIVAL OF NEGROES." As in the Upper South, there were those who tried to stand out with headings like "COME ONE AND ALL WHO WANT NEGROES" and "GREAT EXCITEMENT!! FOUR HUNDRED SLAVES EXPECTED TO ARRIVE BY FIRST NOVEMBER." Others took a simpler but equally effective approach, blaring, "SLAVES! SLAVES!! SLAVES!!!" or "NEGROES! NEGROES! MORE NEGROES!"[110]

Speculators naturally emphasized that they had the types of enslaved men and women that most buyers in the Lower South wanted. As one trader in New

Orleans bluntly put it: "No old people in the lot." Similarly, in Natchez, Griffin & Pullum claimed that their offerings were "selected with great care from the best lots of Virginia and Kentucky Slaves, with reference to age, soundness of body and general healthiness." Others also stressed the care and skill with which their human commodities had been chosen. According to one dealer in Memphis, his slaves came from "good and experienced buyers," while another in Natchez asserted that his had been "carefully selected by the most experienced buyers in the United States." As a result, many advertisements resembled that of John Smith in New Orleans, who proclaimed his lot to be "the best Negroes that can be bought in the Virginia and Carolina markets," or S. N. Brown in Montgomery, who declared his slaves "the likeliest ever offered in this market."[111]

Most speculators likewise mentioned the state origins of the men and women they had for sale. In part, this was because the majority of buyers desired "fresh arrivals" from outside the region, who had not yet been damaged by the harsh realities of slave life on a Deep South cotton or sugar plantation. Yet, it also had much to do with the belief of many planters that slaves from differing states supposedly had varying innate characteristics, in much the same way that many colonists had believed that slaves imported from the Gold Coast were somehow different from those imported from the Congo or other parts of western Africa. The Memphis firm of Bolton, Dickens & Co. was one of many that played upon this bias when, in one of its notices, it agreed "with the Southern Planters that the Virginia and North Carolina Negroes give more satisfaction, less trouble, and make the best servants [in the] South." Traders not only catered to their customers' needs, but they also helped to shape them. This can be seen when the following year the firm decided to shift its buying farther to the west and needed to alter its advertising accordingly. In its new notice, Bolton, Dickens & Co. now announced that it would "concentrate [its] purchases from Kentucky and Virginia to this point, and give the buyers of this country an opportunity of investing their money in good negroes."[112]

Not all buyers, however, desired such "fresh arrivals." When the coffle carrying the former Maryland slave Charles Ball arrived in South Carolina, one local man complained that "all the *niggers* in the drove were Yankee *niggers*." In Louisiana, another planter vowed to "never buy grown negros from Va.," because "one creole will pick as much as two of them." But the majority of planters with this bias against Upper South slaves had concerns about the forced transplants' ability to survive the harsh Deep South summers.[113]

For that reason, traders always mentioned when the men and women they had for sale were acclimated to the region. As the New Orleans dealer Elihu Cresswell noted in one of his advertisements for such a lot, "These Slaves are fully guaranteed, and are less subject to diseases of the climate, and to attacks of the cholera, than those frequently imported into the State." Some innovative dealers, such as Walter Campbell in New Orleans, even set up residences away from the more disease-ridden parts of the region to acclimate their human commodities. In the fall of 1860, Campbell announced, "Over One Hundred NEGROES were brought in last night from my farm within eighty miles of the city and are for sale. A large number of them have been on the place for the past year and longer, and all passed the last summer." Campbell then added a sales pitch that illustrated why such an arrangement proved so beneficial: "Virginia and Maryland negroes, with this advantage of acclimation and trained to plantation labor, offer inducements to purchasers." In other words, unlike most of his competitors, Campbell could now appeal to both the cultural biases and the practical concerns of his customers.[114]

In their notices, speculators did everything they could to attract business. Like in the exporting states, some stressed their reliability. Joseph Bruin of New Orleans emphasized that he had been "a regular trader in this city for the last twenty six years." Others in that market went out of their way to accommodate customers. Womack & Martin offered to save patrons a trip, suggesting that "planters wishing to purchase can have their orders filled upon advantageous terms without coming to the city, should they prefer to do so." Conversely, John Smith took his slaves to the planters, advertising that he would "be at Donaldsonville, La., on September 20th, with 100 likely Virginia and Carolina NEGROES." And there were always those who appealed to buyers' pocketbooks. In Natchez, R. H. Elam operated "on the principle that a 'quick penny is better than a slow shilling,'" while the Nashville dealer Reese Porter claimed that he would "sell so cheap you will hardly know the difference between buying and hiring."[115]

Attracting potential customers with good advertising was one thing; getting them to buy was another matter. Or, as one experienced dealer in Savannah put it: "Buyers are like horses, you can offer the bucket *but can't make them drink.*" Therefore, traders also needed to work their customers to make a sale. This aspect of the business was best expressed by the former slave Charles Ball, who noted that the speculator who bought him "regarded the southern planters as no less the subjects of trade and speculation, than the slaves he sold to them." Some traders did this by offering special arrangements. In the Upper South, they persuaded owners to sell by paying them cash during the summer months and letting them keep their slaves until after the crop had been harvested in the fall. Or, they let buyers take an individual home on trial before actually purchasing. Others worked their customers by befriending them through charm and alcohol. Frederick Douglass described the traders he saw in Maryland as "generally well dressed men, and very captivating in their manners. Ever ready to drink, to treat, and to gamble." The former slave William Wells Brown observed that the speculator he worked for "always put up at the best hotel, and kept his wines in his room, for the accommodation of those who called to negotiate with him for the purchase of slaves."[116]

For many slave traders, working their customers also involved outright trickery and deception. As the former slave John Brown noted, "There are 'nigger jockeys' as well as horse jockeys, and as many tricks are played off to sell a bad or an unsound 'nigger,' as there are to palm off a diseased horse." The most common tactics were fixing up older individuals to look young and out-fitting slaves in new clothes. Almost all traders believed that their merchandise would "sell much better for being well dressed," and this was usually the case, but not always. At least one man had to inform his client that he "dressed up your negroes and made them look their best but could not screw them up any higher."[117] While such practices might be expected, other traders engaged in much less socially acceptable acts, like those indicated by John Brown, and pawned off individuals with known health problems as sound. One trader in Richmond considered purchasing a "naked headed girl" at a discount, believing that he could "put a fals set of hair on her and sell her for as mutch as if she had it growing." Another buyer in Alabama came home with his new purchase only to find "*that the fellow had no toes on his feet.*" The seller had "cunningly stuffed" cotton in the front of the man's shoes "for show." In New Orleans, one trader informed a colleague that "your old man Dick Towley pisses blood—the first offer he gos."[118]

Because of the reputation that slave traders had for engaging in such unsavory practices, a number of dealers also employed creative advertising to help improve their public image as honest businessmen. Nathan Bedford Forrest assured customers in Memphis, "that which we promise or say, we guarantee," while in New Orleans, Thomas Foster made it clear that he conducted his "business in a proper and Strictly Moral manner." Even in tiny Lumpkin, Georgia, J. F. Moses advertised that "being a regular trader to this market he has nothing to gain by misrepresentation, and will, therefore, warrant every negro sold to come up to the bill, squarely and completely." Many speculators also listed references in their advertisements. When Mosely & Spragins opened a new depot in Alexandria, Louisiana, they let it be known that they had "been trading in the Mississippi market for a number of years—and can give the most satisfactory New Orleans references as to their responsibility and character." While most mentioned only local firms, some stressed their national reputation, such as the New Orleans dealer Seneca Bennett, who listed men in Baltimore, Mobile, Norfolk, Charleston, and New Orleans in his notice.[119]

Leading traders also consciously strove to project a positive image in their day-to-day dealings with the public. They dressed and conducted themselves in a professional manner. A visitor to John Armfield's office called him "a man of fine personal appearance, and of engaging and graceful manners," while a former northerner living in Natchez described Isaac Franklin as "a man of gentlemanly address, as are many of these merchants, and not the ferocious, Captain Kidd looking fellows, we Yankees have been apt to imagine them." One visitor to Richmond even noted that the slave auctioneer he met there was "a most respectable-looking person," and "so far as dress is concerned, he might pass for a clergyman or church-warden." Many traders also knew the importance of good customer service. Several were thanked by their clients for their "promptness and Punctuality," and, at least according to his court testimony, one agent working in a New Orleans depot had been instructed by his employer "never to misrepresent negroes and to exchange them any time rather than go to a law suit."[120]

As a result of this public relations effort, most of the leading slave traders managed to create a reputation of honor and respect. One visitor to Alexandria noted that John Armfield "bears a good character, and is considered a charitable man," while another traveler to that city believed that Armfield had "acquired the confidence of all the neighboring country, by his resolute efforts to prevent kidnapping, and by his honorable mode of dealing." This same reliable observer had earlier visited Austin Woolfolk in Baltimore, and he remarked that "the business is conducted by him, and by the other regular traders, in such a manner, that there is never any suspicion of unfairness in regard to their mode of acquiring slaves. In this respect, at least, their business is conducted in an honorable manner." It is important to remember that the vast majority of speculators were not leading traders, nor did they have the same resources or abilities to create such positive public images. In fact, many could not have cared less about what others thought of them. Yet, the most successful traders all knew the importance of effective advertising to promote both their businesses and themselves.[121]

VIII

After arriving in South Carolina via an overland coffle, Charles Ball recalled that "in the State of Maryland, my master had been called a *negro buyer, or Georgia trader*, sometimes a *negro driver*; but here, I found that he was elevated to the rank of merchant, and a merchant of the first order too; for it was very clear that in the opinion of the landlord, no branch of trade was more honourable than the traffic in us poor slaves." Moreover, according to this person who housed them, their speculator was "a public benefactor, and entitled to the respect and gratitude of every friend of the South."[122]

While there was never such a thing as a typical slave trader, and all elements of southern society could be found among them, there was much truth in this South Carolinian's viewpoint, at least as far as the white South was concerned. Numerous speculators certainly took advantage of individual slave owners whenever they could, not to mention all of the pain and suffering they helped to inflict upon the vast majority of black southerners who came under their control. But traders did provide a vital service and possessed important marketing skills that many found useful. Therefore, few were the slave owners who did not come to them for assistance when necessary.

Even more important for the region as a whole was the major role that slave traders played in the economic development of the South. Most important, they infused a significant amount of capital into the southern economy each year. Between 1820 and 1860, interregional slave traders averaged at least $10.8 million worth of sales each year (table 4.1). In addition, to conduct their business, they relied upon an array of supporting personnel, such as bankers, factorage houses, lawyers, doctors, clothiers, provisioners, blacksmiths, insurance companies, and shipping agents. Not only did this ancillary activity draw more people into the marketplace, but it also pumped at least another $1.5 million into the southern economy each year.[123] Therefore, in the four decades preceding the Civil War, the interregional slave trade generated, on average, more than $12.3 million worth of business each year (and more than $17.8 million each year during the 1850s). Furthermore, unlike the money that came from the production of cotton, which only flowed into certain subregions of the South, the cash associated with the slave trade poured into every county in the slaveholding states.[124]

Finally, many of the men who made their living by buying and selling slaves ventured into other aspects of the new market economy. While it was common for slave traders to work as farmers or planters during the off-season, a large number of them also engaged in other business activities, such as owning general stores and buying and selling other types of commodities. Not only did they speculate in humans, but slave traders bought and sold real estate, livestock, bonds, and all types of stock, including bank, railroad, telegraph, insurance, and manufacturing. The versatility of such men can be seen in the report that the credit agency R. G. Dun & Co. gave of the South Carolinian Thomas Weatherly, calling him "quite a bold speculator. Besides merchandise he deals in slaves, Kentucky horses, mules and swine" and "is decidedly a man of bus[iness] talents."[125]

Many of the more successful slave traders also played leading roles in diversifying market development in the South. Several prominent dealers

TABLE 4.1. Estimate of the Minimum Number and Value of Slaves Sold
in the Interstate Slave Trade, 1820–1859

Decade	Minimum Number of Slaves Sold in the Interstate Slave Trade[a]	Lowest Average Price of Slaves Sold in New Orleans[b]	Total Value of Slaves Sold in the Interstate Slave Trade
1820–1829	93,000	$617	$57,381,000
1830–1839	171,000	$838	$143,298,000
1840–1849	110,400	$670	$73,968,000
1850–1859	150,600	$1,046	$157,527,600
Minimum Total Value of Slaves Sold in the Interstate Slave Trade, 1820–1859			$432,174,600
Minimum Average Value of Slaves Sold in the Interstate Slave Trade, 1820–1859			$10,804,000

[a]The figures used for this category come from the estimate that between 1820 and 1859, at least 875,000 slaves were forcibly removed to the importing states and that 60–70 percent arrived there through the interstate slave trade. When determining the figures for this category, the lowest estimate of 60 percent was used. For an explanation of the validity of these figures and their breakdown by decade, see appendix A.
[b]The figures used in this category come from the three slave price indexes compiled by Ransom and Sutch in "Capitalists without Capital," 155–56. When determining the figures for this category, the lowest of the three price indexes was used (see Kotlikoff, "Structure of Slave Prices").

in Charleston, including Thomas Ryan, Ziba Oakes, and Thomas Gadsden, served as directors or vice presidents of banks. In New Orleans, the former butcher turned leading slave auctioneer Joseph Beard was a part-owner of the *New Orleans Commercial Bulletin*, the city's foremost commercial newspaper. Others promoted internal improvements. In North Carolina, the former slave trader Joseph Totten became the president of a local turnpike company, and the Virginian Francis Rives used his slave-trading wealth and political influence to build and manage railroads. Some even became important entrepreneurs and venture capitalists. By the time of his death in 1853, the South Carolinian and former slave trader John Springs III had one of the more extensive investment portfolios in the nation. Among other things, he was an early investor in the largest textile mill in the South.[126]

In many respects, the motivations that attracted these men to the slave trade in the South were not that different from those that drew other men into the increasingly capitalistic business world in the North. In both regions, these men knew that hard work, a willingness to take risks, and mastery over a new set of market skills were the surest way to financial success. And many of them obtained it. In the end, the actions of northern capitalists and southern slave traders would have drastically different results. The first transformed the

North into a society based exclusively upon free labor, while the latter, despite their best efforts at market development, ended up making human property the most valuable form of capital investment in the South, which solidified the white South's commitment to chattel slavery. This major difference aside, these businessmen still shared much in common, and their activities helped to make the values of the marketplace a greater part of people's everyday lives.

FIVE

A Regular Part of Everyday Life:
The Buying and Selling of Human Property

In March 1859, Pierce Butler, grandson of a signer of the Constitution and ex-husband of actress Fanny Kemble, was forced to sell all 460 slaves from his Georgia plantations to pay off creditors. Naturally, an auction of this size drew considerable attention. According to a correspondent for the *New-York Tribune*, "For several days before the sale every hotel in Savannah was crowded with negro speculators from North and South Carolina, Virginia, Georgia, Alabama and Louisiana, who had been attracted hither by the prospects of making good bargains," and "nothing was heard for days, in the bar-rooms and public rooms, but talk of the great sale, criticisms of the business affairs of Mr. Butler, and speculations as to the probable prices the stock would bring." The reporter also noted that "the office of Joseph Bryan, the negro broker who had the management of the sale, was thronged every day by eager inquirers in search of information, and by some who were anxious to buy, but were uncertain as to whether their securities would prove acceptable." Most of the slaves had been brought to Savannah in freight cars and were being held at a local track outside of town where the sale was scheduled to occur: "Little parties were made up from the various hotels every day to visit the Race Course, distant some three miles from the city, to look over the chattels, discuss their points, and make memoranda for guidance on the day of sale." Although hard rains had threatened to reduce the size of the crowd, a Savannah newspaper reported that the two-day affair was still "largely attended," and the local slave trader William Parker noted that Butler seemed "well pleased with the sale." The following week, practically every boat or train that left the city carried individuals who had been purchased at this sale.[1]

The sale of Pierce Butler's slaves was of course unusual, if for no other reason than its size, but interest in slave auctions and the domestic trade was pervasive throughout the South. Auctions always drew a crowd, and in many rural communities they were an important social event. According to a historian of slavery in Baton Rouge, in the 1850s slave auctions were so popular that members of the Louisiana state legislature often left their seats to attend them, and one Missouri man remembered that, especially when young women were advertised, "crowds would flock to the court house to see the sight."[2]

The price of slaves and other aspects of the slave trade were also constant topics of conversation. In Richmond, Frederick Law Olmsted, the New York journalist, "frequently heard people say, in the street, or the public-houses" that "such a nigger is worth such a price, and such another is too old to learn to pick cotton, and such another will bring so much, when it has grown a little more." He added that "evidence of activity in the slave trade of Virginia is to be seen every day."[3]

Information about the domestic trade also filled southern newspapers. Large advertisements placed by professional slave traders and local sheriffs announcing upcoming sales often ran for columns, together with smaller notices placed by individuals wanting to sell a servant or two. During the 1850s, the *Memphis Eagle and Enquirer* even had a regular front-page column entitled "NEGROES," that listed all of the slaves for sale. Newspapers across the South also carried reports of all of the major sales and the prices that the slaves had brought, as well as stories about large and unusual sales from other parts of the country. Not surprisingly, accounts of the sale of Pierce Butler's slaves in Georgia appeared in faraway papers like the Lexington *Kentucky Statesman* and the St. Louis *Missouri Democrat*. When the editor of the Warrenton, Virginia, *Whig* reported that the slave-auctioning firms of Richmond conducted more than $4 million worth of business in 1856, this information was reprinted in the *Savannah Republican*, Baton Rouge *Advocate*, and *New Orleans Bee*.[4]

From the early nineteenth century until the Civil War, the slave trade was a familiar sight throughout the South. In front of every county courthouse, on isolated plantations, in tiny hamlets and large cities, in virtually every southern county, human beings were bought and sold, either at public auction or through private transactions. Every town had its slave "pens" or depots, and in some cities, elaborate auction halls were a source of civic pride. Coffles of slaves heading to market were a frequent sight. In the 1820s, Basil Hall, a British traveler, was told that during certain seasons of the year, "all the roads, steamboats, and packets, are crowded with troops of negroes on their way to the great slave markets of the South." Two decades later, a Richmond man informed his brother in South Carolina that "not a Carr, boat, or stage scarcely comes to this place that does not bring negroes for sale." Similar scenes were also common in the Lower South. Writing from Huntsville, Alabama, a Philadelphia businessman noted that "the country is absolutely flooded with speculators from

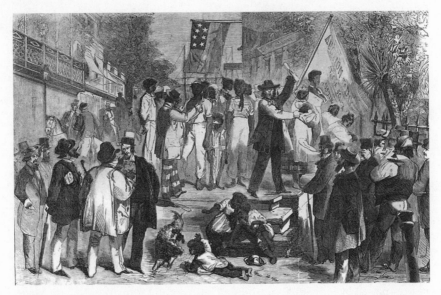

Illustration of a slave auction in the South. Such scenes were common throughout the South, and as many as half of all slaves were sold in this manner. *Harper's Weekly*, July 13, 1861. Courtesy of the Library of Congress.

Virginia, who find a ready market for their 'articles,' and who are always ready to pick up as they go along."[5]

By the early nineteenth century, not only had the domestic slave trade made human property the most valuable form of investment in the South and made many slave traders rich, but it had also transformed southern society in another important way. Namely, it made the buying and selling of men, women, and children a regular part of everyday life. Most well known was the interstate trade, with its long overland coffles and prominent slave depots in all of the major cities. But there was much more to the domestic trade than this infamous long-distance traffic. In many respects, the real glue that held the southern slave system together was the far more prevalent local trade. Despite the tendency of both popular culture and most historians to equate the domestic trade with the interregional trade, the overwhelming majority of enslaved people who were sold never passed through the hands of a professional slave trader nor spent a day in a large New Orleans slave depot. They were sold locally, by one owner to another or by nearby county courts as a way to settle debts or estates. Such sales were not always as visible nor did they constitute the same kind of powerful images that went along with the interstate trade. Hence, they have all but disappeared from view. But local sales made up the great majority of all slave sales, and for those being sold, the consequences could be just as great.[6]

Therefore, despite its large size, the sale of Pierce Butler's 460 slaves was more typical than it might at first appear. This was how as many as half of all slaves in the South were sold: at public auctions initiated by private parties or through the actions of the southern courts. Some of the individuals at this sale found themselves transported to the Southwest by professional slave traders engaged in the interstate trade. Others were purchased by local owners, who still carried them far enough away that they would never see their loved ones again. Together, these two components of the domestic slave trade made the buying and selling of humans a most common form of commerce. Evidence of this traffic pervaded the antebellum South, and in many cities and towns it was an important part of their local economy. Moreover, the values and business practices of the professional slave traders permeated southern society, as countless owners recognized the commercial significance of their human property and regularly bought and sold this valuable commodity. Both the interregional and local sales of slaves were essential for the smooth transferring of property from one owner to another, and without them, the southern slave system could never have survived.

I

Whether on the roads or on the waterways, in the country or in towns, some aspect of the slave trade could always be seen in the antebellum South. This proved especially true for the interregional trade, which by its very nature was on view for anyone who wished to see it. After being gathered in the Upper South, men, women, and children were transported long distances along common thoroughfares and were openly marketed to buyers in the Southwest. All of this was performed in full public view, and few were those who did not encounter its presence.

Slave dealers obtained their merchandise through a variety of means, but most advertised extensively, either through handbills or in the local newspapers. Both resident and itinerant traders placed these notices, and they were a regular feature in most Upper South newspapers. Some, especially those by resident dealers, ran for months. Itinerant traders normally listed how long they would be in town and where they could be found. Usually this was a hotel or tavern, but at least one trader in Baltimore gave his location as "Mr. Michael Jamart's Coffee House." Sometimes their notices made it seem like they were all over town. In its advertisement, the firm of Birch & Jones claimed its principals could "at all times be found at Isaac Beers' Tavern, a few doors below Lloyd's

Tavern, opposite the Centre Market, Washington D.C., or at Mr. McCandless' Tavern, corner of Bridge and High street, Georgetown." Not every slave trader bothered to pay for expensive advertising. One early newspaper in Virginia reported that "several wretches ... have for several days been impudently prowling about the streets of this place with labels on their hats exhibiting in conspicuous characters the words 'Cash for negroes.'"[7]

After purchase, the most common means of transporting slaves south was by overland coffle. As a rule, slave coffles consisted of 30 to 40 individuals, although they sometimes numbered in the hundreds. In southwestern Virginia, the Englishman George Featherstonhaugh came across a coffle driven by John Armfield that had 300 slaves and nine wagons for supplies. A former slave in that state likewise remembered seeing them "come in lines reachin' as far as you kin see." The men were usually handcuffed in pairs and fastened to a long chain that connected each pair. The women and children either walked or rode in a wagon, and the white drivers, carrying guns and whips, rode on horseback at each end of the coffle. The trip normally took seven to eight weeks marching at around twenty to twenty-five miles per day. Generally, they camped in the woods and the fields. As one woman who was forced to march in such a coffle from Richmond to Macon, Georgia, recalled: "Late in the even's we stretched the tents and cooked supper and spread out blankets an' slept. Then after breakfas', bout sunup, we start travelin' again."[8]

At times they also spent the night at farm houses and other accommodations along the way. As one Kentucky man remembered:

> One night a gang of slaves were driven up to my father's house at dusk.
> The slave dealer wanted to put them in the barn for the night, but
> father was afraid of fire and would not allow it. We had a big haystack
> outdoors, and all the slaves, men, women and children were chained
> together and slept on the haystack that night. Some of the women had
> babies in their arms.

Frederick Law Olmsted also met a farmer in northern Mississippi who reported that "in the fall, a great many drovers and slave-dealers passed over the road with their stock, and they frequently camped against his house, so as to buy corn and bacon of him." The man claimed that sometimes there were 200 slaves in these coffles, and "he didn't always have bacon to spare for them, though he killed one hundred and fifty swine." In addition, coffles occasionally spent the night at cheap public roadhouses. One Virginia man recalled staying at a tavern in the western portion of his state when "a drove of 50 or 60 negroes stopped at the same place that night." He noted that "they usually 'camp out,' but as it was excessively muddy, they were permitted to come into the house," where they all slept on the floor.⁹

During the fall and early winter, slave coffles were a frequent sight on most southern highways. One Virginia man even remembered seeing four different droves in a single day. Some southerners found these caravans to be a nuisance, such as the traveler through Tennessee who was "pestered" by all the "negro drivers" he had met on the road. But others welcomed this diversion into their lives and appraised the various coffles they encountered. In the 1830s, one trader testified that the strangers who he met on his way to Mississippi often remarked that his "was the likeliest lot that had passed during the season."¹⁰

With their long string of chained and shackled men and numbers of women and children herded along by men with whips and guns, slave coffles could make for a strange and disturbing sight. Many slave traders tried to mitigate this fact by forcing their captives to sing or engage in other acts of merriment. One day when traveling through central Kentucky, the Reverend James Dickey heard music and saw an American flag in the distance. Thinking that it was a military parade, Dickey pulled off to the side of the road, only to find that it was a coffle of slaves: "The foremost couple were furnished with a violin apiece; the second couple were ornamented with cockades, while near the centre waved the Republican flag carried by a hand *literally in chains*." The spectacle caused by these processions resulted in at least one Lexington, Kentucky, newspaper condemning all of the coffles "driven through the main street of our city." But in other towns, the launching of a slave coffle was apparently cause for public celebration. One North Carolina man, the Reverend Jethro Rumple, remembered that "on the day of departure for the West, the trader would have a grand jollification. A band, or at least a drum and fife, would be called into requisition, and perhaps a little rum be judiciously distributed to heighten the spirits of his sable property, and the neighbors would gather in to see the departure."¹¹

In addition to those traveling overland by foot, many slaves were transported south by water. Besides the important (although less visible) coastal trade, a heavy traffic in slaves developed along the nation's inland waterways. Focusing on the Ohio, Missouri, and especially Mississippi rivers, cities such as Louisville, St. Louis, Memphis, Natchez, and New Orleans all became important slave-trading centers, in large part because of this river trade. As early as 1818, one traveler reported seeing fourteen flatboats outside of Natchez, all loaded with slaves who had been floated down from Kentucky for sale, and by 1830, a New Orleans newspaper could note, "New Orleans is the complete mart for the slave trade—and the Mississippi is becoming a common highway for the traffic." Every type of boat was used in this trade, from small barges to large steamers, and slaves heading to market were a frequent sight. According to the former slave William Wells Brown (who once worked in this river trade), "A drove of slaves on a southern steamboat, bound for the cotton and sugar regions, is an occurrence so common, that no one, not even the passengers, appear to notice it, though they clank their chains at every step."[12]

While the overwhelming majority of slaves in the coastal and river trades were shipped from the Upper South into New Orleans, a small but significant export trade existed out of that city as well. For one thing, if destined for the Mississippi market, slaves in the coastal trade were often transferred to another boat and taken upriver to Natchez. Slaves were also sometimes shipped out of New Orleans by traders working in other Deep South markets. During the 1820s and 1830s, that usually meant such Gulf towns as Bay St. Louis and Biloxi, Mississippi; Mobile, Alabama; and Pensacola, Florida. By the mid-1840s, however, this relatively minor outbound traffic east had been surpassed by sizable shipments of slaves to Galveston and other Texas ports.[13]

By the late antebellum period, carloads of slaves traveling on the South's emerging railway lines had also become a common sight. As early as 1842, while traveling on the cars from Fredericksburg to Richmond, the British writer Charles Dickens encountered "a mother and her children who had just been purchased; the husband and father being left behind with their old owner." Dickens added that "the children cried the whole way, and the mother was misery's picture." Such scenes only escalated in the ensuing years. By the late 1850s, one northern visitor noted that "every train going south has just such a crowd of slaves on board," and, according to a British traveler, an engineer in North Carolina even claimed "that on one occasion he had taken 600 slaves south in one train." While this might have been an overstatement, other sources indicate that this traffic had become extensive. At a station in southern Virginia, Frederick Law Olmsted recalled seeing a trader and his "company of negroes intended to be shipped South; but the 'servants' car' being quite full already, they were obliged to be left for another train."[14]

After arriving in the Lower South, slaves were marketed through a variety of means. When overland coffles were used, traders often set up conspicuous and well-known camps outside of towns or along major roadways. This not only gave the slaves a chance to recuperate from the long trip, but it also provided buyers with a place to obtain their purchases. Depending on the strength of the market, some of these camps lasted until the entire lot was sold, while others moved from place to place. Most of them were set up in rural areas or near small towns, but they could also be found outside the region's largest cities. As one trader informed his partner, who was heading for Montgomery, Alabama: "I think it will be best To camp out on the Stage road Some 4 or 5 miles from Town." He noted that "after crossing the bridge a few hundred yards there is a good Spring neare the road, but Suit your Self as To a place and Stay there untill I get there."[15]

As in the Upper South, advertisements about the slave trade also filled the newspapers of the Lower South. Not only did slave traders advertise in the large urban newspapers, but their notices appeared in most of the smaller papers as well. In addition to placing his ad in all of the major New Orleans dailies, Walter Campbell's notice for the fall of 1857 likewise ran for a year in the following Louisiana papers: *Alexandria American, Baton Rouge Gazette, Donaldsonville Coast Journal, Franklin Journal, Lake Providence Herald, Thibodaux Minerva,* and Vidalia *Concordia Intelligencer;* the following Mississippi papers: Jackson *Flag of the Union, Natchez Courier,* and *Vicksburg Whig;* and the Camden, Arkansas, *Ouachita Herald.*[16]

Finally, newspaper editors in the Lower South helped to promote the trade by occasionally running news stories praising the services of local traders or announcing upcoming sales. In a piece entitled "Good Prices for Negroes," the Tallahassee *Floridian and Journal* attributed the lucrative results of a recent sale to the skills of "Col. Berry, the Prince of Auctioneers." In Natchez, the *Mississippi Free Trader* informed its readers that the firm of Griffin & Pullum had a new lot of slaves for sale, adding that "this is an old established firm known far and near for the probity that has always marked their every transaction." Under the headline "IMPORTANT SALE OF SLAVES," the *New Orleans Bee* called readers' "special attention to the sale of a list of choice cooks, washers, ironers, cotton rollers, plantation hands, brick-yard hands and house servants, which will take place to-morrow, in the rotunda of the St. Louis Hotel, by N. VIGNIE, Esq., auctioneer."[17]

II

While much of the domestic trade's activity occurred beyond the limits of the South's cities and towns—the antebellum South was overwhelmingly rural, and it was there that many of the traders and their agents worked, either buying and selling slaves or transporting them to market—it is important to note the crucial role that the region's urban areas played in sustaining this trade. Slaves were often brought to town, either to be sold out of a dealer's office or to be held in a trader's pen or city jail until shipment south. Moreover, urban markets were places where people came to shop. Most of the dealers and brokers were located there, and all of the larger cities had several auction halls and sales emporiums. Finally, cities and towns were crucial transportation hubs, and many if not most of the slaves in the interregional trade passed through them.

This proved especially true for the major markets like New Orleans, where by the late 1850s one could find 3,000 or more slaves available for sale. But this traffic flooded the region's smaller towns as well. As one trader in Mississippi noted, "This country [is] full of negroes. They are at every village in the country I believe." During the boom years of the mid-1830s, another speculator in tiny Livingston, Mississippi, reported that there were "about 300 in market at this place & Droves passing on below Dayley."[18]

Because so much market activity occurred there, urban areas were places where the domestic slave trade could be frequently seen. Those visiting a city routinely encountered it, often upon arrival, as many traders had facilities near major roads and transportation terminals. In Baltimore, Austin Woolfolk's slave pen was "near the intersection of the Washington and Frederick roads," while John Donovan's notice pointed out that his stand was "immediately in the rear of the railroad depot." Donovan added that "persons bringing negroes by the cars will find it very convenient, as it is only a few yards from where the passengers get out." In Richmond, Pulliam & Betts informed potential customers bringing slaves for sale that it had a "porter always at each depot," and in Memphis, the firm of Bolton, Dickens & Co. advertised that its mart was "opposite the lower steamboat landing."[19]

Those traveling about town could not avoid seeing these establishments. In New Orleans, Joseph Bruin informed readers that the "omnibuses running on Royal and Chartres streets all pass my house," and tourists to the U.S. Capitol often had to walk past the slave depots at the corner of Seventh and Independence, across the street from where the National Air and Space Museum is located today. Resident slave dealers could also be found near the best hotels in town. John Montmollin's office in Savannah was "opposite the Pulaski House," and in Lexington, Kentucky, William Talbott's slave pen was "adjoining the Broadway Hotel." One could likewise always run across the trade in every city's commercial district. As the Montgomery firm of Thomas A. Powell & Co. prudently made known: "Our depot is in the centre of the business portion of the city, convenient to all the banking houses."[20]

Sometimes slave dealers had their pens in surprising locations. While it might be appropriate that R. W. Lucas's depot in Lexington was "opposite the County Jail," Lewis Collier had the misfortune to operate "near the Poor-house" in Richmond. Visitors to New Orleans could find the office of J. L. Carman on Gravier Street, "opposite the Varieties Theatre." But two traders in Baltimore probably raised the most eyebrows with their addresses. John Denning advertised that his establishment was "near the Methodist Episcopal Church," while James Purvis attracted the attention of abolitionists when he made it known that he could be reached at either "SINNER'S HOTEL, water street" or his "residence on Gallow's Hill, near the Missionary church—the house is white."[21]

Photograph of a slave dealer's office on Whitehall Street (currently Peachtree Street) in Atlanta. Such businesses were a common sight in the commercial districts of all southern towns. Courtesy of the Library of Congress.

In addition to easily spotting a slave trader's depot (typically with a big sign stating "Negroes Bought Here"), it was also common in southern cities to witness the marketing of human property. Frederick Law Olmsted was one of many visitors to comment on this sight. In Alabama, he observed that "one of the curiosities to every Northerner visiting Montgomery—the capital of the State—is the parade of negroes, dressed up attractively (the smallest boys provided with the thickest heeled shoes and the tallest hats), which is made every day through the principal streets." In Houston, he remarked that "in the windows of shops, and on the doors and columns of the hotel, were many written advertisements headed, 'A likely negro girl for sale.' 'Two negroes for sale.' 'Twenty negro boys for sale,' etc."[22]

Photograph of a slave auction in Lexington, Kentucky. Courtesy of the J. Winston Coleman, Jr., Photographic Collection, Transylvania University Library.

But the most graphic display of the domestic trade was the buying and selling of humans at public auction. In southern cities and towns, visitors routinely encountered this scene whether they wanted to or not. Anton Reiff, a New York musician, accidentally came upon an auction on a street corner in Mobile, and when walking through Galveston, Texas, another northerner ran into "a negro with a red flag & bell in his hand & a placard on his hat with the legend For Sale in large letters." Together with the pounding of a drum, the man had been used as an advertisement for an outdoor sale that soon commenced nearby.[23] Auctions also transpired at sites where they were least expected. A German tourist reported that a pregnant woman and her two children were placed upon a bench in a Louisville coffee house and sold to the highest bidder, and according to Ralph Waldo Emerson, a slave auction broke out in the neighboring yard as he attended a meeting of the Bible Society in St. Augustine, Florida.[24]

While slaves were sold everywhere (including "at Hawkins & Bassett's Shoe Store" in Lexington), most of the major cities had sections where dealers congregated and much of their business took place. In Richmond, this was in the heart of the city's commercial district, along Fifteenth Street from Franklin to Broad, just two blocks from the state capitol and governor's mansion. In addition to numerous dealers' offices, there were also several large auction halls where many of the sales occurred. Every day, up and down the street (and along several side alleys), red flags were posted, with slips of paper attached listing all of the lots to be sold. Most of the slave dealers in Charleston were also located in that city's business district, primarily along State Street from the Old Exchange on East Bay to the slave mart on Chalmers. Slaves were sold at both of these locations, as well as in the dealers' offices. In Natchez, slave sales could be found all over the city, from the river landing to the front steps of the fashionable Mansion House Hotel. But the main slave-trading center, especially after 1833 when the city prohibited public sales by slave traders within the city limits, was a collection of rough wooden structures just outside of town. Originally known as "Niggerville," by the late 1830s this market was more commonly referred to as the "Forks of the Road." Every year at least four or five large traders operated out of these stands, and one resident remembered seeing as many as 800 slaves in that venue at one time.[25]

None of these places, however, could compare with New Orleans, where the buying and selling of human property had become a major industry. By the late 1840s, there were hundreds of traders in the city and countless others working in related occupations. In 1854, a census of merchants listed eleven "slave dealers" in one square block alone, and by the end of the decade there were at least twenty-five within a few blocks of the St. Charles Hotel, mostly on Gravier and Baronne. As Walter Campbell made known in his notices, his depot was "due west from the St. Charles Hotel, and is convenient to all the merchants and hotels."[26]

Evidence of the slave trade could be found everywhere in the Crescent City. During a visit in the early 1840s, a free black man from Tennessee was struck by a huge billboard bearing the words "Maryland and Virginia Negroes for Sale." While he had seen this legend posted all over town, on one edifice, seventy-five-feet long, "the sign painted on the wall ran the length and around the corner of the building." Throughout the city, men and women were conspicuously exhibited in store fronts and along public streets. According to one British traveler, "We came upon a street in which a long row, or rather several rows, of black and coloured people were exposed in the open air (and under a smiling sun) for sale! There must have been from 70 to 100, all young people, varying from 15 to 30 years of age." This visitor noted that they "were arranged under a kind of verandah, having a foot-bench (about six inches high) to stand upon, and

Illustration of slaves dressed in nice clothing being offered for sale on the streets of New Orleans. *Harper's Weekly*, January 24, 1863. Courtesy of the Library of Congress.

their backs resting against the wall. None were in any way tied or chained; but two white men ('soul-drivers,' I suppose) were sauntering about in front of them, each with a cigar in his mouth, a whip under his arm, and his hands in his pockets, looking out for purchasers."[27]

Unlike the auction halls in Richmond, which most visitors characterized as dirty and dark, similar facilities in New Orleans were elaborate emporiums and sources of civic pride. One visitor described Bank's Arcade, a prominent slave mart on Magazine Street, as "lighted from above by a large sky-light, and paved with marble." But the city's most celebrated auction rooms were located in its two finest hotels. One Englishman called the St. Charles "the largest and handsomest hotel in the world," and it was here, in its famous barroom, where the American Exchange took place. Under a large dome, supported by huge brick columns, were two auction blocks, one on each end of the bar, where men and women were routinely offered for sale. The other was the St. Louis Hotel, equally renowned for its grand rotunda and lively French Exchange. According to one guest, it was "perfectly circular within; and its domed roof, 60 feet in height, [was] beautifully painted, [and] supported by Corinthian columns round the sides." Here up to a half dozen sales took place, all at the same time, with auctioneers alternating between French and English, each trying to drown out the others.[28]

Illustration of the elaborate auction hall in the rotunda of the St. Louis Hotel in
New Orleans, where the sale of slaves and other forms of property took place. From
Buckingham, *Slave States.*

In addition to being a frequent sight, the domestic slave trade was an
important factor in the economies of many southern cities and towns. Simply put, the domestic trade was big business. In the late 1850s, Richmond and
Charleston each had annual slave sales totaling more than $4 million, and it
has been estimated that the figures for New Orleans were larger than the two
cities combined. However, the trade probably played an even greater economic
role in some of the region's smaller towns. The Montgomery city directory for
1859 listed four slave depots, equal to the number of banks and hotels in town.
In 1860, the *Natchez Courier* reported that $2 million worth of slaves were sold
in that city annually—a rather large sum for a town whose population totaled
only 6,600.[29]

The domestic trade was also an important source of income for other urban
businesses. Newspapers received much of their revenue from the trade, as did
other ancillary industries, such as insurance companies, factorage houses,

and physicians (almost all slave depots retained the regular services of a local doctor). Some clothing makers likewise specialized in providing new outfits for those about to be sold. According to the advertisement of Lewis B. Levy, a "MANUFACTURER OF ALL KINDS OF SERVANTS' CLOTHING," his office was in the heart of Richmond's slave-trading district, and "persons bringing their servants to the city for hire or sale, can be supplied on reasonable terms. The attention of traders and others particularly solicited." For references, he listed four of the largest slave-trading firms in the city. One visitor to an auction hall in Richmond reported that the walls were plastered with similar notices. The same proved true for the other end of the trade. In New Orleans, N. C. Folger & Son called "the attention of Traders to their immense assortment" of more than 4,000 blue suits, as well as drawers, undershirts, and socks to be worn by male slaves at their sale. This firm too was located in the midst of the city's slave-trading district, at the corner of Magazine and Gravier.[30]

Arguably the institution most closely tied to the domestic trade was southern banks. In addition to initiating thousands of slave sales through the foreclosure of loans, bank presidents sometimes helped to promote these sales. In North Carolina, the president of the Bank of Tarboro hoped to boost the proceeds from such a sale when he notified a local speculator that his bank was selling $20,000 worth of human collateral. Moreover, bankers often participated directly in this trade. One man in Nashville, who listed his address as the Bank of Commerce, offered "Real Estate in Exchange for Negroes."[31]

But the most important connection between southern bankers and the slave trade came through the issuing and refinancing of bank notes. Some banks had almost all of their resources tied into this commerce. According to one Quaker reformer, "Two-thirds of the funds of the Bank of North Carolina were invested in loans to slave merchants," while another man in Richmond complained that the slave traders there owned "a Bank in this City, and have millions of money under their control." At times, demand for such loans stretched lending institutions to the breaking point. In 1860, the *New Orleans Crescent* noted that the high price of slaves was "demanding through our mercantile community all the resources at the command of the banks."[32]

Such a large commitment of funds into this trade could sometimes put banks at risk. As one bank president in Tennessee acknowledged: "It has been a common subject of complaint against the Union Bank that too large amount of its accommodations have been extended to Negro traders & other speculators to the exclusion of the Planter and Merchant—It is the intention of the Board at least not to *merit* this imputation in [the] future." Reckless investments could even create the threat of bankruptcy. In Savannah, a man posing as a slave trader with forged letters of recommendation managed to swindle the Bank of Georgia out of $21,000. Afterward, the local dealer William Parker quipped, "wish he had Brook the Bank for their carelessness."[33]

Finally, municipalities (as well as states) collected considerable revenue from this traffic through a variety of taxes and fees. Some of these charges were minor, such as a tax of $5 or $10 on each individual sold, but a number of cities levied much higher licensing fees on places where slaves were kept for sale. In Washington, DC, this amounted to $400 a year, and depot owners in New Orleans had to pay an annual fee of $500. Moreover, many southern towns levied additional charges on nonresident traders before they could even offer their slaves for sale. Needless to say, this could become economically crippling for those who wanted to sell in several different cities. Most speculators complained that all of these fees were "an enormous Tax on Traders," but they proved to be a major source of revenue for southern municipalities. By 1851, licensing and taxes on the slave trade brought in more than $10,000 annually to the city of Richmond. Therefore, for the urban residents of the South, the domestic slave trade had become a central and important part of everyday life. Not only did it stimulate their local economy, but it also helped to pay for their public services.[34]

III

Of the more than 2 million slaves who were sold in America between 1820 and 1860, more than two-thirds were sold to local buyers. This includes intrastate sales between planters, commercial sales through agents or brokers, and court-ordered sales. Local sales have not typically been treated, or even generally thought of, as being part of the domestic trade. In all of the published works on American slavery, few have paid more than passing notice to this crucial aspect of the trade, and not one, including those specializing in the interregional trade, have examined it in any depth. By focusing primarily on professionally transacted interregional sales, however, it is easy to forget the crucial role that the local slave trade played in southern society. Without this fundamental ability to transfer property from one owner to another, the southern slave system could never have functioned.[35]

The buying and selling of humans was a frequent occurrence, and virtually all southern slave owners engaged in this traffic at least once. According to one historian of early nineteenth-century Nashville, the local trade was so common that "they used slaves almost as currency." Former slaves also recalled the everyday nature of such sales. One man from Texas noted that his owner "bought and sold them all the time." Moreover, all segments of society engaged in this commerce, including women and other groups not normally associated with the world of business. In 1838, the Reverend Jean Louis Brasseur, curé of the Church of St. Martin in Louisiana, sold a forty-eight-year-old woman named Ellen to a fellow priest, the Reverend C. H. de St. Aubin, curé of the St. Peter Church at New Iberia.[36]

As the commercial values of the professional slave traders spread throughout southern society, countless owners began to view their human property in more market-oriented terms. Most significantly, slave property was increasingly seen as an investment, a valuable type of property that could be purchased and sold like any other. Not all were as blunt as the Alabama man who told his agent to take his slave woman and her child "to some market and cash them as quick as possible," but it was not uncommon to find newspaper advertisements like the one that read "to be sold for no fault, but to change investment." During times of economic depression, such as the mid-1840s, many would agree with the Missouri man who worried that slaves were "one of the most uncertain & unprofitable kinds of stock in the country." But in general, throughout the antebellum period, this type of property was routinely seen as a good investment. As early as 1818, a Louisiana youth explained to his uncle, "For a young man, just commencing in life, the best stock, in which he can invest capital, is, I think, negro Stock. . . . Negroes will yield a much larger income than any Bank dividends." During the 1850s, the peak period of rising slave prices, a South Carolina man even remarked that his mother was "about to sell a piece of property, for the purpose of investing in Negroes."[37]

In addition, many southern slave owners began to speak of their human property in market-oriented language similar to that of the professional traders. As one seller in Kentucky noted, his "only reason for selling is too great an increase in the stock." Another man in Virginia considered his recent purchase "a great bargain," while a Louisiana planter was proud of the "fourteen head of negroes" whom he had just bought. In Louisville, the Reverend L. J. Halsey was grateful for the $33 that he had cleared after selling his slave woman Jane, adding that was "certainly the first and only profit she has ever been to us."[38]

The indifference that accompanied such a perspective naturally led to some callous actions by owners when buying and selling their human property. At the extreme were those who could only view the loss of their slaves in economic terms. After his slave woman hung herself (following two unsuccessful attempts at escape), one Texas planter could only damn her and lament the fact that just two months before he had been offered $900 for her. As this man saw it, "*The fates pursue me.*" But equally hardened were those who sought to limit their losses by selling off those who were the least productive on the plantation. According to William Craft, his former owner sold his parents and "several other aged slaves" because "they were getting old, and would soon become valueless in the market." Arguably the most cold-hearted were those owners who dumped their infirm slaves onto men like Dr. T. Stillman of Charleston for use in his "Medical Infirmary for Diseases of the Skin." Stillman advertised that he would pay "the highest cash price" to "any person having sick Negroes, considered incurable by their respected Physicians, and wishes to dispose of them." In other words, pragmatic owners could turn a loss into a gain by receiving cash for their dying and "worthless" property, who would then be used as involuntary subjects for Dr. Stillman's medical experiments.[39]

While most owners were never so blatantly callous, many still routinely disregarded the sentiments of their slaves (and their family attachments) when the sale of their property satisfied the owners' perceived need or whim. One woman was sold away from her family so her owner's son could go to school; another was likewise traded so her gallant "master" could buy a substitute for the Confederate army. In Virginia, one elderly man sold all of his slaves for the sole reason that he wanted to get rid of them before he died, while in Lexington, Kentucky, a woman and her family were offered "simply because the owner does not desire a servant with children."[40]

Not only did many owners adopt the attitudes and language of the professional dealers, they also became just as skillful at marketing their slaves. One common means of selling slaves locally was through advertisements in the newspapers. Intermingled in the For Sale columns with notices for land and other items, these advertisements usually offered one or two individuals on reasonable terms, although at least one Alabama man was adamant about what he believed his property was worth. In 1821, William Powell claimed that his slave John was "inferior to none," and therefore "$1000 is my price, . . . persons not disposed to give that price need not apply." Most sellers were more flexible, however, and much more typical was the notice found in the Tallahassee *Floridian and Journal* that offered a young woman at private sale (presumably at her owner's desired price), and "if not sold before the 1st of January, she will be sold at Public Auction."[41]

While seldom as flashy, local advertisements frequently employed the same types of effective sales pitches as those found in the notices placed by the large interregional traders. In the Lower South, owners almost always pointed out when the men and women they had for sale were "acclimated" and therefore more valuable. In Natchez, one man offered "a first rate field hand, having been raised on a Plantation in this neighborhood," while in New Orleans, the owner of a fifteen-year-old girl noted that she had "been raised in the country from her earliest infancy and speaks French and English."[42]

Even more so than the interregional dealers, in their notices local vendors often emphasized the skills of the individuals they were selling. One man in New Orleans offered a twelve-year-old girl named Caroline, who was not only "very active and intelligent" but could also speak "English, French and German" and was "a No. 1 waiting maid and something of a seamstress and cook." A young woman near Vicksburg was a "No. 1 cotton picker," who could pick "not less than 300 lbs." According to the notice for a "No. 1 Seamstress" in New Orleans, this woman understood "working on Grover & Baker's Sewing Machine, and when sold, the machine, which cost $150, will go with her."[43]

At times, owners even outdid the traders at their own game. It is hard not to appreciate the irony when one speculator complained that the local sellers "flater the negroes very much in the advertisement." Lewis Clarke recalled that when his owner wanted to sell an old man to an itinerant trader, he ordered another slave "to take Paris into the back room, *pluck out* all his grey hairs, rub his face with a greasy towel, and then had him brought forward and sold for a *young* man." Sometimes these ploys could backfire, however. That nearly happened to one Virginia man who tried to boost the price of some slaves he was selling at auction by pretending to be a potential purchaser. He eventually got his price, but afterward noted that "the traders said I understood the thing a little too well," adding that they thought "it was the plan for a *green horn*. I was the last bider except the purchaser to whom I sold them."[44]

IV

Owners engaged in the local trade because it provided numerous benefits for them. For one thing, special arrangements could be made, such as obtaining a slave on a trial basis before purchase. While professional traders did this as well, it was far more common in the local trade. Conversely, it was also possible in this branch of the trade to sell an individual with the option of buying the person back before a specified period of time.[45] And many a planter volunteered a trade in lieu of cash or to settle his account. In 1849, one Texas man wanted to know if his neighbor would accept a thirteen-year-old boy, "very hearty, & . . . Sound in every respect," in exchange for some land; and twelve years later, due to hard times, D. V. Alexander of Tennessee offered to sell "a Good smart plow Boy, yaler complected, say 10 or 11 years old" to a creditor to pay off his debt. One seller in St. Louis even offered to sell a twenty-year-old man "for cash or exchanged for groceries."[46]

Another big advantage was that slaves could often be purchased on "accommodating terms." While most sellers preferred cash, and some, such as John Carter of Kentucky, demanded it ("owner must realize cash, owing to his removal to West"), it was usually possible to purchase a slave on credit, primarily because this brought more money to the seller in the long run. Terms varied but normally stretched from six months to three years at rates ranging from 7 to

10 percent. Some sellers even left the decision up to the buyer. Richard Byrd of Virginia offered his slaves on twelve months' credit, although "persons preferring to pay cash, will be allowed a discount of 6 per cent, upon doing so."[47]

It was also often cheaper to buy a slave in the local trade. This proved especially true in parts of the Upper South, where dual price structures developed. According to one official from the Eastern Shore of Maryland: "Slaves in this County and I beleive generally upon this Shore have always had two Prices, Viz a neighbourhood or domestic and a foreign or Southern price. The domestic Price has generally been about a third less than the foreign and sometimes the difference amounts to onehalf." One reason for this variation was the type of men and women who were usually available for purchase in this part of the South. As one Virginian noted when advertising a forty-year-old man, this slave was "rather old for the Southern market, and will be sold a bargain." But others also believed that they deserved a preferential price for keeping an individual in the area. This can be seen in the advertisement by a buyer seeking a young enslaved boy on the Eastern Shore of Maryland; he made it clear that "a *home* price will be given."[48]

For many owners, however, the most important benefit of trading locally was knowing the parties with whom they were dealing. Sellers frequently contacted potential purchasers. When John Haywood of Raleigh, North Carolina, wanted to sell his slave woman Sall, he wrote to a Mrs. Brickell, who had previously owned her. Haywood had purchased Sall at a sheriff's sale, and since she was sold through legal action, Haywood believed that Brickell might not have wanted to sell her and would be willing to buy her back again. Such appeals were not unusual, especially when owners had slaves with spouses on neighboring plantations.

For southerners like John Haywood, knowing the buyers of their "people" and possibly being able to satisfy a slave's wishes fit in nicely with their paternalistic ideals and was one of the many advantages of selling slaves locally. Three years after Haywood approached Mrs. Brickell, another man, John Woods, contacted Haywood about selling him a slave named Winton who was "desirus to git Back to his Parants and friends." Woods noted that Winton was "a Boy of Sutch good qualities that I Could not imbrace the thought of parting with him but he has been so faithfull a Slave since I have owned him that I think it My Duty to Let him go." If Haywood were willing "to accomidate the Boy," a "faire price" was all that Woods required.[49]

But even more important was the opposite benefit of knowing the seller of a slave and the character and condition of the person being sold. Unlike buying from an itinerant trader, when a planter bought locally, he usually knew all of the parties involved. This was a big advantage when making such a major, and often risky, investment. As one Virginia man advised when recommending that his son purchase a local woman, "It is best to get one that is well known: For it is hasardous buying strange Negros."[50]

Southerners had good reason to be concerned when purchasing slaves. All across the South, disgruntled buyers kept the courts busy addressing problems that resulted from the sale of slaves. These included everything from cases of outright fraud to discrepancies over titles, health concerns, and "moral" or character issues. Even county sheriffs were sued for holding allegedly rigged auctions at court sales. At least one man in Louisiana tried to rescind the sale of his two slaves by claiming that he was drunk at the time. For a variety of reasons, many sellers agreed to take their property back or change the terms of their original contracts when confronted by a dissatisfied buyer. In New Orleans, two women came to a mutual settlement after one found fault with two of the seventeen slaves she had purchased from the other. Mrs. N. P. Weems agreed to deduct $850 from the first payment if Mrs. S. A. Knapp would relinquish the right to any future claims. Still, many, if not most, of the disputes ended up in court. One study found that in Louisiana the state supreme court spent more time on cases dealing with slave sales than with any other question related to slavery.[51]

Every southern state had laws regulating slave sales, and in general, most tried to protect buyers from unscrupulous sellers. While some states in the Upper South were ambivalent on this issue, in large part because of their slave-exporting interests, slave-importing states were especially careful to put protective legislation in place. Wealthy, influential planters sought as much security as possible for their principal investments. As one man in Louisiana put it, "The citizens of this Country have been so much imposed on with bad negroes that they will not buy without full guarantees in Terms of the Law."

Because buyers were at an informational disadvantage, many states required that sellers disclose known faults at the time of purchase. Of primary concern was the health, or "soundness," of a slave. Therefore, in most states, sellers had to inform purchasers of all known health problems, and if none were listed, it was presumed that the individual being sold was sound. Later, if it could be proven that a preexisting condition had been present, the buyer usually had grounds for a suit. This relatively modern concept of implied warranty, or the rule that a sound price implies a sound product, was most actively followed by the courts of South Carolina, although it could be found at different times and to various degrees throughout the South. In most states, however, the implied warranty only covered title and soundness; only in Louisiana was it expanded to include "vices of character" as well. Primarily, this referred to habitual runaways. While it was also supposed to encompass other faults such as "addicted to theft," these were often difficult to prove. As a state supreme court judge noted: "It is well known that most slaves will steal small articles from their own-

$1175, Richmond Feb 28th 1856.

Received of Mr R. I. Young of Ala ——
Eleven hundred & Seventy five Dollars, being in full
for the purchase of one Negro Slave named Meridith
the right and title of said Slave. I . . . warrant and defend against the claims of
all persons whatsoever, and likewise warrant him ———— sound and healthy
As witness my hand and seal,

Silas Omohundro [SEAL.]

Like many professional slave traders, Silas Omohundro of Richmond used printed
forms to record his bills of sale. Most slave bills of sale also guaranteed the title and
soundness of the individuals being sold unless noted. Courtesy of Mrs. Judy Tuccinardi
and the Virginia Historical Society.

State of Alabama } Received of Henry Stewart one
Autauga County } thousand Dollars in full pay
ment of a cirtin negro man slav by the name
of Edman which cirtin negro I warent to be sound
and healthy both in boddy and mind except his
site for left foot all so I will defend fend the
site of said negro against the claim or claims or
any person or persons January the 10th 1840

Gaines Goodwin

Like many southerners who sold slaves in the local trade, Gaines Goodwin of Autauga
County, Alabama, recorded his bill of sale by hand. This sale was for a man named
Edman to Henry Stewart for $1,000 on January 10, 1840. Edman was warranted sound
except for his left foot. Collection of the author.

ers as well as others when they find an opportunity. . . . If sales were set aside for that, there would be no security in slave sales."[52]

Despite assistance from the southern courts and written warranties on most bills of sale, slave buyers still remained at risk. Court cases concerning slave sales were always uncertain. Buyers usually had to prove that the fault was present at the time of purchase or that the actions of the seller were fraudulent. In addition, as one lawyer in South Carolina noted when advising his brother-in-law, who had been accused of selling an unsound woman at an estate sale, there was the problem of determining "what does or does not constitute unsoundness." While it is impossible to know how many sellers deliberately set out to deceive their customers, the number of cases before the southern courts clearly shows the propensity that some southerners had to pawn their undesirable property off on unsuspecting others. And it also illustrates the fact that slave buyers had a legitimate reason to be concerned when making their purchases.[53]

It is not surprising, then, that when buying slaves many southerners minimized their risks by purchasing individuals who were known or who could be recommended by people they knew and trusted. Often they turned to family members for assistance. One such man was John Brodnax of North Carolina. After informing his mother in Lynchburg, Virginia, that he was looking for a female servant, she suggested a local teenager, adding that the girl was "sold for no fault" and came from "a very likely family, . . . Nancy and Rebecca liveing here are her sisters, they are as good servants as you meet with in these days." Relatives living in more favorable markets were especially called upon for aid. When John Campbell of Richmond was asked to buy a slave for his sister in southwestern Virginia, he promised her that he would make an "inquiry here among my friends & acquaintances and if a boy can be had for a reasonable price of a good character you shall have one." While most buyers usually trusted their family members' judgments, occasionally extra reassurance was needed before purchasing. In 1853, G. L. Ellis of rural South Carolina complained to his cousin in Charleston that a woman he had bought recently had died. Ellis asked his cousin to look for another but added, "before you close a bargain for such a woman let me hear from you & I will come down & see for myself as I have suffered both ways, by selling & now by buying."[54]

Buyers also sought help from friends and neighbors. While visiting Lexington, Kentucky, Will Carr assisted a friend in St. Louis by making inquiries "on the subject of purchasing negroes." Although he found that most were priced too high, Carr reported that if "you should want one with his wife and two small children I think I know of such that might be purchased much below their value and that are said to be exceedingly fine slaves." One Virginian who needed help in obtaining a more stable and secure investment was G. B. Wallace, who wanted to replace "a very unruly negro girl" and asked a neighbor to "be so good as look out for me a breeding negro woman under twenty years of age. Also a young active negro man." Wallace added that a middle-aged couple with children would also be acceptable, but haste was of the utmost importance, "as the negro of whom I wish to dispose is a very dangerous character." Even after purchasing, southerners took comfort in the opinions of others. After buying a forty-two-year-old carpenter, a Virginia man worried that the price he had paid was too high "for a negro of that age, but every body who knows him says that he is one of the most valuable fellows in the country, and that I have bought a great bargain."[55]

When forced to advertise, those seeking to buy sought as much protection as possible. That was why most demanded that "testimonials of character will be required" or that "none but those well recommended need apply." Some had special demands, like the purchaser in Louisville looking for a young woman "who can come well recommended for sobriety." One buyer in Wilmington, North Carolina, even added an extra incentive by offering "a fair price ... for one that is well recommended."[56]

Conversely, when selling their slaves, owners sought to alleviate whatever fears a buyer might have about purchasing an unknown individual. Many of their notices were like that of the Richmond man who simply stated that his slave woman was "of *good character*," but some were more specific, such as the seller of a man in Washington, DC, who pointed out that "to a gentle-man wishing a body or house servant he would be an acquisition, being hon-est and sober in his habits." Many tried to reassure buyers that the men and women they were selling came from good, stable homes. According to one seller, his woman had "been raised with much care and instruction"; another was praised as "a trustworthy, honest house servant" who had "lived in the same family 18 years"; and another was being "sold for the first time; character and qualities good." In some cases, however, the reputations of those being sold spoke for themselves. Among the eleven slaves sold at auction in Mont-gomery was "that well known workman CAESAR," while a New Orleans seller noted that his "Trusty and Faithful" slave had been "advantageously known in the city for many years."[57]

Of primary concern to buyers was the reason for the sale. Therefore, most sellers tried to reassure potential purchasers by mentioning that their slaves were being "sold for no fault." Among the most frequent explanations were "want of money" and "no further use for her," but others included retirement or, as in the case of the Virginia man who was "going to reside North," an own-er's removal to a new location. One South Carolinian listed the inconvenience of the distance between his residence and his planting interest as the reason for his sale, while a man in Frederick, Maryland, sold a family of six simply because he had "too many." Sometimes vendors were candid about the "faults" of the men and women they were selling, especially in those states where they were required by law to declare such known problems before sale. Yet even here, sellers often tried to downplay these "defects." As one man in St. Francisville, Louisiana, explained it, his two men were being "sold for no fault except drinking, which the owner cannot prevent, owing to his peculiar situation."[58]

Southerners also sought protection by buying their slaves through local dealers, brokers, and auctioneers. Some of these men were what one itinerant speculator referred to as "town Traders," slave dealers who provided services for (and sometimes dabbled in) the interregional trade, but who also did extensive business with regular local customers. Others were general merchants who dealt in a variety of goods, and slaves were only one of many items they offered. These included men such as J. C. Gentry of Louisville, who operated a livery stable and sold horses, carriages, cattle, wagons, and slaves on commission, and Louis Miller of Natchez, who dealt not only in slaves and cotton but also handled smoked mackerel, whiskey, flour, bacon, lard, butter, candles, soap, and dry goods. By catering to a neighborhood market, these traders offered many of the same benefits that came from local buying: the knowledge that an owner could purchase a slave at a good price with confidence and trust.[59]

V

In addition to sales by private owners, slaves were also sold by southern states and municipalities. Sometimes these political entities bought slaves for public projects and then had to sell them again when they were no longer needed. In 1834, the state of Georgia sold 190 slaves who had been bought to carry out river and road improvements, and in 1860 the state of Louisiana sold approximately 100 individuals after its general assembly passed "An Act providing for the sale of the Slaves belonging to the Internal Improvement Department of the State." Evidence that at least some of these sales catered to a local market can be found in the advertisement put out by the city of Huntsville, Alabama, when in 1848 it sold off a gang it had bought for grading the streets: "These slaves are stout, healthy, of good character and well known to the citizens of this town."[60]

The largest source of state-sponsored slave selling, however, came from sales ordered by southern courts of law. Not only did southern courts spend much of their time settling disputes over slave sales, but they were also responsible for initiating many of these same sales. Human chattels were the South's most valuable asset and one of its most mortgaged forms of property. A study of East Feliciana Parish, Louisiana, found that slaves accounted for 80 percent of the collateral for secured loans. In addition, they were an easily convertible source of cash. Therefore, it is not surprising that in settling cases, southern courts regularly instructed that slaves be sold and the proceeds distributed to creditors and other interested parties. Historian Thomas Russell has found that roughly half of all the slave sales in South Carolina between 1820 and 1860 were the result of some form of court action. Because of their prominence, Russell has argued that "the courts of South Carolina acted as the state's greatest slave auctioneering firm" and that "court sales were at the center of the business of slave sales." Although similar studies have not yet been done for other states, corroborating evidence does make it seem likely that Russell's findings for South Carolina were not unique and that the actions of the southern courts and the agents of those courts were responsible for an overwhelming number of slave sales throughout the South.[61]

One common type of sale based on legal action was to settle estates. In their wills, many southerners were quite explicit about the distribution of their slaves. They bequeathed specific individuals to various beneficiaries and sometimes ordered one or more slaves sold for the benefit of the estate. Occasionally, they did both, such as the Texas man who left a slave to his wife for eight years, after which this individual was to be sold and the proceeds divided among the heirs. But not all slave owners were so precise. Some only called for an equal division of their estate. In such cases, disinterested commissioners usually made an appraisal of the slaves and if a division could not be agreed upon by the heirs, a sale would follow. In addition, problems arose when settling estates: owners died intestate or in debt; the beneficiary was a minor; or an inheritor desired the sale of a slave not designated for sale. These matters were settled in probate court, often with the slaves being sold by the sheriff or another official of the court. Some executors saw to the selling of the slaves themselves, especially when they were concerned about finding desirable purchasers for favorite servants. While this was possible with small numbers of slaves, it took much time and cut into the proceeds of the estate. At least one executor in South Carolina, after failing at such efforts, "concluded 'twas best to put them in the hands of a Broker, . . . thinking it better to pay a commission, than incur longer delay in accomplishing the Sale." Almost all large sales were conducted by professional auctioneers.[62]

In many ways, there was little difference between an estate and a commercial slave sale. They were advertised in much the same way. Notices for estate sales appeared in newspapers and were plastered on handbills, frequently with screaming headlines similar to those used by professional slave dealers. In Kentucky, Philip Swigert, master commissioner of the Franklin Circuit Court, began one notice for the settlement of a probate case with

"Look At This! ! !
Public Sale of Land & Slaves!"

Some sheriffs could be just as skillful in making sales as professional auction-eers. When describing the high prices that slaves brought at a local estate sale, the Baton Rouge *Gazette and Comet* added:

> We suspect our sheriff Babin must have been a *little extra* in his efforts to get good prices. He has such a pleasing face, and can say '*my dear sir, don't let this property go for nothing*,' with such *plaintive silvery tones*, that one out of pure sympathy bids; and then he is so popular he pleases everybody and we suppose everybody wishes to please him; hence such sales as he makes.[63]

While estate sales were sometimes held at the plantation of the deceased or at the county courthouse, they were also often conducted in the same loca-tions as commercial sales. The administrators of one estate sold seventy slaves out of Franklin & Armfield's pen in Alexandria. Many of Charleston's slave auctioneers also held their estate sales at the slave mart on Chalmers Street, the same place where they ran their regular commercial sales. (The city's two masters in equity held some of their sales there as well.) The place of sale was a crucial decision that could add greatly to the proceeds of an estate. As one man argued when recommending a sale be held at Richmond instead of at the local courthouse in Culpeper: "Richmond would be the more eligible market of the two. The Southern purchasers invariably resort to the latter place for their supplies."[64]

The most common venues for court-ordered sales, however, were the monthly auctions held on the front steps of virtually every county courthouse across the South. In addition to probate cases, the sheriff and various other officials of the state courts conducted all types of sales there, from the settle-ment of lawsuits and debt cases to the selling of runaway slaves. The monthly sale day was a major part of antebellum American society, especially for those living in the nation's numerous small towns and rural areas. It was an occasion when residents from all over came to socialize and look for bargains at the sales. Relatively isolated farmers visited with family and friends and listened to public speeches, attended political meetings, and often consumed large quantities of alcohol. While the court sales were the primary focus, people often brought other items to sell, and many a town square was turned into an open market. But, most important, attendees participated in, and gave their approval to, the sale of human beings on the courthouse steps.[65]

Sale day always drew a crowd, but whenever slaves were to be sold, people flocked to town. In Camden, Arkansas, one man described such an event as a "busy Day, city full of People, Several sales of property at enormous prices. Negroes fellows 17 to $1800, women $1400, children 6 to $800." The same proved true in Jefferson City, Missouri. In its account of a recent slave sale, a local newspaper reported that "a large number of persons were in attendance from all parts of the country, and the bidding was unusually spirited." Even the most respected members of society attended these events. As a man in Culpeper, Virginia, bragged, "There was a large sale of negroes here that day which brought many people to town. Hon. O. R. Singleton a member of congress from Mississippi came up to attend the sale." Nor could bad weather keep people away. According to one small-town newspaper in South Carolina, "Yesterday was sale day, and notwithstanding the inclemency of the weather, a considerable crowd was in attendance. The negros belonging to the estate of Col. H. Miller were sold."[66]

The popularity of such sales can also be found in the accounts written by former slaves. After being transported in a coffle from Maryland to South Carolina, Charles Ball was brought to Columbia for sale. Although the individuals in his group were sold privately and not as a result of legal action, they were kept in the public jail and sold at auction outside the jailhouse door. According to Ball, "The court was sitting in Columbia at this time, and either this circumstance, or the intelligence of our arrival in the country, or both, had drawn together a very great crowd of people." On the first day, "more than a thousand gentlemen came to look at us," and the next day, "the crowd in town was much greater than it had been" the day before. Another probable reason for the especially large turnout was that July 4th fell on the third day. "I understood that the court did not sit this day, but a great crowd of people gathered, and remained around the jail, all the morning; many of whom were intoxicated, and sang and shouted in honour of free government, and the rights of man." At noon there was a large dinner with much singing, drinking, and speeches by politicians. About five o'clock the jailer announced that the sales would resume and "in a few minutes the whole assembly, that had composed the dinner party, and hundreds of others, were convened around the jail door." Ball "perceived much eagerness amongst the bidders, many of whom were not sober," and within a few hours all those in his group had been sold.[67]

Judicial sales drew large crowds for many of the same reasons that southerners were interested in buying slaves from local sellers. They realized that the individuals were being sold for no fault and could be purchased with minimal concern about their character. This assumption can be seen in the request that a Missouri man made of his son to buy a slave family for him: "I wish to have negroes of good repute such as are sometime to be bought at sales by administrators." Officials often stressed this point when advertising their sales, especially in the slave-importing states where apprehension about such matters was more widespread. One notice for an estate sale in Alabama made it clear that the slaves to be sold were "all family negroes,—not bought up by speculators from every State in the South." Southern courts also helped in promoting this arrangement. In 1849, the administrator of one estate was ordered to sell a slave named Lewis, privately and for cash, because Lewis was "a very vicious boy & is so ungovernable, as to be of great disadvantage to the other negroes belonging to the estate."[68]

There were other advantages to buying slaves at court sales as well. As with most local sales, the slaves were normally sold on long credit. While numerous examples of judicial sales for cash exist, they were the exception and in some places apparently quite unusual. According to one man who attended a court sale in south-central Virginia, "The commissioners announced, to the surprise of many, that the terms of sale required *money and nothing but money—no drafts or acceptances*, it mattered not how responsible the men were.... The buyer would have to pay the money in the course of the day or lose the property." The man added that "it was the opinion of many persons that if the negroes had been sold as negroes commonly are, and on a credit of six months, they would have brought thirty thousand dollars," which was $9,000 more than was given.[69]

In addition to the accommodating terms, slaves at judicial sales could usually be purchased for less money and with more confidence than those sold commercially. Thomas Russell found that the average price of a slave sold at a court sale in South Carolina was 3.8–8.4 percent lower than one sold at a noncourt sale. At first glance this may not seem like much of a discount, but it would be roughly equivalent to buying an item today without paying the sales tax, a factor that becomes increasingly important on large purchases. Because the sales were conducted by the state, buyers could also be assured that the title to their property was good and that their purchase would be duly recorded. Therefore, it is not surprising that a Virginia man advised a colleague who was eager to purchase "not to be in haste to buy, certainly one may meet with some at shff's sales by & by on better terms."[70]

The predominance of court sales in the overall number of slave sales further emphasizes the crucial role that southern cities and towns played in sustaining the domestic slave trade. But even more important was the impact that such sales had on defining many of these communities. Judicial sales were open to the public, and buyers from all over attended, especially when the sales were large. One group that frequently made the rounds was the professional slave traders. Although they did not always buy many slaves, these men found court sales helpful in gathering information about current prices and making contacts with potential customers. And they occasionally sold some of their own slaves as well. Sheriffs and other legal officials advertised their sales extensively, in part because they were required by law to do so, but also because it bolstered prices (and, in some cases, their commissions). Sometimes they even made special appeals to such outsiders. As one Virginia executor noted in her auction notice: "Traders will do well to attend the sale."[71]

Nevertheless, judicial sales remained primarily neighborhood affairs. In South Carolina, it has been estimated that 80 percent of all of the slaves sold by legal action went to local buyers. One reason for this was that, in many cases, at estate sales family members of the deceased often bought many of the slaves. In addition, the abilities of the slaves were usually known, which sometimes made them more expensive. As one Virginia man explained, "I had to over-bid the neighbours who were well acquainted with them." The accommodating terms at court sales likewise made it difficult for professional traders. Because slaves almost always sold for more money on credit, speculators preferred to make most of their purchases with cash. Even when court sales were for cash, other factors could make slaves more expensive. One trader in South Carolina believed that he had a good chance of buying at an upcoming court sale, "as the Sale will be for Cash," but only if the creditors did not "come in competition"[72] and drive up the prices.

But, most important, local residents often played an influential role in deter-mining the outcome of these sales. If an auction was being conducted for a rea-son or in a manner that they felt inappropriate, crowds were known to engage in collusive nonbidding or to respond with open threats to bidders, especially when they were from outside of the area. When Harriet Jacobs's grandmother was put up for auction against the well-known wishes of her deceased owner, those in the audience shouted, "Shame! Shame!" at the executor who tried to sell her and refused to offer a bid. Eventually, the grandmother was sold for $50 to a sister of the deceased, who promised to free her. Individuals also sometimes addressed the crowd in an effort to allow a sale to go to a deserving buyer. The Natchez barber William Johnson recorded that one man "made a Long speech" in behalf of a slave girl "and Said Some soft things" that convinced the buyers to let the girl go with her mother. Not all such appeals, however, were so successful. When the two granddaughters of a family slave were put up for sale, one Ken-tucky man tried to relieve the woman's suffering by purchasing them for her. At the sale, he went to the slave traders in attendance and "persuaded a number of them not to bid." He then "stated the facts to the crowd" and the reason for his bidding. He made it clear that he "did not want to defraud creditors, but wished to give a firm price & let the old woman possess her granddaughter[s], & if there was any sympathy to not press the matter." Unfortunately for the grandmother, not all of the traders that day refrained from bidding, and the two girls were sold to different purchasers at prices far higher than the hopeful redeemer could afford.[73]

Court sales were important symbolic events that helped to draw and redraw community lines. Everyone—bidders and nonbidders alike—at such sales played a role, and their behavior both sanctioned the procedure and legitimated the results. In many respects, the sale of slaves at these gatherings was a ritualistic reenactment of the enslavement of black southerners. Prior to their sale, appraisers formally categorized the enslaved men and women as property, no differently than any other type of livestock or implement. Typical was the estate of Ash Thompson of Madison County, Alabama, whose inventory first listed all of his slaves by name and appraised value, then all of his mules by name and appraised value, followed by the rest of the property with its appraised value. At the sale itself, enslaved black southerners were humiliatingly exposed to the white majority, who often expressed their superiority with jeers and insults. According to one visitor who witnessed such a sale in Charleston, "I saw in many present a sneering expression, which I have often noticed in persons who have to look on that which they dare not regard seriously. I thought, too, that I detected a brutality of tone which men do not acquire from dealing in sheep. . . . What the deadening effect might be of seeing such a thing often, I do not care to inquire."[74]

Therefore, not only were court sales a major component in the domestic slave trade, they also helped in both defining acceptable community behavior and in designating who did or did not belong to that community. But these sales did more than simply define the community in relationship to geographic outsiders. More than anything else, they reaffirmed the community's public sanctioning of the institution of chattel slavery.

VI

In 1975, the historian Herbert Gutman offered a startling statistic about the frequency and magnitude of southern slave sales. He noted that "if we assume that slave sales did not occur on Sundays and holidays and that such selling went on for ten hours on working days, a slave was sold on average every 3.6 minutes between 1820 and 1860." In other words, roughly once every 3.5 minutes, 10 hours a day, 300 days a year, for 40 years, a human being was bought and sold in the antebellum South. Since then, historians (including Gutman himself) have revised Gutman's estimate of the total number of slaves sold, and virtually all have suggested that his totals were too low. Therefore, it is quite possible that the average frequency of sale was even greater.[75]

It really does not matter, however, if a southern slave was sold once every two minutes or once every five. The point is clear. This was certainly a common form of commerce. As part of one of the largest forced migrations in world history, more than a half million African-American men, women, and children were transported from the Upper South to the Lower South through the interregional slave trade. More than twice that number were bought and sold between neighbors and within state lines. Evidence of this trade could be found everywhere, in the countryside and in the towns, from coffles on southern highways, waterways, and railroads, to public auctions in elaborate emporiums and on the steps of every courthouse. Both the interregional trade and the local trade were essential for American slavery, and it is impossible to imagine the system surviving without the ability to transfer human property from one owner to another or to transport it to another region where it was more in demand. It is for this reason that the domestic slave trade, in all of its components, was the lifeblood of the southern slave system, and without it, the institution would have ceased to exist.

SIX

Outside Looking In: The Domestic Slave Trade and the Abolitionist Attack on Slavery

The first issue of the *Liberator* is justly famous for William Lloyd Garrison's bold opening manifesto. Virtually every history textbook quotes some part of the well-known passage: "I *will be* as harsh as truth, . . . AND I WILL BE HEARD." But little mention is ever made about the two articles that appeared alongside it on the front page of that famous publication. In "District of Columbia," Garrison described how in the nation's capital, "the worst features of slavery are exhibited; and as a mart for slave-traders, it is unequalled." Also included was a petition to Congress asking for the abolition of slavery in the District of Columbia and "for the preventing of bringing slaves into that District for purposes of traffic." If that article left anyone "unmoved," the next piece was intended to startle the reader out of apathy, "unless he be morally dead—dead—dead." In "The Slave Trade in the Capital," Garrison presented examples of the hardships caused by the domestic trade, concluding with sentiments reminiscent of those in his statement of purpose: "Such are the scenes enacting in the heart of the American nation. Oh, patriotism! where is thy indignation? Oh, philanthropy! where is thy grief? OH SHAME, WHERE IS THY BLUSH!"[1]

The prominent coverage that the domestic slave trade received on the front page of the opening issue of the *Liberator* foreshadowed the important role it would play throughout the entire thirty-five-year history of that publication. Literally hundreds of pieces appeared that touched upon some aspect of the domestic trade. Lengthy in-depth articles described how the slave trade worked, and poems lamented the hardships that slaves endured. Firsthand accounts provided authentic testimony: there were letters from travelers reporting their encounters with the trade, and reprinted articles from southern newspapers gave factual evidence and southern views of it. In the sixth issue, the *Liberator* began the column "Slavery Record," the purpose of which was to exhibit the evils of the system. The first installment contained a list of slave sale advertisements. These public notices would appear again and again throughout the life of the paper.[2]

Perhaps the best example of how important the domestic trade was for the *Liberator*'s message can be found in the masthead for the publication itself. Originally, the masthead contained only the words "THE LIBERATOR." But beginning with the seventeenth issue, a large woodcut illustration appeared together with the title. This drawing was of a "HORSE MARKET" where a distraught family of black slaves was being sold at auction. Upon the auctioneer's stand was the announcement: "SLAVES HORSES & OTHER CATTLE TO BE SOLD AT 12 OC."[3] Over the long run of the *Liberator*, two more mastheads would later replace this one, but in all of them, an auction sale represented slavery. Not everyone agreed with Garrison's decision to include a picture of a slave auction on his masthead. His friends initially cautioned him against it, and southerners found it especially disturbing. In describing the reaction of slaveholders who had seen the paper, one Georgia resident reported that the "engraving in the title is galling to them, and often elicits a deep and bitter curse." Garrison, however, realized the powerful effect that visual images of the slave trade had on his audience, and for all but the first sixteen issues the *Liberator* prominently featured an illustration of a slave auction in its masthead.[4]

One reason that Garrison and the other abolitionists focused so heavily on the domestic trade was because of the larger social and economic changes that had taken place in America during the first half of the nineteenth century. For northerners, this market revolution resulted in an increased commitment to a social system based upon a diversified economy and free labor. But, in

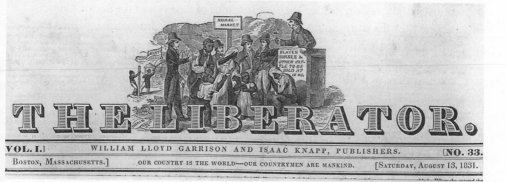

First illustrated masthead for the *Liberator*. Courtesy of the Library of Congress.

the South, these same forces led to the development of the Cotton Kingdom with its reliance upon chattel slavery. Consequently, many northerners began to view that region and its way of life as not only backward and old-fashioned, but as downright cruel. This proved especially true by the 1830s, as more and more young northerners came of age with no personal recollection of slavery or without even the experience of having seen an enslaved person. This made all of the horrors associated with the institution seem that much more pronounced and brutal. And few features of the system had a bigger impact upon a northern audience than the dramatic accounts of humans being sold on an auction block, or the tearing of husbands away from their wives or screaming children from their mothers' arms. Therefore, what had become commonplace in the South, such a normal part of everyday life, came to be seen far differently by those outside the region.[5]

The growing isolation of northerners from the domestic trade also helps to explain why seeing it firsthand had such a dramatic impact on so many people, and why they frequently cited an encounter with a slave coffle or an auction sale as a major turning point in their understanding that slavery was wrong. Many of the leaders of the abolitionist movement, including Garrison himself, had such encounters, as did countless other northerners who traveled into the slaveholding states. This was also why the Upper South unwittingly played such a crucial role in converting so many people to the antislavery cause. Being closest to the North and most accessible to visitors from that region, it was there, in the states of Maryland, Virginia, and Kentucky, that the majority of outsiders saw the workings of slavery for themselves. Much to the white South's dismay, it was also in these states that many of the worst features of the slave system took place. These states had come to rely upon the sales of thousands of their enslaved residents to the Deep South each year, and it was impossible to hide all of the wrenching scenes that this produced. For that reason, the Upper South came to be an important and influential "middle ground," where people from outside of the region formed their impressions of slavery and the South. Unfortunately for the white South, many of these visitors went home transformed by what they had seen.[6]

Over the years, the abolitionists have often been denounced as idealistic dreamers or trouble-making rabble-rousers out to destroy the American Union. Yet, from the very beginning, the abolitionists had a clear and realistic plan for bringing about an end to slavery. In this too, the domestic trade played a prominent role. Primarily, abolitionists focused on areas where they believed Congress had undisputed legal authority, most notably, in regulating interstate trade. They also relied upon the power of petition and their knowledge of how the interregional trade served as the lifeblood of the southern slave system. In the end, their efforts did not turn out exactly as they had planned. But, in many ways, they still were successful, as their actions politicized apathetic whites in the North and heightened tensions within the slaveholding South, eventually leading to secession and to war.

Therefore, while William Lloyd Garrison and the northern abolitionists employed many different strategies in their long effort to eliminate slavery, their strategies that centered around the domestic trade carried special importance. The slave trade was crucial in the development of antislavery theory and tactics, and it remained a prominent feature throughout the life of the movement. It was the aspect of American slavery that most people outside the South found most difficult to accept. Not only did the buying and selling of humans exemplify the harsh reality of the slave system, but by turning people into marketable property, it brought into question the very definition of what it means to be human. Through their efforts, the abolitionists were able to challenge the accepted way of life for whites inside the South, and they did so by making the domestic slave trade a powerful symbol of the evil inherent in the slaveholding world.[7]

I

The antislavery movement in America had its origins in opposition to the slave trade. When this effort began, however, the objection was mainly against the African trade. The first known white protest against slavery in America, a paper issued by the Germantown Friends Meeting of 1688, began with a list of "the reasons why we are against the traffick of men-body." Among the grounds cited was the Golden Rule, in relation to which the Friends asked, "Pray, what thing in the world can be done worse towards us, than if men should rob or steal us away, and sell us for slaves to strange countries; separating housbands from their wives and children." Also, the Friends wondered what people in Europe must think when they hear "that ye Quakers doe here handel men as they handel there ye cattle."[8]

During the revolutionary era, the African trade came under heavy attack and developed into a source of conflict in the early republic. Much of the anti-slavery effort during the 1780s and 1790s centered on abolishing this trade. Newly formed antislavery societies petitioned both the state and national governments, and community leaders spoke out against it. These early abolitionist societies also worked on manumitting slaves and protecting the rights of free blacks in both the North and Upper South. The kidnapping of free blacks and the selling of northern slaves soon to be freed by changing laws to slave traders heading for the Deep South proved especially troublesome and often received much of these groups' attention. But after the banning of the African trade in 1808, there was a curtailment in antislavery activity by whites. In part this was

due to the belief of many reformers that once the African trade had been abolished, slavery itself would soon wither away. Except for the formation of the
American Colonization Society in 1816, there was little organized effort against
slavery until the 1830s.[9]

The African slave trade continued to play an important role in the antislavery struggle for many years following its legal prohibition in 1808. Northern
churches and African-American organizations frequently celebrated the anniversary of its abolition in sermons and public speeches.[10] The Society of Friends
made the foreign slave trade a prominent feature in its antislavery efforts, and
antebellum abolitionists often referred to its horrors and complained about
the supposedly rampant practice of smuggling. Nevertheless, while the African
trade always remained a component in the antislavery movement, its importance declined over time.[11]

Opposition to the domestic slave trade began to appear and then mushroomed as the trade itself rapidly increased after 1808. One of the earliest tracts
to focus primarily on the internal trade was *A Portraiture of Domestic Slavery,
in the United States* (1817) by Jesse Torrey. In many ways this work illustrated
the transitional nature of the white antislavery movement at the time. Torrey, a
Pennsylvania physician, did not believe in racial equality and hinted that some
form of colonization to a distant part of the United States might be necessary,
but he strongly opposed slavery and argued vigorously against the domestic
trade and the evils that resulted from it. Like so many other visitors to the
South, Torrey claimed that seeing the slave trade firsthand made him feel physically ill, and it was this reaction coupled with witnessing the slave traders in
Washington, DC, that propelled him to write his tract. While Torrey's treatment of the domestic trade was new, his connection to the earlier abolitionists
can also be seen in his emphasis upon the uncontrolled nature of this traffic and how it encouraged the widespread kidnapping of free blacks and their
transportation south into slavery.[12]

By the mid-1820s, many new African-American organizations had developed
in the North. Much of their efforts went toward promoting issues of immediate
importance, such as mutual aid and cultural awareness, but they also fought
against the racism that was so rampant in American life, even among those
whites who were sympathetic toward their cause. For this reason, the struggle
against colonization preoccupied much of their time. Still, many of these free-
black groups likewise fought against slavery, and they too began attacking the
internal trade. In October 1828, the first black newspaper, the *Freedom's Journal*
of New York, called for an immediate end to the domestic trade and during its
two years of publication printed more than forty articles on the topic.[13]

Among white abolitionists, however, few paid much attention to this activity except for the influential Benjamin Lundy. During the 1810s and 1820s,

Lundy almost single-handedly among white Americans tried to organize some form of opposition besides colonization to a rapidly growing and ever more deeply entrenched slave system. Few abolitionists placed greater emphasis on the evils of the domestic trade than Lundy. Beginning with the first issue of his *Genius of Universal Emancipation* in 1821, Lundy printed a list of slaves sold at auction from a Charleston newspaper and gave accounts of slaves who committed suicide after being purchased by slave traders. Almost every issue of the paper thereafter made some mention of the domestic trade, including occasional woodcut illustrations of slave coffles with titles such as "Hail Columbia, Happy Land!" and "A Picture, Which Kings Might Laugh At!"[14]

One reason for Lundy's obsession with the slave trade was personal experience; it was an encounter with this traffic that had first converted him to abolitionism. Lundy had moved from his native New Jersey to Wheeling, Virginia, at the age of twenty and was shocked at seeing a coffle of slaves being driven south. He later recalled how this sight made "his young heart bound within his bosom, and his heated blood boil in his veins." The frequent repetition of such scenes caused him to make "*a solemn vow to Almighty God,* that, if favored with health and strength, he would break at least one link of that ponderous chain of oppression" and devote his life to abolishing slavery.[15]

Lundy had an acute awareness of the changes that were occurring in the economy of the Upper South. He understood that the interregional trade, and its effect on the price of slaves, would be the economic link upon which that subregion would commit itself to slavery. He also realized that, as the connection strengthened, "neither the moral force of precepts and examples, nor the enactment of penal laws, will have their proper effect while the 'breeding' of slaves is considered lucrative." Therefore, Lundy continuously stressed the dubious role that the Upper South played in the southern economy and referred to the region's slaveholders as "the most disgraceful whoremongers upon earth; they make a *business* of raising bastards and selling them for money; . . . [and] they oppose the work of emancipation *on this ground.*"[16]

Lundy likewise attacked the local slave traders, even though it almost cost him his life on one occasion. After moving from Tennessee to Baltimore in 1824, Lundy's criticisms fell especially hard on Austin Woolfolk and his family, the area's largest slave-trading operation. Lundy hounded them relentlessly until eventually, in January 1827, Woolfolk retaliated by accosting Lundy on the street and, according to the official report, "beat and stamped upon his head and face in a most furious and violent manner, until pulled off by the byestanders." Lundy sued for assault. Woolfolk admitted his actions, but in his defense exhibited articles written by Lundy which stated that the domestic slave trade was "barbarous, inhuman and unchristian" and that Woolfolk was "equally guilty in the sight of God with the man who was engaged in the African Slave Trade." While the judge was forced to fine Woolfolk $1 plus costs, he noted that the slave trade was a legal business in Maryland and also "beneficial to the state, as it removed a great many rogues and vagabonds who were a nuisance in the state."[17]

Most important, Benjamin Lundy was the man responsible for converting William Lloyd Garrison into an abolitionist. The two men met in 1828 and Garrison quickly became enthralled with Lundy's cause. A turning point came when Lundy delivered a speech in Boston centered on the extent of the domestic trade. When Lundy was rebuffed by a local minister who argued that the trade was beneficial because it was gradually abolishing slavery in the Upper South, Garrison sent a bitter letter to the editor of the *Boston Courier* defending Lundy and pointing out the dangers of "this profligate and inhuman traffic." Not long after, Garrison headed south and joined Lundy in his work on the *Genius of Universal Emancipation.*[18]

In Baltimore, the ever-present reality of the slave trade, as well as Lundy's strong influence, helped to make the domestic trade a prominent feature in Garrison's work. He revived an old column called the "Black List" and included in its accounts of the evils of slavery advertisements for slave sales and other horrors of the domestic trade. Garrison also attacked the local slave dealers and even went so far as to provoke a trader from his hometown of Newburyport, Massachusetts. After seeing Francis Todd's ship in the Baltimore harbor with its cargo of slaves bound for New Orleans, Garrison angrily wrote that men such as Todd, who were engaged in this "nefarious business," deserved to be "SENTENCED TO SOLITARY CONFINEMENT FOR LIFE; *they are the enemies of their own species—highway robbers and murderers.*" Todd sued Garrison for libel, and Garrison served two months in prison for inability to pay his fine. In jail, Garrison took full advantage of his situation. He wrote a vivid account of his trial and composed numerous public letters, including one to Todd, in which he asked: "Is not this horrible traffic offensive to God, and revolting to humanity?" Garrison also harassed the slave traders who came to the jail looking for bargains to purchase. In this he proved partially successful. Baltimore's largest slave trader, the thin-skinned Austin Woolfolk, had normally visited the jail each day. But during Garrison's tenure, he refused to enter.[19]

As with so many of the early abolitionists, the domestic slave trade was one of the few aspects of slavery that William Lloyd Garrison witnessed personally. His experience with Benjamin Lundy and firsthand exposure to the slave trade in Baltimore proved influential in developing his views about slavery and the need for its abolition. By the time he began publication of the *Liberator*, Garrison had acquired a full understanding of the crucial role that the slave trade played in perpetuating American slavery, as well as the powerful impact it had upon audiences, in both the North and South.[20]

II

In the 1830s the abolitionist movement exploded with new organizations and members, and virtually every group included the domestic trade somewhere in its antislavery efforts. At the first American Anti-Slavery Society meeting in December 1833, delegates approved a "Declaration of Sentiments" expressing the association's goals and intentions. Written by Garrison, this document praised the nation's revolutionary ancestors but noted that "*their* grievances, great as they were, were trifling in comparison with the wrongs and sufferings of those for whom we plead. Our fathers were never slaves—never bought and sold like cattle" nor "recognized by the laws, and treated by their fellow beings, as marketable commodities—as goods and chattels—as brute beasts." In the society's constitution, one of the organization's stated objectives was "to influence Congress to put an end to the domestic slave trade." The opening statement in the group's first periodical, the *American Anti-Slavery Reporter*, listed making "merchandize of God's image" among its criticisms of slavery, and in its first annual report the association called on all members to persevere "in the face of all opposition, till the seat of our nation's power and honor is no longer a slave-mart—till the coffle of the domestic traffic no longer stains with blood its weary track from the Potomac to the Mississippi."[21]

Several early antislavery publications focused exclusively on the domestic trade. One of the first was a public letter composed by Henry B. Stanton in the spring of 1834, shortly after the founding of the American Anti-Slavery Society. Stanton gathered information from his southern colleagues at the Lane Seminary in Ohio and, using their inside knowledge, described how the slave trade operated and gave numerous examples of the hardships that blacks suffered because of it. In this widely reprinted article, Stanton noted that "there has been no time when the domestic slave trade was so brisk as at present," and because of this trade he concluded that "the system is wrong at the foundation—and there the reform must commence."[22]

An even more comprehensive examination of the domestic trade was produced by the New England Anti-Slavery Society at its annual meeting in May 1834. A special committee, led by David Lee Child, compiled a lengthy document complete with numerous firsthand examples showing the extent of various atrocities resulting from the trade. Included in this portrait were tales of murder, suicide, rape, and kidnapping. The committee also asserted Congress's ability to stop it, made comparisons with the African trade, and explored the interregional trade's role in the Upper South, arguing it was "chargeable with the whole guilt of the continuance of slavery in several of the States." The report concluded with a resolution, which was passed unanimously, stating that the domestic trade "involves the crimes of murder, kidnapping and robbery, and is equally worthy with the foreign to be denounced and treated by human laws and tribunals as piracy, and those who carry it on as enemies of the human race."[23]

There were many reasons that the domestic slave trade played such a prominent role in the early years of organized antislavery activity. In addition to the personal experiences of Garrison and many of the other abolitionists, by the 1830s the interstate trade had become a pronounced feature of American life. As previously shown, the cotton boom of the 1820s and 1830s had led to a surging of the slave trade in the South, which not only supplied the abolitionists with more victims to use as examples but also supported the argument that slavery was not going to disappear on its own. Due to the basic nature of the trade, its horrors were likewise difficult to conceal. It would have been highly unusual if the antislavery movement had not taken advantage of this most public aspect of the institution. Finally, the slave trade was national in its operation. In his initial call for a nationwide antislavery society, Garrison argued that this organization should "take up those branches of the subject which are acknowledged to be of a national character," such as "the criminal and disgraceful commerce between the States, in slaves." Therefore, when abolitionist activity escalated in the early 1830s, it focused in large part on the domestic trade. Even foreign visitors commented upon this development. As the Swedish writer Carl Arfwedson noted in 1834: "The slave-trade is now become more than formerly a subject of discussion."[24]

The domestic trade's prominence in the early years of Garrisonian abolitionism foreshadowed the crucial role that this feature of slavery would play throughout the entire history of the movement, and the arguments developed at that time became the cornerstone of antislavery thought. The abolitionists based their call for the immediate abolition of slavery on their belief that slavery was a sin. And, for them, slavery was a sin because it was a crime against nature and a rebellion against God. According to the abolitionists, by transforming humans into property, by making them articles that could be bought and sold, slavery essentially turned people into "things." This not only contradicted God's intentions, it also interfered with man's relationship to God. Slavery destroyed the moral accountability of humans by making slaves answerable to their earthly masters and not to God. In effect, slavery had reversed the order of creation by putting man above God, and both slaveholders and God were competing for control over humankind. This is what they meant when the abolitionists continually referred to slave owners as "man-stealers." Slaveholders had stolen both the humanity from their slaves and humankind from God. Therefore, as one antislavery tract explained it, turning "*men into merchandise*" was a principle "openly at war with all the relations which God has established between His creatures, and between Himself and them," and any attempt to justify it was "sin."[25]

The abolitionists never tired of charging that slavery turned humans into property, and they frequently commented on the vital role that the ability to transfer this property from one owner to another played in sustaining the entire slave system. Beriah Green called it "the very root of American slavery," and in a lecture entitled "The Sin of Slavery," Amos Phelps contended that "*holding man as property*" was "the *starting point* whence all slavery originates—the *fundamental principle* on which it is based, and the *sustaining principle* by which alone its continued existence is secured." Gerrit Smith likewise made this argument, contending that "man's right to property in man" was the "foundation doctrine" of the institution. But Smith also noted the importance of the marketable quality of this property, when he insisted that the "traffic in human flesh" was "the very life-blood of slavery."[26]

The best illustration of the centrality of this issue for the abolitionist argument can be found in the work of Theodore Weld. When training new agents for the American Anti-Slavery Society, Weld defined slavery as "*holding & treating persons as things*." He maintained that this was "the essential sin of slavery" because "it takes man out of the sphere in which God placed him & puts him in a sphere designed to be occupied by others." In *The Bible against Slavery* (1837), Weld added that this process did "not merely unhumanize *one* individual, but UNIVERSAL MAN" because it annihilated all rights and destroyed man's relationship with God. Weld also made it clear that the sin of slavery was in large part based on the transformation of humans into commodities when he asserted that "ENSLAVING MEN IS REDUCING THEM TO ARTICLES OF PROPERTY, making free agents chattels, converting *persons* into *things*, sinking intelligence, accountability, immortality, into *merchandize*."[27]

For Weld and many other abolitionists, the transformation of humans into things was more sinful than any of the physical cruelties found in slavery, and for them, it formed the heart of their argument against the institution. Not only did they claim that slavery deprived the enslaved of their humanity on a spiritual level, but they also pointed out that slave owners frequently equated their human property with animals on a day-to-day basis, especially in market activity. They noted that both slaves and livestock were listed on the same sale notices and sold on the same auction blocks and that identical terminology was used for both. Weld observed that "the same terms are applied to slaves that are given to cattle. They are called 'stock.' So when the children of slaves are spoken of prospectively, they are called their 'increase;' the same term that is applied to flocks and herds," and "the female slaves that are mothers, are called 'breeders' till past child bearing." Most abolitionists used these same terms when attacking southern slavery. But, for them, using animal metaphors not only pointed out that humans were indeed being turned into things, but by illustrating how common these terms had become and by showing how easily people thought of their fellow humans in bestial images, they also emphasized how far slavery, and especially the slave trade, had gone toward "unhumanizing" everyone involved.[28]

III

In addition to playing a fundamental role in abolitionist ideology, the domestic trade also became an important symbol of the inherent cruelty of American slavery. By constantly presenting heartrending examples of slaves being sold, the abolitionists proved that such events were not isolated incidents but a common occurrence in the South. It is also important to note that slavery was no longer a part of everyday life in the North, and unlike previous generations, which had frequently witnessed slave sales, by the 1830s few northerners had any real experience with the trade. This made descriptions of such scenes all the more shocking. The sale of humans outraged most outsiders' perceptions of civilized behavior, and the abolitionists understood the effect that this distasteful feature of the system had on their audience, especially those individuals who may not have previously supported their cause. As one abolitionist put it: "I wish every pro-slavery man and woman in the North could witness one slave auction." The slave trade epitomized American slavery at its worst, and tales of families being divided, children torn from their mothers, and humans on an auction block simply could not be defended. No explanation was needed to show that such actions were wrong. Garrison explained this best when he stated, "I know that their bodies and spirits (which are God's) are daily sold under the hammer of the Auctioneer as articles of merchandize; I need no nice adjustment of abstractions, no metaphysical reasonings, to convince me, that such scenes are dreadful, and such practices impious."[29]

Subsequently, most antislavery publications included either copies of sale notices or some mention of the devastating scenes that the domestic trade produced. Often the abolitionists provided estimates of the number of slaves exported to the Deep South each year (as high as 120,000) to show the extent of this traffic. The rise of the cheap mass press during this period allowed the movement to flood the country with newspapers, pamphlets, almanacs, books, and broadsheets. One of its primary goals was to get every northerner to think of the whip, rampant sexual improprieties, and especially the auction block and slave trade whenever they thought of the South.[30]

One common practice was the use of pictorial illustrations. These items made the point vividly clear and helped the audience to visualize the evils of slavery. Often the subject was some aspect of the slave trade. In one poster, "Views of Slavery," four of the six pictures depicting the slave system were of the domestic trade. The purpose and effect of these drawings can best be understood in a note that appeared in the July 1836 issue of the *Anti-Slavery Record*. Usually the editor of the *Record* would create an "incendiary picture" of the more brutal aspects of slavery, but due to his absence no illustration was made for that number. So the paper instead printed a small woodcut drawing that was in use at that time in the southern press to announce upcoming slave sales. It depicted a black man on an auction block in the process of being sold. The *Record* criticized the hypocrisy of the South and its northern supporters who opposed the abolitionists for using similar illustrations, and noted: "Now, how does it come to pass, that this said picture when printed in a southern newspaper is perfectly harmless, but when printed in the Anti-Slavery Record is perfectly incendiary? We have nothing further to say about it till this question is answered."[31]

Also popular were firsthand reports by those who had witnessed the trade. Travelers' narratives always attracted readers in the antebellum era, and the abolitionists relied on them extensively. For most visitors, observing the slave trade was an unpleasant event that affected them deeply. Writers reported their disgust at seeing a slave coffle or witnessing a slave auction, and they used terms like "shocking" and "horrifying" to describe their reactions. When the Englishman George Featherstonhaugh encountered a slave coffle in western Virginia, he claimed he "had never seen so revolting a sight before," and the British author Harriet Martineau called a trip to a slave auction in Charleston "the most infernal sight I ever beheld."[32]

Throughout the antebellum period, exposure to the slave trade often influenced foreigners' views on American slavery. After visiting a slave mart in New Orleans, the British poet Charles Mackay explained: "I felt a sensation something similar to that of the first qualm of sea-sickness" and "entertained at that moment such a hatred of slavery that, had it been in my power to abolish it in one instant off the face of the earth by the mere expression of my will, slavery at that instant would have ceased to exist." The New Orleans market also caused the Swedish feminist Fredrika Bremer to sum up the feelings of many when she remarked that "no sermon, no anti-slavery oration could speak so powerfully against the institution of slavery as this slave-auction itself."[33]

It is not surprising, then, that abolitionists capitalized on this widely available and powerful indictment of the slave system and frequently reprinted excerpts from the more famous accounts. In addition, they also published reports submitted by readers relating their encounters with the trade. Some-times abolitionists even made journeys of their own into the South and observed the system for themselves. One of the more influential accounts was by Joshua Leavitt, editor of the *New York Evangelist* and founding member of the Ameri-can Anti-Slavery Society. In 1834, Leavitt visited the Franklin & Armfield offices in Alexandria and inspected both the jail and one of the firm's slave ships. His findings were later widely circulated in antislavery publications.[34]

Even more effective and fascinating for northern audiences were accounts by former residents of the South. Unlike tourists, who had to make their impressions from scant observations, native southerners could explain slavery's workings with a greater empathy and depth. They had experienced the slave system on an everyday basis and their descriptions had an air of authenticity that few outside accounts could. For this reason, individuals like the Grimké sisters and James Birney became important figures in the antislavery move-ment. The Grimkés attracted attention not only for their gender and speaking abilities but also because they had an intimate knowledge of the role that slav-ery played in Charleston society. The same was true for Birney. Here was a man who had lived in both Kentucky and Alabama and who had bought and sold slaves. He became one of the most popular abolitionist speakers of the 1830s, in part because of his experience with slavery and the slave trade throughout the South.[35]

The tactic of using firsthand accounts to show the evils of southern slav-ery reached its culmination with the appearance of Theodore Weld's *American Slavery As It Is* in 1839. Wanting to attack slavery using the slaveholders' own words, Weld tied together statements from hundreds of witnesses, including both former and present residents of the South, travelers' accounts, articles from the southern press, and speeches from Congress. While this work was an entire encyclopedia of horrors, much of the testimony centered around the domestic trade. There were heartrending descriptions of overland coffles and slave auctions, accounts of forced breeding and families divided, and high esti-mates as to the number of free blacks kidnapped and foreign slaves illegally smuggled into the country. Advertisements for slave sales filled pages, and there were even statements from former slave traders. The slave trade's importance can best be seen in the introduction, in which Weld argued that everyone knew intrinsically that slavery was wrong, and "whoever denies this, his lips libel his heart." Weld asked the reader to imagine himself a slave: "Give him an hour to prepare his wife and children for a life of slavery; bid him make haste and get ready their necks for the yoke, and their wrists for the coffle chains, then look at his pale lips and trembling knees, and you have *nature's* testimony against slavery." *American Slavery As It Is* was an immediate success, selling more than 100,000 copies the first year and eventually more than any other antislavery tract, making it the most important publication produced in the first two decades of the movement.[36]

During the 1830s, the antislavery movement also began to recognize the importance of another group of ex-southerners—former slaves. Northern-born black abolitionists had been active since the beginning of organized anti-slavery activity and played a crucial role in the early years of the movement. By the end of the decade, however, a new type of black abolitionist appeared as more and more former slaves went public about their experiences under slavery.[37] Some abolitionists, such as Theodore Weld, understood the impact that black speakers (especially former slaves) had on northern audiences and promoted their use.[38] By the early 1840s, both black lecturers and slave narratives had become extremely popular. Former slaves at an antislavery meeting always drew a crowd, and many of the slave narratives became instant bestsellers and were reprinted again and again. Because of their sincerity and unique perspective, former slaves did much for spreading the argument against slavery and were important in converting many northern whites.[39]

The primary goal of the black abolitionists was to inform those outside of the South of the inherent cruelty of American slavery, and, not surprisingly, the domestic trade played a central role in their work. Virtually all of the major written accounts mentioned the sale of either the authors themselves or members of their families. One of Moses Grandy's earliest memories was of his mother being beaten for the scene she made when his brother had been sold. Josiah Henson fled when threatened with sale, and Henry Box Brown carried out his famous escape after witnessing his wife and children driven away in a coffle. Because of the "chattel principle" and the ever-present possibility of sale, James W. C. Pennington ridiculed the notion of slavery being milder in the Upper South or some owners being kinder than others: "They are not masters of the system. The system is master of them; and the slaves are their vassals."[40] Both Henry Bibb and Solomon Northup gave detailed and gripping accounts of being transferred by slave traders from the Upper South to New Orleans, and William Wells Brown spent the longest year of his life when he was hired out to a slave trader and forced to prepare other slaves for sale. Even Lunsford Lane, who admitted that his lot had been "a favored one for a slave," lived in constant fear of being sold south, a fate that he called "infinitely worse than the terrors of death."[41]

The most famous and influential of the black abolitionists, however, was Frederick Douglass. After escaping from slavery in 1838, Douglass made his first public speech three years later, and in 1845, his first autobiography appeared. While Douglass had never been sold himself, the slave trade still played a fundamental role in his life. As a child in Maryland, Douglass was haunted by the threat of sale, and many of his immediate family members had been sold south. Some of the most moving passages in his *Narrative* were those relating to the domestic trade: the forcible separation from his mother as a small child; the trauma and indignity associated with the division of his owner's estate; being harassed by the local slave traders outside the Easton jail; and the painful knowledge that his grandmother was living in isolation after having her children, grandchildren, and great-grandchildren sold away from her.

The buying and selling of humans was also a major element in Douglass's speeches. He frequently spoke about families being torn apart and argued that in the Upper South the domestic trade was "the most cruel feature of the system." For effect, Douglass even used the image of himself upon the auction block and claimed that he had been sold. But, most important, the slave trade was a central theme in what one biographer has called "perhaps the greatest antislavery oration ever given." In this speech, "What to the Slave Is the Fourth of July?" Douglass used the internal slave trade as his foremost example of the "revolting barbarity and shameless hypocrisy" of American society. He described in detail the horrible realities of this trade and noted that, while equal in condemnation to the African trade, it was "sustained by American politics and American religion." Douglass saw little reason to celebrate the nation's independence when such a "murderous traffic" was "in active operation in this boasted republic."[42]

IV

Another important theme in the abolitionist argument was the destructive effect that slavery, and especially the slave trade, had on southern families. Despite the paternalistic arguments used by many white southerners to defend their way of life, abolitionists continually reminded their audience of the "strange misnomer" of referring to slavery as the "domestic institution." In their eyes, nothing could have been further from the truth, as they saw the disruption of southern families, both black and white, as central to the institution of slavery. Consequently, they filled their publications with tales of children torn from their mothers and husbands from their wives, women sold for prostitution, forced breeding farms, and the depravity of licentious planters and their sons.[43]

While the abolitionists directed this aspect of their argument to both male and female audiences, it played an especially prominent role in their appeals to northern women. Special tracts were written for female readers and virtually all focused on the destructive effect that slavery had on southern families. In one article that appeared in the *Anti-Slavery Record*, women were asked: "Do the mothers of our land know that American slavery, both in theory and practice is nothing but a system of *tearing asunder the family ties?*" In *Slavery Illustrated in*

Its Effects upon Woman and Domestic Society (1837), these same female readers were told that it was "the duty and privilege of women" to correct this.[44]

One reason that both male and female abolitionists emphasized slavery's effect upon families in their appeals to women was their belief that issues concerning the domestic sphere were of special importance to women and that this was an area in which women had both a right and a moral responsibility to act. Female abolitionists also used this argument when justifying their presence in the public sphere. In its opening address, the New York Female Anti-Slavery Society argued that "whatever else it may be, slaveholding must be eminently *a domestic evil*. It works its mischiefs among the sweet charities which naturally flourish in the family circle. . . . Can it be pretended that here is ground in which *woman* has no interest?" Because of its harmful effect upon families, for most women, the slave trade was the harshest of all of the evils of slavery, and even those who disagreed with the abolitionists could concur that this was an aspect of the institution that women had a responsibility to oppose. In her essay attacking the antislavery movement as being too extreme and outside the proper sphere of women, Catharine Beecher conceded that the internal trade was a wrong that Christian women, through their gentle persuasion, could do much to bring to an end.[45]

One important argument used when appealing to women was the idea of an interrelated sisterhood and that injustices to women in slavery were injustices to women everywhere. At the first national female antislavery convention, Angelina Grimké claimed that northern women needed to become more involved, because the women in slavery "*are our sisters*; and to us, as women, they have a right to look for sympathy with their sorrows, and effort and prayer for their rescue." Sarah Grimké also voiced this idea in her letter "On the Condition of Women in the United States" (1837). After giving numerous examples of how "women are bought and sold in our slave markets, to gratify the brutal lust of those who bear the name of Christians," she then wondered, "Can any American woman look at these scenes of shocking licentiousness and cruelty, and fold her hands in apathy and say, 'I have nothing to do with slavery'? *She cannot and be guiltless.*"[46]

The abolitionists often told of the hardships suffered by slaves and asked their audiences to change places and imagine how they would react if placed in a similar situation. While this question was posed to both men and women, once again, it proved especially effective with female audiences. One popular speaker on the women's issue in the 1850s was Susan B. Anthony, who often made reference to the slave trade in her speeches. In "Make the Slave's Case Our Own" (1859), Anthony asked her audience to "feel that it is our own children, that are ruthlessly torn from our yearning *mother* hearts, & driven in the 'coffle gang,' through burning suns, and drenching rains, to be sold on the auc-

tion block to the *highest bidder.*" The abolitionists usually focused their attention on women in the North, but occasional efforts were also made to reach southern women. In her *Appeal to the Christian Women of the South* (1836), Angelina Grimké described how southern men sold their own daughters, and then asked her readers to imagine how they would feel if their children were enslaved.[47]

The domestic slave trade also played a prominent role in the abolitionist message to children. The *Liberator* had a regular "Juvenile Department" that was headed by a woodcut drawing of a slave auction. The sketch featured a small black child standing alone on the block crying for his mother, who stands to the side looking on in agony. Among the crowd watching is a white child holding his mother's hand. The column often featured copies of advertisements of young people for sale. After such pieces, readers were asked, "Are you not very thankful that you are not slaves? Can't you do something for these slave children?" The *Anti-Slavery Almanac* also had a "Children's Department." In the 1837 issue, the column featured an illustration of two black sisters holding each other tight. The accompanying text told of slaveholders who "sometimes tear such little children away from their parents, and sell them to cruel men who will never let them see their mothers while they live." Following this piece was another illustrated story of a mother who killed her own children rather than see them sold.[48] One regular tract for young people was the *Slave's Friend.* This inexpensive monthly was simply written on small-sized pages to fit into little hands. It was described as containing "pretty pictures, sweet hymns, and interesting stories." In addition to reprinting numerous advertisements for the sale of children, the "interesting stories" were often about the domestic trade and had titles such as "The Slave-trader," "The Public Auction," "Selling Human Beings," and "Taking Away a Baby." The "pretty pictures" included "Stolen Children," "The Afflicted Mother," "The Coffle-Yoke," and "Soul-Drivers." Abolitionists also emphasized the slave trade in their personal appeals to children. When Angelina Grimké visited the Boston Juvenile Anti-Slavery Society in 1837, she told of seeing twenty children marched through the streets of Charleston in chains on their way to New Orleans for sale.[49]

The abolitionists' message to children might sound harsh to modern ears, but they wanted to make a dramatic and lasting impression on their young audiences. By asking small children to imagine the horrible realities of slavery, such as being torn from their parents, abolitionists personalized the slave experience and persuaded them that slavery was wrong. While this tactic was employed on people of all ages, it carried special importance with the young. They were the future, and it was hoped that they would carry with them a lifelong understanding of the evils of slavery and fight for its demise.

After the 1830s, the moral suasionist wing of the abolitionist movement became increasingly eclipsed by political antislavery. The domestic trade, however, continued to play an important role in the moral argument against slavery. This can be best seen in Harriet Beecher Stowe's *Uncle Tom's Cabin* (1852). From the opening scene, when the slave trader Haley convinces the paternalistic planter Shelby to part with his two favorite slaves, to her concluding remarks about how the internal trade was "at this very moment, riving thousands of hearts, shattering thousands of families, and driving a helpless and sensitive race to frenzy and despair," Stowe continually made the point that the buying and selling of humans was not an isolated occurrence but a fundamental and frequent requirement of American slavery. Virtually every black character experienced the devastating effects of sale. Uncle Tom himself was forced into a slave coffle and sold three times, including once at a New Orleans auction house. More than any other writer, Stowe was able to convey the trauma associated with the forcible separation of mother and child. Not only did her readers hold their breath as Eliza, clutching her son, skipped across the frozen ice, but they certainly understood when she earlier asked: "If it were *your* Harry, mother, or your Willie, that were going to be torn from you by a brutal trader, to-morrow morning, . . . how fast could *you* walk?"[50]

Stowe's main goal, however, was more than just getting her audience to empathize with the sufferings of a few individuals or to recognize that the slave trade was a constant presence in southern life. She was also arguing that as long as humans were objects of trade, slavery would always be an inherently evil institution and that even the best intentions of well-meaning people were powerless to prevent its destructive effects. As she noted in the first chapter, "So long as the law considers all these human beings, with beating hearts and living affections, only as so many *things* belonging to a master, . . . it is impossible to make anything beautiful or desirable in the best regulated administration of slavery." Time and again, Stowe illustrated this point, that it did not matter what type of owner one had or where in the South one lived, as long as slaves were salable property and could be taken to settle debts, families would be destroyed and the notions of kind masters or mild forms of slavery were meaningless.[51]

Uncle Tom's Cabin hit a responsive chord among the American public, selling more than 300,000 copies in its first year of publication. Although the majority of northerners did not consider themselves to be abolitionists, Harriet Beecher Stowe undoubtedly strengthened whatever reservations they previously had about the South's peculiar institution. More than any other work, her book used the domestic slave trade to present the moral argument against slavery, and it most certainly helped to influence many outsiders' impressions of slavery and the South.

Besides being essential for abolitionist ideology and a prominent symbol of the inherent cruelty of American slavery, the domestic slave trade also played a fundamental role in the development of the abolitionists' political attack against slavery. Important to their argument was their acute understanding of the regional differences within the South and how the interregional trade functioned as the lifeblood of the southern slave system. The abolitionists recognized the crucial economic relationship that the slave trade had created between the Upper South and the Lower South and how this served to strengthen the institution throughout the region. They also realized that this relationship was subject to congressional regulation, and it was here that they sought a political solution for abolishing slavery.

One of the most effective speakers on the regional differences within the South was James Birney. His experience as a slaveholder in both Kentucky and Alabama made him an expert on the relationship between the slave-selling and slave-buying states, and he often discussed this in his speeches and writings. In one of his first public appearances, at the second annual meeting of the American Anti-Slavery Society in 1835, Birney told his audience that, contrary to popular opinion, slavery was not any milder in the Upper South than in the Lower South, nor less harsh than in the past. According to Birney, however, slavery was changing. The number of "coffles of slaves traversing the country to a market" was increasing daily, and "the system now growing into practice is for the farming states to supply those farther south with slaves, just as regularly and systematically [as] the slave coast of Africa used to supply the colonists of Brazil or St. Domingo." A few months later, Birney even claimed that slavery in the Upper South "would, long since, have been relinquished, had it not been for the establishment of the American Slave trade, intoxicating the holders of the marketable commodity, every where, and by its great profits, blinding them to the inhumanity of the traffic."[52]

In spite of what many northerners believed, Birney and the other abolitionists made it clear that slavery was not declining in the Upper South, but becoming more entrenched, mainly because of the interregional slave trade. This trade kept the Upper South committed to the slave system by providing a means for transferring labor that it found excess, or "undesirable," to other parts of the country that had a greater demand for it. And the slave trade even strengthened the institution in the Upper South by providing an incentive for slaveholders to encourage breeding among their slaves. Children were reared specifically to be shipped to the Deep South market, and human chattel had become the main export from the states in that region.

Given this keen understanding of the importance of the interregional trade for maintaining the southern slave system, it is not surprising, then, that the abolitionists saw the domestic trade as the key to the political destruction of slavery. In an 1838 tract, Birney argued that if the slave-selling states "could be restrained from the *commerce* in slaves, slavery could not be supported by them for any length of time, or to any considerable extent."[53] Others pushed this line of reasoning even further, asserting that the interstate slave trade was the linchpin that held the entire system together, and as such, it was here that they needed to focus their attack. In a speech before the sixth annual meeting of the American Anti-Slavery Society, Henry B. Stanton called the internal trade "the great jugular vein of slavery" and argued that if they could "cut this vein, slavery would die of starvation in the southern, and of apoplexy in the northern slave states." The abolitionist who most thoroughly developed this argument, however, was Alvan Stewart of New York. Stewart made the interstate trade a major topic in his speeches and even referred to it as "the great door to the slave Bastile." In an 1836 speech, Stewart claimed that if the interregional trade could be abolished, "slavery would come to an end by its own weight, in Virginia, Maryland, Kentucky, Tennessee, and the western parts of North and South Carolina" and that within ten years, two-thirds of the slaves in the United States would be freed.[54]

Alvan Stewart, and most other abolitionists, believed that banning the interregional slave trade was not only desirable but also legally possible. While the majority of abolitionists did not think that Congress had the right to interfere with slavery in the states, from the beginning of the movement, the American Anti-Slavery Society and virtually every other antislavery group had argued that Congress had the right to regulate the interstate trade. They based this opinion on constitutional interpretation and historical precedent. They believed that the nation's founders had wanted to eliminate slavery and had given Congress the power to do so in the Constitution.[55]

Much of their argument was based on the nation's previous actions against the African slave trade. The abolitionists noted that earlier in the century the country had declared the African trade to be a great moral crime and treated it as piracy, made punishable by death. In their eyes, the domestic trade was no different, and they often argued that it was even worse because it dealt in American-born slaves. The abolitionists also used the nation's earlier actions against the African trade as the basis for arguing that Congress had the power to abolish the interstate trade. As Alvan Stewart put it: "The same words, clauses and sections of the Constitution, which gave Congress the power to abolish the African slave trade, give Congress the ability to pass a law to abolish the internal slave trade now carried on between the slave States, in defiance of the loudest cries of humanity."[56]

The main clause of the Constitution to which Stewart referred was Article 1, section 8, which grants Congress the power "to regulate Commerce with foreign Nations, and among the several States." The abolitionists believed that this clause gave Congress the power to regulate all forms of commerce, including the traffic in human property, and it was primarily on this point that they based their argument that Congress had the right to abolish the interstate trade. One of the most prominent abolitionist writers on this subject was William Jay, a New York judge and son of the first chief justice, John Jay. In *A View of the Action of the Federal Government, in Behalf of Slavery* (1839), Jay argued that the commerce clause was the sole authority for Congress's power to abolish the African trade, and he noted that when it did so in 1808, few people questioned its right. Jay then made a similar claim for the domestic trade, asking, "By what logic then will it be shown that the power to regulate the commerce among the several States, does not include the power to interdict a traffic in men, women, and children? Is it more wicked, more base, more cruel, to traffic in African savages than in native born Americans?"[57]

Also important for the abolitionists' argument was Article 1, section 9, which states that "the Migration or Importation of such Persons as any of the States now existing shall think proper to admit, shall not be prohibited by the Congress prior to the Year one thousand eight hundred and eight." According to the abolitionists, this clause was added because at the time of the Constitution's framing it was so well understood that Congress had the power to abolish the African trade, that another clause was felt necessary to protect the slave-owning interests in the Deep South for a limited number of years. In other words, by denying Congress the power to prohibit the African trade for twenty years, this was proof that Congress did have the power to destroy it. Otherwise, there would have been no need to temporarily restrict Congress's right to do so if it did not already have this power. As Gerrit Smith phrased it in a public letter to Henry Clay, "The implication in this clause of the existence of the power in question, is as conclusive, as would be the express and positive grant of it." Smith also noted that this clause made the founders' intentions clear as to what this power entailed: "The power of Congress over 'migration or importation,' which this clause implies, is a power not merely to 'regulate,' as you define the word, but to 'prohibit.'" Therefore, according to the abolitionists, Article 1, section 9, proved that Congress had the power to prohibit as well as to regulate the slave trade, and, in addition, by using the words "migration" and "importation" this clause had granted to Congress, after 1808, the power to prohibit not only the importation of slaves from Africa but also the migration of slaves across state lines.[58]

Besides constitutional arguments, there were several historical precedents for congressional regulation of the interstate slave trade. In the Louisiana

Ordinance Bill of 1804, Congress had prohibited the importation of slaves into the territory for sale. Also, when the African trade was banned, Congress set limitations on the coastal trade, making it illegal to transport slaves in ships of less than forty tons. After citing this earlier example, William Jay noted that Congress clearly had the power to destroy the entire coastal slave trade, if for no other reason than "it would not be easy to show that the Constitution forbids its prohibition in vessels *over* forty tons." Moreover, if Congress could regulate the coastal trade, the same power should apply to the overland trade as well.[59]

The most influential precedent, however, came from the Missouri debates of 1819–1820, when congressmen argued over the question of Congress's ability to prevent the spread of slavery, and the slave trade, into the new states and territories. Although much of this debate focused on the migration and importation clause and on the question of planters migrating with their slaves, numerous speeches were made concerning the regulation of the interstate slave trade, and practically all of the arguments that the abolitionists were later to use appeared at this time. Representative John Sergeant of Pennsylvania maintained that "slaves are every where articles of trade, the subject of traffic and commerce," and "the general power to regulate commerce, includes in it, of course, a power to regulate this kind of commerce." Senator William Trimble of Ohio was one of many northerners who made comparisons to the African trade, claiming that "if Congress has the power to prohibit the importation of slaves from foreign countries, (which I believe has not been doubted,) they have the same power to prohibit the migration or transportation of slaves from one State to another State. . . . The terms in which the powers are granted are in both cases precisely the same." Southerners, however, disagreed, in part arguing that the word "migration" did not refer to slaves at all but instead to the influx of white immigrants who had entered the country. The northerners scoffed at this argument, countering that the founders' intentions were, as Senator David Morril of New Hampshire put it, "too clear to admit a doubt." Not wanting to taint the Constitution with the word "slave," they had substituted the phrase "such Persons," and everyone knew that this clause referred to the migration and importation of slaves. The founders had desired the eventual elimination of slavery and had sought to do so by granting to Congress, after a twenty-year delay, the power to prohibit both the importation of slaves from Africa and the migration of slaves across state lines. Included in this power was the ability to regulate the interstate trade in slaves. Among the well-known politicians of the time who endorsed this opinion were John Jay, Daniel Webster, and John Quincy Adams.[60]

The abolitionists also claimed that Congress had control over slavery and the slave trade in the District of Columbia. They pointed to Article 1, section 8, of the Constitution, which grants Congress the power to "exercise exclusive Legislation in all Cases whatsoever" over the District of Columbia. While most Americans generally agreed that Congress had jurisdiction over DC, by the 1830s many southerners were arguing that Congress had no right to regulate issues relating to slavery in the District of Columbia without the consent of Virginia and Maryland.

Once again, the abolitionists had several precedents to support their argument, including the fact that Congress was already regulating the slave trade in DC. As William Jay noted, "The very fact that slave traders are *licensed in the District*, is a full and complete acknowledgement that there is authority competent to forbid their nefarious business."[61] The abolitionists also had several precedents from southerners themselves. As early as 1802, in a grievance to Congress, a grand jury from Alexandria demanded "legislative redress" from slave traders coming into DC to pursue "a traffic fraught with so much misery." In 1829, after more than 1,000 residents petitioned Congress, another Washington grand jury asked Congress to exclude "this *disgusting traffic* from the District." Congress responded with a resolution, introduced by Representative Charles Miner of Pennsylvania, to "inquire into the slave trade as it exists in and is carried on through the District." Although no action was ultimately taken, Miner exposed many of the hardships caused by the trade and demonstrated how prevalent it had become in the nation's capital.[62]

From the beginning of the movement, the abolitionists understood the symbolic importance of slavery, and especially the slave trade, in the District of Columbia. Such activities in the nation's capital were disconcerting to all and an embarrassment to the entire country. According to Lydia Maria Child, "the disgrace of such scenes in the capital of our republic cannot be otherwise than painful to every patriotic mind; while they furnish materials for the most pungent satire to other nations," and "foreigners, particularly those who come here with enthusiastic ideas of American freedom, are amazed and disgusted at the sight."[63]

It is not surprising that the abolitionists constantly pointed out the hypocrisy of buying and selling humans in the capital of the so-called land of the free. Or, as one broadside proclaimed, the District of Columbia had become "ONE OF THE GREATEST AND MOST CRUEL SLAVE MARKETS IN THE WORLD!"[64] Abolitionists frequently described how the slave pens could be seen from the Capitol and how the voices of auctioneers and slaves being sold mingled with the oratory of the republic's statesmen legislating in Congress. One recurrent account told of an enslaved man raising his chained fist and singing out "Hail Columbia, happy land!" as he passed by the Capitol steps in a coffle bound for the Deep South. The importance of the slave trade's presence

Illustration showing the exodus of a slave coffle from Joseph Neal's slave pen on Seventh Street in Washington, DC, across the street from where the National Air and Space Museum is located today. From the broadside "Slave Market of America" published by the American Anti-Slavery Society in 1836. Courtesy of the Library of Congress.

in the nation's capital can be seen as early as the first issue of the *Liberator*, in which two articles on the subject appeared on the front page, and it continued to be a prominent theme in abolitionist publications thereafter. One of the more graphic works devoted solely to the problem was a large broadside entitled "Slave Market of America." This poster contained numerous facts about the slave trade in the capital, including copies of advertisements of slaves for sale, a map of the city noting all of the traders' addresses, and a variety of woodcut illustrations featuring slave ships, coffles, auctions, and slave traders' jails—with views from both inside and out.[65]

But the presence of slavery and the slave trade in the District of Columbia was also important because, according to the abolitionists, it was one portion of the slave system where northerners bore partial responsibility and over which they did have some control. The abolitionists occasionally noted how

Illustration of free people of color being sold into slavery in Washington, DC, for failure to pay their jail fees. From the broadside "Slave Market of America" published by the American Anti-Slavery Society in 1836. Courtesy of the Library of Congress.

northerners contributed to supporting the domestic trade through their business investments or inheritances in the South.[66] Even more common, however, was their complaint that northern tax money went to building and maintaining public jails in the nation's capital, which, according to one abolitionist, were used by the slave dealers to store "the victims of their infernal traffic." In addition, the $400 licensing fee that these traders paid, or the "price of blood" as the Grimké sisters put it, was "thrown into the coffers of the nation." But the main problem was that northern congressmen allowed this to happen and refused to act upon their constitutional right to prevent it. Therefore, many abolitionists argued that the guilt for these evils rested not just on the South but upon the entire nation.[67]

The primary action that the abolitionists proposed was petitioning both the state and federal governments for relief. Petitions against slavery and the slave trade had appeared as early as the Washington administration, but during the 1830s their numbers soared, especially after the passage in 1836 of the infamous "gag rule" that prohibited the reading of antislavery petitions on the floor of Congress.[68] The topics represented in the petition drives covered a range of subjects, but as a circular to antislavery women noted, the most important object was "obtaining petitions for the abolition of slavery in the District of

"THE HOME OF THE OPPRESSED."

CAPITOL OF THE UNITED STATES. "HAIL COLUMBIA."

Illustration of a slave coffle marching past the U.S. Capitol on the way to the Lower South, where the slaves will be sold. The abolitionists used such powerful images to expose the hypocrisy of slavery in the so-called land of the free. From the broadside "Slave Market of America" published by the American Anti-Slavery Society in 1836. Courtesy of the Library of Congress.

Columbia and the Territory of Florida, and the cessation of the internal slave-trade; all of which are generally conceded to be perfectly within the power of Congress." While the issues often overlapped, and multiple petitions were common, the largest number concerned banning slavery in the nation's capital. Few people questioned Congress's jurisdiction over the District of Columbia, and they naturally felt more comfortable supporting this measure than the far more radical proposal to prohibit the interstate slave trade. Some abolitionists, such as Alvan Stewart, protested, arguing that "slavery never can be abolished in the District of Columbia or the Territories, with any expectation of advantage, until the internal slave trade is abolished between the States."[69]

Nevertheless, in many ways, the petition drive proved to be a limited success, if for no other reason than it increased the growing sense of a threatening "Slave Power" out to deprive northerners of their right to petition and other constitutional rights. But, in addition, it also heightened awareness that the domestic trade was, as one New Hampshire group put it, "an enormous abuse which calls loudly for redress" and that the people had a duty to speak out

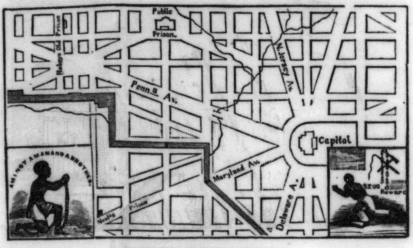

THE RESIDENCE OF 7000 SLAVES.

PART OF WASHINGTON CITY.

Illustration of the location of the three main slave pens in Washington, DC, where slaves were kept while awaiting their transport to the Lower South for sale (*top left*, William Robey's Old Prison and the Public Prison; *lower left*, Joseph Neal's Prison). From the broadside "Slave Market of America" published by the American Anti-Slavery Society in 1836. Courtesy of the Library of Congress.

against it. On the 1,496 petitions presented to the House of Representatives between December 1838 and March 1839, 54,547 people signed their names to petitions calling for a ban on the interstate slave trade, second only to the 80,755 signatures for the abolition of slavery in the District of Columbia.[70]

VI

The response to the petition drives stimulated many abolitionists to pursue political action elsewhere, and the domestic trade remained an integral part of their campaign. One tactic that increased during the late 1830s was the practice of "calling out," or canvassing political candidates. Those running for office were asked to supply their answers to questions such as "whether Congress ought not forthwith to exercise its whole Constitutional power for the suppression of the Domestic slave trade?" The individual's response would then be published and readers were asked to vote accordingly. Candidates often refused to answer, but in areas with high abolitionist sentiment, the tactic proved effective. There were also some successes on the state level. In 1838, in response to abolitionist pressure, the Massachusetts state legislature passed resolutions instructing its congressional delegation that, among other things, "Congress has, by the Constitution, power to abolish the traffic in slaves, between different States of the Union" and "that the exercise of this power is demanded by the principles of humanity and justice." Later that year, the Vermont legislature adopted similar resolutions.[71]

A few individuals also spoke out on this issue in Congress. Representative William Slade of Vermont and Senator Thomas Morris of Ohio both delivered speeches on the floor of Congress condemning slavery and the slave trade in the District of Columbia. Although he was no abolitionist, one of the most notable early supporters was John Quincy Adams, who presented thousands of petitions to Congress, including those for the prohibition of the interstate trade. Once, Adams even offered a resolution to have an official count made of the number of slaves exported from and imported into the various southern ports by the coastal trade. But, as he noted, "There was what Napoleon would have called a superb 'No!' returned to my request from the servile side of the House."[72]

When the Liberty party was formed in 1840, all of the original founders thought that Congress had the right to abolish the interstate slave trade and advocated that it do so. The program they developed was a continuation of the ideas and tactics they had formed during the previous decade. They called for congressional action against slavery in all areas under federal control, which included abolishing slavery in the District of Columbia and the territories, as well as prohibiting the interstate trade. In addition, the political abolitionists continued to give the slave trade a prominent place in their speeches and writings, and for many, it was still seen as the key to the destruction of the institution. According to one of their political tracts, once the slave trade was removed, slavery would die of "*surfeit*" in the Upper South and of "*starvation*" in the Lower South, and "thus by *your vote*, and the votes of Northern men, can slavery be struck lifeless at both extremes."[73]

Despite the importance that members of the Liberty party gave to abolishing the interstate trade, by the late 1840s and 1850s this issue began to receive less attention, even as the political and economic critique of slavery took on greater prominence in the North. One reason was that some abolitionists, such as William Goodell and Gerrit Smith, had developed more extreme views about the federal government's power over slavery and now argued that Congress had the right to abolish slavery not only in areas under federal control but also in the states where it already existed. Therefore, they did not see an attack on the interstate trade as a "practical aim" when they believed that Congress had the power to abolish slavery everywhere.[74]

The main reason for this change can be found in the decision that the political abolitionists made in the late 1840s to broaden their base of support. The inevitable result was a dilution of antislavery principles. To attract as many voters as possible, new issues were added and the more radical ideas, such as abolishing the interstate trade, were given less attention. The best example of this was in the alterations that occurred in the party platforms. Beginning with the Free Soil platform of 1848 and continuing through the Republican platforms of 1856 and 1860, the abolition of the interstate slave trade was no longer explicitly called for, but only implied in the demand that the federal government "relieve itself from all responsibility for the existence or continuance of slavery."[75]

Despite its decreased prominence, the elimination of the domestic slave trade continued to play an important role in antislavery politics. While it was touted less and less as the key to the removal of slavery and advocated by only a minority of Free Soil and Republican politicians, many still believed that the interstate trade was an essential goal in the political attack against slavery. This was especially true for the radicals, who interpreted their parties' platforms as calling for the slave trade's prohibition.[76]

In addition, the domestic trade became a special issue for some politicians, such as Joshua Giddings of Ohio. In 1838, Giddings was elected to the House of Representatives after campaigning on the platform that Congress had both the moral duty and legal power to abolish slavery and the slave trade in the District of Columbia and to prohibit the coastal slave trade. Within weeks of his arrival in Washington, his opposition to the domestic trade intensified after he witnessed a coffle of slaves heading south. The event affected him deeply, and he responded by making a major speech in Congress attacking the slave trade in the District of Columbia and arguing, among other things, against continuing "the seat of Government in the midst of a magnificent slave market."[77]

Southerners reacted with an uproar, but it was nothing compared to the anger that Giddings instilled in them three years later. In 1841 an American ship, the *Creole*, was transporting slaves from Virginia to New Orleans when several slaves revolted, killed one owner, and forced the captain to sail to the Bahamas. When the British freed the slaves, southerners demanded compensation, angering many northerners who did not want their government involved in protecting the coastal slave trade. Giddings fueled this resentment by presenting nine resolutions to Congress (which had been written by Theodore Weld, then working for Giddings as a researcher). In these resolutions, Giddings argued that the coastal trade was illegal and that all slaves became free once they left territorial waters. Therefore, the persons on board the *Creole* had violated no laws and were only protecting their natural rights of personal liberty when they attacked their captors. The House responded by censuring Giddings, who immediately resigned his seat. In a special election, Giddings was overwhelmingly reelected, carrying 95 percent of the vote. Giddings's reelection, for all practical purposes, ended the gag rule in Congress, and upon his return, he praised the "heroism" of the *Creole* slaves and continued his attack on the interstate trade.[78]

The slave trade also remained an important enough issue to be included in the famous Compromise of 1850. Most important, northerners had managed to get a resolution approved that prohibited bringing slaves into the District of Columbia for sale. While this legislation disturbed many southerners, who thought it might set a dangerous precedent, it also angered most abolitionists, who believed that it did not go far enough. Not only did it not abolish slavery in DC nor prohibit the local traffic in slaves already there (which continued as before), but as William Jay later pointed out, while "something was indeed gained to the *character* of the national capital, by prohibiting the importation of slaves for sale," nothing was done for "the cause of humanity, since the traffic was only transferred from Washington to Alexandria."[79]

Finally, despite the fact that by the 1850s fewer and fewer northern politicians were talking about the interstate trade, and no major party called for its prohibition, many southerners continued to believe that it was still a part of the Republican program and that it would be among the antislavery measures that the party would enact if it ever took power in Washington. In an 1860 editorial, the Lexington *Kentucky Statesman* informed its readers that "the prohibition of the inter-State slave trade" was among "the avowed purposes of the republican party," and "its history leaves no doubt that it will undertake to carry out these purposes."[80]

While such views were contrary to the Republicans' platform and frequent statements that they would not interfere with this traffic, many southerners doubted their sincerity. Vice President John Breckinridge, of Kentucky, tried to warn his constituents that abolishing this trade was one of the "present and ulterior purposes of the republican party." According to Breckinridge, "As soon as they obtain power they will not only prohibit slavery in the Territories, but will abolish it in the District of Columbia, . . . and will put an end to the coastwise and internal trade" in slaves. Edmund Ruffin of Virginia likewise believed that after gaining power a Republican administration would quickly outlaw the interstate trade, "as long threatened," and "the institution of slavery would be hastened toward its doomed extinction." Southerners, however, sometimes found justifiable reason to question the Republicans' true intentions. Under the heading "Why We Resist, and What We Resist," *DeBow's Review*, the South's influential proslavery journal, reprinted a November 1860 speech by John Jay, son of William Jay, namesake of his famous grandfather, and a founding member of the Republican party. Among his predictions for a Republican administration, Jay acknowledged that it would not be long before they sought "the abolition of the internal slave-trade of the United States."[81]

Although it is ultimately impossible to ascertain what overall effect the abolitionists had on shaping northern opinion, by looking at which items they chose to use in their attack, it is possible to determine what aspects of the institution they thought would have the strongest impact upon their audience. And there were many reasons that they made the domestic slave trade such a central part of their campaign. Not only did it play a key role in sustaining the southern slave system, but it could never be hidden nor defended, and examples of its devastation were easy to find. But, most important, the abolitionists knew that there was definitely something about the American slave trade that disturbed most people outside of the South, even if they seldom spoke out against it or never joined their cause.

Perhaps the best illustration of this effect can be found in the example of Abraham Lincoln, who never spoke out publicly against the interstate trade, and during his 1860 presidential campaign even explicitly stated that he would not call for its abolition. Yet the domestic trade did have an impact on his life. As a young man in 1841, Lincoln encountered a slave coffle on a riverboat outside St. Louis. He commented only briefly on the experience at the time and did not write about it again for fourteen years. But in 1855 he recalled the incident in a letter to a southern friend. According to Lincoln, "That sight was a continual torment to me; and I see something like it every time I touch the Ohio, or any other slave border." Lincoln also spoke for many, and helped to explain their later actions, when he added that southerners had better "appreciate how much the great body of the Northern people do crucify their feelings, in order to maintain their loyalty to the constitution and the Union."[82]

VII

In February 1865, two war correspondents, Charles Carleton Coffin of the *Boston Journal* and James Redpath of the *New-York Tribune*, accompanied federal troops as they entered Charleston, South Carolina. Knowing the interests of their readers, the two men quickly headed to Ziba Oakes's large slave mart on Chalmers Street and, after breaking down the door, ransacked the premises. Spying the auction block, Coffin thought "that perhaps Governor Andrew, or Wendell Phillips, or William Lloyd Garrison would like to make a speech from those steps," and he "determined to secure them [the steps]." In addition, Coffin climbed a post and wrenched down the gilt star that hung over the front of the mart, and he took the lock from the iron front gate. The two men also carried off a bell and a sign, as well as most of Oakes's business papers, with Redpath noting "what a tale of wickedness these letter books do tell!" Before departing, the two correspondents scribbled "TEXTS FOR THE DAY" on the walls, leaving quotes from Garrison, the Bible, and John Brown.[83]

It is no surprise that Coffin and Redpath headed immediately to a slave mart and brought back evidence of its workings. They understood the power that their "mementoes" and "trophies" would have as symbols of the evil inherent in the American slave system, a system that the North had just paid such a terrible price to defeat. Most of the souvenirs were sent to Boston and used to raise money for the freedmen. But some of these items were also given to William Lloyd Garrison in honor of his role in the antislavery movement.

The first public appearance of these "relics of barbarism" was on March 9, 1865, at "AN IMMENSE MEETING" at Music Hall in Boston. Despite the bad weather and admission charge, a huge crowd gathered to see Charles Coffin present the Charleston auction block to the Eleventh Ward Freedman's Aid Society. According to the *Liberator*, "The steps of the slave auction-block were placed upon the stage, and in front of the organ were suspended the large gilt letters—'MART,' which was the sign of the auction establishment where human beings were bought and sold. Upon the desk was placed the lock of the outside iron door where women were examined before the sale." The audience listened as Coffin read from Oakes's papers and cheered when he described how he and Redpath had looted the slave trader's place of business. Although Governor John Andrew could not be present, other dignitaries followed with speeches. Finally, Garrison ascended the steps, and, as he did so, the crowd went wild. As the *Liberator* described it: "The scene was one of unusual interest and excitement, the audience raising thunders of applause and waving hundreds of white handkerchiefs for a considerable interval."

This event proved not only a personal triumph for Garrison and a fitting culmination to his career, but also the perfect symbolic ending to the abolitionist cause. From the beginning of the movement, the domestic slave trade had figured prominently in the antislavery crusade. It was an essential component in abolitionist ideology and tactics, and few other aspects of the system were as influential in affecting northern opinion about slavery and the South. The auction block was the most graphic symbol of American slavery, and for the abolitionists, the presence of Garrison and other dignitaries upon it was visual proof of the superiority of their cause. As Garrison appropriately told the cheering crowd when he climbed upon the auction block, finally he was "putting the accursed thing under his feet."[84]

SEVEN

Inside Looking Out: The Slave Trade's Effect upon the White South

On Saturday, July 4, 1857, a large crowd gathered on the top of Lookout Mountain in southeastern Tennessee. The occasion was the opening of a convention to establish a proposed "University for the Southern States." Such a project, where southern youths could get a good Christian education in a university away from northern influences, had long been the dream of Episcopal bishops Leonidas Polk of Louisiana and James Otey of Tennessee. While the group had intentionally chosen July 4th for its symbolic importance, and the speakers talked of national unity, Bishop Otey had earlier made it clear that this new university would "materially aid the South to resist and repel a fanatical domination which seeks to rule over us." In addition to a band, 400–500 spectators were in attendance that day, as were seven Episcopal bishops, seven clergymen, and six laymen, representing seven predominantly Deep South states, who served as the convention's official delegates.

Among the lay delegates, none proved more influential in bringing the University of the South to fruition than the former slave trader John Armfield. In the early 1850s, Armfield and his wife purchased the famous mountaintop resort and watering hole for the Deep South elite at Beersheba Springs, Tennessee. When he heard of his friend Bishop Polk's proposed university, Armfield made his resort available for the early planning meetings, and his efforts helped to determine the university's eventual location at the relatively isolated but nearby community of Sewanee, where it still operates today. But, most important, it was Armfield's money that bankrolled the university's founding. While one donor endowed a professorship at $2,000 per year, and another contributed $25,000, Armfield far surpassed them all, pledging $25,000 per annum during his lifetime. It is no surprise, then, that a Nashville newspaper praised his "princely offer" and "generous heart."[1]

In many ways, John Armfield's part in the founding of the University of the South mirrors the larger role that he and other slave traders played in southern society and in the creation of southern wealth. For one thing, this was not the only southern university funded by the sale of American-born slaves. In 1838, Georgetown College in Washington, DC, was saved from financial ruin only after the Jesuits there sold all of the 272 bondspeople whom they owned for $115,000. Even more significant is that, despite his central role in its establishment, Armfield's contributions to the University of the South, an institution that supposedly symbolized southern ideals, have all but been forgotten (as have the earlier actions of the Jesuits at Georgetown). The initial reports and histories of the university barely mention him, and except for a bluff named in his honor, there is no other commemoration for Armfield on the campus today. The same has proven true for slave traders as a whole. While it is impossible to imagine the creation of the Cotton Kingdom without them, their place in southern society has always remained ambiguous, and their contributions, at least those to white southerners, have been consciously ignored.[2]

The main reason for this ambiguity is because the buying and selling of men, women, and children was unlike any other form of commerce in the nation, and it (along with the traders) always posed a problem for the slave-owning South. On the one hand, this trade was essential for the smooth running of the slave system, and it was the foundation of the region's primary source of wealth. Yet the very nature of the business was offensive to many people, including numerous whites within the South itself. Moreover, the long-distance trade was interstate commerce and, according to the U.S. Constitution, subject to congressional regulation. For that reason, slaveholders needed to protect this traffic from the political abolitionists' constitutional assault. They were able to do this, but only at a cost. While defending the domestic trade as legitimate commerce, slave owners also had to somehow downplay its importance in order to defend the institution from the abolitionists' moralistic attacks. Consequently, unlike the North, which was able to recognize its main source of wealth—free-labor capitalism—and celebrate it, white southerners always remained on the defensive about their most valuable form of property and were never able to acknowledge and tout the market activity that made their economic system such a great financial success.

By the 1830s, southern slave owners increasingly found themselves in a bind. Most important, they needed to employ whatever political or legal arguments were necessary to protect the lifeblood of their institution or face economic and social collapse. Yet, at the same time, they also had to counter the abolitionists' charges that their way of life, and the trade responsible for it, were morally wrong. Through the arguments they developed during the Missouri debates and with the aid of helpful northern politicians, white southerners prevented the abolitionists from ever regulating the interstate trade. Countering their moralistic attacks against the trade, however, proved much more difficult, and southern slaveholders found this the most troubling aspect of their slave system to defend. They tried a variety of approaches, including denying its impact and horrors as best they could. But for the most part, they blamed others for its worst evils and claimed that they almost never voluntarily sold their slaves.

Central to their defense of the slave trade (and the entire slave system) was the ideology of paternalism. According to southern slave owners, paternalism was a system of hierarchies, in which everyone had a place, and each had a set of duties and obligations to others. For the self-proclaimed "masters," this meant looking after their charges, or their "people," as owners liked to call them. Not only did they have to provide them with food and shelter, but they also took an interest in their personal lives and cared for their well-being. In return, the grateful slaves performed whatever labor their beloved masters required and were expected to show them respect, obedience, and loyalty. As the owners described it, this relationship was a loving one similar to that of a father and his children. Therefore, masters saw their slaves as inferior members of their extended households and constantly spoke of their "families, white and black."

It is important to remember that paternalism was simply an ideology and never an accurate description of the relationship between owners and their slaves. The vast majority of the enslaved never accepted this system, and the slave-owning class frequently did not live up to its responsibilities. Nor did this ideology truly govern southern society. But paternalism did provide slave owners with an effective means to defend their region's slave system and the southern way of life. With it, white southerners could portray their society as a more caring and civilized one, in contrast to the increasingly capitalistic North with its cold competitiveness and crude materialism.[3]

While paternalism never described historical reality, it was still a prevailing ideal that provided an important set of norms which influenced southern society. Many slave owners acted upon its principles when entering the domestic trade. It was not uncommon for some owners to accept less money so that their slaves could remain with loved ones, and countless sellers preferred the local trade (with its lower financial compensation) so that they could have greater control over getting their people a good home. The public displays of the horrors of the trade (which appeared to contradict southerners' paternalistic ideals) also offended many people, and communities across the South did their best to hide its worst features.

Yet, while belief in the paternalistic ideal definitely caused anguish for some white southerners, it also proved to be an extremely flexible ideology that ultimately provided the most effective and enduring defense of the domestic trade. Most important, it allowed slaveholders to argue that they were not the ones responsible for the vast majority of slave sales that took place; blame for these sales could be shifted onto the slaves themselves or the men who were simply carrying out the owners' desires. Therefore, paternalism allowed slavery's defenders to claim that few owners ever willingly sold their people and that those sales that did take place usually only involved "unruly" slaves, who deserved to be sold, or were the result of manipulative slave traders, who were always viewed as outcasts in southern society.

Unfortunately, this paternalistic defense of the slave trade proved so successful that many of its basic tenets linger in American historical memory today. The large number of slave sales that took place has long been forgotten (along with all of the hardships they entailed), and slave traders are still usually thought of in only the most simplistic and stereotypical terms. Even more enduring has been the myth of the planters' reluctance to sell their people, despite the reminders embedded in our culture of the slaveholders' overwhelming failure to live up to their own paternalistic ideals.

I

Nothing proved more crucial for southern slave owners to the survival of their slave system than the need to refute the political abolitionists' constitutional assault against the interregional trade as interstate commerce. They too knew that this was the lifeblood of their institution and the foundation upon which the whole system rested. As such, this was an issue that could never be compromised, and every effort was taken to prevent any federal regulation of this trade.

As with northern critics of this trade, southern defenders developed most of their legal arguments during the tumultuous Missouri debates of 1819–1820. Central to their defense was the fifth paragraph in Article 1, section 9, of the Constitution, which states, "No preference shall be given by any regulation of commerce or revenue to the ports of one state over those of another." They used this clause to argue that any regulation of commerce must apply to all of the states equally and that Congress did not have the power to regulate the commerce of a limited number of states. According to southerners, that was the reason that the founders had given Congress the right to regulate commerce in the first place: to prevent individual states from abusing one another through state-issued regulations. As Representative Louis McLane of Delaware noted, "Partial regulations of commerce was precisely the evil which the power vested in the Congress was intended to guard against." Southerners also expanded upon this argument by claiming that only the states had the right to regulate the internal slave trade and many of them had already done so. Representative James Pindall of Virginia added an interesting twist to this defense when he pointed out that if only Congress had the right to regulate the interstate movement of slaves, then all state laws on this subject would be void, including those outlawing slavery in the northern states. Finally, southerners argued that the power to regulate commerce did not equal the power to destroy commerce. Many likewise noted that northerners did not want to simply ban the commerce in slaves; they were ultimately seeking the destruction of the entire institution of southern slavery.[4]

The Missouri Compromise never settled this constitutional question, and it would continue to be an issue of concern to white southerners all the way up to the forming of their own confederacy. When the question next arose, during the great petition campaign of the mid-1830s, southerners were able to get a northern Democrat, Representative Charles Atherton of New Hampshire, to help them. In his series of resolutions to renew the gag rule in 1838, Atherton noted that "petitions for the abolition of slavery in the District of Columbia and the Territories of the United States, and against the removal of slaves from one State to another, are a part of a plan of operations set on foot to affect the institution of slavery in the several States, and thus indirectly to destroy the institution within their limits." Arguing that Congress had no right to do indirectly what it could not do directly, he included a resolution stating "that all attempts on the part of Congress to abolish slavery in the District of Columbia or the Territories, or to prohibit the removal of slaves from State to State, . . . are in violation of the Constitution, destructive of the fundamental principle on which the Union of these States rests, and beyond the jurisdiction of Congress."[5]

While passage of the Atherton resolutions temporarily eased southern concerns, the matter was troubling enough by 1850 for Henry Clay to include it in his famous compromise that year. Clay had long feared the abolitionists' intent on this issue. As early as 1838, he worried that the abolitionists would "begin by prohibiting the slave trade, as it is called, among the slave States, and by abolishing it in the District of Columbia, and the end will be ———." Consequently, in a major speech on abolition the following year, Clay argued that Congress did not have the power "to abolish what is called the slave-trade."[6] Given this background, it is not surprising that Clay sought to protect this trade in his 1850 compromise. His initial proposal contained a resolution declaring "that Congress has no power to prohibit or obstruct the trade in slaves between the slaveholding states." What is surprising, however, was the pressure from northerners who refused to make such a concession. Not only did they force Clay to drop this resolution, but northerners also demanded another resolution (which was approved) that granted Congress the power to prohibit the slave trade within the District of Columbia. Needless to say, many white southerners were outraged by such an agreement. They believed that this was the first step on the road to the complete abolition of slavery.[7]

Finally, the interstate trade played a role in the various proposed compromises that emerged after the election of Abraham Lincoln in the winter of 1860. Senator Andrew Johnson of Tennessee proposed a constitutional amendment that, among other things, would prohibit Congress from touching "the inter-State trade, coastwise or inland." As a lesser-known part of his more well known compromise, Senator John Crittenden of Kentucky also proposed an amendment stating, "Congress shall have no power to prohibit or hinder the transportation of slaves from one State to another, or to a Territory in which slaves are by law permitted to be held, whether that transportation be by land, navigable rivers, or by the sea." The importance of protecting this form of commerce can ultimately be seen in the constitution that southerners adopted after forming their own confederacy. They granted their Congress the power "to regulate commerce with foreign nations, and among the several States." However, they also included two separate provisions guaranteeing their citizens the right to carry their slave property from state to state, as well as into whatever territories the new nation might acquire in the future.[8]

II

While slaveholders successfully prevented outsiders from politically destroying the interstate trade, the lifeblood of their slave system, they still faced a dilemma in defending their institution from the charge that it routinely tore families apart and turned humans into things. On this moral front, the task proved more difficult and the defense more diverse. Part of the problem was the very public nature of the slave trade. Auction sales needed to be advertised and were open to anyone who chose to attend. Traders likewise advertised their businesses and carried their merchandise, often shackled and chained, along public roads and waterways. Such activity was necessary for the smooth running of the system, but it was also distasteful and seemingly at odds with the way that southerners liked to depict their institution as a loving one based upon paternalistic relationships.

By offering an array of explanations, the white South attempted to deflect these charges. One common strategy was to argue that outsiders did not understand the reality behind such events. In a series of sketches of southern life, the Virginia journalist Edward Pollard wrote: "I can assure you that the inhuman horrors of the slave auction-block exist only in imagination. Many instances of humanity may be observed there." Pollard and others claimed that instead of tearing families apart, slave auctions were frequently occasions where humane owners, often at great expense to themselves, stepped in to purchase individuals for the purpose of reuniting families or keeping them together, such as at estate sales. Even in those cases where an owner's change of fortune forced his human property onto the auction block, men and women of good character were almost always purchased by local owners who kept them in the neighborhood. According to the essayist George Frederick Holmes, "They will never be removed from the district in which they have lived, but will either be bought with the place on which they have worked, be transferred *en masse* to some neighboring locality, or scattered about within easy distance of each other in the same vicinity."[9]

Southerners also argued that many of the sales that took place were simply for the benefit of those being sold. In addition to sales to reunite spouses and family members, some defenders claimed that many of the advertisements in the newspapers involved individuals who had been rescued from abusive owners and were now being sold by the public authorities for their own protection. Likewise, the Baltimore slave trader Hope Slatter informed the British abolitionist Joseph Sturge "that slaves would often come to him, and ask him to purchase them, and that he was the means of transferring them from worse masters to better."[10]

While southern defenders could not deny that some slave families were destroyed by the domestic trade, they once again argued that outsiders did not really understand such events and overestimated the impact of these partings. As the New York journalist Frederick Law Olmsted observed on his travels throughout the South, "It is frequently remarked by Southerners, in palliation of the cruelty of separating relatives, that the affections of negroes for one another are very slight. I have been told by more than one lady that she was sure her nurse did not have half the affection for her own children that she did for her mistress's." Some even insisted that selling slave children away from their parents was a good thing, because adult slaves were too careless and indifferent toward their offspring to properly raise them. Moreover, white southerners claimed that due to innate differences between the races, blacks did not feel the pain of separation as deeply as a white person would and quickly got over whatever sorrow they may have initially felt. According to one Maryland man, "Their grief will be as transient as it is violent."[11]

Southerners also liked to compare the treatment that their slaves received to the conditions of the laboring poor in other parts of the world, especially in the North and in England. They noted that family breakups occurred in those areas as well and argued that families in slavery were more stable than the families of any other laboring group. According to one female writer, it was "a *fact*" that there was "less separation among negro families than among whites." Furthermore, they argued that there were individuals who abused any system.

Just because some men battered and even murdered their wives did not mean that the institution of marriage should be abolished. Finally, even in those cases where slaves were sold, defenders argued that only their labor was sold and that, unlike northern laborers who lost their jobs, slaves were taken care of and did not have to seek further employment or starve. As William Harper of South Carolina explained it:

> The slave is certainly liable to be sold. But, perhaps, it may be questioned, whether this is a greater evil than the liability of the laborer, in fully peopled countries, to be dismissed by his employer, with the uncertainty of being able to obtain employment, or the means of subsistence elsewhere. With us, the employer cannot dismiss his laborer without providing him with another employer. His means of subsistence are secure, and this is a compensation for much.[12]

One of the most effective arguments that southerners used to counter the horrors that the domestic trade produced was to simply deny that such events took place, or at least not on as widespread a scale as the abolitionists liked to claim. They argued that most owners were reluctant to sell their slaves and almost never did so purely for economic gain. The author Maria McIntosh claimed that the majority of slaveholders would "resist any temptation and submit to much privation" before resorting to such a practice. Southerners insisted that owners loved their people and would just as soon part with a member of their family as with one of their slaves. As one Texas owner explained to his son, "My Slaves to me, are part of my Family and I would as soon think of Selling one of my own Children as one of them." Even in the Upper South, where the sale of surplus slaves could not be denied, southerners claimed that such sales supposedly brought greater anxiety and suffering to the owner than to the person being sold. According to Henry Clay, an owner "takes care of his slaves; he fosters them, and treats them often with the tenderness of his own children. They multiply on his hands; he can not find employment for them, and he is ultimately, but most reluctantly and painfully, compelled to part with some of them because of the increase of numbers and the want of occupation."[13]

Finally, southerners attacked northerners for being hypocrites and accused them of also having played a part in the slave trade. In *An Inquiry into the History of Slavery* (1841), the Reverend Thomas C. Thornton argued that it was slave traders from the North who had earlier forced slavery upon the southern states against their will. Aversion to this traffic supposedly still remained, and Thornton insisted that it was the slaveholding states, not the North, that had the most "resistance to the slave trade." Moreover, by the abolitionists' claiming that the interstate trade could be regulated as commerce, Thornton believed

Yet, while all of this was true, upon closer examination, the situation does become more complex than it would at first appear. Despite the facts that the idea of paternalism was most effectively used to defend the southern slave system from outside attack and that virtually every owner bought and sold slaves (and thought of them as valuable property), there is also no denying that numerous white southerners did take their society's paternalistic principles to heart. The close contact that most owners had with their slaves meant that they did get to know them as people. This not only helped to reinforce the notion that there was more to the master-slave relationship than simple economic gain, but it also fostered a paternalistic sense of obligation in many toward those under their care (and often living in their homes), even if it was based on racist assumptions about black inferiority.

Therefore, for some owners, tension did exist at times between their desire to advance financially and their sense of responsibility toward their human property. This does not mean that they always put their people's best interests above their own, which they seldom did. Nor does it imply that the majority of owners felt any sense of guilt over profiting off the sale of their slaves. It does, however, mean that trading in humans was different than dealing in livestock and that not all those southerners who expressed anguish over doing so were hypocrites. And, some of these owners did act against their own best financial interests when buying or selling slaves.

On this last point, the record is filled with cases in which owners, often at a loss to themselves, acted upon paternalistic principles in the slave trade. When forced to sell, some took less money to make sure that family members stayed together. Typical was the man in South Carolina who needed to sell his slave York. Instead of going to a trader, he contacted his aunt, informing her that he could "obtain a high price for him to go to the Western country, but I am willing to sell him to you for several hundred dollars less so that he may be with his family." The same proved true for an owner in Georgia. After selling all of his slaves to the same buyer, this man was glad they were sold together despite the fact that more could have been obtained had they been sold separately. As he told his wife, "Conscience is better than money."[20]

Owners also frequently entered the domestic trade to reunite family members. After purchasing four slaves at an estate sale, one Tennessee planter admitted that he would "have bought none of those people but for their intermarriages with my servants & their appeals to me to do so." While such actions were common in the local trade, efforts were also made to prevent family separations through the interregional trade. One North Carolina man contacted a Richmond trader who had a woman from the man's neighborhood and offered $100 more than her value, explaining that "she wishes to come back to her husband and he is also very anxious to have her near him." Even after long-distance sales were made, some new owners attempted to bring dispersed family members together. One such case was a planter near Natchitoches, Louisiana, who purchased a man and his wife from a trader in New Orleans. The couple, who had previously been owned by different persons in North Carolina, had been forced to leave their three children behind. The Louisiana planter not only united the couple with his purchase, but he also traveled back to North Carolina and made it known that he was "very desirous of gratifying the parents by restoring their children to them, and would therefore freely pay their full value for them."[21]

Not all southerners who bought slaves to reunite families did so for purely altruistic reasons. For one thing, in some cases there were financial benefits. When encouraging his brother to sell a slave so that the man could be with his wife, one North Carolinian pointed out that "he is very likely & if you wish to sell him he will Bring you a Big pile of money." More important, as one Mississippi man phrased it: "It is much better for the Negroes & for us that their wives should be with them." From a strictly practical standpoint, purchasing the spouse or children of a slave helped to guarantee better cooperation in the workplace. Moreover, bringing family members together minimized runaways and ensured ties to the plantation, as well as provided capital gain from any new offspring. Subsequently, there was often more than one motive when owners thought they were acting benevolently.[22]

In addition, for many owners, their paternalistic sensibilities only went so far. Some put limitations on their financial generosity. As one Virginia man informed his agent in reference to a small girl named Polly, he wanted the man to sell the girl with her mother, "unless there should be a great sacrifice." Others had boundaries to their patience. After spending two years in trying "to please her in getting a good home," a Kentucky man had enough with his slave woman and decided to sell her wherever he could, believing that he had "done all that duty requires in that respect." There were also those who thought they were acting paternalistically, yet failed to recognize the devastating effect their actions still might have on enslaved families. Typical in this regard was the Louisville owner who wanted to sell a slave woman and her two children. While stipulating that these individuals would "not be sold to go down the river," he showed less concern about the other member of the family, adding that "her husband, a fine man, can be had also."[23]

When buying and selling slaves, a number of southerners likewise deceptively played upon the paternalistic sentiments of others for their advantage. One former Virginia slave recalled that, when his mother's owner moved to Mississippi, her owner convinced the owner of the slave's father to sell the man at a reduced price, ostensibly to keep the family together, only to sell the slave's father again (presumably at a higher price) before the party reached their final destination. Another man in North Carolina likewise made a similar appeal

sequently, for all but a small percentage of owners, virtually all of their slaves could be thought of as key slaves. The vast majority of slaveholders lived in close contact with the handful of people they owned and knew them quite well. Even on large plantations, where the majority of slaves lived, most owners had some interaction with their work force and knew their field hands by name. Therefore, the small size of their slaveholdings, and the personal familiarity that most owners had with their human property, makes any idea of selective paternalism meaningless for the majority of southern slaveholders.[30]

In addition, southerners frequently expressed paternalistic sentiments when dealing with men and women who could not be considered privileged slaves. For one thing, it was common for sellers of large lots to show concern for their property's personal needs. Typical was the seller from Pensacola, Florida, who demanded that his entire work force of sixty "not be separated under any circumstances." The same proved true when buying unknown individuals. One Tennessee man was hesitant about purchasing a slave named Jack without his wife, noting that he "would prefer buying both together or not at all, as I would not like to be instrumental in separating them." And buyers often took their new property's preferences into consideration before purchasing. In South Carolina, one man would only buy a slave from a Charleston dealer, if "*he is still willing to come.*"[31]

The widespread influence of the paternalistic ideal was also one of the reasons that so many owners found the local trade attractive; it gave them more control over the destiny of the men and women they were trying to sell. All across the South, newspapers were filled with advertisements offering slaves for sale with the restriction that the person being sold must remain in the neighborhood. Most simply stated this requirement, such as the fourteen-year-old girl who was "*Not to be carried out of the City of Richmond,*" or the couple in Louisville who would be sold "to city or suburban residents only." Other sellers provided more in-depth explanations of their motives. One Augusta, Georgia, man demanded that his slaves "not be sold out of the city or its immediate neighborhood" because he wanted "to avoid the necessity of separating husbands and wives." Many offered economic incentives, like the Charleston owner who advertised that his man would "be sold low to remain in the city." Some even sought legal protection. When selling a seventeen-year-old girl, one Virginia man noted, "Bond and security will be required of the purchaser not to carry her out of the Corporation and county of Fairfax."[32]

Others preferred the local trade (and accepted less income from a sale) because they believed it gave them a greater opportunity to find a "good home" for their people. Typical was the owner of a middle-aged woman in Baltimore who offered her "low to a good home," or the seller of a young man in Natchez who would also accept a reduced price "to a good master living in the city."

The only reason that some owners even sold particular slaves was because of their property's discontent with their current homes. Such was the case with two men offered for sale in Charleston; apparently they had "a dislike to a Rice Plantation." And many owners left the decision up to the men and women they were selling, like the man in Cambridge, Maryland, who wanted his three slaves to "have a choice of masters." Throughout the South, it was common to allow slaves to find their own purchasers. While one reason for doing so was the decreased expense and effort required for making a sale, a number of owners did this for more humanitarian reasons. As one man in St. Augustine, Florida, explained, his enslaved man had permission to look for a new owner because he was "unwilling to be removed to Savannah, having a wife here whom He says cannot be purchased."[33]

Numerous owners also refused to sell their slaves to professional traders. While it was possible to find advertisements like the one that read, "No objection will be made to traders purchasing," far more common were the ones that said "traders need not apply" or that the individuals offered would be "sold to any gentleman for his own use, but not to speculators." Once again, some owners willingly accepted a loss of revenue for this benefit. As one Virginia man explained to his father in reference to his slaves, "I shall sell them for what they will bring to some farmer in Va. I do not wish to sell them to a negro trader." While it is easy to dismiss such statements as mere rhetoric, many sellers did act upon this sentiment. According to a Louisiana planter on a slave-buying trip to Virginia, some of the farmers there "don't like to sell to Negro traders butt will to anybody that buys for their own use." Such restrictions could even be found at court sales. After attending a sale near Charlottesville, one speculator complained that "they would not let a trader have the negroes."[34]

When purchasing slaves, especially in the Upper South, many advertisers also thought it important to make known that they were buying for their personal use and not for speculation. One common way of doing this was by referring to themselves as "GENTLEMEN" (often capitalized) and by offering proof that their purchase was not intended for resale. Typical was the notice of a man near Alexandria that read, "A GENTLEMAN is desirous of purchasing, for HIS OWN USE, thirty efficient Field Hands," or the one in Washington, DC, where the buyer promised "satisfactory evidence that the purchase is not intended for speculation." This effort to differentiate themselves from professional traders proved especially relevant for planters from the Deep South when traveling to the Upper South to buy slaves. Not only did they too refer to themselves as "gentlemen," but they also often conducted their business through a local newspaper editor or friend who could vouch for their intentions. Therefore, alongside the "CASH FOR NEGROES" notices placed by professional traders were numerous advertisements like the one stating, "A

other commodity. In fact, despite the widespread presence and importance of the domestic slave trade for the southern economy, its existence was often condemned or publicly denied. It was never embraced and praised in the same manner as was similar commercial activity in the North. Not only did numerous white southerners express their discomfort with this trade, but they also took steps to eliminate it from public life as much as possible.

While newspapers all across the South at one time or another opposed this form of commerce for practical concerns (such as fears of possible insurrection), several papers also denounced the trade for moral reasons. The Baltimore Quaker Hezekiah Niles routinely attacked the interregional trade in his influential *Weekly Register*. As he argued in one 1817 editorial, "If there is any thing that ought to be supremely hated, it is the present infamous traffic that is carried on in several of the middle states, and especially in *Maryland*, in negroes, for the *Georgia* and *Louisiana* markets." As a printer, Niles felt ashamed whenever he saw "advertisements published in the newspapers, openly avowing the trade, and soliciting business, with the indifference of dealers in horses." Articles against the trade likewise regularly appeared in the *Western Luminary*, a publication of the Presbyterian church out of Lexington, Kentucky. This weekly was filled with stories reminiscent of those found in the abolitionist press. Under the heading "Disgraceful Scenes," one 1831 story began with the complaint, "Our streets have lately exhibited scenes which we consider disgraceful, and altogether inconsistent with our character as a civilized and christian community. We allude to the barbarities connected with the merciless traffic in human flesh, which is continually carried on, by beings in human shape, in our midst." The paper could only conclude that "such scenes are revolting to humanity, and must sicken every feeling heart."[39]

Stories like this were common in the religious-based newspapers of the Upper South in the early decades of the nineteenth century. During that time, some evangelical southerners in that subregion were alarmed at the rapid growth of the trade and shocked at how it contrasted with their ideal view of slavery. Others supported the colonization movement, and as the *Western Luminary* frequently pointed out, the interregional trade proved detrimental to this effort by raising the price of slaves in the Upper South. By the 1830s, the number of such pieces in religious publications declined, with the rise of the proslavery argument and most southern churches becoming strong defenders of slavery. They never disappeared entirely, however, and continued throughout the antebellum period.[40]

Articles attacking the trade for moral reasons also appeared in the more mainstream southern press. In 1822 the Paris, Kentucky, *Western Citizen*, a newspaper that regularly contained advertisements by slave traders, published a letter to the editor condemning "the diabolical, damming practice of SOUL-

PEDDLING, or the purchasing of negroes, and driving them like brutes to market." Three years later, a paper in Raleigh, North Carolina, likewise spoke "with abhorrence" against the "too frequent occurrence" of slave coffles passing through town. Even as late as 1849, the *Louisville Courier* printed a story with the heading "BEAUTIES OF THE TRADE," that complained that "a gang of some fifty or sixty negroes, handcuffed and chained together, were driven down Main street, bound, we suppose for a market."[41]

While most stories of this nature appeared in the Upper South, newspaper articles critical of the trade could also be found in the importing states. One of the more interesting commentaries opposing the trade was a parody of a slave-trader advertisement that ran for one issue only in the *Memphis Eagle* in October 1845. In an attempt to criticize the growing public presence of the slave trade at a time when Memphis was becoming a major market in the interregional trade, the author of this fictitious ad ridiculed the marketing practices of the professional traders while simultaneously demonstrating how they were an affront to community standards. At first glance, this notice appeared to be a normal advertisement with the common typographical symbol employed by many traders of a black man running. A closer look, however, revealed the author's true intention. Instead of "NEGROES" or "SLAVES," the bold-type heading read "NIGGERS!" and the seller's name was listed as "BLACKEY TOUGHSKIN." Among other things, this supposed trader threatened to make his business unavoidable by promising to "take out his stock of Niggers, consisting of Men, Women, Children and crying babies, and occupy the whole pavement on the south side of Jefferson street, where he will exhibit them to those wishing to purchase." To make sure that readers got his point, the author also sarcastically added, "Ladies wishing to visit any of the stores or the 'Commercial Hotel' on Jefferson street, are requested to provide themselves with a bottle of Eau de Cologne, and walk in the middle of the street."[42]

Some southern citizens were so offended by the slave trade that they petitioned their respective governments to abolish it. Nowhere did this prove more true than among the residents of the District of Columbia. As early as 1802, a grand jury in Alexandria demanded a ban on slave traders in DC, because "they exhibit to our view a scene of wretchedness and human degradation, disgraceful to our characters as citizens of a free government." Twenty-five years later, the Benevolent Society of Alexandria published a tract likewise calling for a prohibition of "this cruel traffic." Among other things the society feared that "these enormous cruelties cannot be practiced among us, without producing a sensible effect upon the morals of the community." The following year, in March 1828, a petition signed by more than 1,000 residents of the District of Columbia was presented to Congress calling for the gradual emancipation of slaves and a ban on the domestic slave trade within the District of Columbia. Unfortu-

this project into effect." A traveler to New Orleans managed to get an acquaintance to take him to that city's slave pens, but only if he agreed "not to say a word, but merely to listen" so as not to give away that he was British. As was often the case, however, no other southerner expressed this sentiment better than the South Carolina socialite Mary Boykin Chesnut. As she remarked to a visiting Englishwoman when passing a slave auction in Charleston, "If you can stand that, no other Southern thing need choke you."[48]

Such negative attitudes by the public to the more unsavory aspects of their business forced some slave traders to adjust their operations and make them less visible. One northern visitor to the South noted that "the trade is not a clandestine one, but being offensive to the feelings of a large portion of the community, it is in a great measure withdrawn from public observation." For one thing, Frederick Douglass remembered as a young boy in Baltimore seeing all of the slave coffles passing down Pratt Street toward the docks at midnight. As he explained it, "A growing civilization demanded that this hell black crime should not be displayed in public." A former slave in Missouri likewise recalled that "the traders used to drive the slaves through the streets in the day time, but Public sentiment eventually turned against that sort of thing. A great many people in St. Louis discountenanced the slave traffic and the traders were afraid they would be mobbed." Consequently, they started driving their slaves to the boats "between 4 and 5 o'clock Sunday morning, when nobody was stirring."[49]

The most indicative sign, however, of white southerners' uneasiness with the domestic trade can be seen in the treatment that it received in the southern commercial press. Like the major markets in the North, southern cities like Charleston, St. Louis, and New Orleans printed regular "prices current," which listed up-to-date reviews of their various commodity markets. The *New-Orleans Price-Current, Commercial Intelligencer and Merchants Transcript* of 1842 listed sixty-seven different commodities from anchors to wool, but nowhere did it relate the state of the city's market in human commodities. Except for the printed circulars released by the leading slave auctioneers in Richmond, no commercial paper in the South listed this type of commodity, nor was it regularly reported in the market sections of the region's newspapers. This is quite telling, especially given that this form of commerce was perfectly legal and also the leading source of capital investment in terms of economic value in the South. But southern whites were not alone in this silence. The slave trade was the only branch of commerce for which the U.S. federal government provided no statistical information. As the American Anti-Slavery Society remarked, "It would be unseemly for a republican government to publish these things, but not at all for a republican people to do them."[50]

VI

The conflicting attitudes toward the slave trade make it obvious that the new values of the commercial marketplace, values that so easily took hold in the North and that were being disseminated by slave traders in the South, were not the only values present in southern society; the ideology of paternalism also had an effect upon the actions of many white southerners. On the one hand, southern slaveholders appreciated the benefits that the domestic trade provided and regularly participated in its operation, yet at the same time, many also found it offensive and even acted against their own best interests when buying or selling slaves. Given this seeming contradiction, it is hard not to believe that the clash between the desire to achieve economic benefit at the expense of others and the paternalistic obligation to look after one's charges had to have caused mental anguish for at least some white southerners.

On at least one occasion, this conflict over the benefits and social costs of the slave trade even threatened to tear a community apart. During the spring of 1860, the citizens of Natchez engaged in a heated public debate over whether or not to repeal their city's ban on slave traders operating within the city limits. This debate began in late February when the *Natchez Courier* printed an editorial calling for a repeal of the ban, saying that the slave trade was no longer a nuisance and that returning it would increase city revenues and stimulate the local economy. A letter to the editor of the city's competing paper, the *Mississippi Free Trader*, by "Planter" strongly disagreed, arguing that the increased revenue would be minimal and that instead of benefiting the economy it would hurt it by making it more difficult for nearby merchants to attract customers. But, most important, Planter also attacked the morality of the trade, calling it "a deadly poison" and arguing that he and "any man of any sensibility" had an "unutterable disgust for the whole trade!" This debate in the press continued, with the *Courier* eventually declaring that the domestic trade was "no sin and no wrong" and that Planter's expressions were "at war with Southern principles."

This debate soon spread throughout the community and became an issue that the city council was forced to confront. In early March seven local slave traders petitioned the council calling for a repeal of the ban. Accompanying this petition was a memorial signed by a citizens group also asking for a repeal, arguing among other things that the current ban cast "a stigma upon the institution of slavery itself, and furnishes a handle of argument and abuse to our political and domestic enemies." The council did not vote on this issue for another three months, but before it did another petition, "signed by a number of citizens," argued against the repeal "*under any conditions.*" In the end,

ordered the man sold to "negro purchasers from Georgia" or from "any other quarter so distant as never more to be heard of among us." Fifty-five years later, a rural South Carolina planter had a similar response after he caught one of his men setting fire to his house. As this man angrily informed his cousin: "I would not have such a wretch about me for the world. Such an act must be crushed & the actors made an example of. I send Harry to Charleston by Munday's vessel, for sale immediately." One frustrated Virginian even felt compelled to sell his enslaved man because the fellow had committed "so many outrageous thefts in the neighborhood that I feel that it is due to the community to rid them of such a pest." Moreover, he was no longer able "to endure the mortification and humiliation of having my neighbors continually coming to search for & find the fruits of his repeated robberies."[56]

But most times, owners punished slaves with sale for relatively minor offenses. One Maryland woman was sold for her "Impertinent Language to her Mistress"; a New Orleans woman was "very saucy" and "had too much jaw [lip]." The owner of a Missouri slave named Sam got rid of him "for general bad conduct," while a South Carolina man was put up for "his imprudence." Sadly, the owner of a fourteen-year-old boy in Frederick, Maryland, sold him for too frequently running off to his mother, who lived nearby.[57]

Not surprisingly, supposed sexual improprieties annoyed some owners. This proved to be the case for two Alabama women, who were sold for being "incorrigible strumpets," and for the woman in Savannah whose owner wanted her sold out of the city "because of her liking the men too well." One young light-skinned Tennessee woman was even sent to a slave trader because of her fondness "for white men" and her owner's refusal "to raise a gang of white children [who were] negroes too."[58]

While some owners deplored the supposed sexual licentiousness of their female slaves, others punished enslaved women for scorning their own sexual advances. After Harriet Jacobs refused what her owner called his "kind offers," this man then threatened to sell her child away from her, warning, "Perhaps that will humble you." A former slave in Virginia also recalled what happened to the enslaved cook on her plantation when their owner tried to rape the woman while she was making soap. After the man attempted to rip the cook's dress off and throw her on the floor, the woman "took an' punch ole Marsa, . . . an' den she gave him a shove an' push his hindparts down in de hot pot o' soap." Their owner sold the cook to a slave trader a few days later. Unfortunately, most enslaved women were never able to fight off such advances. Yet, some women did resist their consequences, albeit in a painfully extreme way, by destroying any children produced by their rape. It is impossible to know how widespread infanticide was among enslaved women, or to discern all of the complex motives behind such acts. But it did occur, and when caught, the women were usually punished with sale. One such case involved a woman in southern Virginia. According to another slave on her plantation, the woman had gotten "rid of" her two mulatto children "in a way that excited suspicion against her and she was consequently sold."[59]

Running away, however, constituted the most common offense for which an individual was sold. Not only did owners regularly sell those individuals who committed this action, but they also sometimes similarly punished the offender's family as a deterrent to others. After a Louisville man ran away, his owner "immediately sold his wife and children" to an interregional trader. Ironically, a recent sale was also one of the most frequent incentives for flight, as many bondspeople took off in an effort to reunite with separated family members and loved ones. Such was a case in Montgomery, Alabama, although the owner interpreted the motives of his human property somewhat differently. After having two men run away as soon as he purchased them, this man decided to "sell them and Lay the money out in like property," adding, "I am resolved not to keep a mean negro."[60]

This individual's attitude was typical of slave owners all across the South, as most of them made it standard policy to sell off troublesome slaves. For one thing, it made good economic sense. One owner in South Carolina thought it "a great piece of folly for any person to keep a negro that will not behave himself, particularly when they can [get] more for them than they are worth." Another owner in Alabama agreed, adding that he "had rather sell a bad Negro than be harrassed & fretted, especially when for the same sum that he would bring a good one might be purchased to supply his place." Even more important, though, this policy removed potentially corrupting influences from the rest of the work force. The New Orleans philanthropist John McDonogh spoke for many when he wrote that his "practice throughout life, has been to sell the vicious, to separate them from the good and well disposed, (no matter what their talents, or qualifications)."[61]

Because the practice of selling unruly slaves as a form of punishment was also well known to the enslaved themselves, owners were able to use the threat of sale as an effective form of labor control. Historian Norrece Jones has even argued that this threat was "the most powerful long-term technique of control—short of death—that masters possessed." As one former South Carolina slave put it: "Every slave know what, 'I'll put you in my pocket, sir!' mean." It was the ever-present threat of sale. This fear allowed many owners to rule like the man in Louisiana, who bragged that he was able to govern his slaves "without the whip, by stating to them that I shall sell them if they do not conduct themselves as I wish."[62]

The reason that this threat proved so effective was because of what a forced sale, especially a long-distance sale, meant to most American slaves. One former

and he demanded that she be sold at least 100 miles from her home. Porter was determined to punish Mary for "her conduct by keeping things concealed from me respecting her children." Mary's family was obviously important to her. Not only had she kept information about her children from her owner, but when Porter had earlier tried to sell Mary through a local Savannah trader, he failed after she managed to get a letter written "to her Mistress to beg for her." Therefore, Porter now warned Oakes that "she will do every thing to prevent any one purchasing her." Apparently, she was once again successful, at least temporarily, since one week later Porter wrote another letter to Oakes angrily demanding that the slave trader's failure to sell Mary was

> owing entirely to her conduct which you measurably can control by say[ing] to her if she acts in that way you will sell her to the worst man you can find. And that you will punish her also. Again let her know that she is not to be brought back. And nothing will enduce me to take her home, and that she had better alter her conduct or you will send her further from home where she can never hear from any of her people.

It is uncertain what became of Mary, or if she ever saw her children again, but it is known that Porter's desires in this case were satisfied. The following week, he sent another letter to Oakes stating that the price he had obtained for Mary was fine and that he would soon be sending another of his slaves to the Charleston slave trader for sale.[69]

Therefore, the selling of slaves in the Old South was not only common, but, in many cases, it was also a devastatingly cruel form of punishment. While sanctioned by a number of state governments, it was primarily carried out by individual owners across the region. The threat of sale proved to be the most effective form of long-term labor control, as owners frequently used precious family bonds to hold their human property in check. White southerners justified this system by telling themselves that what they were doing was not their fault and the responsibility for this brutal action rested upon those who were being punished. The result was a sense of betrayal on the part of the owner and family devastation and heartbreak for those being sold.

VIII

In order for the proslavery argument to be truly efficacious (both to the outside world and to the slaveholders themselves) an important distinction had to be drawn between what owners termed "voluntary" and "involuntary" sales. Southern slaveholders argued that they seldom sold their people voluntarily.

In the vast majority of cases, owners only sold their slaves out of "necessity" and not from any desire to profit at the expense of others. This distinction may seem minor, but it was crucial for the paternalistic defense of slavery. Voluntarily speculating in human property negated the special bond that supposedly existed between master and slave. Therefore, southerners had to blame all slave sales on forces beyond their control or onto someone else.

Most important, this distinction provided an excuse for the largest number of slave sales: those done from financial necessity and those ordered by the southern courts. According to the slaveholders, they did not voluntarily enter into these sales for profit; the sales were forced upon them by creditors or by an impersonal entity known as the law. An owner could still love his people, but misfortune and an intervening court order made their sale necessary. Of course, one could always argue that reckless investments, or using slaves as collateral, implied the risk that an owner's human property might someday have to be sold, but southerners did not see it that way. The ideology of paternalism required that the responsibility for all slave sales had to be shifted somewhere else. It also allowed owners to justify their actions (at least in their minds) to those whose lives they were about to destroy. As one Alabama man instructed his wife about informing their slaves that they were to be sold to pay off debts, "Let them understand that it is impossible for us to keep them," and "Let them know too that it lacerates our hearts as much as it does theirs to be compelled to the course we suggest."[70]

Southerners also frequently placed the blame for their slave sales onto someone else, which likewise allowed them to see such sales as involuntary. Most often, owners held the enslaved responsible for their own sale; they believed they had no choice but to punish those who failed to live up to their part in the paternalistic bargain. In addition, the Reverend Nathan Rice offered another scapegoat when he blamed the abolitionists for the increased evils of the interstate trade. According to Rice, these outsiders "have sought to make the slaves discontented in their condition; they have succeeded in decoying many from their masters, and running them to Canada. Consequently masters, for fear of losing their slaves, sell them to the hard-hearted trader; and they are marched to the South."[71]

But the most effective scapegoat for the evils of the domestic trade was the professional slave trader himself. Slave owners constantly tried to make the distinction between the sales that they had to do from necessity versus those done by commercial dealers for profit (although the difference between these two types of sales existed more in their imaginations than in reality). They did this because unlike the majority of southern slave owners, who claimed to love their people, the trader did not even pretend to have a paternalistic relationship with his slaves. His relationship with them was purely speculative

thize with their fate. Such was the case with the former North Carolina slave Sella Martin. After his former owner refused to speak with his mother concerning her sale, Martin recalled that "the trader did all in his power to soothe the irritated and wounded spirit of my mother. He tried to console her by mention of the fact that her children were spared to her, and with the promise of tender treatment, with the pledge that he would try to get her a kind master, and that he would sell her and her children together." Upon their arrival in Georgia, this man "kept his word to my mother, and not only succeeded in getting us a kind master, but one who bought the three of us—my mother, my sister, and myself." According to Martin, his "mother remembered and spoke of this kindness, from such an unexpected quarter, till the day of her death."[77]

Slave traders also sometimes acted more humanely than owners when it came to reuniting black families. This is not to say that the majority of speculators felt any compunction about dividing slave families when it was to their advantage, because they frequently did that. After two of the slaves in his coffle had "taken up with each other as man and wife," a trader in Alabama noted that as soon as he had an "opportunity of selling either of them they go certain." Still, there were cases where interregional traders bought a married couple who had separate owners and lived on different plantations in the Upper South and then sold them together as man and wife to a single owner in New Orleans. Others occasionally sidestepped the wishes of previous owners who wanted their property punished with an out-of-state sale. After purchasing a young man whose owner made it clear that he desired such a punitive sale, one agent in upcountry South Carolina informed his boss in Charleston that the agreement had not been put in writing. Therefore, they could now, he hoped, find a new owner for him in the city where the young man's wife lived. Some traders even sacrificed profits so their slaves could get a "good home." R. M. Owings & Co. of Hamburg, South Carolina, sold a woman named Lydia for "Something Less than we Would of like to of had for her but in Consideration of her getting a good home and at a point where she will be able to see her relatives & friends we concluded to let her go for the above price."[78]

At times, slave traders likewise exhibited a surprising understanding of the humanity of the men and women they were dealing in as property. The Charleston broker Ziba Oakes was once admonished by a colleague for being "too sensitive" with his slaves. According to this associate, Oakes had "too great a desire to please negroes. By allowing them to visit their friends in your office, you give them trouble, and also annoyance to purchasers." While most of these men simply raped the young women under their control, or kept them as temporary concubines, a few developed meaningful relationships with black women that lasted well after Emancipation. Such was the case with the Richmond jailer Robert Lumpkin. After the war, he legally married one of his former slaves, a woman named Mary Jane. The couple had two daughters together, both of whom Lumpkin had previously sent north for their education and protection (they were considered slaves under Virginia law). The Charleston dealer John S. Ryan did not formally marry his black mistress, but he did have several children with her, and after the war he donated $500 to the erection of a school for black youth. Finally, at a dinner she attended in New Orleans, the British author Harriet Martineau reported that there were three black servants and a former slave trader among the guests. After "a gentleman of very high official rank" told a racist joke, all of the party but one broke into laughter. According to Martineau, "While every other American at the table laughed without control, I saw my neighbour, the former slavetrader, glance up at the negroes who were in attendance, and use a strong effort not to laugh."[79]

While there is no record of any slave traders feeling guilt over what they did for a living, the actions taken by the New Orleans dealer Elihu Cresswell do raise some questions. Cresswell was a successful trader who owned his own depot on Common Street before dying from disease in 1851 at the age of thirty-eight. While his death was not that unusual, the contents of his will were, at least for most people today (although most people at the time gave it little notice). Cresswell's estate was valued at more than $65,000 and more than half of that amount was in slaves. Having no other heirs, he left his entire estate to his mother in South Carolina, with two important exceptions: first, he manumitted his personal servant, Gabriel, whom he had inherited from his father, and provided this man with $50 for his "long and faithful services"; and second, he freed all of his other slaves (a total of fifty-one) and provided them with money for their transportation to the free states. Despite some legal challenges from his mother, in the end, virtually all of his former slaves made it to the free states.[80]

Obviously the case of Elihu Cresswell was not typical, nor does his story imply that the majority of southern slave traders were great humanitarians. They were not. They engaged in a despicable business that caused pain and suffering to millions of people. The consequences of their actions helped to solidify one of the most vicious and dehumanizing slave systems the world has ever known. However, they were not all the stereotypical monsters that many of their contemporaries made them out to be. While many of these men certainly fit that mold, there were others who occasionally acted far more humanely than their compatriots who proclaimed themselves to be such great paternalists.

Slave traders had a legitimate complaint when they sometimes accused owners of being hypocrites who eagerly took advantage of their services but then condemned them in the abstract as the scapegoats for their slave system. As traders well understood, they were not the only southerners responsible for the evils and horrors of this traffic. Equally to blame were the hundreds of

for the Upper South's slaveholding class because they supposedly reaffirmed the belief that their people still loved them. Despite the fact that they had not lived up to their part of the paternalistic agreement by selling their slaves down the river, despite the fact that they had torn apart the families of their people and sent them to a harsh and deadly environment hundreds of miles from their families and friends, in their minds their people still loved them and deep down truly wanted to be with them again. Not only did slaveholders sing these songs themselves, but they even forced the enslaved to sing them on their overland coffles to the Deep South. According to one British traveler, John Armfield encouraged the slaves in his coffle to sing "Old Virginia never tire" as they were leaving that state. Slaveholders in the Upper South needed these songs to somehow convince themselves that what they were doing was not wrong. They had to reassure one another that they had not failed to live up to their paternalistic ideal. Despite all of the pain and suffering they had caused, they managed to deceive themselves into thinking that their people still loved them and that they longed to be carried back to Old Virginny or to their old Kentucky home.[84]

EIGHT

"The Nastiness of Life": African-American
Resistance to the Domestic Slave Trade

In her Pulitzer Prize–winning novel, *Beloved*, Toni Morrison writes that in the antebellum South, African-American "men and women were moved around like checkers." In addition to being "rented out, loaned out,... mortgaged, won, stolen or seized," they were also frequently bought and sold like any other form of property. In the book, the family's matriarch, Baby Suggs, knew all about the harsh realities of sale. Six different men had fathered her eight children—five of whom had been sold away, and two of whom had fled before a sale could occur. Baby Suggs understood the system well, and, according to Morrison, "what she called the nastiness of life was the shock she received upon learning that nobody stopped playing checkers just because the pieces included her children." Although Morrison based her novel on the true story of Margaret Garner, this is a work of fiction and not historical "fact." But the problems that her characters face are representative of those that confronted millions of African-American men, women, and children in the antebellum South.[1]

It is important to note that not every black person in the South was a victim of the domestic trade; many spent a lifetime in slavery without ever being sold, and others used the trade to better their condition under slavery. Some forced their own sale to get away from abusive owners. One enslaved woman in Baltimore even got a court order requesting to be sold out of state (she was eventually sold to a new owner in Florida). Many more slaves initiated their own sale to reunite with family members and loved ones. And a few found their future spouses while traveling overland in a coffle and were lucky enough to stay together after their sale in the Deep South.[2]

Some free blacks in the South profited from the buying and selling of enslaved African Americans. In 1830 in the South, there were 3,684 black slaveholders, who owned a total of 11,916 slaves. While the majority of these black slaveholders owned family members and lived in states that prohibited them from manumitting their relatives, a small number of free blacks owned sizable holdings of slaves whom they bought and sold at the same rate, and with the same callousness, as their white neighbors. Typical of these individuals was William Ellison of Stateburg, South Carolina, who bought at least thirty-five slaves (and possibly twice that number). It has been estimated that he also sold off roughly twenty young girls who had been born on his plantation to invest in more land and in young men to work his fields. A few free blacks even operated as professional slave traders. In the 1830s, A. F. Edwards bought slaves in Maryland, Virginia, and North Carolina and sold them in the Deep South markets of New Orleans, Natchez, and Mobile. South Carolinian Thomas Inglis made nearly $20,000 speculating in slaves. Others could be found at the bottom end of the trade. In 1818, one "colored fellow" in Maryland was sentenced to three years in prison and fined £300 for kidnapping three free blacks and then selling them for slaves.[3]

Still, for the vast majority of African Americans, the domestic slave trade was a dreadful reality that posed a constant threat to their lives. Most important, virtually every enslaved person faced the possibility of sale. While the interregional trade was highly age-specific, people of all ages could be found there. Moreover, the widespread nature of the local trade put all age groups at risk. Especially destructive were the large number of court-ordered sales in which families were frequently divided to maximize revenue. As a result, few families were untouched by this trade. It has been estimated that at least half of all slave families in the Upper South were broken through the interstate trade through the sale of either a spouse or a child. Yet, when combined with the even larger local trade, the percentage was almost certainly much higher, and sales destroyed countless families in both the Upper and Lower South.[4]

The consequences of sale could be devastating, both for those being sold and for those they left behind. As one former slave in South Carolina put it, "People wus always dyin' frum a broken heart." Many never got over this loss. After his entire family was sold, Charles Ball remembered that his "father never recovered from the effects of the shock, which this sudden and overwhelming ruin of his family gave him." Another former slave in Virginia recalled that her "mother never did git over dis ack of sellin' her baby to dem slave drivers down New Orleans."[5] A sad few broke down entirely. Solomon Northup reported that after her two children were sold, his companion Eliza constantly talked "of them—often *to* them, as if they were actually present," while a woman in Arkansas who lost her children through sale continued to "make clothes and knit for them." One Kentucky woman who was sold away from her children and taken to Louisiana not only refused to eat or drink on Fridays, but she once stripped off all of her clothing and threw it into a fire. As one witness testified, "She was melancholly, dejected and always weeping, and speaking of her children from whom she was separated."[6]

It is not surprising, then, that enslaved black people lived under a continual fear of being sold. Thomas Jones recalled that he and his wife "constantly dreaded a final separation," and Lewis Hayden noted that "the trader was all around, the slave-pen at hand, and we did not know what time any of us might be in it." Arguably the best description of this apprehension came from the interviewer of the former slaves Tabb Gross and Lewis Smith, who claimed:

> The continual dread of this separation of husband and wife, parents and children, by sale, ... is inseparable from a state of slavery. It may happen at any moment, and is one of the greatest miseries hanging over the head of a slave. His life is spent in the fear of it. The slave may forget his hunger, bad food, hard work, lashes, but he finds no relief from the ever-threatening evil of separation.[7]

For most American slaves, little could be done to prevent this terrible threat. Some responded by shielding themselves from the inevitable pain that a sale would produce. As Toni Morrison's fictional character Paul D expressed it: "You protected yourself and loved small. Picked the tiniest stars out of the sky to own. ... Grass blades, salamanders, spiders, woodpeckers, beetles, a kingdom of ants. Anything bigger wouldn't do. A woman, a child, a brother—a big love like that would split you wide open in Alfred, Georgia." For a few, simply the fear of sale proved more than they could bear. During his travels through the United States in 1831, Alexis de Tocqueville came upon a black man in the Baltimore almshouse, whose "madness [was] extraordinary." Apparently the man imagined that one of the local slave traders "sticks close to him day and night and snatches away bits of his flesh." According to Tocqueville, "his eyes rolled in their orbits and his face expressed both terror and fury. From time to time he threw off his blanket, and raised himself on his hands shouting: 'Get out, get out, don't come near me.' It was a terrible sight."[8]

But the majority of enslaved African Americans were able to live with this ever-present fact of life, and they maintained meaningful family relationships in spite of it. As young children, they learned of the horrors of the trade and often became victims of it. They also sought to resist its more devastating effects, especially as they got older. Even those who had never previously struck out against slavery fought back when sale forced them to confront the reality of being torn away from family and friends. Some attempted to manipulate a sale or openly rejected its completion, while others were forced to rely upon more subtle forms of resistance, such as retaining familial ties through naming practices, memory, and various forms of communication. As with most forms of slave rebellion, resistance to the domestic trade was overwhelmingly individualistic and not meant to overthrow the slave system. But it did make the system, and one of the South's most common forms of commerce, run less smoothly than many owners would have liked. More than anything else, by resisting their sale, the enslaved exposed the white South's paternalistic ideal for the cruel fantasy that it ultimately was.

I

From an early age, most African-American children in the South were forced to confront the devastating realities that the domestic trade brought into their lives. For one thing, they made up an especially large component in this traffic. It is impossible to know exactly how many enslaved boys and girls were actually sold, but one study claims that between 1820 and 1860, at least 10 percent of all teenagers in the Upper South fell into the hands of speculators in the interregional trade. In addition, young children made up a disproportionate percentage of the southern slave population. More than two-fifths of antebellum slaves were younger than age fifteen, and one-third were younger than age ten. Therefore, they had an even greater chance of being sold in the local trade. Typical was the experience of Louis Hughes, who was born in 1832 and was sold for the first time at the age of six. Within the next six years, he was sold three more times to different owners within his native state of Virginia before being placed on an auction block in Richmond and sold to a planter in Mississippi at the age of twelve.[9]

Many enslaved children found themselves being sold at an extremely young age. While most slaves sold into the interregional trade were between the ages of fifteen and twenty-five, young children were always present. This proved especially true during times of economic prosperity when demand for slaves in the Deep South was greater. Young girls tended to be sold at an earlier age than young boys (they usually matured sooner), although young boys were frequently in greater demand (and brought a higher price) because of their labor potential. It was even more common to find very young children in the local trade. While owners generally sold toddlers with their mothers (they were easier to care for that way), they sometimes sold infants as young as twelve, ten, or even two months old on their own. Newspapers regularly listed small children for sale, including one advertisement in Washington, DC, for a "Negro boy, 4 years of age, well grown." When one Louisiana man asked his lawyer in New Orleans to be on the lookout for "an orphan girl of eight or nine years of age," he tellingly added that "they are frequently offered."[10]

Unlike adult slaves, who were often sold as punishment for a supposed infraction, owners usually sold enslaved children when they needed cash. Ironically, many of these self-proclaimed paternalists sold their black children to help finance the education of their own privileged white children or to help in other ways to support their lavish lifestyle. In Georgia, the enslaved boy John Brown was sold at the age of ten to finance the construction of a new plantation house for his owner. Another former slave recalled that his brother "wuz sold ter dress young Missus fer her weddin.'"[11]

Legal action likewise forced the sale of many young children. As a prevalent form of collateral, they were commonly sold to settle debts. And very little worried enslaved Americans more than the deaths of their owners, since that often meant that sales would occur to divide up and settle their estates. As the former slave Frederick Douglass noted, the death of an owner was a time of "high excitement and deep anxiety" for most American slaves. Sometimes the human property was split up among their former owner's descendants, but it was also common to sell the slaves individually at public auction to bring the biggest return for the estate. Therefore, at such times it was not unusual for boys and girls as young as four or five to be sold away from their family and friends for the rest of their lives.[12]

It was at this point in their young lives that southern slaves began to learn how to resist such sales as best they could. The former slave Henry Watson remembered that, when a strange white man arrived on his plantation in Virginia, he "ran with the rest of the children to hide ourselves until the man had gone," while another former Virginia slave recalled that "young'uns fout an' kick lak crazy folks" when they were placed on the auction block. Some even learned how to use other ploys to negotiate a sale. At the age of fifteen, Ambrose Headen was forced to leave his family in North Carolina, walk fourteen miles to a slave market, and place himself upon an auction block before a crowd of 500 people. After three hours of intense bidding, he was sold to a local planter who was known for his cruelty. Headen began crying and sobbing until the planter, at the urging of others, resold him to another buyer, just as he had hoped.[13]

Despite the efforts of individuals such as Headen, who were able to alter a sale to their liking or even to negate an undesirable one by running away or causing a scene, there was little that most slave children could do to prevent their sale and forced departure from their loved ones. Most parents tried to soften the blow of separation for their children as best they could. Thomas Jones recalled that his parents were aware of the "inevitable suffering in store for their beloved children," and they "talked about our coming misery, and they lifted up their voices and wept aloud, as they spoke of our being torn from them and sold off to the dreaded slave trader." Henry Box Brown remembered that his mother would take him "on her knee, and pointing to the forest trees adjacent, now being stripped of their thick foliage by autumnal winds, would say to me, 'my son, as yonder leaves are stripped from off the trees of the forest, so are the children of slaves swept away from them by the hands of cruel tyrants.'" John Brown's mother simply "took to kissing us a good deal oftener" when she realized that her children were about to be sold.[14]

Many slave parents made special efforts to prepare their children for their eventual fate. Some emphasized the need to be stoic when faced with suffering and to never complain. Others were like the Virginia mother who advised her daughter before the girl's departure to "Be good an' trus' in de Lawd." At such times, parents frequently told their children to be polite and obey their elders in their new home. Laura Clark's grandmother counseled the little girl to "be er good gal, and mine bofe white and black." That way, "ev'body will like you." This was important advice for the six-year-old Laura, who was about to be taken from her home in North Carolina by a slave trader and sold in Alabama. Such young children needed to depend upon complete strangers (both black and white) for their survival.[15]

A few slave parents managed to find adult substitutes to look after their children in their absence. When Mingo White was sold away from his family to a slave trader at the age of four, his father arranged for another slave named John White "to take care of me for him," which he did. Small children also needed someone to look after them when their parents were sold away. Before a mother in Arkansas was carried away from her children, she asked another enslaved woman to "be a mother to my children, will you? I hate to leave them, poor little things, but I can't help myself. Their poor father is dead and only God knows what will become of them when Master Bill and Miss Tessie dies."[16]

Despite their parents' best efforts to protect them, sale for the vast majority of young children was still a traumatic experience. This proved especially true for those who were sold at public auction. As one former slave recalled when describing her sale as a little girl, "I was scared and cried, but they put me up there anyway." Sometimes when young people were too fearful, the crowd might ridicule them for their inability to handle their fate. According to one visitor to an auction in Washington, DC, a sixteen-year-old boy "trembled all the while" before his sale, which resulted in "a good deal of laughing and talking amongst the buyers, and several jests." If youths could maintain the proper decorum on the stand, however, they might win over the respect of the bidders. Such was the case with a fifteen-year-old boy in St. Louis. As a visitor to this sale reported, "The little fellow appeared to realize his condition and when the big tear rolled down his cheek would meekly brush it aside and hold up his head with an air & manner which won him the sympathies of a great number of the spectators." Unfortunately, this young man could hold his strong front only so long, for "as soon as he was sold, his feelings were vented in floods of tears."[17]

After the humiliation of the auction block, those boys and girls sold in the interregional trade were usually manacled to other slaves in a coffle and forced to march overland to their destination in the Deep South. While such a journey was difficult for most adult slaves, it was especially challenging for young children, who lacked the same physical strength to endure the long trek (only the smallest children got to ride in the wagons along with others who required such assistance). In addition, at times they also had to defend themselves from other slaves who sought to take advantage of them.

One boy who later chronicled his experiences in a slave coffle was John Parker. After being sold at the age of eight, Parker was chained next to an old man and marched from Norfolk, Virginia, to Richmond for resale to the Deep South. This elderly man took pity on the young boy and made Parker's "weight of the chain as light as he could." Despite this helpful example, though, on his next journey to Alabama, Parker at first acted in just the opposite manner, taking out his frustrations by attacking those creatures weaker than him. He knocked the blooms off the shrubs in his path and threw a stone at a bird hoping to kill it—only to have the other slaves laugh at his anger. He also beat up a smaller boy in his coffle named Jeff, who continually cried at being taken from his mother. Fortunately, Parker soon recognized the foolishness of his actions and came to the younger boy's defense. When another bigger and stronger boy in the coffle tried to steal the smaller boy's food, Parker began "pummeling and clawing him, until he was glad to release Jeff's dinner."[18]

Upon their arrival in the importing states, enslaved boys and girls also faced other painful challenges. As one former slave recalled, he "was jes' a little chap" when he was placed with a hundred other slaves in a New Orleans slave pen, but he still remembered "like it happened yesterday" how "the dirt and smell was terrible, terrible." Moreover, while most adult slaves from the Upper South considered sale into the Deep South a fate worse than death, with the region's frontier conditions, subtropical climate, rampant diseases, and extreme working conditions, for small children, it likewise meant being exposed to potentially abusive adults (both black and white) without the protection of family and friends. It was no surprise, then, that James Franklin reported from his slave depot in Natchez that "the small fry look at me as though they are allarmed &c," adding that he supposed "they will have some cause when F & A's [Franklin & Armfield's] lot arrives."[19]

While this lack of family protection was costly for all slave children, it proved especially so for young girls. Enslaved women throughout the South were routinely raped by white men; however, threats of retaliation by a woman's family or friends could, at times, offer some security from this violence. Young girls caught in the slave trade lacked even this minimal level of protection and were particularly vulnerable to sexual abuse, both by the enslaved men around them and by their new owners. After her sale in Missouri, a fourteen-year-old girl named Celia was raped on the way home by the sixty-year-old widower who had purchased her. Another young girl in Georgia met the same fate. As this girl's sister later explained, her new owner made "her go out and lay on a table and two or three white men would have in'ercourse with her befor' they'd let her git up." The sister then sadly added that "she wus jes' a small girl hone. She died when she wus still in her young days, still a girl."[20]

The domestic trade had devastating consequences for the young boys and girls who were caught up in it. For most enslaved children, especially those sold into the interregional trade, sale meant that they would almost certainly never see their families or friends again, and in many respects, it brought the same type of finality as death. According to Louis Hughes, he continually grieved for his mother after his sale as a small boy, and "it came to me, more and more plainly, that I would never see her again. Young and lonely as I was, I could not help crying, oftentimes for hours together."[21]

Their experience in the slave trade was also something that most enslaved children remembered for the rest of their lives. After being sold at the age of four, Charles Ball had to watch as his owner whipped his mother when she tried to plead with the man not to take her young child away. More than fifty years later, Ball admitted that "the terrors of the scene return with painful vividness upon my memory." Some, such as John Brown, were haunted by their childhood experiences in large New Orleans slave pens. As he later wrote, "I cannot think of it without a cold shiver. I often dream of it, and as often dwell upon it in the day-time." Most, however, focused on never forgetting their families and friends. After being torn from his family in Virginia at the age of seven, Lewis Clarke noted that his "thoughts continually by day and my dreams by night were of mother and home." In his later life, the former South Carolina slave Caleb Craig acknowledged that he still had "visions and dreams" of his mother "in my sleep, sometime yet."[22]

Even if the majority of enslaved children never experienced the trauma of sale personally, the slave trade still had a constant effect upon their lives. For one thing, it was quite likely that they would have had family members or friends who were sold away from them, and it is hard to overemphasize the impact that having a parent sold away would have upon a young child's life. Also, most children at one time or another witnessed the slave trade and heard stories about its operations and effects. For those living in southern cities or near county courthouses, slave auctions were common and both black and white southerners were present at the proceedings. Others lived near country roads and frequently observed the many slave coffles as they trudged their victims, including many children, toward the slave markets of the Deep South. According to one former slave from Texas, Calvin Moye, he was constantly in fear of the many slave traders who passed by his place: "Dey was lots of dem speculators coming by de road in front of de plantation, and ever' time I see dem coming, cold chills run over me till I see dem go on by our lane."[23]

The slave quarters were likewise always full of tales of child snatching and kidnappers enticing little children into their wagons with trinkets and food. While such stories were often based more on suspicion than reality, cases of slave kidnappings were common enough to give credence to these fears. Naturally, these stories exacerbated the feelings of fear already present within many enslaved families. At the same time, however, they also helped to keep numerous young boys and girls from wandering too far from home. Both slave parents and meddlesome owners used such fears to help restrain enslaved children. As one former Texas slave recalled, "Old Massa warned us to look out and not let the trader catch us, cause the trader'd just as soon steal a nigger as sell him."[24]

The fear of sale influenced virtually every enslaved child in the South, and they were forced to cope with this anxiety as best they could. Like countless children in other societies, many young slaves attempted to neutralize what they feared most through imitative play. Children have always acted out real-life events in their play as a way to nullify things that trouble them or that make them anxious about their forthcoming lives. Therefore, slave children did more than just play house and dramatize their future roles as parents. Both outside observers and former slaves noted that enslaved children played the game of "auction." Upon entering an otherwise empty slave-auctioning hall in Richmond, one visitor found three small children at play: "An intensely black little negro, of four or five years of age, was standing on the bench, or block, as it is called, with an equally black girl, about a year younger, by his side, whom he was pretending to sell by bids to another black child, who was rolling about the floor." Such activities by slave children not only demonstrated the powerful influence that the domestic trade had upon their lives, but it also showed the extent to which they would go to mitigate, and in their own way resist, that which they feared most.[25]

II

Upon reaching adulthood, most southern slaves continued resisting the domestic trade as best they could. At the extreme were those individuals who responded to an unwanted sale by violently attacking those whom they saw as responsible for their fate. After the owner of a slave in St. Louis sold the man's wife, the enraged slave took a double-barreled gun and fired one shot each at his master and mistress in the middle of the night, killing his male owner. Another enslaved man in Arkansas responded to his upcoming sale in a similar fashion. While being transported to a local slave market, this man fractured his owner's skull and slit his throat. In Alabama, a black man killed two of his children and wounded his former owner with a knife. According to the newspaper report, the owner "had but a few days before sold the negro, without his children. It is supposed he was urged to the horrid deed by the idea of parting with them."[26]

Desperate slaves took out their anger against all manner of people associated with their sale or the sale of a loved one. Some struck out against their new owners. After his wife and children were sold by their Maryland owner, a male slave shot and killed one of the two men who came to pick them up, while in Kentucky a recently sold man stabbed the agent sent to apprehend him three times with a knife, killing him instantly. Others attacked neighboring owners whom they saw as responsible for the sale of their family or friends. Such was the case with a Missouri man who learned that the woman who had owned his mother and brother had sold them away. The furious slave barged into the white woman's home during dinner with a drawn gun only to be killed first by a white family member who had his own firearm. One enslaved man in Virginia even killed his owner with a tobacco hoe for refusing to sell him back to the vicinity of his former home.[27]

Such violent responses were not confined to younger, more impetuous slaves; enslaved southerners of all ages committed them. In Virginia, after a sixty-year-old man named Jesse and his wife were sold to a trader, Jesse armed himself with several knives, a razor, an ax, and a hatchet and went looking for John Jenkins, his wife's former owner. In the struggle that ensued, Jesse intentionally cut himself seriously enough to prevent sale and burned down Jenkins's house. At his trial, Jesse reportedly said that "he did not want to go to the traders and would not go if he could prevent it—said too many were sold to go with their wives and did not go" and that "he would be perfectly satisfied himself to die if he could have satisfaction out of Mr. Jenkins."[28]

A number of slaves fought back while being carried to the Deep South for sale. As early as 1799, two Georgia traders had their throats slit when the slaves in their coffle revolted. In 1825, five men escaped from a coffle outside Raleigh, North Carolina, after one of them felled their speculator with a stone. Three years later, Robert Carlisle, a trader from Kentucky, was killed by a bondsman along the National Road in western Pennsylvania. The following year about ninety chained and handcuffed slaves were being driven through Kentucky when suddenly two of the manacled men dropped their shackles and commenced fighting. As the traders moved in to stop them, it quickly became apparent that this was a diversion and all of the slaves were at liberty, thanks to a file they had somehow appropriated. Before it was over, two of the three white men had been killed and about $2,400 had been stolen. The slaves involved in this incident were all soon captured and the four ringleaders were executed, although they remained unrepentant until the end. Before their execution, one of the men reportedly exclaimed, "Death—death at any time, in preference to slavery."[29]

By the 1830s, the killing of slave traders by their human cargoes had become so common that some whites in Virginia worried that it was having a negative effect upon the interregional trade, as well as on their most important export. After a slave in that state killed a Mississippi trader in 1836, local citizens petitioned for the enslaved man's relief, claiming that "hatred to the south and southern purchasers of their Race has been increased to a degree of *desperation* so much so that the *best* of them has no *morral* hesitancy in killing what they call a sole driver." This fear of rampant assaults upon traders did have some credence; just two years earlier, two traders, Jesse and John Kirby of Georgia, were attacked in Virginia by several Maryland slaves they were transporting south. As a local newspaper put it, in addition to robbing the two men of about $3,000, "their throats were cut, and the head of one cleft open with an axe." Such attacks appear to have tapered off by the end of the decade, or at least they received less coverage in the southern press. Still, violence against speculators continued throughout the antebellum period. In 1849, John Ponder was murdered with an ax by the slaves in his coffle while asleep in his tent in Georgia.[30]

Uprisings occurred when slaves were transported by water as well. The most famous insurrection in the coastal trade was in 1841, when 135 slaves on the *Creole* killed one trader, wounded several others, and forced the captain to sail to the Bahamas. Earlier, in 1826, while sailing from Baltimore to New Orleans, about 30 men and women on the *Decatur* also revolted. They killed two crew members and attempted to navigate to Haiti, only to be recaptured and taken to New York. Four years later, a cargo of slaves on a similar voyage likewise nearly captured the *Lafayette*. According to a contemporary report, "They were subdued, after considerable difficulty, and 25 of them were bolted down to the deck, until the arrival of the vessel at New Orleans."[31] Bloody attacks also took place in the river trade. In 1826, while heading down the Ohio River on a flatboat for Mississippi, seventy-five slaves broke free and killed all five white men on board, including early Kentucky trader Edward Stone.[32]

Finally, those caught in the domestic trade struck out violently against slave traders in other important ways. In 1825, a newspaper in Washington, DC, reported that "a serious riot" had broken out between blacks and local slave dealers in Alexandria. In 1859, a man recently imported into Mississippi ran away three times within six weeks of his purchase. After he was captured the second time, he tried to slit his jailer's throat. According to one former slave, at least one enslaved woman got the ultimate revenge against her tormentor.

When the speculator who purchased her tried to rape this woman, she grabbed a knife and "sterilized him," from which injury the man died the next day. While the woman was initially charged with murder, officials eventually released her and granted her freedom.[33]

In addition to the slaves who lashed out violently against those whom they saw as responsible for their sale, there were also some who responded to the domestic trade by engaging in more self-destructive behavior. A few men and women tried to prevent their sale by lessening their market value through self-mutilation. In Richmond, the Swedish visitor Fredrika Bremer met a man who had chopped off the fingers of his right hand after his owner had determined to sell him away from his wife and children, and in Missouri, a newspaper reported that a man had cut off the fingers of his left hand after learning of his sale to a New Orleans trader.[34]

There were also those who sought solace by taking their own lives. *Niles' Register* reported that "a negro man, at the moment of his transfer to one of these blood-merchants cut his own throat, on a public wharf in Baltimore— and a few days ago a negro woman, near Snow Hill, in this state, on being informed that she was sold, first cut the throat of her child and then her own, by which both of them immediately died." This was not the only enslaved woman to take her and her children's lives because of the domestic trade. In Louisiana, a recently sold woman named Agnes drowned herself and her infant daughter "in a deep water hole" rather than live with her new owner, while a newspaper in Nashville reported that another woman there jumped into the river with a child in each arm. According to the report, "Her master had threatened to sell her, and she was determined not to be sold." Some desperate men like-wise responded to an unwanted sale in this manner. After one man in Alabama had been sold, he "commenced crying" and begged his owner to rescind the sale. When the man did not, the distraught slave hung himself. Another man in South Carolina ended his life in an even more dramatic fashion when he slashed his own throat in front of the seller, buyer, and all others in attendance at his sale.[35]

It needs to be noted that the overwhelming majority of black southerners did not respond to the domestic slave trade with violent resistance. Most per-ceived such behavior as futile, especially when committed in fits of anger. They knew that practically all who resisted in this manner were eventually caught and punished, which usually meant either sale to the Deep South or death. But for some, violent resistance seemed the only choice available—and not all were found guilty for their actions. In 1848, in order to prevent their being sepa-rated through sale, a man in Covington, Kentucky, killed his wife and child and attempted to kill himself. Not only did a jury find the man innocent of murder, but the community also agreed to purchase his freedom.[36]

III

A far more common form of resistance to sale was flight. All across the South, thousands of enslaved men and women fled their owners because of sale, the threat of sale, or the sale of a loved one. It was arguably the most prevalent reason for running away. Even one former slaveholder in Alabama later acknowledged that the separation of families through sale was "the cause of about half of the runaways." According to one fugitive who made it into Canada, "The fear of being sold South had more influence in inducing me to leave than any other thing." The same proved true for most black expatriates. Of the 117 former slaves living in Canada interviewed by the abolitionist Benjamin Drew, 60 gave a reason for their decision to flee, and of this group, 53 percent mentioned the threat of sale or the consequences of a sale as their primary motivation. Of those who gave another reason for flight, 68 percent had been sold at least once in their lives or knew of a close friend or family member who had been sold. Therefore, not only was the fear of sale a powerful incentive against flight, as the owners had intended, but, ironically, for many it could also be a major cause for escape.[37]

Slaves frequently ran away after being told that they were going to be sold, and some left at just the possibility of such an event. As one Missouri owner noted when advertising for his absent man, he believed "that nothing but the fear of being sent to New Orleans induced him to run away." Sometimes entire slave communities fled when threatened with sale. After 155 slaves living on a plantation in St. Augustine, Florida, learned they had been sold and were about to be transported to Louisiana, the majority of people in that community decided to flee. According to the agent assigned to transport the slaves, when the time came for removal, "they declined going to New Orleans" and "that night about forty of the Negroes absconded." Soon only about twenty of the slaves remained. As the worried agent reported to his boss, this was "an act of revolt on the part of the Negroes, and I fear we have not seen the worst of it."[38]

Others absconded not long after sale, with some even disappearing before their new owners could get them home. Typical was the notice placed by a Louisiana planter for five runaway men who "were lately purchased at the Slave Depot on Moreau street." Many owners lost individuals even more quickly. One disappointed purchaser complained that he had "bought George in St. Louis, and he left me the night after I got to Vicksburg"; another noted that his runaway would still "probably have on a suit of trader's blue cloth clothes and fur hat"; while a third said his man "had on handcuffs when he left." Such quick departures also occurred at court-ordered sales. One buyer at a public sale in Lexington, Kentucky, told the man he had just purchased to meet him at the stables at three o'clock, only to have his new property never show up because he had already run away.[39]

Recognizing the effect that sale had on precipitating flight, many owners took steps to prevent it. The most common means was by withholding advance knowledge of an upcoming sale. When ordering the sale of a troublesome man named Owen, one Alabama planter warned his agent in Mobile that "this must be done with surprize & secracy lest he make his escape." Another seller in Missouri went so far as to keep his identity hidden from those who were advertising the sale. As he explained in a letter to the local sheriff: "Not wishing my negroes to know of my intention to sell lest they might slip off or be out of the way when wanted, you will see the reason that no name was attached to the advertisement nor to this, that you might not be able to answer any inquires that might be made as to the owner lest they might hear of it." Some owners also engaged in deceptive ploys, such as tricking a slave into unknowingly handing himself over to a new owner. As the former slave William Parker recalled, a childhood friend was sent to deliver a letter to a family acquaintance, only to learn "at the end of his journey that he had parted with parents, friends, and all."[40]

Because of their fear of being sold to the Deep South, slaves were especially anxious to get away from professional traders. Even the hint of such a sale could cause people to flee. That was why slaves always got nervous, and talked about flight, whenever they saw strange white men hanging around their owners' property. Some dealers, like John Denning of Baltimore, sought to reassure prospective clients that such elopements would not occur when dealing with them. As Denning told a Maryland planter, if he came out and appraised the man's slaves, they "would never suspect me as a trader." Still, most speculators recognized the fears that their actions instilled in black southerners. Therefore, when a trader in Savannah inquired if a colleague in Charleston would send him two slaves who were working on a boat there, he noted that the men were to be sold and cautioned "if they have the slightest hint of it they will give you trouble and probably make their escape."[41]

Once slaves were in their possession, most experienced slave traders took extra precautions to make sure that everyone was well secured. That is why slaves were usually held in jails or pens and chained when transported south. Traders also alerted their partners to potentially troublesome individuals. When sending a man to Richmond for sale, one Baltimore dealer warned his associate in that city to "*be sure to put him into jail*, allow me to urge that point"; on an earlier occasion, this man had also advised the Richmond auctioneer to keep another slave under heavy guard, "otherwise he will run away sure as hell." Some slaves attempted to flee even when they had no chance of making their escape. On one occasion, an enslaved man ran out of Jones & Slatter's jail in Richmond and, according to a competing trader who witnessed the incident,

Photograph of handcuffs and leg irons used to shackle slaves to prevent them from escaping during transport to the Lower South in overland coffles. Courtesy of the Audio-Visual Archives, Special Collections and Archives, University of Kentucky Libraries.

Photograph of the interior of the Franklin & Armfield slave pen on Duke Street in Alexandria. During the Civil War, this was one of several former slave pens that the Union army used to house Confederate prisoners of war. Courtesy of the Audio-Visual Archives, Special Collections and Archives, University of Kentucky Libraries.

one of the firm's principles ran "right after him & hollowing, ketch him! ketch him, & away they both went down the street." The man was eventually caught, but the competitor still thought it "very amuseing to see Slater run & to hear him hollow & when he came up the street with the boy he had him by the Collar & now & then he would give him a little shake."[42]

Despite all of the efforts to prevent flight, enslaved men and women still managed to get away from professional traders. As one speculator reported from Charlottesville, Virginia: "I had bought a boy the same day and had him up in my Room and stript him, and told the man I would take him, & He give him a order to go and get his Cloathing, and that was the Last I have seen of him." Two Virginia men, Levi Douglass and James Wright, managed to escape from a slave coffle after convincing the trader to unshackle them. Others walked off steamboats or jumped ship before sailing to New Orleans in the coastal trade. In February 1819, one captain made an addendum to his slave manifest, noting that a man and woman "done ran away before leaving Savannah"; three months later, another captain farther north made a similar correction, adding that one slave had "run away before leaving the port of Baltimore." Railroads offered opportunities for flight as well. While being transported to Richmond, one man named Andrew exited the train. Apparently he was fastened by himself which facilitated his escape. Other runaways received aid in getting off "the cars." After a slave he was sending to Charleston disappeared, one South Carolina trader threatened to sue the railroad, as the train's conductor had earlier removed the man's handcuffs.[43]

Some individuals even managed to escape from a slave trader's depot. In New Orleans, one recently arrived man ran away from the dealer James White after he convinced the trader that he had forgotten his clothing on board a steamboat. When White allowed the man to return to the boat, the new arrival eluded his guard and got away. Another slave named Archy similarly disappeared from the dealer Thomas Foster. When Archy agreed to carry some clothing to a steamboat for a woman Foster had just sold, Archy never returned. Women likewise fled from such facilities. Not only did one woman break out of a New Orleans slave pen (through three locked doors), but she also disguised herself well enough to secure passage aboard a vessel to France. Another woman named Angeline successfully escaped from a Richmond jail. According to the trader who advertised for her, he thought Angeline would return to "where she was raised, either by the Canal or Central Rail Road." Finally, in Memphis, Nathan Bedford Forrest and his then partner Byrd Hill offered a $25 reward for a man named Nat Mayson who "RANAWAY from our Negro Mart." Remarkably, Hill & Forrest claimed that the man had run away "without a cause."[44]

While it is common to think of runaway slaves as fugitives heading north, the vast majority remained in the South, with many crisscrossing the region, trying to reunite with family and friends. Owners understood this and frequently looked to a prior residence when attempting to locate and capture their property. This can be seen in the numerous runaway-slave advertisements, many of which listed the fugitive's former home. Sometimes this was only a county or two away, such as the owner in Virginia who noted that the young man he had just purchased in Richmond "was raised near Fredericksburg; near which place I suppose he is now lurking." Others had much greater distances to travel. One Mississippi planter advertised for his runaway in the *Louisville Courier*, believing that the man had "returned to Kentucky about forty miles back of Louisville where he was raised."[45]

Most of these notices listed individuals trying to get back to former homes; however, there were also many men and women who fled in an attempt to find others who had been sold away. As one Alabama owner noted in reference to his absent man: "I think it quite probable that this fellow has succeeded in getting to his wife, who was carried away last Spring out of my neighborhood." Contrary to the common stereotype of all slaves fleeing to the North, the owner of one Kentucky runaway thought it "highly probable" that his man would go the other way and "make for New Orleans, as he has a wife living in that city, and he has been heard to say frequently that he was determined to go to New Orleans." While such elopements obviously angered most owners, at least one Missouri woman found the absence of her family's man excusable. After the husband of a recently sold slave had fled, this woman admitted that she was "glad to hear he had so good a reason for running away. Most men run *from* instead of *to* their wives."[46]

While flight was a relatively common response to sale, as with violent resistance, the prospect for success was not very promising. The trip was filled with hazards, and those who remained in the South had little chance of going unnoticed even if they did reach their destination. Failed escape could also be costly, especially for those who tried to flee from professional traders. Many received gunshot wounds or other injuries in their recapture. When a man ran away from a trader in New Orleans, he ended up in the Baton Rouge jail after being "shot in the legs by those who stopped him." In addition, a number of speculators guarded their coffles with dogs. As Henry Bibb later reported, the man who transported him to New Orleans "had a very large savage dog, which was trained up to catch runaway slaves."[47]

Most of those recaptured also faced punishment for their actions. One especially severe torture occurred in Florida after a woman named Katy ran off following her sale to a Pensacola man against her wishes. According to the local newspaper report, after she was caught, the man had Katy "tied behind a wagon, by a chain fastened to her neck by a leather string, and with her arms tied fast behind her, ... ordered the driver of the horse attached to the wagon, to drive about the streets, and to whip the horse so as to make it go fast." This he did until the exhausted woman "became insensible."[48]

The greatest risk involved with flight, however, was simple survival, as some of those who fled came to tragic ends. Not long after being sold by a New Orleans trader, one man ran off, lasting about three months before succumbing to an illness caused by exposure and "eating indigestible food." Others lost their lives attempting to elude capture. Within days of being sold by a Charleston trader who had carried him to New Orleans for sale, a ten-year-old boy named Ben ran off from his new owner. Ben returned to the slave trader's yard, only to be reclaimed by his purchaser. Once more the young boy fled, and this time he drowned while making his escape. Considering all of the possible consequences, then, it is not surprising that some runaways experienced a change of heart and returned to face their fate. According to one South Carolina owner, after informing a slave named Nat that he was going to be sold, "his lordship left." But after thinking about it for a few hours, Nat "came in and set about making his arrangements for moving."[49]

Still, despite the dangers and risks, thousands of enslaved men and women did flee their owners, and many were successful in their efforts. That some were able to escape the system entirely is confirmed by the dozens of fugitive slave narratives, almost all of which mention sale as a motive for their flight. Many others blended in with the southern urban population or were protected by someone in their former neighborhood. At least one Virginia man who ran off after being sold to a trader managed to hide in the woods for twelve months before a neighboring woman bought him from the trader. After word of this transaction reached him, this man returned from the woods and his new owner reunited him with his family. Therefore, while flight always remained an uncertain proposition, at least for some individuals, it was an effective form of resistance to the domestic trade.[50]

IV

In addition to running away, bondspeople also engaged in other forms of overt resistance when faced with an unwanted sale. Several former slaves recalled the courageous actions of their mothers when they and their siblings were about to be sold. Moses Grandy remembered that his "mother often hid us all in the woods, to prevent master selling us." According to Henry Stewart, his mother did the same thing and once even blocked the sale of his brother to a trader. Apparently, when their owner came to pick the boy up, she defied him, stating "the first man that comes into my house, I will split his head open." Most women were not so successful, although many did have to be forcibly restrained when their children were taken away. After Grandy's brother was sold, his mother resisted so strenuously that she had to be held down, and she was later tied to a peach tree and flogged.[51]

This desperate attempt by women to keep their families together was commented upon by numerous white observers of slaves being sold at auction. According to a visitor in Memphis, after the mother of two children was sold, "She begged and implored her new master on her knees to buy her children also, but it had no effect, he would not do it. She then begged him to buy her little girl (about 5 years old) but all to no purpose, it was truly heart rending to hear her cries when they were taking her away." Given such efforts, it is not surprising that the slaveholding congressman John Randolph of Roanoke once remarked: "The greatest orator I ever heard was a woman. She was a slave and a mother and her rostrum was an auction block."[52]

In addition to losing their families, enslaved women had to confront other degrading aspects of the domestic trade. Not only were many of them raped by the white men who owned them, but a number then found themselves being sold (along with their children, who had been fathered by their abusers), either at the insistence of the owner's wife or as a way of removing a troublesome reminder for the man. At least one Mississippi woman tried to do something about such an unwanted sale. In 1853, Virginia Boyd sent a letter from a slave depot in Houston to the former slave dealer Rice Ballard. This woman had apparently been the slave and mistress of Ballard's partner, Samuel Boyd, and even though she knew that Ballard had arranged for her sale, she still sought his assistance in getting Boyd to bring her and her children back to Mississippi. She appealed to Ballard's paternalistic sensibilities, noting all that she had gone through with Boyd and how hard it was "for the father of my children to sell his own offspring, yes his own flesh & blood." She likewise alluded to Ballard's feelings as a father and praised his ability "to simpathize with others in distress." But the enslaved woman then made a not-so-subtle threat. She assured Ballard that she had taken "every precaution to prevent others from knowing or suspecting any thing" about her relationship with Boyd, and she would "not seek ever to let any thing be exposed." That is, however, "unless I am forced from bad treatment &c." Unfortunately for this woman, neither her paternalistic appeals nor her threat to expose Boyd's indiscretions had their desired effect; three months later she was sold along with her youngest child to parts unknown.[53]

Women also had to confront embarrassing assaults upon their modesty and dignity, especially when sold at public auction. According to one visitor to an auction in Richmond, he had "never looked upon a more disgusting sight, young girls are put on the stand, & undergo the most indecent examination & questioning." While women were not generally examined in as intimate a detail as men, they still had strange men grabbing their arms, legs, and breasts and sticking dirty fingers in their mouths to check their teeth. And if a potential purchaser desired, he could examine a woman's genitals (normally, behind a screen) to check for venereal disease or a prolapsed uterus, both of which were common enough to elicit concern. Moreover, slave auctioneers went out of their way to create a sexually charged atmosphere for their predominantly male customers. As one visitor to New Orleans noted when describing one of these men: "When a woman is sold, he usually puts his audience in good humour by a few indecent jokes." That was why a former male slave later recalled that the women at such sales "always looked so shame and pitiful up on dat stand wid all dem men standing dere lookin' at em wid what dey had on dey minds shinin' in they eyes."[54]

While women had little choice but to accept this degradation, some individuals did their best to resist. Particularly insulting were the examinations to check a young woman's nursing ability. As one former slave explained, they would "take her by her breasts and pull dem to show how good she was built for raisin' chillun." Although women could not prevent such violations, some did make their displeasure known. One visitor to an auction in Richmond reported that when the men in the room began examining the breasts of a woman for sale, "her eyes flashed fire, and I sincerely believe, had a knife been within her grasp she would have plunged it in the hearts of her tormentors." A few women even used their sexuality to turn the insult around and shame the men. According to a former Virginia slave, when the buyers of one enslaved woman began sticking their fingers in her mouth checking her teeth, the woman "got awful mad, and she pult up her dress an' tole ole nigger traders to look an' see if dey could fin' any teef down dere."[55]

A number of slaves, both male and female, resisted the more arbitrary nature of sale by taking an active part in determining who their new owners would be. All across the South hundreds of men and women managed to talk their masters into letting them find their own purchasers. While one motive for allowing such liberty was to facilitate a sale, it did offer many individuals the chance to control their fate. Others appealed to family members for help in finding a buyer. In 1852, one "quite heart sick" Virginia woman wrote to her husband that their son had just been sold to a trader and she and another child were to be offered at the next court sale. She wanted him to act quickly and ask "Dr Hamilton [and] your master if either will buy me," adding, "I don't want a trader to get me." Occasionally, professional traders used these connections to help to complete a sale. When one Savannah dealer had trouble selling a man named Ben, he contacted a colleague in Charleston. Apparently the enslaved man had a wife who lived in that city and the Savannah dealer thought his colleague "may be able to find some one to purchase him as she is very anxious that Ben should be owned in Charleston." Several slaves also recommended their own sale rather than being carried away by migrating planters. When their absentee owner planned on moving them, two Missouri women informed him that "we have a great many friends in this place and would rather be sold than go to Texas."[56]

Slaves could also sometimes influence a sale at public auction. One widow in Alabama canceled the sale of her human property after the first woman to be sold "overcame us all by her tears & promises." Moreover, just as purchasers acquired as much information as possible about the men and women they were buying, those being sold did the same for the people who were looking at them. As one former slaveholder admitted when remembering his first slave auction, "It was surprising to see how thoroughly they all seemed to be informed concerning the men who were bidding for them." Through signals, both subtle and overt, those on the block frequently made their desires known. Usually this entailed looks of encouragement or open pleas for a particular member of the audience to buy them, but it could also be conveyed in blunt expressions of displeasure. According to one British visitor, a woman prevented her sale to an undesirable bidder by warning him: "Buy me if you please; but I tell you openly, if I become your slave, I will cut your throat the first opportunity."[57]

Slaves had an even greater chance of affecting a sale when sold out of a slave dealer's depot. Once again, not only did buyers base their decisions on first impressions, but so did the enslaved. Given the longer time that most individuals spent in these facilities, that gave them a greater opportunity to evaluate purchasers and do what they could to acquire an acceptable owner. As John Brown, a former slave who spent three months in a New Orleans pen, explained, "The price a slave fetches depends, in a great measure, upon the general appearance he or she presents to the intending buyer. A man or a woman may be well made, and physically faultless in every respect, yet their value be impaired by a sour look, or a dull, vacant stare, or a general dulness of demeanour." He added that this was the reason that those being sold were "instructed to look 'spry and smart:' to hold themselves well up, and put on a smiling, cheerful countenance." Dealers demanded this behavior and often punished those who refused, yet most slaves sized up purchasers as well and decided for themselves how far they would comply. According to John Parker, another young man who found himself in a New Orleans depot, "I made up my mind I was going to select my owner, so when anyone came to inspect me I did not like, I answered all questions with a 'yes,' and made myself disagreeable."[58]

Some men and women sought to prevent sale entirely by feigning illness or physical disability. As one Virginian remarked after being told by a Richmond dealer that a female slave was telling possible buyers that she was unsound: "I believe it is all pretentious & false representations she is making with the hope of returning to King George [County] to live with her husband which she will never do." Even after arriving in the Deep South, some individuals employed this ruse, usually in the hope of being carried back to their former homes. After transporting a man from South Carolina to Alabama, one trader complained, "I could Sell him like hot Cakes if he would talk Right. . . . the Boy is trying to make himself *unsound.* He Says he wore a trust [truss] in Charleston." Sometimes just the possibility of such behavior could be used against a master considering a sale. According to a trader in Virginia, the owner of a man he had recently bought had warned him that "the negro has made some threats that if he went to sell him that he would tell that he was unsound."[59]

Owners understood that their property could deliberately sabotage a sale and often took action to prevent it. Sometimes that meant a gentle enticement. When sending his man to a Charleston broker, one South Carolina planter noted that "a little bribe to him will make him speak up, for he is a fellow inclined to extol his capabilities above their merits." A North Carolina trader also paid his slaves from $1 to $3 each, explaining that "it was understood that I should give the negroes a Present if they would try to get homes and not do any thing against the intrust of their sales."[60]

But far more often, this "enticement" took the form of a beating. When selling through dealers, owners frequently believed that their property might need a little "correcting" before they would bring a good price. As one Virginia planter recommended in reference to the man he was trying to sell, "Try and get him to talk right. Probably you will have to have him whiped a few times before he will do." Others, such as John Campbell of Baltimore, were less specific, stating simply, "Paddle all the crazy ones untill their senses are right." One Lynchburg, Virginia, man instructed the Richmond auctioneer selling his troublesome woman to "tell your Boy Homer to Present her my compliments and at the same Time to turn her coat over her head & give her 25 licks well Laid on her naked *Ass.*"[61]

Professional traders also routinely "healed" those who claimed sickness and other ailments. After one man complained of being ill, the New Orleans auctioneer Joseph Beard remarked that he would "thrash that out of him," while a speculator selling enslaved Virginians in Louisiana assured buyers that his "Slaves were good, healthy, and serviceable Slaves, and promised that if they were not sound he would *make them so.*" Some traders even had their own special "cures." After two women he owned prevented their sale by fabricating health complaints, one Richmond speculator reported to his partner in North Carolina: "I will hav to use som of Dr Halls Medson of NC, you know what kind of medcin that is. . . . they want braking and I had as well brake them as any body."[62]

Still, despite all of the efforts by owners to get their human property to "talk right" and make a good sale, many bondspeople were able to manipulate these transactions and sometimes even prevent them entirely. When sending several individuals to Richmond for shipment south, one Virginia trader complained: "I did intend to leave Nancy's child but she made such a damned fuss I had to let her take it." A visitor to a slave auction in Nashville reported that one woman who had already lost two children made such a convincing appeal that the crowd forced the auctioneer to accept a low bid so her three-year-old daughter could be sold to her purchaser. In Maryland, one mistress noted that "the old witch Sara and her granddaughter" had managed to prevent a long-distance sale: "We tried to sell her in Baltimore but couldn't; [she was] afraid of being sold to some Georgian and took it in her head to make herself look bad. Finally, she made so many fine promises that she persuaded Ben Lowndes [presumably a neighbor] to buy her." In Virginia, no purchasers could be found for one woman because of her "hysterical, low spirited situation" and "depression of spirits." Apparently this struck a sympathetic chord in her owner, who told a Richmond firm to send her back home and "assure her I will keep her myself, or sell her in Falmouth. But my desire, and that of the family is to keep her."[63]

Many enslaved men and women made direct appeals to an owner's paternalistic sensibilities when trying to influence a sale. Expressions of "love" for a master and praise for an owner's supposed humanitarian qualities were common when slaves attempted to obtain the purchase of a spouse or family member. The same proved true for those seeking a similarly wanted sale of themselves. When one elderly Virginia slave contacted his absentee mistress in Missouri asking to be sold to the owner of his wife, he began by telling the woman what she wanted to hear, stating that "*although I know very well that I can never get another mistress that will do for me as you have done or would do, if it was in your power to do still . . . allow me to choose a home for the remainder of my life.*" He assured her that he just wanted to live out the few years he had left with his wife and concluded by wishing his owner "all the happiness this world can give and a future existence may bring." He signed his letter "your old and devoted Servant, Lewis."[64]

While the historical record is filled with such paternalistic appeals for the reunification of loved ones, lesser known are the similar pleas that were often made as a last-ditch effort to prevent an unwanted sale. When one Richmond slave feared that the man to whom he was hired also wanted to purchase him, the slave contacted his owner to let him know that he did not want "to be the property of any body but yourself." On one occasion, an entire slave community in South Carolina got their master to change his mind about an upcoming sale. Their owner had intended to sell a troublesome man, "but he seemed so penitent & promised so fairly & the other negroes promising to see that he would behave himself in future that I concluded that I would try him once more."[65]

Much more tragic were those appeals made by individuals who had already been sent off or sold away. Some managed to contact their former owners or others while still in the hands of a trader. One North Carolina slave somehow telegraphed his wife's mistress, informing her that the train he was being carried on to Richmond was passing through Raleigh and asking if she would please come to the station and purchase him so he would not be sold to the Deep South. In 1854, one Charleston broker informed the owner of a man he was commissioned to sell that "your instructions are for him to go out of the state; [but] Jack begs me to ask you to carry him back, he says he is sorry for what has occurred and will behave himself better for the future." Another man writing to his former owner from a dealer's pen in Mobile, Alabama, pleaded: "I Would like werry much master for you to get me Back for you no me and I no you. You would be douing me a grat favor for I would lik to live with you the Remander part of my life and mor on the account of my wife." The man had been sold for running away and said he was "werry sorry it was so that I and you had to part, but I hope that you wil over look that." He added that the trader "ses If you wil buy me Back he wil let me go cheap or at cost" and concluded "pleas sir try and get me if you can."[66]

Even after being sold in the Deep South, some individuals managed to contact their previous owners and begged to be brought back to their former homes. In 1838, Samuel Tayler, who was in Mobile, wrote to his ex-mistress in South Carolina. He noted that he had been in that city about three years and his current owner was "remarkably kind," "but Still my mind is always dwelling on home, relations, and friends which I would give the world to see." Tayler believed that his purchase price had dropped considerably since he was originally sold and added, "If you my Dear Mistress, can buy me, how happy I would be to serve you and your heirs."[67]

A Georgia woman, Vilot Lester, likewise contacted her former owner in North Carolina. She was pained at having "to leav my Long Loved home and friends" and explained in detail how she had arrived at her current location through the domestic trade. She stated that her present master "will keep me til death Siperates us without Some of my old north Caroliner friends wants to buy me again" and added, "my Dear Mistress I cannot tell my fealings nor how bad I wish to See you and old Boss and Miss Rahol and Mother." But, of special concern, Lester wanted "to now what has Ever become of my Presus little girl." She said her current owner was willing to purchase the child if her former mistress would consent to sell and requested an answer as soon as possible. She closed her appeal with "your long loved and well wishing play mate as a Servant until death."[68]

It is unknown if any of these individuals ever made it back to their former homes, just as it is impossible to determine how sincere they were in their expressions of feeling for their previous owners. While it is possible that some form of affection might have existed for a few, it is important to remember that these people had been brutally torn from their families and friends. Some of their owners may have thought of themselves as benevolent paternalists, but it is hard to imagine enslaved men and women seeing those who had sold them in that light. Still, they were obviously able to play the game when it was to their advantage. Evidence of this manipulation can be found in the example of one Georgia couple, William and Kate, who were married in 1856. The two had lived on separate plantations but were united in 1863 after William persuaded his owner, Charles Jones, to purchase Kate and the couple's three children. Undoubtedly, William had appealed to Jones's paternalistic nature when making this request and told the man what he wanted to hear. Not surprisingly, then, Jones became both embittered and confused when William and Kate refused to stay with him following the war.[69]

V

While many men, women, and children were able to mitigate, and sometimes even prevent, the harsh realities of the domestic trade, most had little choice but to accept the consequences of an unwanted sale, however unpleasant. This realization was perhaps best described by the former slave Samuel Hall. After being sold away from his wife and children, Hall noted that "his soul rebelled against such subservience to men who called themselves masters and his temper was aroused to such a pitch that he was like a wild animal in a cage, conscious, in a way, of the hopelessness of his situation, but none the less tamed, or willing to admit that he was justly restrained."[70]

Still, this does not mean that most African Americans accepted the white South's belief that they were simply human commodities who could be moved around like pieces on a giant checkerboard. Although the majority of southern slaves could not negotiate or negate their sale, there were other forms of resistance to the domestic trade (and to the slaveholders' view of the enslaved), even if they were less overt. And most essential for the survival of many individuals was the strength they found in elements of their black culture.

One important rock of support, and subtle form of resistance to the system, was slave religion. Christians took comfort in their trust that they would someday be reunited in the afterlife with departed loved ones, and many a bondsperson sought relief in the power of prayer. Usually this was an isolated act or family matter. As one former Tennessee slave recalled, "When the slaves got a feeling there was going to be an auction they would pray. The night before the sale they would pray in their cabins. They didn't pray loud but they prayed

long and you could hear the hum of voices in all the cabins down the row."
Sometimes they also came together in a form of group ministration. One former slave remembered a secret "praying time" that he and his fellow inmates
held while in a New Orleans slave pen, and the former Maryland slave John
Bruce once attended a prayer meeting on a neighboring plantation with forty
other slaves on the night before fifteen of them were shipped off to Georgia.
As he later noted, "Like the last supper where our Lord met, and identified his
betrayer—Judas, this last meeting of those blacks was to them a harbinger of
evil which they had foreseen but could not avert."[71]

Also important was the solace that could be found in song. All across the
South, music played a prominent role in the slave community, and one of its
primary functions was its ability to provide cathartic relief. As Frederick Douglass explained: "The songs of the slave represent the sorrows, rather than the
joys, of his heart; and he is relieved by them, only as an aching heart is relieved
by its tears." Therefore, understandably, the domestic trade was one of the most
frequently recurring themes in slave music. When working in the river trade,
William Wells Brown often heard such songs, one of which included the verse:

> See wives and husbands sold apart,
> Their children's screams will break my heart;—
> There's a better day a coming,
> Will you go along with me?
> There's a better day a coming,
> Go sound the jubilee!

Another former slave remembered the following song as "one of de saddest
songs we sung en durin' slavery days. . . . It always did make me cry":

> Mammy, is Ol' Massa gwin'er sell us tomorrow?
> Yes, my chile.
> Whar he gwin'er sell us?
> Way down South in Georgia.[72]

Most important in helping enslaved southerners to withstand the harsh
realities of the domestic trade was the African-American family. Since the 1970s,
much work has been done demonstrating the strength of this institution and
the special part that such alternative arrangements as extended families and
fictive kin like adoptive "aunts" and "uncles" played in aiding those individuals
caught in the trade. Moreover, the formation of a family, and especially moth-
erhood, provided a certain amount of protection against sale, since single men
and infertile women were usually sold before child-producing couples. This

point, however, should not be overemphasized since at best a woman could expect to keep small children for only a few years, and the prevalence of court sales put everyone at risk.[73]

Even more significant was the determination of many bondspeople to keep their families together, if only in memory, despite being separated by sale. One practice for remembering loved ones was naming newborns after those who had been recently sold. Others encoded family memory by naming their children after important relatives, especially fathers, who were more likely than mothers to be sold away. Such naming practices helped to sustain family memory across generations and across geographical space. Individuals transported to the Deep South also educated their children about the larger kinship group they had left behind. Many years later, former slaves in Louisiana were able to recollect stories of family members in the Upper South, some of whom they had never met. Even when forced into other living arrangements, some slaves kept their families alive in memory. In Georgia, Frances Kemble encountered a woman who had nine children (and two miscarriages) with a man named Tony. When asked, however, she made it clear that "he was not her *real* husband." The man whom she continued to think of as her *real* husband had been sold from the estate many years before for running away.[74]

In addition to keeping a family alive in memory, several men and women made efforts to stay in contact through the mail. Some managed to get word back to their loved ones while still in the hands of a trader, often by obtaining the assistance of the trader himself. Halfway through his journey to Alabama with a coffle of slaves, one trader wrote to his partner in North Carolina, "Luc wants you when you write to me to write how her child is. . . . She is doing very well though she would be better satisfied to here from her child." Another husband and wife sent a note to a "Mr Delions" back in Georgia from a slave depot in New Orleans. Apparently written by Phoebe, the wife, she asked him, "Pleas tell my daugher Clairissa and Nancy a heap how a doo for me," and requested that he "please answer this Letter for Clairssa and Let me know all that has hapend since i left." She added, "Clairssa your affectionate mother and Father sends a heap of Love to you and your Husband and my Grand Children." After listing them all by name, she concluded with "I have no more to say untill i get a home. I remain your affectionate Mother and Father."[75]

Even more poignant was the 1858 letter written by a man being held in a Savannah depot to his wife on a Georgia plantation. He began, "My Dear wife I take the pleasure of writing you these few [lines] with much regret to inform you that I am Sold to a man by the name of Peterson atreader and Stays in new orleans. I am here yet But I expect to go before long but when I get there I will write and let you know where I am." He told her, "Give my love to my father & mother and tell them good Bye for me. And if we Shall not meet in this world

I hope to meet in heaven. My Dear wife for you and my Children my pen cannot Express the griffe I feel to be parted from you all. I remain your truly husband until Death, Abream Scriven."[76]

Others got in touch with family members after reaching their final destinations, usually through the assistance of their new owners. Sometimes these
new masters also conversed with a slave's loved ones back home. Upon his
arrival in Texas, one recently purchased man named Dave received a letter from
his enslaved father and mother in Missouri. Dave's new owner, T. T. Bradley,
allowed Dave to write a return letter in which he informed his father, Gabe,
that he "had got home safe" and that he was "very well pleased with my home."
Dave noted that he "would like to se you and mother and my Sisters and Brothers but we are two fur a part to think a bout that." Still, he told his family not to
"be uneasy a bout me for I would not Swap my home for no other." Following
this message, Dave's owner, Bradley, then added a few lines himself to Dave's
father, assuring him, "well Gabe I Suppose I own your Sun Dave. I did not no it
when I bought him tho I am well pleased with him. I never have had to Speak
a Short word to him yet and I am in hopes I never will. I Bought him to keep
and if Dave holds out to be a good boy I will keep him as long as we Both live
and I will treat him well."[77]

While most recently sold slaves did not have this kind of cooperation from
their new owners, many still reached out to loved ones they had left behind.
Writing from a Louisiana sugar plantation, Thomas Ducket contacted a sympathetic white person back in the District of Columbia, demanding "for god
sake let me hear from you all. My wife and children are not out of my mine nor
night." When one woman in Tennessee contacted her former mistress in North
Carolina asking for information about her family and friends, she ended her
appeal with the paternalistic blandishment, "Please Pray for me and help me
to do right for i love you much. I am yours in the bonds of affection." Sadly,
an elderly woman in Kentucky had her new owner send a letter to her children
in Virginia, telling them that she now lived "at a great distance from you and
probably I shall never see you any more and this is to let you know that I have
not forgoten you." She added, "I often think of you, and should be glad to see
you, but if we cannot see each other, we should desire to hear from each other."
She concluded her letter, "O that I could see you all but if I cannot fairwell,
remember me to all that enquire after me and be certain to send me a letter. No
mor, your loving Mother till Death, Nancy."[78]

Many slaves who received letters from those sold away were able to correspond with their loved ones in return. The owner of one enslaved couple in
North Carolina sent a letter to the new owner of at least two of their children,
relating to them that their parents were "very glad to here from them and was
glad to here that they had a good home and were satisfied there." They conveyed

all the local news and asked their children "to write them something about nancy and Julia who was sold with them, if they knows where they were sold and who bought them and if they have herd anything from there sisters who was sold some years ago." They ended their message by asking their children to "please rite again."[79]

A Tennessee woman likewise sent a similar message to her husband in Louisiana. She informed him, "We received the letter that your Master so kindly wrote to us and you can not ever think how glad we was to hear from you and Jake. I had almost given up the thought of ever hearing from you again. . . . We did not even [know] in what part of the world you was, so you may know I was glad to hear that you and Jake was together." She added that everyone was doing well, and "our boy growes finely. I do wish you could see him but as that can not be I will learn him to always remember you, he has not forgot you. . . . Even now if we aske him where you are he will say you are on the cars. His grand Father sends his love to you." She signed her letter, "your loving wife, Hannah Blair."[80]

Others sent to the Southwest through the interregional trade made gallant efforts to reunite their families. In 1860, Eliza Jones received a letter from her former owner in Maryland that acknowledged her request to have him sell her remaining daughter Jennie to her new owner in Louisiana. The man noted that the little girl "seemed glad to hear from you, & her countenance lightened up with a smile at the names of Aunt Liza & Tillie Anne (as she calls you and her sister.)" Unfortunately, there is no record of whether or not the man ever agreed to sell the young girl, although it does seem unlikely. While her former owner claimed "to appreciate the affection of a mother for her child," he also considered her mother an "ungrateful servant" and told her, "if you had conducted yourself faithfully, no offer would have tempted me to part with you." But sad as Jones's probable fate was in her efforts to procure her daughter, it does appear likely that she may have had greater success in getting to see another member of her family who had also been transported to Louisiana in the domestic trade. One year after the message from Maryland, Jones received a note from her mother who had been living in a nearby parish for the past five years. The elderly woman was glad to hear from her daughter, although she had to explain, "I am too old to go and see you [and] I therefore wish your mistress would let you come and see me." She told her daughter that she "should like very much to see you once more before I die" and signed her letter, "Hoping to hear from you soon, believe me, your affectionate mother."[81]

It is important to remember that only a small number of enslaved southerners were able to communicate with loved ones who had been torn away through the domestic trade. Still, some were able to do so, and a few even managed to correspond with one another for years. One such couple was an elderly

Virginia man and his sister (appropriately named Memory), who had been sold away to Tallahassee, Florida. After a silence of several years because of illness, the man once again contacted his sister, informing her of his recent heart troubles, as well as all of the news about her family and friends in Virginia. But it was obvious that he had thoughts of mortality on his mind. In a passage that conveyed the love and fondness that the two still maintained for one another, this enslaved man concluded, "I ardently long to meet you in Heaven, may it be our happy lot. Write to me soon and I will answer your letters. Affectionately, your brother Lenn."[82]

VI

In his 1855 autobiography, Frederick Douglass made the perceptive observation that "the grand aim of slavery, . . . always and everywhere, is to reduce man to a level with the brute," and the primary means of doing so was by "obliterating from the mind and heart of the slave, all just ideas of the sacredness of *the family*, as an institution." Douglass argued that his forced separation as a young boy from his mother and siblings destroyed all such bonds of affection for him. It seems that Douglass's experience was not the norm, however, and tremendous efforts were made by many others to retain these familial ties. Moreover, by making these efforts, thousands of men and women refused to accept the white South's belief that family connections had little meaning for African Americans. Ultimately, they were resisting the basic premise of American slavery—that men and women could be turned from rational beings into simple commodities who could be moved around at will.[83]

While the threat of sale remained a constant reality for all enslaved African Americans, few calmly accepted it as a legitimate part of the slave system. From an early age, they were forced to confront this devastating fact of life. When faced with an unwanted sale, many did resist and they were sometimes able to mitigate its more pernicious effects. Some fought back violently. Others ran away. And many more feigned poor health or played upon the sympathies of paternalistic planters to negotiate or negate a sale. Most, however, were unable to totally prevent an unwanted sale, and thousands, if not millions, were forcibly separated from their families and loved ones. Still, many of these people made valiant efforts to keep their families together, even if it was only in memory or through the mail. By doing so, they were refusing to accept the white South's definition of them and affirming that their familial relationships had deep meaning.

Perhaps most typical was the response in a letter written in 1857 by a South Carolina woman to her husband, who had just been sold away. The woman's owner was shipping her husband's trunk to the slave trader who had just bought him, and in the accompanying letter the owner noted: "As his so-called wife wishes to send some message to him, I will append it to this." Enclosed at the bottom was the following note: "Dear Tom, . . . Howdee & good-bye for I never expect to see you again. Try and do the best you can, and if you have a good Master, behave properly to him, and try to think about your Master in Heaven." She then added, "If I had known you were going to be sold I would have been better satisfied, but I am very much distressed now at being seperated from you. Remember me and I will think of you. Write to me after you are settled. Your wife, Fatima."[84] Unfortunately for many, this was often all that could be done when faced with this "nastiness of life."

Epilogue

In March 1865, one month after federal troops entered Charleston, South Carolina, the black population of that city held a giant procession, more than two and a half miles in length. Included in this parade were marshals and bands, the Twenty-First Regiment of the U.S. Colored Troops, clergymen, women's groups, schoolchildren, and various trade organizations. But as James Redpath, the special correspondent for the *New-York Tribune*, reported: "The most original feature of the procession was a large cart, drawn by two delapidated horses. . . . On this cart there was an auctioneer's block, and a black man, with a bell, representing a negro trader, a red flag waving over his head; recalling the days so near and yet so far off, when human beings were made merchandise of in South Carolina." According to Redpath, "This man had himself been bought and sold several times; and two women and a child who sat on the block had also been knocked down at public auction in Charleston. As the cart moved along, the mock auctioneer rang his bell and cried out: '*How much am I offered for this good cook?* . . . '*Who bids? who bids?*'" The vivid memories of this sight proved more than many of those along the roadway could bear: "Old women burst into tears as they saw this tableau, and forgetting that it was a mimic scene, shouted wildly: '*Give me back my children! Give me back my children!*'" The mock auctioneer was followed by a contingent of sixty men tied together by a rope, representing the numerous slave coffles that had marched through that city on their way to Louisiana. Following this mock coffle was a hearse, on which was written, "Slavery is Dead."[1]

The important role that the domestic trade played as a symbol of the southern slave system for African Americans could be seen over and over again in the years following Emancipation. Within hours of the fall of Richmond, a large crowd of black soldiers and local residents had assembled on Broad Street, near Lumpkin's Jail, the largest boarding house for traders and their slaves. As they did so, both those locked inside the compound and those congregating outside began to sing:

Slavery chain done broke at last!
Broke at last! Broke at last!
Slavery chain done broke at last!
Gonna praise God till I die!

According to one black soldier, when the prison's doors were opened, those inside poured out onto the street, "shouting and praising God and . . . master Abe" for their freedom. As this man later reported, "I became so overcome with tears, that I could not stand up under the pressure of such fulness of joy in my own heart. I retired to gain strength."[2]

All across the South, former slave jails and auction rooms were converted to religious and educational facilities for the freedmen. The symbolic importance of these establishments was seen even during the war itself, when the Union army used several of them for holding Confederate prisoners of war. As one northern soldier noted to his wife after being stationed at the old Franklin & Armfield mart in Alexandria, "Today I find myself at the *slave pens* where for years human beings have been sold at auction by the slave dealer. . . . The pens are now used to confine rebel prisoners and a fine mess of them we got."[3] Following the war, the First Congregational Negro Church in Lexington, Kentucky, was set up on the location of Lewis Robards's old slave jail, and in Savannah and New Orleans, schools for the freedmen were organized in former slave markets. In 1867, two years after the fall of Richmond, Lumpkin's Jail became the first home of what would later become the Richmond Theological Seminary, a school set up by the Baptist church primarily to train former slaves for the ministry. As one founder noted, "The old slave pen was no longer the 'devil's half acre' but God's half acre."[4]

After the war, men and women throughout the South sought to reunite families torn apart by sale. Some wandered the countryside, trying to get back to their former homes or to locate family members. Others flooded the Freedmen's Bureau, seeking aid in finding their relatives. As one bureau agent explained, "In their eyes, the work of emancipation was incomplete until the families which had been dispersed by slavery were reunited." The bureau did the best it could, writing letters and acting as a clearinghouse for information. But in most cases the time and distance gone by was simply too great. Often it had been several years since family members had seen one another. Not only had people been sold several times, but physical features had also changed, especially in the case of children. And others met with disappointment after finding out that former spouses had remarried or made new attachments.[5]

Despite the fact that most of these searches resulted in failure, many people persisted in their efforts to reunite their broken families, whatever the odds. One such attempt was made by a Texas man who had been sold away from his

Virginia family decades before. In his 1867 letter to the Freedmen's Bureau, this man stated that he was "anxious to learn about my sisters, from whom I have been separated many years. I have never heard from them since I left Virginia twenty four years ago. I am in hopes that they are still living and I am anxious to hear how they are getting on." Enclosed in this letter was another note addressed to "Dear Sister Jane" that began: "Your little brother Hawkins is trying to find out where you are and where his poor old mother is. Let me know and I will come to see you. I shall never forget the bag of buiscuits you made for me the last night I spent with you. Your advice to me to meet you in Heaven has never passed from my mind." He asked his sister to "please send me some of Julia's hair whom I left a baby in the cradle when I was torn away from you. I know that she is a young lady now, but I hope she will not deny her affectionate uncle this request, seeing she was an infant in the cradle when he saw her last." He also wanted her to say hello to his "old playmate Henry Fitz who used to play with me and also to all the colored boys who, I know, have forgotten me, but I have not forgotten them." He added, "Thank God that now we are not sold and torn away from each other as we used to be," and concluded his letter, "Your loving and affectionate brother, Hawkins Wilson." Unfortunately, Freedmen's Bureau records indicate that his letters never found their destination.[6]

Even as late as the turn of the twentieth century, many former slaves had not given up hope and continued to search for their long-separated loved ones. In 1892, one Mississippi woman named Peggie got a local minister to write to her former owner in Tennessee to try to find her mother and father from whom she had been sold decades before. Many others placed advertisements in the "Information Wanted" section of African-American newspapers, seeking knowledge about individuals who had long been sold away. While hundreds of these notices appeared in the years immediately following the war, they could still be found as late as the 1890s.[7]

Finally, the pain of sale was something that most people never forgot. When elderly blacks in the 1930s recalled their experiences under slavery, they frequently commented upon the anguish that still lingered from such events. According to one Texas man, "The only thing I remember about all that is that there was lots of crying when they took me away from my mammy. That's something I will never forget." A woman in Virginia reported that losing her sister through sale "was the saddes' thing dat ever happen to me," while another woman in South Carolina broke into tears after recalling that she "don' know who bought my brothers, George en Earl." When thinking about the horrors of the domestic trade, one Virginian remarked, "Truely, son, de haf has never been tol'," and another stated simply, "Chile, it gives you de creeps up yo' spine to think 'bout it."[8]

Therefore, it should come as no surprise that some found it difficult to forgive those who had caused them so much pain and suffering. One man who successfully made his escape into Canada believed "that the place of punishment was made for those who separate husbands and wives, and traffic in their fellow men." After being reunited with her former husband at a contraband camp during the war (both had since remarried), one woman proclaimed, "White folk's got a heap to answer for the way they've done to colored folks!" Even as late as the 1930s, one Virginia woman declared, "No white man ever been in my house. Don't 'low it. Dey sole my sister Kate. I saw it wid dese here eyes. Sole her in 1860, and I ain't seed nor heard of her since. Folks say white folks is all right dese days. Maybe dey is, maybe dey isn't. But I can't stand to see 'em. Not on my place."[9]

. . .

While the domestic slave trade continued to play an important role in African-American life following Emancipation, the opposite proved true for white Americans. Mainstream American society went out of its way to forget that this essential component in the southern slave system had ever existed. In large part, this was because of the uneasy feelings that many white Americans (in both the North and South) had about the trade before the war, as well as the need to reunite the country afterward. Controversial subjects like the real cause of the war (i.e., the South's need to maintain slavery and expand it into the West) were ignored, and attention was focused instead on the bravery and sacrifices of the fighting men on each side. During the postwar period, there was simply no place for grim reminders of what life had really been like in the Old South when white Americans seemed so determined to accept the fantasized version as portrayed by the former slaveholders.

After the war, one notable form of selective amnesia was in forgetting who the slave traders actually were. True, speculators in the abstract continued to be scapegoated by southern society. As one early twentieth-century southern historian wrote, "In all the category of disreputable callings, there were none so despised as the slave-trader. The odium descended upon his children and his children's children." Yet the existence of anyone who had actually been a slave trader seemed to disappear from public memory. Following the war, many of these men just switched to other forms of business, such as brokering, retailing, general auctioning, or selling insurance, bonds, or real estate. And upon their deaths, some of the more successful ones were recognized for their accomplishments. In their public accolades, however, no mention was ever made about how they had acquired their early wealth. When the Charleston slave trader Ziba B. Oakes died in 1871, his death made front-page news, although his obituary only stated that he made the bulk of his fortune in "the Commission and

Auction business." In 1899, the death of another dealer in that city, John S. Riggs, likewise made the newspapers. The Charleston *News and Courier* called him "one of the city's pioneers in progress" and "a self-made man in every sense of the word," but said nothing about his early days as a slave trader. Consequently, many of these businessmen finally received recognition for their entrepreneurial skills, although it was only after southern society had agreed to whitewash their previous careers.[10]

Other speculators transformed themselves through their achievements on the battlefield. One such man was John H. Morgan, a prominent hemp manufacturer in Lexington and slave-trading investor before the war, but who is now most well known for his exploits as a Confederate cavalry leader. The most famous of these warrior slave traders, however, was Nathan Bedford Forrest, who also rose to national notoriety as a Confederate cavalry officer. Following the war, hagiographic biographers somehow managed to successfully defend Forrest's lifelong actions against black people. Not only was Forrest the largest slave trader in Memphis prior to the war, but he also led the Fort Pillow Massacre, which killed up to 300 U.S. Colored Troops in cold blood, and he then served as the first grand wizard of the Ku Klux Klan after the war. Despite this atrocious record (or perhaps because of it, for some people), Forrest still commands the adoration of many today, and in some circles he has a more devout following than Robert E. Lee.[11]

Wealth from the slave trade has woven its way into American society so thoroughly that few have any knowledge of its origins. One of the Louisiana plantations that Isaac Franklin bought with his slave-trading earnings was "Angola," on which land is now located the infamous state penitentiary of the same name. While it is well known that many nineteenth-century banks, insurance companies, and other businesses profited from slavery (and the domestic trade), less known is the extent to which money from the slave trade has also benefited families, communities, and institutions of all types, including churches, colleges, and even the profession of history itself. Two prominent traders in Richmond from 1857 to 1864 were the brothers Silas and Richard Omohundro. Descendants of this family today have been generous supporters of historical causes, including the prestigious Omohundro Institute of Early American History & Culture at Williamsburg, Virginia. While it is uncertain how much of this family money came from the slave trade (the current benefactor descends from a younger brother of the two principles of the firm), it is hard to imagine that some of that money did not work its way into the family estate.[12]

Finally, just as slave traders and their profits have disappeared from view, so too have most traces of their business. Few physical remnants of the domestic trade remain. An auction block from the old St. Louis Hotel is one of the featured exhibits at the Louisiana State Museum in New Orleans, and this facility (as well as several others) proudly displays a set of iron chains used to restrain slaves in coffles. Yet, the sites themselves have almost all been transformed, and there seems to be little desire by most contemporary southerners to commemorate them, although in Charleston there is a museum erected where Ziba Oakes's slave depot and auction hall once stood. The building currently sitting on the spot (and advertised as an authentic slave depot) is not, however, the original building that was used by Oakes. The building currently referred to as the Charleston Slave Mart was actually constructed after the war.[13]

In the overwhelming majority of southern cities, there are no markers nor any other trace that the slave trade ever existed. In most, this once-ubiquitous component of southern urban life has been paved over by modern development. Probably the best example of this is in Richmond, where Robert Lumpkin's Jail and the other depots on Fifteenth Street now lie under the Franklin Street off-ramp of Interstate 95. In other cities, the same holds true. In Baltimore, most of the slave pens were located on Pratt Street, and their remains are now under the current convention center and across the street from the city's much-heralded Camden Yard baseball field. Many of the traders in New Orleans were congregated around Gravier and Baronne, an area now dominated by banks. The other major sales emporium was Banks' Arcade on Magazine Street. While this building has been designated an Orleans Parish Landmark, there is no mention on the plaque of the type of sales that took place there. Interestingly, the building now houses a "luxury boutique hotel."[14] Not to be outdone in irony, in Memphis, the Shelby County Court House now sits where Bolton, Dickens & Co. had its last establishment and across the street from Nathan Bedford Forrest's old stand. This latter building does have a plaque stating that Forrest had his office there, but once again, no mention is made as to what type of business he operated.

There have been indications, however, that this selective amnesia is changing. Several towns have erected markers noting the location of their main auction blocks. In Sharpsburg, Maryland, there is a stone at the corner of Church and Main that reads: "From 1800 to 1865, This Stone Was Used as a Slave Auction Block. It has been a famous landmark at this original location for over 150 years." At the corner of Charles and William streets in downtown Fredericksburg, a memorial was dedicated in 1984 stating that this was "Fredericksburg's Principal Auction Site in Pre–Civil War Days." But the city whose changes have had the most far-reaching impact is Natchez, Mississippi, where in 1998 a state historical marker was placed at the old Forks of the Road slave market. Although the neighborhood today is rather run down, the city has bought most of the land and is turning it into an interpretive center. The site has also been nominated for National Historic Landmark status. If it achieves that, then the Forks of the Road will join Franklin & Armfield's slave depot in Alexandria

One of the few public markers commemorating the domestic slave trade today. This state historical marker in Natchez, Mississippi, was dedicated in 1998. Courtesy of Ben Hillyer and the *Natchez Democrat.*

and Isaac Franklin's plantation home in Tennessee as historical slavery sites of national significance.[15]

While the actions at Natchez and elsewhere have certainly been important first steps toward remembering this nation's past and healing its racial wounds, far more is needed to fully comprehend the role that the domestic trade has played in American life. Public reminders of the trade's existence help us to realize how widespread its presence was in our past, however, it is of even greater significance to recognize (and to admit) that the slave trade had a tremendous impact upon the formation of this country. Originating with the birth of the nation itself, the domestic trade was an essential component of the southern slave system. It produced great wealth for many people, and it also helped to tear the country apart. But, most important, it brought unconscionable pain and suffering to millions of this nation's inhabitants. Only by acknowledging the centrality of the domestic slave trade to the early history of the United States can we truly understand the many complexities of antebellum American life and the lingering effects that this traffic still has on American society today.

APPENDIX A

Total Slave Migration, 1820–1860, and Percentage of Migration Attributable to the Interregional Slave Trade

Over the years, historians have generally been in agreement in their assessments of the overall trends in the southern slave migration which occurred between 1820 and 1860. Virtually all have acknowledged that this movement mirrored the general economic conditions in the South: it took off with the prosperity of the 1820s, mushroomed during the 1830s, only to decrease somewhat in the early 1840s following the Panic of 1837, and escalated again in the late 1840s and 1850s. For the most part, even the differences in their estimates of the total number of individuals involved have not been that great. Determining what percentage of this movement was attributable to the interregional slave trade, however, is a question that has been subject to much debate.

The first historian to examine this issue was Winfield Collins. In his 1904 work on the domestic slave trade, Collins used decennial growth-rate calculations to estimate the total number of slaves transported from the slave-exporting to the slave-importing states. He first determined the growth rate for the entire southern slave population and then multiplied this rate times the population of the slave-exporting states at the beginning of each decade and subtracted the actual slave population of those states at the end of that decade from the amount that they should have attained had they experienced the average growth rate. Using this method, Collins calculated that approximately 124,000 slaves were removed from the selling states in the 1820s; 265,000 in the 1830s; 146,000 in the 1840s; and 207,000 in the 1850s, for a total of 742,000 over the four decades. Collins argued, however, that most of this migration was attributable to slaves accompanying their owners as they relocated to the Southwest. He estimated that the interregional slave trade was responsible for only 40 percent of the movement, although it may have climbed to 50 percent during the 1850s.[1]

For many years Collins's work shaped the discussion of this issue. Ulrich B. Phillips agreed with his assessment that the domestic trade was of minor importance, arguing that "the long-distance slave trade was essentially a part of the westward movement, supplementing the flow of people who went without involving purchase and sale." Although Lewis Gray questioned Collins's statistical technique and hinted that he believed the slave trade played a greater role, Gray still relied upon Collins's estimates for total slave movement.[2]

The first historian to challenge Collins's interpretation was Frederic Bancroft. In his classic study, *Slave Trading in the Old South* (1931), Bancroft also used decennial growth-rate statistics to calculate the overall movement of slaves and came up with numbers considerably larger than those of Collins (e.g., 283,000 in the 1850s). Bancroft's most influential contribution, however, was his argument that the interstate slave trade dominated this movement. He correctly noted that Collins had failed to consider, as part of the trade, Lower South planters who traveled to the Upper South to purchase slaves for their own use. In addition, he examined hundreds of advertisements placed by slave traders in southern newspapers and, in large part based on this evidence, argued that, at least for the 1850s, fully 70 percent of this migration was a consequence of the domestic slave trade.[3]

For several decades, Bancroft's work on the slave trade and his argument of its widespread nature dominated most historical discussions of slavery. His views were included in the major books in the field, including Kenneth Stampp's *The Peculiar Institution* (1956), Stanley Elkins's *Slavery* (1959), Richard Wade's *Slavery in the Cities* (1964), and Eugene Genovese's *The Political Economy of Slavery* (1965).[4] In addition, other historians produced similar works, which seemed to confirm many of Bancroft's findings. In their study of the economics of slavery, Alfred Conrad and John Meyer argued that the institution was profitable in large part because the widespread "sales of slaves provided an important capital gain for the [slave] exporting states." Robert Evans also recalculated Collins's estimates for the total slave migration and came up with numbers that were more in agreement with those of Bancroft. Evans pointed out that in his computations, Collins only included those states that he deemed to be slave-selling states. Following Collins's growth-rate technique, but including as a slave-exporting state any state that experienced a relative loss in slaves, Evans found that the total number of slaves exported from 1830 to 1860 was roughly a third greater than what Collins had estimated. For the 1850s alone, he concluded that 279,500 slaves had been transported—or approximately the same number as Bancroft.[5]

Not every historian, however, has been in agreement with the findings of Bancroft, and it was inevitable that some would eventually question his work. Prominent among these critics was William Calderhead, whose 1972 article on the slave trade in Maryland directly challenged Bancroft and the influence he had on so many important historical works. Calderhead was especially critical that Bancroft had not made any effort to "note the amount of sales actually consummated." Calderhead believed that by combing through the extensive records for eight of Maryland's nineteen counties (which had a total of 45 percent of the state's slave population), it was possible to find information about every slave sale that had occurred in those counties between 1830 and 1860. He could then project that information and make more accurate generalizations about the state as a whole. Following this procedure, Calderhead determined that between 1830 and 1860, a total of only 18,500 slaves had left the state (including both movement with migrating owners and the slave trade). This was one-fourth of the amount estimated by Bancroft. Even more striking, Calderhead argued that in the 1830s—the decade of greatest slave-trading activity—only 3,601 slaves, or 3.5 percent of the state's slave population, had been "sold south," and of this group, only 1,896, or 52 percent, had been purchased by professional slave traders (the rest went with visiting planters from the Lower South or were sold out of jails). Therefore, Calderhead concluded that "contrary to Bancroft's view, Maryland did not participate extensively in the interstate trade," and he brought into question the extent and importance of the entire border-state slave trade.[6]

Calderhead's findings proved extremely influential, in part because they were incorporated by Robert Fogel and Stanley Engerman in their controversial work, *Time on the Cross* (1974). Among their many questionable claims, Fogel and Engerman argued that the total slave migration from 1820 to 1860 consisted of only 686,000 individuals, a figure lower than that estimated by Collins. Even more shocking, however, was their assertion that only 16 percent of all slaves who were forced south went via the interstate slave trade—the other 84 percent supposedly traveled with migrating owners. Although not completely clear in the original text, they based this conclusion on three factors: a breakdown of New Orleans slave-sale invoices, a combination of Calderhead's findings for Maryland with their estimates of slave migration out of the state, and a comparison of the sex ratios of the coastal slave trade from the Chesapeake to New Orleans against data for overall slave migration.[7]

Time on the Cross met with a firestorm of criticism, and much of it dealt with Fogel and Engerman's striking claims about the interstate slave trade. One of the earliest and most vocal critics was Herbert Gutman. In *Slavery and the Numbers Game* (1975), Gutman questioned Fogel and Engerman's finding that the New Orleans slave-sale invoices indicated that only 25 percent of all slaves sold in the city had been imported from the exporting states. Gutman noted that this was a "poorly-described source," and by failing to recognize that many interstate slave traders were residents of the city, the authors had seriously undercounted the number of interregional sales.[8]

In an essay written with Richard Sutch, Gutman also questioned the extremely low figures presented in *Time on the Cross* for total slave migration. Fogel and Engerman had relied upon a study that used a new survival-rate technique for determining migration patterns over time. While this method was more sophisticated and advanced than the simple growth-rate calculations employed earlier by Bancroft and others (instead of looking at a whole population, separate age and sex cohorts were examined), the totals cited by Fogel and Engerman were considerably lower than those that Sutch had found in his own earlier study, which used this same survival-rate technique. (Sutch had estimated that 269,287 slaves were transported in the 1850s—or about 76,000 more than Fogel and Engerman and 13,000 fewer than Bancroft.) Gutman and Sutch argued that this discrepancy and the low figures cited by Fogel and Engerman in general were attributable to their failure to account for the migration of children under the age of ten, who constituted nearly 18 percent of Sutch's estimate. In addition, their study had failed to include those slaves who had been carried to other states but had died before the census was taken at the end of the decade. According to Sutch, these individuals were approximately 10 percent of the total moves made by slaves over ten years of age.

Gutman and Sutch were also critical of Fogel and Engerman's use of Calderhead's study of Maryland for their claim that the interstate slave trade constituted only 16 percent of the overall slave migration. They pointed out internal inconsistencies in Fogel and Engerman's calculations and questioned "the propriety of applying an estimate for Maryland to the entire South." Even more important, however, they raised serious doubts about the validity of Calderhead's study itself. Gutman and Sutch argued that "it is likely that Calderhead's estimate of the slaves 'sold south' from Maryland is too low." They noted that Calderhead made his calculations, in part, on his claim to have known of every professional slave trader in Maryland, which, in all probability, he did not. In addition, they questioned how representative of the state as a whole were the counties at which Calderhead looked. Gutman and Sutch were especially critical of the data Calderhead used for Baltimore County. Not only were calculations for Baltimore City probably excluded, but lacking any records prior to 1852, Calderhead simply projected backward data from after that date, undoubtedly undercounting the number of slaves sold in the interstate slave trade from that county.[9]

Several other historians have expanded upon Gutman and Sutch's criticisms of Calderhead's study. In 1980, Donald Sweig questioned Calderhead's claim that during the 1830s only 179 slaves were sold south in Prince George's County, Maryland. Using coastal slave manifests, Sweig noted that during the same decade, in six years alone, nearly 3,000 slaves were shipped from Alexandria, Virginia, which lies directly across the river from Prince George's County. Since many Maryland slaves were shipped from Baltimore, and most slaves in southern Virginia were transported out of Richmond and Norfolk, that meant that "a significant portion of Maryland slaves, particularly from nearby Prince George's County, [were] shipped south from Alexandria." Therefore, at least for southern Maryland, Calderhead's estimates were simply too low.[10]

In 1993, Thomas Russell expanded upon this criticism and convincingly argued that Calderhead's entire method was "fundamentally flawed," and his data suffered from problems of both over- and underinclusion. In his study, Calderhead had claimed that there were "three means by which slaves were legally sold south. The most common was by a standard bill of sale" (which was Calderhead's primary source of documentation). The other two means were the settlement of estates and through the state's legal authorities. Russell correctly noted, however, that bills of sale were not a "means" of sale, they were simply evidence, or proof, that a sale had occurred. Bills of sale could be, and often were, given at the other two types of sale that Calderhead used for determining his number of sales. Therefore, it is quite possible that a given transaction could have been counted as two sales by Calderhead, and it was for this reason that his data suffered from overinclusion.

Even more troubling, though, was Calderhead's claim that he had evidence for every slave sale that had occurred in the counties that he had studied. Russell noted that this was highly unlikely, "because far from every slave sale would have been accompanied by the recording of a bill of sale with the county clerk." Bills of sale cost money and often demanded an inconvenient trip to the county courthouse. And, while bills of sale might be beneficial for local slave sales (where the question of ownership might be more likely contested), there was little incentive to go through the cost and bother for the purchase of a slave who was soon to be shipped out of state. Therefore, Russell argued that Calderhead's data also suffered from an even more serious problem of underinclusion; not only was it probable that over the years some of the records had been lost or destroyed, but in all likelihood, many, if not most, of Maryland's slave sales were never recorded in the first place—especially in the case of interstate sales.[11]

Russell's argument that many interregional slave buyers never bothered to obtain legal bills of sale in Maryland before transporting their human cargoes to New Orleans is supported by another study. In their 1991 article on the New Orleans slave trade, Herman Freudenberger and Jonathan Pritchett attempted to overlap records (certificates of good character) of 352 slaves who had been purchased in Maryland and brought to New Orleans for sale in 1830.

Knowing the date of original purchase, name of the original owner, his or her place of residence, a description of the slave, and frequently the name of the buyer in Maryland, Freudenberger and Pritchett searched through the Maryland records for bills of sale that corresponded to these known transactions. Of the 352 sales, they were able to find bills of sale for only 54 slaves, or 15 percent. Especially damaging to Calderhead's claim that he had evidence of every slave sale was the fact that they were able to find records of only 6 of 83 sales (or 7 percent) in Kent County, a county Calderhead had used in his sample. Freudenberger and Pritchett's inability to find bills of sale for 85 percent of their known slave sales in Maryland and 93 percent of such transactions in one of Calderhead's sample counties gives strong credence to the argument that Calderhead seriously underestimated the number of interstate slave sales in his study.[12]

Finally, in his study *Speculators and Slaves* (1989), Michael Tadman has challenged the third factor on which Fogel and Engerman based their claim that the slave trade was of only minor importance in the overall slave migration. Fogel and Engerman had observed that 60 percent of the New Orleans slave trade was male, but when they looked at the census data, they found that only 51 percent of the overall slave migration was male. Therefore, they argued that the slave trade could not have comprised more than 16 percent of the total slave migration. Tadman pointed out, however, that Fogel and Engerman had seriously miscalculated the sex ratio of the entire interregional slave trade because they had assumed that it was all 60 percent male. According to Tadman, the New Orleans market was an exceptional branch of the slave trade. Because of the nearby sugar plantations and their unusual demand for male laborers, the New Orleans trade was more sex selective than the rest of the trade, which had a more balanced sex ratio. While I believe that Tadman has overestimated the exceptional nature of the New Orleans trade, in their study of this specific market for the year 1830, Freudenberger and Pritchett did find some support for Tadman's argument on this issue.[13]

Tadman also supplied his own estimates for both the total slave migration and the magnitude of the interregional slave trade. Using modified survival-rate techniques, Tadman calculated that roughly 155,000 slaves were exported in the 1820s; 285,000 in the 1830s; 184,000 in the 1840s; and 251,000 in the 1850s, for a total of 875,000 individuals transported over the four decades. In addition, Tadman employed three different methods for estimating the size of the interregional slave trade: an examination of coastal slave manifests for the New Orleans market (primarily in the 1840s), an age-structure analysis comparing the slave trade against planter migration (in the 1820s and 1850s), and a study of slave traders in South Carolina (in the 1850s). Combining these three methods, Tadman concluded that there was a clear "dominance of trading over planter migration," and he estimated that between 60 and 70 percent of the total slave migration was attributable to the interregional slave trade.[14]

Therefore, in light of the most recent work, it is possible to discredit the extremely low figures found in William Calderhead's study of Maryland and in Robert Fogel and Stanley Engerman's *Time on the Cross* for both the total slave migration and the percentage of this migration attributable to the interregional slave trade.[15] The numbers provided by Michael Tadman seem to be a far more accurate assessment and are the most convincing to date. His analytical methods and statistical techniques appear to be sound, and his totals are in line with the material examined elsewhere in this study. Moreover, his estimates for both the total slave movement and the magnitude of the interregional slave trade have the benefit of falling in between the relatively low numbers given earlier by Winfield Collins and the higher figures of Frederic Bancroft. Because Tadman's final totals would have been even greater if more allowance had been made for importing and exporting subregions within states (as he himself indicated), I believe it is safe to conclude that between 1820 and 1860 at least 875,000 American slaves were forcibly removed from the Upper South to the Lower South and that between 60 and 70 percent of these individuals were transported via the interregional slave trade.[16]

Estimated Number of Local Slave Sales and Total Number of Southern Slave Sales, 1820–1860

Unlike the interregional slave trade, there have been surprisingly few studies of the magnitude and importance of slave trading among neighbors and within state lines. Most of the early works on the domestic slave trade barely touched upon the local trade, if at all, and treated it as peripheral to the interstate trade. Winfield Collins never even mentioned local slave trading; Frederic Bancroft did estimate that it "involved as many *slaves* as all the *interstate* trading," but he failed to elaborate in much detail. The local slave trade was ignored in most general works on slavery as well. Ulrich B. Phillips simply noted that "the slave trade was partly systematic, partly casual." Only Kenneth Stampp in *The Peculiar Institution* (1956) provided any hint of its importance, pointing out that "much of the traffic in slaves involved private transactions between neighbors."[1]

The first historian to provide any quantitative evidence about the magnitude of the local slave trade, albeit somewhat inadvertently, was William Calderhead in his 1972 study of Maryland. Calderhead was primarily concerned with the interstate trade and his argument that Maryland's role in it had been minor, but buried in his statistics were figures with amazing implications about the extent of the local trade. According to his data for slave sales based on bills of sale between 1830 and 1840, only 1.7 percent of Maryland's slaves had been sold south. However, if all types of sale are included, a total of 10.8 percent of the state's slaves would have been sold during this period. Considering that this source was only one of his three "means" of sale, this certainly indicates that a large number of the state's slaves had been sold during this decade. In addition, according to these bills of sale, the ratio of local sales to interstate sales was 5.2 to 1. To put it another way, for every person sold south from Maryland, at least five others had been sold within the state. While Calderhead had focused on his claim that only 16 percent of Maryland's slaves who had been sold were sold south, he failed to notice that other, rather large 84 percent. The implications of such an enormous, and previously unknown, local slave trade were staggering. If true, and if the data for Maryland were typical for other states in the South, that meant that millions more people had been bought and sold than ever before imagined.[2]

Robert Fogel and Stanley Engerman were the first to pick up on Calderhead's calculations in their work *Time on the Cross* (1974), although they too failed to see its importance. Without stating clearly how they had derived this figure, except to say that it came from Calderhead's local to interstate sales ratio of 5.2 to 1, Fogel and Engerman asserted that 1.92 percent of the southern slave population had been sold each year. They noted that, over the period 1820 to 1860, this averaged out to around 50,000 transactions per year. From this, they calculated that "on average, only one slaveholder out of every twenty-two sold a slave in any given year." Therefore, based on these statistics, they concluded that "this low sales rate clashes with the notion that speculative purchases and sales of slaves were common among southern planters."[3]

Herbert Gutman was quick to point out that, as with so much of their work, Fogel and Engerman had misplaced the focus of their research. In *Slavery and the Numbers Game* (1975), Gutman argued that instead of looking at the average number of sales conducted by slaveholders, Fogel and Engerman should have noticed that, according to their calculations, roughly 2 million people would have been sold (50,000 × 40). To emphasize the magnitude of this number, Gutman noted that "if we assume that slave sales did not occur on Sundays and holidays and that such selling went on for ten hours on working days, a slave was sold on average every 3.6 minutes between 1820 and 1860." However, Gutman simply could not believe that such a figure was correct. Not only was it greater than any estimate provided by Bancroft or Stampp, but "even Frederick Douglass and William Lloyd Garrison never hinted at so large a volume of slave sales between 1820 and 1860." Gutman therefore concluded that Maryland was exceptional, and the 1.92 percent annual sales rate was too high for the South as a whole. He offered a more moderate estimate of 1 percent, which still would have amounted to more than 1 million slave sales over the forty years.[4]

The following year, in an essay with Richard Sutch, Gutman revised his earlier assessment and now argued that Fogel and Engerman's annual sales rate of 1.92 percent had not been too high but too low. Gutman and Sutch had recalculated Calderhead's data and found that Fogel and Engerman were off in their numbers; according to Calderhead's study, the annual sales rate for Maryland during the 1830s should have equaled 2.45 percent. When questioned as to how they had arrived at their rate of 1.92 percent, Stanley Engerman replied that they had based their estimate on data for only one of Maryland's counties (over only one decade) and had excluded from their totals those slaves who had been sold by their owners after leaving the state. Gutman and Sutch correctly noted that basing a regionwide, forty-year annual sale rate upon such flimsy evidence was "at best, a very dubious procedure." Gutman and Sutch also realized that Calderhead had drastically undercounted the number of Maryland's interstate sales. When they retabulated the data after revising the figures to compensate for this, they determined that the annual sales rate was actually 3.46 percent. If this rate were applied throughout the South, that would mean that close to 4 million slaves would have been sold over the forty-year period.

Gutman and Sutch pointed out, however, that even their own revised figures should be used with caution, as "they too are based upon a number of unsupported assumptions." Foremost among them was calculating a region-wide annual sales rate from data for only one state. But even more trouble-some was the fact that, despite some revisions, Gutman and Sutch had essentially relied upon Calderhead's findings for determining their estimated rate. As is pointed out in appendix A of this volume, there are enough serious problems with this work to eliminate its reliability as a credible source. Therefore, any precise calculation based upon it, including that of Gutman and Sutch (or Fogel and Engerman), is itself suspect and cannot be accepted as a trust-worthy estimate.[5]

Nevertheless, although Calderhead's study is of little value in determining the total number of slaves sold or the exact annual sales rate, it is helpful in illustrating one point. If the main flaw in his work was the undercounting of interstate sales, that means that the ratio of local sales to interstate sales was not as drastic as Calderhead's data would suggest. However, it also means that the number of people bought and sold in the state of Maryland during the 1830s had to have been at least equal to, and was most likely even greater than, the totals we have been discussing. Therefore, while Gutman and Sutch were probably correct when they concluded that the high sales rate in Maryland was atypical of the entire South, their estimates were probably not that far off. And, at least for one state, it seems certain that the buying and selling of humans was a very common affair.

The only other state where the rate of slave sales has been studied in any depth is South Carolina. In his work *Speculators and Slaves* (1989), Michael Tad-man focused almost exclusively on the interregional trade, although he did note that "there was also a very high rate of *local* sales, at least as high and probably higher than the per capita rate of interregional sales of Upper South slaves." He even hinted at the magnitude of this intrastate trade, arguing that during the 1850s, at judicial sales alone, local buyers in South Carolina purchased 30 percent more slaves than interstate traders in the state bought from all sources combined. Still, Tadman did not seem to recognize the importance of this large local trade and touched on it only briefly. He offered no estimates as to the total number of slaves sold nor an annual sales rate for either South Carolina or the South as a whole.[6]

Nevertheless, Tadman's work does offer valuable clues for obtaining this information. In his 1993 dissertation on slave sales and the South Carolina courts, Thomas Russell noted that buried in Tadman's footnotes were figures about South Carolina in the 1850s which could be used to determine the state's total slave sales volume. Tadman had estimated that 67,500 slaves had been sold through court-ordered sales. He calculated that 54,000 of them, or 80 percent, had been sold to local buyers. In addition, he estimated that another 36,000 slaves had been sold from one South Carolina resident to another through various noncourt means. Therefore, according to Tadman's figures, 90,000 slaves had been sold on the local market. When combined with the other 39,000 individuals sold out of state through the interregional trade, that added up to a total of 129,000 slaves sold over the decade. Divided by the state's mean population, that equaled a brisk annual sales rate of 3.28 percent (or more than 3.5 million slave sales if projected nationally over forty years). According to Tadman's estimates, the ratio of local to interstate sales was 2.3 to 1, and court-ordered sales made up 52.3 percent of all slave sales in the state.[7]

Despite his unquestioned expertise in the South Carolina slave trade, Russell believed that Tadman had significantly overcounted the number of court-ordered sales in the state. In his own work, Russell had examined the records of five upcountry districts and found that the annual percentage of court-ordered sales was much lower than Tadman had estimated. Unable to find any explanation for this discrepancy, except that Tadman had included Charleston District in his sources, Russell settled upon a compromise annual percentage rate (0.85 percent) for court-ordered sales, weighted to include Tadman's numbers for Charleston and his figures for the rest of the state. The net effect of this compromise rate was to cut Tadman's totals for court-ordered sales in half. Using Tadman's other calculations for local and interregional sales, Russell then projected these figures back to the 1820s and was able to determine estimates for the total number of slaves sold in the state and an average annual sales rate.

Unfortunately, when tabulating his data, Russell made several mathematical errors, including a drastic miscounting of the number of local noncourt sales, which seriously marred his final estimates. Nevertheless, I believe his methodology is still solid. Therefore, I have taken Russell's revised rate for court-ordered sales, together with Tadman's figures for local and interregional sales, and reworked them into a new estimate for the total number of slaves sold (table A.1). Breaking it down between court and noncourt and between local and interregional sales, I have determined that from 1820 to 1860, more than a

TABLE A.1. Total South Carolina Slave Sales and Average Annual
Sales Rate, 1820–1860[a]

COURT SALES	1820s	1830s	1840s	1850s
Interregional	4,878	5,461	6,052	6,693
Local	19,512	21,843	24,209	26,771
Total	24,390	27,304	30,261	33,464
NONCOURT SALES				
Interregional	7,432	28,549	11,316	32,339
Local	13,008	14,562	16,139	17,847
Total	20,440	43,111	27,455	50,186
Decennial Sales	44,830	70,415	57,716	83,650
Population Mean	286,938	321,220	356,011	393,695
Annual Rate	1.56%	2.19%	1.62%	2.12%

Total Court Sales	115,419	(45%)
Total Noncourt Sales	141,192	(55%)
Total Interregional Sales	102,720	(40%)
Total Local Sales	153,891	(60%)
Total Slave Sales, 1820–1860	256,611	
Average Annual Sales Rate, 1820–1860	1.94%	

[a]Total court sales are determined by using Russell's average annual rate of 0.85 percent of
the slave population. This figure is then divided into interregional and local totals based on
Tadman's estimate that 80 percent of such sales went to local buyers. Interregional noncourt
sales are based on 60 percent of Tadman's estimated total out-of-state slave migration, less
the number of interregional court sales. Finally, local noncourt sales are based on Tadman's
estimate that these sales equaled 40 percent of the total local sales. The mean population
from 1820 to 1860 was 330,441. The somewhat low ratio of local to interregional sales is
attributable, I believe, to Russell's rather low rate for court sales. In addition, Tadman
acknowledged that his figures of 80 percent of court sales to local buyers was probably low.
Tadman, *Speculators and Slaves*, 12, 120; Russell, "Sale Day in South Carolina," 65–74.

quarter million South Carolina slaves were sold, at an average annual sales rate
of 1.94 percent of the state's slave population. Once again, this figure is using
Russell's revised rate for court-ordered sales. If Tadman's original rate had been
used, the overall totals would have been much higher.[8]

Based upon the high quality of Tadman's work and Russell's insightful
methodology, I am confident that these estimates for South Carolina slave sales
are the most reliable numbers currently available. That being said, I still feel
the need to repeat Gutman and Sutch's earlier warning and note that these
figures too must be viewed with a degree of caution. Not only are they based
upon several unsupported assumptions, but these estimates, as with the earlier
works, cover only one state. Therefore, any projection for the entire South is

certainly suspect. However, unlike Maryland, I believe that South Carolina was representative of the region, at least as far as the buying and selling of slaves is concerned. From the late eighteenth century, Maryland was almost exclusively a slave-exporting state, and by the end of the antebellum period, the status of slavery itself had become problematic within the state.[9] While it is true that during the years under study here, South Carolina was also a net slave-exporting state, unlike the other slave-exporting states, South Carolina was in the Lower South, and pockets of slave importation always existed. And there was no question about the status of the institution within its borders. Still, one can question how representative any one state was of the South as a whole, or if the estimates from a slave-exporting state can apply to the slave-importing states of the Southwest. Although no in-depth quantitative studies have been done for the states in that region, several secondary sources do indicate that the level of slave trading was also high there, on both the interstate and intrastate levels. Moreover, while it is quite likely that some states had a lower annual sales rate than South Carolina, it is certain that other states, such as Maryland, had a higher one. Finally, it should be noted that the lowest possible estimates were used here and that the actual annual sales rate could have been much higher.[10]

Therefore, until further studies can be done (and this appendix should make it clear how desperately other work is needed), these estimates appear to be the most reliable numbers available. Projecting an annual sales rate of 1.94 percent across the South would average out to more than 2.1 million slave sales for the forty-year period. While this may appear high to some, it is roughly equal to the figure offered back in 1974 by Robert Fogel and Stanley Engerman and much lower than the estimates provided by most of the other works completed since then. In addition, it seems certain that a large number of these sales occurred between neighbors and within state lines. Even using Michael Tadman's highest estimate of the total number of interregional sales (slightly more than 600,000), that leaves at least twice as many sales in the local trade as in the far more well known interstate trade. Because the most conservative figures have been used throughout, I believe it is safe to conclude that between 1820 and 1860, at least 2 million American slaves were bought and sold and that more than two-thirds of these transactions involved the local trade.

NOTES

Abbreviations

AAS	American Antiquarian Society, Worcester, MA
ADAH	Alabama Department of Archives and History, Montgomery
BPL	Boston Public Library
CHS	Chicago Historical Society
CU	Columbia University, Butler Library, New York
DU	Duke University, Perkins Library, Durham, NC
EI	Essex Institute Library, Salem, MA
FSU	Florida State University, Strozier Library, Tallahassee
HU	Harvard University, Houghton Library, Cambridge, MA
LOC	Library of Congress, Washington, DC
LSU	Louisiana State University, Hill Memorial Library, Baton Rouge
MAHS	Massachusetts Historical Society, Boston
MDAH	Mississippi Department of Archives and History, Jackson
MDHS	Maryland Historical Society, Baltimore
MOHS	Missouri Historical Society, St. Louis
MSA	Maryland State Archives, Annapolis
NA	National Archives, Washington, DC
NCSA	North Carolina State Archives, Raleigh
NONA	New Orleans Notarial Archives
NOPL	New Orleans Public Library, Louisiana Collection
NYHS	New-York Historical Society
OSMM	Old Slave Mart Museum, Charleston, SC
RL	Rosenberg Library, Galveston, TX
SC	Schomburg Center for Research in Black Culture, New York Public Library
SCHS	South Carolina Historical Society, Charleston
SCSA	South Carolina State Archives, Columbia
SHC	Southern Historical Collection, University of North Carolina, Chapel Hill
TSL	Tennessee State Library and Archives, Nashville
TUL	Tulane University, Howard-Tilton Memorial Library, New Orleans, LA
UF	University of Florida, Smathers Library, Gainesville
UGA	University of Georgia, Hargrett Rare Book and Manuscript Library, Athens
UK	University of Kentucky, King Library, Lexington
UNO	University of New Orleans, Long Library
USC	University of South Carolina, Caroliniana Library, Columbia
UVA	University of Virginia, Alderman Library, Charlottesville
VHS	Virginia Historical Society, Richmond

VSL   Virginia State Library, Richmond
XU   Xavier University, University Library, New Orleans, LA

Introduction

1. Sturge, *Visit to the United States*, 32–35.

2. While the definitions of these regions changed over time, in general, the Upper South included the states of Delaware, Maryland, Virginia, Kentucky, and Missouri, along with the District of Columbia. The Lower South frequently included the Middle South states of North Carolina, Tennessee, and Arkansas, as well as the Deep South states of South Carolina, Georgia, Florida, Alabama, Mississippi, Louisiana, and Texas.

3. For accounts of the development of the domestic slave trade, see Bancroft, *Slave Trading*, chaps. 1–2; Kulikoff, "Uprooted Peoples," 143–71; and Tadman, *Speculators and Slaves*, 11–21.

4. For a full discussion of the total slave migration to the Lower South and the percentage attributable to the interregional slave trade, as well as a discussion of the estimated number of local slave sales and total number of southern slave sales, see appendixes A and B.

5. The Chesapeake region included the states of Delaware, Maryland, and Virginia, along with the District of Columbia.

6. While this region gradually changed over time, the Old Southwest included the states of Alabama, Mississippi, Louisiana, and Texas.

7. For a look at the role that southern slave property played in the American economy, see table 2.1.

8. Not everyone agrees with this relatively new market-revolution paradigm. But it is safe to say that a majority of historians today do find the paradigm useful, at least as an umbrella concept for describing the numerous economic changes that defined American society in the first half of the nineteenth century. As James Henretta recently noted, "The 'Market Revolution' threatens to supersede 'The Age of Jackson,' 'The Era of the Common Man,' and 'The Industrial Revolution' as the leitmotif of an era." Henretta, "The 'Market' in the Early Republic," 289. The pivotal work on this topic is Sellers, *Market Revolution*. Also influential are two special editions of the *Journal of the Early Republic*: "A Symposium on Charles Sellers' *The Market Revolution*" and "Capitalism in the Early Republic." In addition, I have found the following useful for understanding this topic: Hahn and Prude, eds., *Countryside in the Age of Capitalist Transformation*; Watson, *Liberty and Power*; Clark, *Roots of Rural Capitalism*; Henretta, *Origins of American Capitalism*; Rothenberg, *From Market-Places to a Market Economy*; Kulikoff, *Agrarian Origins of American Capitalism*; Merrill, "Putting 'Capitalism' in Its Place"; Stokes and Conway, eds., *Market Revolution in America*; Feller, "The Market Revolution Ate My Homework"; and Bushman, "Markets and Composite Farms in Early America."

9. Even those individuals who write about the market revolution and the South, most notably Harry Watson, have focused on other issues, such as the "dual economy" of the region and how planters and backcountry yeomen farmers experienced this economic development differently. It is true that several historians, including Watson, have men-

tioned how the rise of the domestic slave trade was an important consequence of the economic changes that swept the country in the first half of the nineteenth century, but they have not yet explored the implications that this entailed. See, especially, Watson, "Slavery and Development in a Dual Economy"; Genovese, *Political Economy of Slavery*; Fogel, *Without Consent or Contract*; Oakes, *Slavery and Freedom*; and Egerton, "Markets without a Market Revolution." Other useful works on economic development in the South during the early nineteenth century include Rothstein, "Antebellum South as a Dual Economy"; Wright, *Political Economy of the Cotton South*; Hahn, *Roots of Southern Populism*; Fox-Genovese and Genovese, *Fruits of Merchant Capital*; Weiman, "Farmers and the Market in Antebellum America"; Siegel, *Roots of Southern Distinctiveness*; Ford, *Origins of Southern Radicalism*; Escott, "Yeoman Independence and the Market"; Klein, *Unification of a Slave State*; Reidy, *From Slavery to Agrarian Capitalism*; Chaplin, *An Anxious Pursuit*; Watson, "Common Rights of Mankind"; and Dupre, *Transforming the Cotton Frontier.*

10. Most historical works that examine the domestic trade mention the importance of the local trade, but pass over it quickly and focus almost all of their attention on the interstate trade; see Bancroft, *Slave Trading*, 403–4; Tadman, *Speculators and Slaves*, 118–20, 136–40; and Johnson, *Soul by Soul*, 6–7.

11. A number of present-day historians have also held this view of the South. The historian who has most explored the premodern nature of the Old South is Eugene D. Genovese; see especially *Political Economy of Slavery*; *World the Slaveholders Made*; and *Roll, Jordan, Roll.*

12. For accounts of the Revolution's effect upon slavery in the South, see Dunn, "Black Society in the Chesapeake"; Kulikoff, *Tobacco and Slaves*; Frey, *Water from the Rock*; Berlin, *Many Thousands Gone*; and Morgan, *Slave Counterpoint.*

13. For accounts of the Revolution's effect upon slavery in the North, see Zilversmit, *First Emancipation*; Nash and Soderlund, *Freedom by Degrees*; White, *Somewhat More Independent*; Berlin, *Many Thousands Gone*; and Hodges, *Root and Branch.*

14. The literature on paternalism is extensive and controversial. Its most effective advocate is Eugene D. Genovese, especially in *Roll, Jordan, Roll.* For other, more critical accounts, see Oakes, *Ruling Race*; Jones, *Born a Child of Freedom*; and Tadman, *Speculators and Slaves*, chap. 8. For attempts to resolve the debate, see Morris, "Articulation of Two Worlds"; and Young, *Domesticating Slavery.*

15. The best descriptions of the slave trader as scapegoat can be found in Tadman, *Speculators and Slaves*, 180–84; and Gudmestad, "A Troublesome Commerce," 361–69.

16. Dumond, ed., *Birney Letters*, 1:108; Fladeland, *James Gillespie Birney*, chaps. 1–5.

17. The only historian who has explored the long-term consequences of the interstate trade in depth is William W. Freehling; see *Road to Disunion* and "Complex Career of Slaveholder Expansionism." Eugene D. Genovese has also examined this question somewhat in *Political Economy of Slavery*, esp. chaps. 6 and 10.

18. For a good account of how the Old South was romanticized in an effort to reunite white America after the Civil War, see Silber, *Romance of Reunion*; and Blight, *Race and Reunion.*

19. Phillips, *Life and Labor in the Old South*, 158; Phillips, *Slave Economy of the Old South*, 141. Phillips's most influential work was *American Negro Slavery.*

20. Bancroft, *Slave Trading*; Stampp, *Peculiar Institution*; Elkins, *Slavery.*

21. Stampp, *Peculiar Institution*, chap. 6. For other major works on this topic that were published during the 1970s, see Rawick, *From Sundown to Sunup*; Gutman, *Black Family*; Owens, *This Species of Property*; Levine, *Black Culture and Black Consciousness*; Webber, *Deep Like the Rivers*; Raboteau, *Slave Religion*; and Blassingame, *Slave Community*.

22. Fogel and Engerman, *Time on the Cross*. For two books criticizing the findings of *Time on the Cross*, see Gutman, *Slavery and the Numbers Game*; and David et al., *Reckoning with Slavery*. For other works by economic historians on the slave trade since *Time on the Cross*, see Kotlikoff, "Structure of Slave Prices in New Orleans"; Greenwald and Glasspiegel, "Adverse Selection in the Market for Slaves"; Fogel, *Without Consent or Contract*; Tadman, *Speculators and Slaves*; Freudenberger and Pritchett, "Domestic Slave Trade"; Pritchett and Freudenberger, "A Peculiar Sample"; Pritchett and Chamberlain, "Selection in the Market for Slaves"; Komlos and Alecke, "Economics of Antebellum Slave Heights Reconsidered"; Pritchett, "Interregional Slave Trade and the Selection of Slaves"; and Pritchett, "Quantitative Estimates of the Interregional Slave Trade."

23. Tadman, *Speculators and Slaves*; Johnson, *Soul by Soul*; Gudmestad, "A Troublesome Commerce."

Chapter 1

1. Mifflin to Adams, Sept. 24, 1798, Adams Papers, MAHS. I would like to thank David Mattern for drawing my attention to this letter.

2. For a good overview of slave trading in British North America, see Deyle, "By farr the most profitable trade." For work on individual colonies, see Coughtry, *Notorious Triangle*; Lydon, "New York and the Slave Trade"; Wax, "Negro Imports into Pennsylvania"; Wax, "Black Immigrants"; Klein, "Slaves and Shipping in Virginia"; Westbury, "Slaves of Colonial Virginia"; Kulikoff, *Tobacco and Slaves*; Littlefield, *Rice and Slaves*; and Richardson, "British Slave Trade to South Carolina."

3. The best overall accounts of the American Revolution's effect on slavery may be found among the essays in Berlin and Hoffman, eds., *Slavery and Freedom in the Revolution*. See also Robinson, *Slavery in American Politics*; MacLeod, *Slavery, Race and the American Revolution*; Davis, *Problem of Slavery in the Revolution*; and Frey, *Water from the Rock*.

4. The earliest attack on the African trade came in the late seventeenth century from Pennsylvania Quakers. But, except for a few isolated cases such as Samuel Sewall's *The Selling of Joseph* (1700), the Quakers remained the only group to argue against the trade during the colonial period. A good collection of early abolitionist writings is Bruns, ed., *Am I Not a Man*, part 1. See also Soderlund, *Quakers and Slavery*.

5. Otis pamphlet in Bruns, ed., *Am I Not a Man*, 104; Hart, *Liberty Described and Recommended* (1775), in ibid., 345; Jefferson quote in Kaminski, ed., *A Necessary Evil?* 3. See also Quarles, *Negro in the Revolution*, chap. 3; Bailyn, *Ideological Origins of the Revolution*, 232–46; Zilversmit, *First Emancipation*, chaps. 3–5; and Jordan, *White over Black*, chap. 7.

6. Kaminski, *A Necessary Evil?* 4; Du Bois, *Suppression of the Slave-Trade*, chap. 5; MacLeod, *Slavery, Race and the American Revolution*, 31–36.

7. Du Bois, *Suppression of the Slave-Trade*, 48–52; Jordan, *White over Black*, 365–74; Goldfarb, "Inquiry into Prohibition."

8. Du Bois, *Suppression of the Slave-Trade*, chap. 6; Davis, *Problem of Slavery in the Revolution*, 122–31; Finkelman, "Slavery and the Constitutional Convention"; Goldfarb, "Inquiry into Prohibition," 26–27.

9. For good accounts of South Carolina's closing and reopening of the African trade, see Brady, "Slave Trade in South Carolina"; and Shugerman, "Louisiana Purchase and the Slave Trade."

10. Petition of the delegates promoting the abolition of slavery, Jan. 7, 1795, General Assembly Papers, SCSA. See also the numerous other petitions in the same collection. Du Bois, *Suppression of the Slave-Trade*, 70–86; Jordan, *White over Black*, 325–31, 372–402; Robinson, *Slavery in American Politics*, 295–323; Fladeland, *Men and Brothers*, chap. 3; Coughtry, *Notorious Triangle*, chap. 6. For a good account of the reaction that these petitions received in Congress, see Newman, "Prelude to the Gag Rule."

11. *Charleston Courier*, Dec. 26, 1803. An indication of the many conflicts and regional differences within the state can be found in the numerous petitions to the state assembly; see Presentments to the Grand Jury; and General Assembly Papers, both SCSA; Brady, "Slave Trade in South Carolina," 612–17; Morgan, "Black Society in the Lowcountry," 83–93; Kulikoff, "Uprooted Peoples," 149–51.

12. Charleston District Petition, Dec. 8, 1807, and General Assembly Resolution, Dec. 12, 1807, General Assembly Papers, SCSA; Du Bois, *Suppression of the Slave-Trade*, 94–108; Robinson, *Slavery in American Politics*, 324–38; Mason, "Slavery Overshadowed."

13. William McIntosh to William Crawford, Mar. 14, 1818, Secretary of the Treasury Report, *Annals of Congress*, 16th Cong., 1st sess., 904–10; Du Bois, *Suppression of the Slave-Trade*, 108–30; Robinson, *Slavery in American Politics*, 338–46; Coughtry, *Notorious Triangle*, 203–37.

14. Davis, "American Slavery and the Revolution," 265. For a good account of the United States' mostly successful efforts at controlling the illegal African trade, see Fehrenbacher, *Slaveholding Republic*, chaps. 5–6.

15. The best overall accounts of Indian relations in the early republic may be found among the essays in Hoxie et al., eds., *Native Americans and the Early Republic*. See also Prucha, *American Indian Policy*; Horsman, *Expansion and American Indian Policy*; Sheehan, *Seeds of Extinction*, esp. chap. 9; Berkhofer, *White Man's Indian*, 134–66; Merrell, "Declarations of Independence"; and Wallace, *Jefferson and the Indians*.

16. Kulikoff, *Tobacco and Slaves*, 77. For accounts of the effect that large-scale migration had on various counties and regions within Virginia during the late eighteenth and early nineteenth centuries, see Schlotterbeck, "Plantation and Farm"; Beeman, *Evolution of the Southern Backcountry*; Siegel, *Roots of Southern Distinctiveness*; and Morgan and Nicholls, "Slaves in Piedmont Virginia."

17. Jacob H. Jeffreys to Robert N. Jeffreys, Mar. 23, 1837, Rogers Collection, NCSA; Brady, "Slave Trade in South Carolina," 615–17; Klein, *Unification of a Slave State*, esp. chap. 6.

18. Appleby, "Commercial Farming and the 'Agrarian Myth'"; Kulikoff, *Tobacco and Slaves*, 157–61.

19. Gray, *History of Agriculture*, chap. 29; Woodman, ed., *Slavery and the Southern Economy*, 17; Bruchey, ed., *Cotton and the Growth of the American Economy*, parts 1–2; Chaplin, "Creating a Cotton South."

20. Goodstein, "Black History on the Nashville Frontier"; Dunn, "Black Society in the Chesapeake," 59–62; Kulikoff, "Uprooted Peoples," 147–48; Kulikoff, *Tobacco and Slaves*, 77; Morgan, "Black Society in the Lowcountry," 83–85; Eslinger, "Slavery on the Kentucky Frontier."

21. Peter Manigault (1772), quoted in Morgan, "Black Society in the Lowcountry," 84n. In 1763, Henry Laurens, Charleston's largest slave trader, explained that it was from the backcountry "folks that we have always obtain'd the highest prices"; Laurens to Richard Oswald & Co., Feb. 15, 1763, in Hamer, ed., *Laurens Papers*, 3:260.

22. U.S. Census, *Negro Population*, 57.

23. Weld, *Travels Through the States*, 1:150; Washington to Robert Lewis, Aug. 18, 1799, in Fitzpatrick, ed., *Washington Writings*, 37:338.

24. Other short-term methods were also employed to help alleviate the problem of a slave surplus in the Upper South. For a good account of the role that slave hiring played, see Hughes, "Slaves for Hire." Another means of relieving the threat of rebellion which a surplus of slaves posed can be found in the rising number of convicted slave criminals who were transported out of Virginia by the end of the eighteenth century; see Schwarz, *Twice Condemned*.

25. Robinson, *Slavery in American Politics*, 295–96; MacLeod, *Slavery, Race and the American Revolution*, 31–34.

26. Martin and Mason quoted in Farrand, ed., *Records of the Convention*, 2:364, 370; Finkelman, "Slavery and the Constitutional Convention," 214–25. Luther Martin and George Mason both refused to sign the Constitution.

27. *Annals of Congress*, 14th Cong., 2d sess., 14–15; ibid., 15th Cong., 2d sess., 12; Robinson, *Slavery in American Politics*, 324–46; McColley, *Slavery and Virginia*, 163–67; Egerton, *Charles Fenton Mercer*, 164–68, 179–81.

28. Jefferson secretly wrote to Senator John Breckinridge of Kentucky, head of the committee to organize the territory, and asked that a clause prohibiting the foreign slave trade but allowing the domestic trade be inserted into the bill. Also, Virginians were later the most vocal supporters of slavery during the Missouri crisis. Scanlon, "A Sudden Conceit"; Robinson, *Slavery in American Politics*, 386–423.

29. *Annals of Congress*, 9th Cong., 2d sess., 528, 626–27, 636–37 (quotation on 626); Mason, "Slavery Overshadowed," 70–71.

30. Robinson, *Slavery in American Politics*, 313; Brady, "Slave Trade in South Carolina," 601–20.

31. McColley, *Slavery and Virginia*, 77–81, 114–21, 182–89; MacLeod, *Slavery, Race and the American Revolution*, 31–40.

32. Pinckney quoted in Farrand, ed., *Records of the Convention*, 2:371; *Charleston Courier*, Jan. 22, 1806; Plumer, *Memorandum of Proceedings*, 130.

33. "Draft of Declaration of Independence" (1776) in Ford, ed., *Jefferson Works*, 2:210–11; Cooke, ed., *Federalist*, 281–82; *Annals of Congress*, 1st Cong., 1st sess., 336; ibid., 9th Cong., 2d sess., 14.

34. For a good example of proslavery Virginians who helped create this antislavery image, see Finkelman, "Jefferson and Slavery"; and Wallenstein, "Flawed Keepers of the Flame." See also McColley, *Slavery and Virginia*, 114–18, 186–89; MacLeod, *Slavery, Race and the American Revolution*, 31–40; and Miller, *Wolf by the Ears*, 6–11.

35. *Annals of Congress*, 5th Cong., 2d sess., 1308–11 (quotation on 1308–9); Jefferson to John Holmes, Apr. 22, 1820, in Ford, ed., *Jefferson Works*, 12:159. See also McColley, *Slavery and Virginia*, 173–75; Miller, *Wolf by the Ears*, chap. 25; and Freehling, *Road to Disunion*, part 3.

36. Henry to Robert Pleasants, Jan. 18, 1773, in Bruns, ed., *Am I Not a Man*, 221–22.

37. Washington to John F. Mercer, Nov. 6, 1786, in Fitzpatrick, ed., *Washington Writings*, 29:56; Washington to Robert Lewis, Aug. 18, 1799, in ibid., 37:338; McColley, *Slavery and Virginia*, 66–70; MacLeod, *Slavery, Race and the American Revolution*, 132–34.

38. Beeman, *Patrick Henry*, 96–97. For good accounts of the difficulties that two other early Virginians faced when forced to sell their slaves, see Cohen, "Jefferson and the Problem of Slavery"; and McCoy, *Last of the Fathers*, 253–60.

39. *New-York Gazette; or, the Weekly Post-Boy*, May 17, 1756; *Pennsylvania Gazette*, Feb. 26, 1767; *South-Carolina Gazette and Country Journal*, Apr. 23, 1771; Deyle, "By farr the most profitable trade," 117–18.

40. Morgan and Nicholls, "Slaves in Piedmont Virginia," 235; White, *Ar'n't I a Woman?* 67; Wood, "Female Resistance to Slavery in Georgia."

41. *Virginia Gazette* (Purdie), Nov. 21, 1777; entry of Mar. 28, 1771, in Greene, ed., *Landon Carter Diary*, 1:554; Bayard, *Voyage dans l'Intérieur des États-Unis*, 289.

42. One indication of the success that Virginia planters had in encouraging their human chattel to reproduce can be found in the high growth rate of the state's black population. Between 1780 and 1820, the black population of Virginia almost doubled, despite heavy black migration out of the state; Greene and Harrington, *American Population before the Census*, 141–42; U.S. Census, *Negro Population*, 57. On the other hand, in urban areas of the South such as Baltimore, some owners continued to sell off women simply for having children well into the nineteenth century; see Whitman, *Price of Freedom*, 82; Will of William Watson, Dec. 3, 1751, Amelia County Will Book 1:78–79, VSL; *Virginia Gazette* (Rind), Nov. 23, 1769; *Virginia Gazette* (Purdie and Dixon), Feb. 18, 1773; Jefferson to John W. Eppes, June 30, 1820, in Betts, ed., *Farm Book*, 46; Morgan and Nicholls, "Slaves in Piedmont Virginia," 235–36.

43. Although changes were occurring in the Lower South, it is important to note that between 1763 and 1795 none of the advertisements in the *Georgia Gazette* concerning slave women mentioned their "breeding" ability, unlike those in Virginia; Wood, "Female Resistance to Slavery in Georgia," 608; Laurens to Richard Oswald, Oct. 16, 1767, in Hamer, ed., *Laurens Papers*, 5:370; Janson, *Stranger in America*, 363–64; Lambert, *Travels through Canada, and the United States*, 2:167–69; Charleston *City Gazette and Daily Advertiser*, Mar. 3, 1796; Robin, *Voyages dans l'Intérieur de la Louisiane*, 3:199.

44. There are no known cases of any individual in Virginia being executed for kidnapping a free person of color. See Essah, *A House Divided*, 84–86, 121–23 (quotation on 85); Phillips, *Freedom's Port*, 230–31; Bogger, *Free Blacks in Norfolk*, chap. 4.

45. "Minutes," Apr. 14, 1807, New York Manumission Society, NYHS; *Boston Gazette*, Oct. 19, 1772 to Apr. 12, 1773; Zilversmit, *First Emancipation*, chaps. 7–8; McManus, *Black Bondage*, chaps. 10–11; Fogel and Engerman, "Philanthropy at Bargain Prices," 391–93;

Nash and Soderlund, *Freedom by Degrees*, 196–201; White, *Somewhat More Independent*, 81–85; Hodges, *Root and Branch*, 191.

46. Wright and Tinling, eds., *Secret Diary of Byrd*, passim. For examples of the many ways that later planters used sales to control their work force, see the entries for Jan. 18, Apr. 14, Apr. 26, 1770, Sept. 23, 1773, July 9 and July 10, 1777, in Greene, ed., *Landon Carter Diary*, 1:347, 389, 396–97; 2:779, 1109, 1110; Washington to Anthony Whiting, Mar. 3, 1793, in Fitzpatrick, ed., *Washington Writings*, 32:366; and Jefferson to Thomas M. Randolph, June 8, 1803, in Betts, ed., *Farm Book*, 19.

47. *Virginia Gazette and Weekly Advertiser*, July 12, 1787.

48. Ball, *Slavery in the United States*; Grimes, *Life of William Grimes*; Davis, *Travels*, 2:148–60. Two other eighteenth-century narratives that mention frequent sale are those of George White, who was born in Virginia in 1764 and sold at the age of eighteen months, again at six, and once more at fifteen; and the Delaware-born Abraham Johnstone, who had five different owners before his death in 1797. Starling, *Slave Narrative*, 87–89.

49. *Virginia Gazette and Weekly Advertiser*, May, 20, 1790.

50. Randolph to Byrd, Sept. 20, 1757, in Tinling, ed., *Correspondence of Three William Byrds*, 2:628.

51. *Virginia Gazette* (Rind), Aug. 4, 1768, and Nov. 8, 1770; Grimes, *Life of William Grimes*, 16; Davis, *Travels*, 2:154; *Richmond Enquirer*, May 21, 1805.

52. McColley, *Slavery and Virginia*, 77–81; Kulikoff, *Tobacco and Slaves*, 70–74.

53. McColley, *Slavery and Virginia*, 82–83; Frey, "Between Slavery and Freedom"; Morgan, "Black Society in the Lowcountry," 108–12.

54. Madison to Robert Walsh, Mar. 2, 1819, in Hunt, ed., *Madison Writings*, 8:426–27; Keim, "Primogeniture and Entail in Virginia"; Smith, *Inside the Great House*, 119–20, 231–48; Kulikoff, *Tobacco and Slaves*, 199–203.

55. A. Drummond to [Col. John Coles], Apr. 5, [1780], Carter-Smith Papers, UVA; *Virginia Independent Chronicle*, Dec. 19, 1787.

56. *Gazette of the State of Georgia* (Savannah), Jan. 17, 1788; *Georgia Gazette* (Savannah), July 16, 1789.

57. Lee to Robert Goode, May 17, 1792, Virginia Executive Letter Books, VSL; *Knoxville Gazette*, Feb. 11, 1792, quoted in Eslinger, "Slavery on the Kentucky Frontier," 10; Siegel, *Roots of Southern Distinctiveness*, 19; anonymous and undirected letter of a slave trader, Jan. 24, 1795, in Phillips, ed., *Plantation Documents*, 2:55–56.

58. Grimes, *Life of William Grimes*, 21–22; Davis, *Travels*, 2:152–53; Ball, *Slavery in the United States*, 16–36.

59. Grand jury report of 1802 quoted in Alexandria *Phenix Gazette*, June 22, 1827; *A Tour in Virginia* (1808?), in Phillips, ed., *Plantation Documents*, 2:55; Bancroft, *Slave Trading*, 19–24.

60. Jefferson to Thomas M. Randolph, June 8, 1803, in Betts, ed., *Farm Book*, 19; Natchez *Weekly Chronicle*, Apr. 2, 1810, quoted in Phillips, *American Negro Slavery*, 189–90; MacLeod, *Slavery, Race and the American Revolution*, 149.

61. Kulikoff, "Uprooted Peoples," 151–53; Kulikoff, *Tobacco and Slaves*, 77; *Federal Intelligencer and Baltimore Daily Gazette*, 1819, quoted in Phillips, *Freedom's Port*, 46.

62. Evans, *A Pedestrious Tour*, 213–14.

Chapter 2

1. Freehling, *Drift toward Dissolution*.

2. Gholson's speech in *Richmond Enquirer*, Jan. 24, 1832. See also Freehling, *Drift toward Dissolution*, chap. 5.

3. It should be noted that the low increase in the Virginia slave population was not attributable to a sizable increase in the state's free black population. In 1820, free blacks comprised 8 percent of the state's black population; in 1860 this figure had only increased to 11 percent. In 1820, the slave population of Louisiana was 69,000. U.S. Census, *Negro Population*, 57.

4. Gutman, *Slavery and the Numbers Game*, 103. Estimates for the total number of slaves removed from the slave-exporting states for each decade are roughly 155,000 in the 1820s; 285,000 in the 1830s; 184,000 in the 1840s; and 251,000 in the 1850s. For a detailed explanation of the figures used in measuring this total movement of slaves, see appendix A. The exact ratio of Virginia slaves removed during the 1830s was 1 in 3.96. U.S. Census, *Negro Population*, 57; Tadman, *Speculators and Slaves*, 12.

5. Tadman, *Speculators and Slaves*, chap. 2. For a detailed explanation of the figures used in measuring the magnitude of the interregional slave trade, see appendix A.

6. Torrey, *Portraiture of Domestic Slavery*, 33; Tadman, *Speculators and Slaves*, 12; McGettigan, "Boone County Slaves," 182–83.

7. Weld, *American Slavery As It Is*, 184.

8. *Farmers' Register* (Petersburg, VA), May 1835.

9. Richard Gooch to Philip Gooch, Jan. 22, 1845, Gooch Papers, UVA; *DeBow's Review* (New Orleans), June 1859, 655.

10. Weston, *Progress of Slavery*, 147–48.

11. Tadman, "Demographic Cost of Sugar," 1541. Tadman also made this same argument in *Speculators and Slaves*, 121–29.

12. Henry Clay quoted in Weston, *Progress of Slavery*, 113; Dew, *Review of the Debate*, 49, 55; *Farmers' Register*, Sept. 1834. It should be noted that this piece in the *Farmers' Register* attempted to disprove this belief.

13. Olmsted, *Journey in the Seaboard States*, 57.

14. Olmsted, *Journey in the Back Country*, 283–84.

15. A. Durnford to John McDonogh, July 6, 1835, McDonogh Papers, TUL.

16. Barkley Townsend to Joseph Copes, June 28, 1835, Copes Papers, TUL.

17. Unnamed Georgia newspaper quoted in New Orleans *Picayune*, Feb. 9, 1851; Catterall, ed., *Judicial Cases*, 3:534–35.

18. Augusta (GA) *Constitutionalist* quoted in *Liberator* (Boston), Sept. 29, 1854; Palestine (TX) *Trinity Advocate*, July 29, 1857.

19. The actual number of convicted Virginia slaves officially transported out of the state was 983. Schwarz, *Slave Laws in Virginia*, chap. 4; Collins, *Domestic Slave Trade*, 122–25; Maryland Pardon Papers, 1818, box 18, folder 104, MSA.

20. *Charleston Courier*, July 12, 1806; Catterall, ed., *Judicial Cases*, 2:352.

21. *Niles' Register* (Baltimore), July 2, 1825. For a reprint of this article in a newspaper from the Deep South, see the Huntsville (AL) *Southern Advocate*, July 22, 1825.

22. Bans on the importation of slaves for sale were in effect in the Upper and Middle South states for the following years: Delaware, 1776–1865; Maryland, 1783–1850; Virginia, 1778–1819; Kentucky, 1798–1849; North Carolina, 1786–1818; and Tennessee, 1812–1855. States in the Deep South had similar bans in effect for the following years: South Carolina, 1800–1803, 1816–1818; Georgia, 1817–1824, 1829–1841, 1842–1848, 1852–1855; Alabama, 1827–1829, 1832; Mississippi, 1833–1846; and Louisiana, 1826–1828, 1831–1834. For a good summary of all the laws relating to the importation and exportation of slaves in the South, see Collins, *Domestic Slave Trade*, chap. 7. See also Bancroft, *Slave Trading*, 269–75.

23. Collins, *Domestic Slave Trade*, chap. 7; Essah, *A House Divided*, 40–41; Whitman, *Price of Freedom*, 78.

24. Bancroft, *Slave Trading*, 197–201; Pritchett, "Interregional Slave Trade and the Selection of Slaves," 68–69; Schwartz, *Born in Bondage*, 89–90. In his study of shipping manifests, Donald M. Sweig found that immediately after the passage of Louisiana's 1829 law, the percentage of the slaves arriving in New Orleans from Virginia who were children under the age of ten dropped from 13.5 percent to 3.7 percent; "Reassessing the Interstate Slave Trade," 11–14.

25. Alexander L. C. Magruder, "Would it be policy in the state of Mississippi to prohibit the importation of slaves (for sale)," Apr. 19, 1828, Magruder Papers, MDAH; Report of the Grand Jury of Perry County, 1845, quoted in Sellers, *Slavery in Alabama*, 178; T. S. Johnston to Thomas Butler, Mar. 12, 1832, Butler Papers, LSU.

26. Milledgeville *Georgia Journal*, Dec. 4, 1821, quoted in Phillips, ed., *Plantation Documents*, 2:68; Catterall, ed., *Judicial Cases*, 3:289. For a good account of the effect that Nat Turner's revolt had on instigating changes in Louisiana law, see Schafer, "Immediate Impact of Nat Turner's Insurrection."

27. Joseph D. Eads to George Huie, Nov. 9, 1839, Miscellaneous Manuscript Collection, MDAH. Mississippi's law requiring certificates of good character was in effect from 1808 until the Civil War. Signers had to swear that the person being sold had not "been guilty of any murder, crime, arson, burglary, felony, larceny to their knowledge or belief." It also required a signature by the county clerk of the slave's former residence. Louisiana's law was only in effect from 1829 until 1831 and required signers to swear that the individual being sold was of "a good moral character and [was] not in the habit of running away." Collins, *Domestic Slave Trade*, 126–31; Sydnor, *Slavery in Mississippi*, 162–71; Pritchett and Freudenberger, "A Peculiar Sample," 112–13. For a summary of the duration of the various bans in the Lower South, see n. 22 in this chapter.

28. Committee Report (Judiciary), Nov. 30, 1821, General Assembly Papers, SCSA.

29. *Savannah Republican*, Jan. 30, 1849; Bancroft, *Slave Trading*, 273–74.

30. John T. Foster to Joseph Gilliam, June 29, 1859, Gilliam Papers, UVA.

31. In the local slave trade, it was also common to use the "round" price for reporting sales or assessing property. This figure calculated the average price of a large group of individuals of mixed ages and sexes. Phillips, *American Negro Slavery*, 368–71; Evans, "Some Economic Aspects of the Slave Trade," 330; Kotlikoff, "Structure of Slave Prices in New Orleans"; Ransom and Sutch, "Capitalists without Capital"; Freudenberger and Pritchett, "Domestic Slave Trade."

32. *Richmond Enquirer*, July 29, 1859; Phillips, *Life and Labor in the Old South*, 177.

33. W. D. Jeffreys to William A. Jeffreys, Jan. 28, 1845, Howell Papers, SHC; Waters & Co. to W. K. Lathim, Aug. 4, 1847, Snyder Collection, MOHS; Kotlikoff, "Structure

of Slave Prices in New Orleans," 503–4; Tadman, *Speculators and Slaves*, 70–71; Freudenberger and Pritchett, "Domestic Slave Trade," 463–67. The 10.8 percent figure comes from Kotlikoff.

34. William Wright to Z. B. Oakes, Oct. 25, 1853, Oakes Papers, BPL; Francis Kinloch to Wilson Waties, Apr. 29, 1825, Waties Papers, USC; A. J. McElveen to Z. B. Oakes, Nov. 1, 1856, Oakes Papers; Samuel Browning to Archibald H. Boyd, Dec. 29, 1848, Boyd Papers, DU.

35. A. Gunn to J. S. Totten, Nov. 23, 1833, Totten Papers, NCSA; H. Bishop to S. R. Fondren, Nov. 8, 1859, Slavery Collection, CHS.

36. William Dickenson to Langhorne Scruggs, Mar. 8, 1851, Scruggs Papers, DU; Tyre Glen to Isaac Jarratt, Nov. 9, 1833, Jarratt-Puryear Papers, DU; Thomas Harrison to James Harrison, Jan. 12, 1836, Harrison Papers, SHC.

37. Rogers, *Incidents of Travel*, 247; Mrs. Walter Lenoir (1835), quoted in McGettigan, "Boone County Slaves," 280; A. Durnford to John McDonogh, July 6, 1835, McDonogh Papers, TUL.

38. Bacon Tait to R. C. Ballard, Aug. 2, 1836, Ballard Papers, SHC; R. H. Berry (1836), quoted in Mooney, *Slavery in Tennessee*, 36; Robert H. Carson to Henderson Forsyth, Dec. 3, 1836, Forsyth Papers, DU.

39. A. P. Merrill to William N. Mercer, Mar. 29, 1837, Mercer Papers, TUL; Asa Biggs to William Yellowby, Oct. 26, 1837, Biggs Papers, NCSA; Milledgeville (GA) *Federal Union*, Dec. 31, 1844.

40. B. R. Owen to William Campbell, Feb. 5, 1840, Campbell Papers, DU; R. H. Pender to Jesse Mercer, Apr. 30, 1841, Mercer Papers, DU.

41. Ransom and Sutch, "Capitalists without Capital," 156; Tadman, *Speculators and Slaves*, 289–90; Inscoe, *Mountain Masters*, 82; Campbell, *Empire for Slavery*, 69–73.

42. McCusker, *How Much Is That in Real Money?* 328–32.

43. In 1860 the total slave population was approximately 4 million. Goldin, "Economics of Emancipation"; Atack and Passell, *New Economic View of American History*, 356; Ransom and Sutch, "Capitalists without Capital," 149–52.

44. The *assessed value* of real estate refers to the amount at which real estate was assessed for taxation. Therefore, the true value of the property may be, and most likely was, somewhat higher. Still, it seems highly unlikely that in 1860 the true value of southern real estate was greater than the value of the slave population. The slaveholding states included Alabama, Arkansas, Delaware, Florida, Georgia, Kentucky, Louisiana, Maryland, Mississippi, Missouri, North Carolina, South Carolina, Tennessee, Texas, and Virginia, as well as the District of Columbia.

45. While there were many factors involved in the decision to secede, it is important to recognize the magnitude of the wealth that slave property represented and how that helped to motivate slave owners following Abraham Lincoln's election. In a recent article, James L. Huston has reminded us that economic historians have been making this point for years, although their arguments have been "insufficiently heeded by historians." Huston, "Property Rights in Slavery," 250. See also Gunderson, "Origin of the American Civil War"; Wright, *Political Economy of the Cotton South*, esp. chap. 5; and Ransom, *Conflict and Compromise*, esp. chap. 3.

46. Charleston *Southern Patriot* quoted in *Niles' Register*, Nov. 23, 1822; *St. Louis Herald* quoted in Milledgeville *Federal Union*, Feb. 14, 1860. In 1857 the *Richmond Exam-*

iner also bragged that "the slave wealth of our State figures in the handsome item of $237,500,000," but since the editor used an average price of only $500 per slave, he noted that "we believe we give too low an aggregate value for the slaves"; *Examiner* quoted in *Richmond Enquirer*, Apr. 24, 1857.

47. Townsend, *Doom of Slavery in the Union*, 19; Stephen F. Hale to Gov. Beriah Magoffin, Dec. 27, 1860, quoted in Dew, *Apostles of Disunion*, 92; "Declaration of Immediate Causes" (1861), quoted in ibid., 13. For an account of the prominent role that Townsend's pamphlet played in the pro-secession movement, see Sinha, *Counterrevolution of Slavery*, 233. For other accounts by contemporary southern politicians who openly worried about losing the enormous economic value of the slave population with Lincoln's election (albeit at estimates of less than $4 billion), see the 1860 speeches of William L. Yancey and Albert G. Brown, quoted in Huston, "Property Rights in Slavery," 253, 260.

48. *New-York Tribune*, Dec. 8, 1854.

49. Ambert O. Remington to "Dear Mother," Nov. 27, 1862, Remington Letters, TUL.

Chapter 3

1. *Charleston Courier*, Nov. 30, 1860.

2. *Wilmington* (NC) *Journal*, July 15, 1853.

3. While historians have long made the connection between westward expansion in the 1840s and 1850s and the coming of the Civil War, scant attention has been given to the increasing tensions that this movement created within the South and even less to the important role that the domestic slave trade played in this development. For the best exploration of this topic, see the works of William W. Freehling, *Road to Disunion* and "Complex Career of Slaveholder Expansionism." In his early work, Eugene D. Genovese also explored some of these issues; see *Political Economy of Slavery*, esp. chaps. 6 and 10. Finally, Lacy K. Ford examined the divisions within the various subregions of the South. His main focus, however, was on the differing constructions of race in the Jacksonian period and not on how these divisions led to civil war; see "Making the 'White Man's Country' White."

4. Charles Vaughan to the Earl of Aberdeen, Oct. 1, 1829, quoted in Roeckell, "Bonds over Bondage," 263. When Walker's letter first appeared in the Washington *Globe*, it covered three full seven-column pages. The best account of Walker's letter and its impact on the debate over annexation is Merk, *Fruits of Propaganda*, part 2. See also Shenton, *Robert John Walker*, chaps. 1–3; and Freehling, *Road to Disunion*, 418–24. The most recent history of how the Texas annexation debate helped to lead to secession is Morrison, *Slavery and the American West*. Like most political histories of the period, however, there is no discussion in this work of Walker's letter or of the role that the domestic slave trade played in bringing about disunion.

5. "LETTER OF MR. WALKER, Of Mississippi, in reply to the call of the people of Carrol county, Kentucky, to communicate his views on the subject of the annexation of Texas," Washington *Globe*, Feb. 3, 1844.

6. *United States Magazine and Democratic Review* (New York), Feb. 1845; Sedgwick, *Thoughts on Annexation*, 8. For a good account of the distribution and impact of Walk-

er's letter, along with a reprinted copy of its first pamphlet edition, see Merk, *Fruits of Propaganda*, 121–28, 221–52.

7. Sedgwick, *Thoughts on Annexation*, 40, 38. Sedgwick's attack first appeared in a series of articles in the New York *Evening Post*. In April 1844, it was reprinted as a pamphlet and soon reprinted again in another edition. William Wilkins's *Address to the People of the 21st Congressional District of Pennsylvania* (1844) was reprinted in the *National Intelligencer* (Washington, DC), July 6, 1844. Charles Ingersoll's letter first appeared in the Washington *Globe*, May 1, 1844, and was reprinted by the *Globe* in pamphlet form. Merk, *Fruits of Propaganda*, 107–11. Walker also threatened northerners with what would happen if Texas were not annexed. He argued that the slave owners would soon go bankrupt, freeing 3 million enslaved blacks, who would then flood to the North and cause an array of social evils.

8. Freehling, *Road to Disunion*, 420–23. Lacy Ford also claimed that in the "Upper South sentiment in favor of gradual emancipation, though always conditional, retained significant strength throughout the Jacksonian era," however, he focused almost exclusively on the Virginia slavery debates of 1832 and never discussed the Walker letter nor the 1840s. I would agree that this antislavery sentiment could be found in the Upper South, but I would argue that it was only "significant" during periods of social or economic stress, such as after the Nat Turner insurrection (1831) or the economic depression of the early 1840s; Ford, "Making the 'White Man's Country' White," 721.

9. "TO THE PEOPLE OF LOUISIANA," *National Intelligencer*, May 25, 1844; Merk, *Fruits of Propaganda*, 113. South Carolina had the highest percentage of slaves of any state, and Louisiana had the third highest; see table 2.2.

10. "TO THE EDITORS," *National Intelligencer*, July 6, 1844; Merk, *Fruits of Propaganda*, 112–14. Thompson's letter was also reprinted in *Niles' Register* (Baltimore), July 13, 1844.

11. Gholson quoted in *Liberator* (Boston), Aug. 30, 1850; *New-York Tribune*, July 24, 1846; Ransom and Sutch, "Capitalists without Capital," 155–56. The former slave Louis Hughes remembered being driven from Virginia to Mississippi in a coffle in 1844. According to Hughes, "as we passed along, every white man we met was yelling, 'Hurrah for Polk and Dallas!'" and "the man who had us in charge joined with those we met in the hurrahing"; Hughes, *Thirty Years a Slave*, 13.

12. William Freehling has argued that the lack of support for Thompson in the South was based on the widespread acceptance of, and rejoicing over, Walker's overall argument. While I agree that the number of people who questioned the future of slavery in the South in 1844 was higher than normal (because of the depression), I believe that he overestimates the number of southerners who actually thought that Walker's plan would really work. Most people supported Walker (and not Thompson) not because they thought that annexation would rid the country of slavery, but because they knew that the first component of his plan would prove true: annexation would lead to an increased demand for slaves, which would raise the capital value of their estates. This was also the explanation offered by Frederick Douglass in an 1845 speech: "In 1836 slaves brought from 1000 to 1,500 dollars; but a year ago, the price was reduced to 600 dollars. The slaveholders saw the necessity of opening a new country where there would be a demand for slaves." Freehling, *Road to Disunion*, 421–24; Douglass quoted in *Liberator*, Dec. 12, 1845.

13. Ransom and Sutch, "Capitalists without Capital," 155–56; Olmsted, *Journey in the Seaboard States*, 58.

14. A. J. McElveen to Z. B. Oakes, Jan. 2, 1854, Oakes Papers, BPL; Baltimore *Sun*, Apr. 29, 1856; *Charleston Mercury*, Dec. 9, 1859.

15. Milledgeville (GA) *Federal Union*, Jan. 17, 1860; *Oxford* (MS) *Mercury* quoted in *Mobile Advertiser*, Jan. 18, 1860; *Lake Providence* (LA) *Herald* quoted in *Washington Union*, Mar. 11, 1856.

16. Nashville *Republican Banner*, May 22, 1858; *Savannah Republican*, Feb. 18, 1859; Austin (TX) *State Gazette*, Oct. 15, 1859.

17. Wright, *Political Economy of the Cotton South*, 139–44.

18. William Conner to Lemuel Conner, Feb. 14, 1857, Conner Papers, LSU.

19. Richmond *Dispatch*, July 22, 1856; New Orleans *Picayune*, July 6, 1860. During the summer months, Hatcher kept the majority of his slaves at "a very healthy and convenient location in the Piny Woods, 2 1/2 miles from Tickfaw Station, on the Tangipahoa River, and only 3 1/2 hours' ride from the city, on the Jackson Railroad." Individuals looking for slaves to purchase could see a list of the men and women kept at the remote location by visiting Hatcher's depot; New Orleans *Picayune*, July 6, 1860. Another example of year-round trading in the Upper South can be found in the advertisement that R. W. Lucas placed in the Lexington *Kentucky Statesman*, Jan. 13, 1860: "A LARGE NUMBER OF NEGROES WANTED! the undersigned wishes to purchase throughout the year, a large number of SOUND AND HEALTHY NEGROES OF BOTH SEXES." Another New Orleans dealer who set up an arrangement similar to Hatcher's was Walter Campbell. According to his notice, he too now had "Negroes for Sale all the Time," adding that "from this time till the fall trade opens in New Orleans, planters can purchase NEGROES by visiting my farm, five miles from Osyka, Miss., on the New Orleans and Jackson Railroad, where I will have a large body of choice hands for sale"; New Orleans *Picayune*, July 1, 1860.

20. *New Orleans Bee*, Mar. 12, 1857; Thomas Bleckley to Sylvester Bleckley, Feb. 10, 1857, Bleckley Papers, USC; entry for Feb. 2, 1859, Leak Diary, SHC.

21. *New Orleans Crescent*, Jan. 30, 1860; Tallahassee *Floridian and Journal*, Feb. 11, 1860.

22. New Orleans *Picayune*, May 20, 1859; *Mobile Register*, Jan. 19, 1859; Athens (GA) *Southern Banner*, Jan. 11, 1855, quoted in Phillips, *American Negro Slavery*, 374; Milledgeville *Federal Union*, Jan. 17, 1860. For other newspapers in the Deep South that warned against the high price of slaves, see Montgomery (AL) *Confederation*, Jan. 13, 1859; and *Savannah Republican*, Jan. 22, 1859. The *Republican* also reprinted the *Picayune* editorial on May 27, 1859.

23. *Charleston Mercury*, Nov. 8, 1854. For a good letter to the editor signed by "South," which noted "that of the six millions and more of whites residing in the South, there are but three hundred and forty-seven thousand five hundred and twenty-five slave owners—not quite one in twenty," see *Mercury*, July 28, 1858.

24. Macon *Georgia Citizen*, Aug. 12, 1859, quoted in Flanders, *Slavery in Georgia*, 193; *Tuskegee* (AL) *Republican* quoted in *Liberator*, Feb. 4, 1859; *Ouachita* (LA) *Register* quoted in New Orleans *Delta*, Apr. 3, 1858; *Sparta* (LA) *Jeffersonian* quoted in *New Orleans Crescent*, Sept. 17, 1859.

25. Austin *State Gazette*, Feb. 12, 1859; *Savannah Republican*, Mar. 14, 1859; Montgomery *Confederation*, Jan. 13, 1859. For some of the other major newspapers in the Deep South that reprinted portions of this editorial, see *Mobile Register*, Jan. 19, 1859; and Jackson *Mississippian*, Jan. 28, 1859.

26. *Savannah Republican*, Jan. 22, 1849.

27. Jackson *Mississippian*, Jan. 28, 1859. This piece by "COMMON SENSE" was reprinted from the *Montgomery Advertiser*.

28. Aberdeen (MS) *Sunny South*, Feb. 25, 1858; *Charleston Mercury*, Apr. 9, 1859.

29. *Mobile Register*, Sept. 30, 1859; *New Orleans Crescent*, Nov. 16, 1857.

30. *St. Louis Democrat* quoted in *Liberator*, Jan. 21, 1859; *Richmond Enquirer*, Apr. 28, 1857. This piece in the *Enquirer* was attacked by the New Orleans *Delta*, which resulted in an exchange of views on Virginia's loyalty to the South; see *Delta*, May 1, 1857; and *Enquirer*, May 12, 1857.

31. Norfolk (VA) *Southern Argus* quoted in New Orleans *Delta*, May 23, 1857.

32. New Orleans *Picayune*, June 22, 1859.

33. *New Orleans Crescent*, Apr. 16, 1857.

34. *Memphis Eagle and Enquirer* and *Richmond Whig* both quoted in *Charleston Mercury*, Jan. 16, 1857; Gov. James H. Adams quoted in *DeBow's Review* (New Orleans), Aug. 1857, 211.

35. *New Orleans Crescent*, Jan. 12, Feb. 17, 1857.

36. For a summary of the various statewide bans on the importation of slaves for sale, see chap. 2, n. 22.

37. *Savannah Republican*, Jan. 22, Feb. 2, 1849; *New Orleans Crescent*, May 2, 1857; New Orleans *Delta*, Apr. 28, 1857.

38. Hancock County petition quoted in *Savannah Republican*, Feb. 23, 1849; Committee Report (Colored Population), Dec. 5, 1851, General Assembly Papers, SCSA.

39. For a summary of the various earlier prohibitions and why they were unenforceable, see chap. 2, sec. III.

40. *Charleston Mercury*, June 6, 1857. Lincoln gave his "House Divided" speech on June 16, 1858, while accepting the Republican nomination for the U.S. Senate. For a good account of the origins and purpose of this speech, see Fehrenbacher, *Prelude to Greatness*, chap. 4.

41. Williamsburg District, Fall 1854, Presentments to the Grand Jury, SCSA; South Carolina House, *Report of the Special Committee*, 25. The *Charleston Mercury* first came out in favor of reopening the African trade in a series of articles dated Oct. 24, 27, 31, Nov. 4 and 8, 1854. *DeBow's Review* first published an article discussing the need to reopen the trade in Aug. 1856, 177–86. Despite its importance in explaining the road to secession, there has been relatively little written by historians on the movement to reopen the African slave trade. The best work on the topic is Takaki, *A Pro-Slavery Crusade*. For other accounts, see Du Bois, *Suppression of the Slave-Trade*, chap. 11; Williams, "Southern Movement to Reopen"; Bernstein, "Southern Politics and the African Trade"; and Sinha, *Counterrevolution of Slavery*, chap. 5.

42. Charleston *Standard* quoted in *Richmond Enquirer*, May 25, 1858; Augusta (GA) *Dispatch* (1859), quoted in Takaki, *A Pro-Slavery Crusade*, 67. For good summaries of the argument in favor of reopening the African slave trade, see the five-part series in

the *Charleston Mercury* beginning Oct. 24, 1854, and the various writings of Leonidas W. Spratt, including his twelve-part series in the New Orleans *Delta* beginning Oct. 2, 1857; the report he wrote for the Southern Convention at Montgomery, Alabama, reprinted in *DeBow's Review*, June 1858, 473–91; his *Speech upon the Foreign Slave Trade*; and his pamphlet *Foreign Slave Trade*.

43. Jackson *Mississippian*, Jan. 28, 1859; *Richmond Whig* quoted in *DeBow's Review*, July 1858, 80; New Orleans *Delta*, Oct. 2, 1857.

44. New Orleans *Picayune*, Dec. 4, 1856; *Savannah Republican*, Dec. 6, 1856.

45. *Lynchburg Virginian*, Oct. 17, 1860; *Richmond Enquirer*, May 25, 1858.

46. South Carolina House, *Report of the Minority Committee*, 11; Foote quoted in *DeBow's Review*, Aug. 1859, 219.

47. Gregg quoted in *Debow's Review*, Feb. 1861, 222; *Charleston Courier*, Sept. 4, 1858.

48. New Orleans *Delta*, Nov. 20, 1857.

49. *Charleston Mercury*, Nov. 8, 1854; South Carolina House, *Report of the Special Committee*, 28. See also Spratt's article in New Orleans *Delta*, Oct. 17, 1857.

50. *Charleston Mercury*, Oct. 27, Nov. 8, 1854. See also Spratt's three articles in the New Orleans *Delta*, Oct. 24, 28, and Nov. 5, 1857.

51. New Orleans *Delta*, Dec. 10, 1856; Adams letter, Aug. 30, 1858, quoted in *Charleston Mercury*, Sept. 15, 1858; *Sunny South*, June 3, 1858.

52. *New Orleans Crescent*, June 29, 1858.

53. Letter of John S. Palmer, *Charleston Mercury*, Nov. 3, 1859; Charleston *Standard* quoted in *Liberator*, Dec. 12, 1856. Leonidas Spratt further elaborated upon this argument in his pamphlet *Foreign Slave Trade*, esp. sections 5–6.

54. Tallahassee *Floridian and Journal*, Feb. 19, 1859; *DeBow's Review*, Jan. 1859, 51; *Tuskegee Republican* quoted in *Liberator*, Feb. 4, 1859.

55. Du Bois, *Suppression of the Slave-Trade*, 178; *Liberator*, July 29, 1859; *Petersburg (VA) Intelligencer* quoted in *New Orleans Crescent*, June 29, 1858; Williams, "Southern Movement to Reopen," 28; Takaki, *A Pro-Slavery Crusade*, chap. 2. Several prominent individuals in the Upper South, most notably, George Fitzhugh of Virginia, also spoke out in favor of reopening the African trade; see his numerous writings in *DeBow's Review*, Dec. 1857, 587–96; Feb. 1859, 144–48; and Oct. 1859, 382–87. Finally, in her recent work, Manisha Sinha has correctly noted that "most historians have failed to fully appreciate the nature and extent of the movement"; *Counterrevolution of Slavery*, 136. Her work is a valuable corrective to this trend.

56. *Charleston Courier*, Sept. 4, 1858; *Charleston Mercury*, Mar. 9, 1859. Even after the *Mercury* declared that it would no longer endorse the African slave trade, it still continued to print letters from readers who advocated this policy.

57. New Orleans *Delta*, May 18, 1858; Du Bois, *Suppression of the Slave-Trade*, 169–73; Williams, "Southern Movement to Reopen," 24–28; Bernstein, "Southern Politics and the African Trade," 24–29; Takaki, *A Pro-Slavery Crusade*, chap. 7; Sinha, *Counterrevolution of Slavery*, 144–51. The southern commercial conventions that addressed the issue of the African trade were held in New Orleans (1855), Savannah (1856), Knoxville (1857), Montgomery (1858), and Vicksburg (1859). For a good account of the speeches at the Montgomery convention, see *DeBow's Review*, June 1858, 574–606.

58. *Savannah Republican*, Mar. 7, 1849.

59. *Charleston Mercury*, July 24, 1858, July 2, 1857; New Orleans *Delta*, Apr. 28, 1857. By the late 1850s, whites in the Upper South also sometimes spoke of themselves as being on the frontier, such as when the *Richmond Enquirer* noted in response to an article by the *Delta* that "our station is much nearer the frontier than his." But this was almost always used in reference to a physical location (with its implications about the North) and not as a description of their lack of commitment to the southern way of life. *Enquirer*, May 12, 1857.

60. Speech of Gov. Benjamin F. Perry, Dec. 11, 1850, in Meats and Arnold, eds., *Perry Writings*, 1:365; *DeBow's Review*, June 1858, 481; *New Orleans Crescent*, June 19, 1858.

61. The slave population in Delaware in 1860 was 1,798. The slave population in Maryland in 1800 was 105,635. By 1860, it had dropped to 87,189. In that year 50.9 percent of Maryland's black population was enslaved. U.S. Census, *Negro Population*, 57.

62. Thomas P. Copes to Joseph Copes, Oct. 31, 1846, Copes Papers, TUL.

63. *New Orleans Crescent*, July 5, 1858, Apr. 16, 1857, Apr. 19, June 30, July 9, 1858; Foner, *Free Soil, Free Labor, Free Men*, 121.

64. *New Orleans Crescent*, July 17, 1858.

65. Unfortunately, despite its importance, there has been little historical study of the Thayer movement. The best secondary information can be found in Hickin, "John C. Underwood." For the best primary account, see the numerous articles that appeared in the *New York Herald*, Feb. 28, Mar. 10, 30, and Apr. 11, 1857.

66. *Richmond Examiner*, May 22, 1857; *Richmond Whig* quoted in *New York Herald*, Mar. 10, 1857; Hickin, "John C. Underwood," 162–63.

67. New Orleans *Delta*, Apr. 28, Aug. 18, Sept. 2, 16, Nov. 17, 1857.

68. *Charleston Mercury*, July 2, 1857, July 24, 1858. For an account of how the term was applied to other frontier states, see "Thayerism in Missouri," New Orleans *Delta*, Nov. 20, 1857.

69. The Richmond *South* was responding to a letter by William Lowndes Yancey of Alabama. *Lynchburg Virginian* quoted in New Orleans *Delta*, May 23, 1857; Richmond *South* quoted in *Charleston Mercury*, July 24, 1858.

70. *Richmond Enquirer*, June 22 and July 5, 1858.

71. Ibid., May 25, 1858.

72. Columbia (SC) *Southern Guardian* quoted in *Richmond Enquirer*, July 5, 1858; *Charleston Mercury*, July 31, 1858; New Orleans *Delta*, June 29, 1858.

73. Richmond *South*, July 8, 1858, quoted in *Liberator*, Aug. 27, 1858; *New Orleans Crescent*, July 17, 1858.

74. New Orleans *Delta*, Oct. 1, 1857; *Charleston Mercury*, July 24, 1858.

75. *Memphis Appeal*, Apr. 4, 1858.

76. *New Orleans Crescent*, June 6, 1857.

77. Ibid., Nov. 16, 1857; New Orleans *Delta*, Apr. 28, 1857.

78. *New Orleans Crescent*, May 2, 1857.

79. Message of Gov. William H. Gist from South Carolina is quoted from the tele-graphic dispatch received by and reprinted in the *Richmond Enquirer*, Nov. 30, 1860; also see ibid., Jan. 8, 1861.

80. Confederate constitution quoted in Thomas, *Confederate Nation*, 313; Yancey quoted in Takaki, *A Pro-Slavery Crusade*, 236; Commissioner Henry Benning quoted

in *Richmond Enquirer*, Feb. 22, 1861. Not all pro-secession southerners agreed with the Montgomery convention's decision to prohibit the African trade. Leonidas Spratt believed that without the foreign trade, "our whole movement is defeated"; *Charleston Mercury*, Feb. 13, 1861.

81. Charlottesville (NC) *Observer* quoted in *National Intelligencer*, Dec. 15, 1860.

82. *Richmond Whig* quoted in *Richmond Enquirer*, Oct. 19, 1860. Unfortunately, far too many historians of Virginia have failed to note the crucial role that the inter-regional trade and slave property values played in that state's decision to secede. In a recent example of this oversight, Daniel W. Crofts has surprisingly proclaimed that Virginia's secession from the Union "is almost a cause for wonderment." The only explanation he could find was that "Virginia's political leaders exaggerated the Old Dominion's affinity for Deep South particularism. Even though economic and social trends indicated otherwise, Virginia Democrats liked to pretend that their state was as southern as any"; Crofts, "Late Antebellum Virginia Reconsidered," 253. See also Crofts, *Reluctant Confederates*; and Shade, *Democratizing the Old Dominion*, chap. 8.

Chapter 4

1. *Memphis Eagle and Enquirer*, Oct. 27, 1855.

2. Bancroft, *Slave Trading*, 252–53; Mooney, *Slavery in Tennessee*, 46–48.

3. *Memphis Eagle*, May 30, Sept. 20, 1849, Jan. 10, 1850.

4. St. Louis *Missouri Democrat*, July 28, 1854; *Lexington Observer and Reporter*, Dec. 1, 1855; *Knoxville Whig* quoted in *Memphis Eagle and Enquirer*, Apr. 20, 1858. In addition to widespread newspaper advertising, Bolton, Dickens & Co. also ran a full-page ad in the *Memphis City Directory and General Business Advertiser* (1855), 212.

5. Stowe, *Uncle Tom's Cabin*, 86. One of the few historians who has fully appreciated the role that slave traders played in promoting the southern economy is Edmund Drago, ed., *Broke by the War*, 9.

6. An indication of how many slave traders were southern-born can be found in the 1860 city census of New Orleans, which listed thirty-four slave dealers as permanently residing in the city: twenty-one were born in the South Atlantic states of Maryland, Virginia, North Carolina, South Carolina, and Georgia; six were born in the Upper and Middle South states of Kentucky, Missouri, and Tennessee; three were born in New England; two were born in the Middle Atlantic states; and two were born abroad; Tansey, "Bernard Kendig," 161.

7. John Hammett to John Preston, May 25, 1820, Preston Papers, VHS; Ball, *Slavery in the United States*, chaps. 3–8.

8. Calderhead, "Role of the Professional Slave Trader," 195–211; Gudmestad, "A Troublesome Commerce," chap. 1. The John Woolfolk who helped Austin to sell slaves in the late 1810s was definitely a relation, and it is assumed that this was the same uncle John from Georgia who advertised for slaves for his personal use fifteen years later; *Baltimore Republican and Commercial Advertiser*, Apr. 18, 1835. Another early trader who began shipping large consignments from Richmond to New Orleans as early as 1817 was Abner Robinson; Tadman, *Speculators and Slaves*, 21.

9. Freudenberger and Pritchett found that in 1830 the average cost of shipping a slave by sea from Norfolk, Virginia, to New Orleans was $17. At the same time, the average cost by land was $15; "Domestic Slave Trade," 472–75. These figures correspond with contemporary estimates. In an 1851 Louisiana court case, the slave trader James White testified that slaves could be transported from Virginia to New Orleans by land for "$15 to $18 per head." David Wise was somewhat more optimistic, claiming it could be done for "$8 per head." Seneca Bennett testified that slaves could be transported by water from Baltimore for "$12 per head" and from Richmond for $15. Testimony of White, Wise, and Bennett, Aug. 20, 1851, Succession of Elihu Cresswell, No. 2423, 8 La. Ann. 122 (1853), UNO.

10. Freudenberger and Pritchett found that in 1830 the trip by sea from Norfolk, Virginia, to New Orleans took on average nineteen days; "Domestic Slave Trade," 467–72. See also Tadman, *Speculators and Slaves*, 71–82.

11. While Woolfolk's bookkeeping records have not survived, remaining slave manifests indicate that between 1824 and 1829, he shipped at least 230–460 slaves south each year. "Speech of July 5, 1852," in Blassingame, ed., *Douglass Papers*, 2:373–74; unknown New Orleans paper quoted in *Genius of Universal Emancipation* (Baltimore), July 1825; *New-Orleans Argus*, Nov. 17, 1828; Calderhead, "Role of the Professional Slave Trader," 195–202; Gudmestad, "A Troublesome Commerce," chap. 1.

12. Stephenson, *Isaac Franklin*, chaps. 2–3; Howell, "John Armfield, Slave-trader," 3–29; Gudmestad, "A Troublesome Commerce," chap. 1.

13. Alexandria *Phenix Gazette*, May 15, 1828; *New York Evangelist*, Feb. 1, 1834; Andrews, *Slavery and the Domestic Slave-Trade*, 135–43; Abdy, *Journal of a Residence*, 2:179–80.

14. Andrews, *Slavery and the Domestic Slave-Trade*, 148. The first vessel on which Franklin & Armfield offered shipping service to New Orleans was the *Jefferson*. Initially, the firm also provided shipping aboard the *United States*, the *Lafayette*, the *James Monroe*, the *Ariel*, and the *Renown*; Alexandria *Phenix Gazette*, Oct. 8, 1828, Dec. 11, 1829, Dec. 18, 1830, Feb. 25, 1831, Feb. 15 and Apr. 16, 1833. By the fall of 1833, however, all of its advertisements were for the three ships that it definitely owned. Its first offering aboard the "new brig TRIBUNE" was on Nov. 3, 1831. Advertisements announcing the *Uncas* first appeared on Oct. 5, 1833, and the *Isaac Franklin* on July 14, 1835 (all *Phenix Gazette*). Wendell Stephenson has argued that Franklin & Armfield also owned the *United States*, however, the company only advertised shipping aboard that vessel once (*Phenix Gazette*, Dec. 11, 1829), and I have not been able to locate any other documentation confirming its ownership of this brig. The company's ownership of the *Tribune*, *Uncas*, and *Isaac Franklin* was confirmed in advertisements placed by the slave-trading firms who purchased them after Franklin & Armfield's dissolution (William H. Williams bought the *Tribune* and *Uncas* and George Kephart the *Isaac Franklin*); *National Intelligencer* (Washington, DC), Nov. 7, 1836, and Feb. 18, 1837; Stephenson, *Isaac Franklin*, chap. 4.

15. The first packet line was the Black Ball Line, which began regular service between New York City and Liverpool in 1818. For a good account of the transforming effect that packet lines had on the American economy, especially in the North, see Taylor, *Transportation Revolution*, 104–7; Stephenson, *Isaac Franklin*, chap. 4; Sweig, "Reassessing the Interstate Slave Trade," 5–21.

16. Alexandria *Phenix Gazette*, Oct. 5, 1833, and July 14, 1835. While all of Franklin & Armfield's shipping announcements listed a specific date for departure, they first noted

that "one of the REGULAR PACKETS" would leave in January 1833 and offered a vessel to New Orleans each month that spring. The following fall, they placed their first advertisement for "Alexandria and New Orleans PACKETS," announcing that either the *Tribune* or the *Uncas* would leave port "every thirty days throughout the shipping season." Ibid., Jan. 4 and Oct. 5, 1833.

17. Stephenson, *Isaac Franklin*, chap. 4. It should be noted that by 1834, other competitors in the DC area were also advertising regularly. Nevertheless, from May 15, 1828, until November 1836, Franklin & Armfield's notices appeared almost continuously in the Alexandria *Phenix Gazette* and other area newspapers.

18. For a good account of the important role that James Franklin played in the selling market, see the numerous letters from him in the Ballard Papers, SHC. The firm's other permanent agents were Rice C. Ballard (Richmond), J. M. Saunders (Warrenton), A. Grimm (Fredericksburg), George Kephart (Frederick), William Hooper (Annapolis), Thomas M. Jones (Easton), and John Ware (Port Tobacco). Alexandria *Phenix Gazette*, Aug. 27, 1833; Stephenson, *Isaac Franklin*, 26–27.

19. Frederic Bancroft has convincingly argued that the firm of Birch & Jones probably worked as an unnamed agent for Franklin & Armfield. According to Bancroft, "the advts. of the two firms repeatedly began on the same day and bore the same directions to the printer as to continuance, and in an advt. for a pair of horses, presumably for the overland trip to Natchez, Armfield requested persons in Washington to apply to Birch & Jones"; *Slave Trading*, 59n.

20. When the firm reorganized in 1835, it took on the name of Armfield, Franklin & Co. in Alexandria, and Ballard, Franklin & Co. in Natchez and New Orleans. Both firms dissolved on November 10, 1841. Articles of Agreement, Mar. 15, 1831, and July 10, 1835, Ballard Papers, SHC; Stephenson, *Isaac Franklin*, 67.

21. Austin Woolfolk was out of the slave-trading business by 1836, if not before. Armfield to R. C. Ballard, Mar. 26, 1832, Ballard Papers, SHC; Stephenson, *Isaac Franklin*, 70; Calderhead, "Role of the Professional Slave Trader," 200; Phillips, *Freedom's Port*, 295.

22. Ingraham, *The South-west*, 2:245; Franklin to R. C. Ballard, Dec. 25, 1833, Ballard Papers, SHC; *New York Evangelist*, Feb. 1. 1834; Andrews, *Slavery and the Domestic Slave-Trade*, 148; Isaac Franklin to R. C. Ballard, Mar. 10, 1834, Ballard Papers.

23. Alexandria *Louisiana Democrat*, Nov. 16, 1859.

24. Forrest began as an itinerant slave trader in 1853. The following year, he established himself in Memphis, and working occasionally with a partner (and at least four of his brothers), he stayed in that market until 1860. *Charleston Courier*, Jan. 23, 1860; *Memphis City Directory* (1855), 251; *Memphis Eagle and Enquirer*, Jan. 21, 1857; *Memphis Avalanche*, Jan. 3, 1860; Bancroft, *Slave Trading*, 256–64; Mooney, *Slavery in Tennessee*, 49–50.

25. Philip Thomas to William Finney, Nov. 26, 1859, Finney Papers, DU.

26. Henry G. Daniel to Isaac Jarratt, Oct. 23, 1835, Jarratt-Puryear Papers, DU; Brown, *Slave Life in Georgia*, 15.

27. Stone was involved in the slave trade from as early as 1816 until his death in 1826. A. J. McElveen to Z. B. Oakes, Oct. 21, 1856, Oakes Papers, BPL; Coleman, *Slavery Times in Kentucky*, 173–76. For an example of slave traders living in their tents while purchasing slaves in Virginia, see the testimony of George D. Thorn, Feb. 13, 1840, *Nelson v. Lillard et al.*, No. 800-1, 16 La. 336 (1840), UNO.

28. Samuel F. Adams to David S. Reid, Feb. 26, 1844, Reid Papers, DU; Gunn to Joseph S. Totten, Oct. 14, 1835, Totten Papers, NCSA.

29. Brown, *Slave Life in Georgia*, 18, 20; A. J. McElveen to Z. B. Oakes, Oct. 21, 1856, Oakes Papers, BPL; Henry Lewis narrative in Tyler and Murphy, eds., *Slave Narratives of Texas*, 29; Flanders, *Slavery in Georgia*, 187.

30. Peter Stokes to William H. Hatchett, Jan. 16, 1846, Hatchett Papers, DU; Fields to Jane M. Fields, Nov. 29, 1822, Fields Papers, DU; Chief Justice Chilton quoted in Sellers, *Slavery in Alabama*, 154.

31. Miles Norton to "My Dear Wife," Nov. 18, 1854, Norton Papers, USC; Brown, *Slave Life in Georgia*, 20–21; Peter Stokes to William H. Hatchett, Mar. 4, 1846, Hatchett Papers, DU.

32. Kephart to John Armfield, Mar. 16, 1838, Ballard Papers, SHC; Thomas W. Burton to William Long, Jan. 31, 1845, Long Papers, NCSA; A. J. McElveen to Z. B. Oakes, Sept. 16, 1856, Oakes Papers, BPL. For examples of formal partnership agreements between the country traders Tyre Glen and Isaac Jarratt and between Tyre Glen and William Martin, see Articles of Agreement, Nov. 13, 1831, and June 6, 1836, Glen Papers, DU.

33. R. C. Puryear to Isaac Jarratt, Mar. 3, 1834, Jarratt-Puryear Papers, DU. Michael Tadman has erroneously argued that Jenny was Glen's wife (*Speculators and Slaves*, 76). According to the background notes for the Tyre Glen Papers (DU), Glen married a woman named Margaret Bynum in 1836. Moreover, there are two previous letters from Glen saying that he was trying to secure the services of Jenny and a man named Andy; Tyre Glen to Isaac Jarratt, Jan. 9 and Feb. 2, 1834, Jarratt-Puryear Papers. The firm of Jarratt & Glen was in business from 1830 to 1835.

34. John R. White, Slave Record Book (1846–1860), Chinn Collection, MOHS; Brown, *Narrative of William W. Brown*, chap. 6.

35. Philip Thomas to William Finney, Oct. 6 and Nov. 8, 1859, Finney Papers, DU; Alvarez, *Travel on Southern Railroads*, 118, 134–37.

36. On his journey from Washington to Richmond, Northup was also carried by steamboat and stage before boarding a train in Fredericksburg for the remainder of his trip. Northup, *Twelve Years a Slave*, 34–36; *Boston Whig*, Apr. 26, 1848; Philip Thomas to William Finney, Nov. 19, 1859, Finney Papers, DU; Z. S. Finney to William Finney, Nov. 1, 1859, Finney Papers.

37. [J. J. Toler] to Elias Ferguson, Mar. 4, 1859, Ferguson Papers, NCSA; A. J. McElveen to Z. B. Oakes, Oct. 15, 1856, Oakes Papers, BPL; J. P. Pool to Samuel Wood, Mar. 19, 1860, Wood Papers, DU.

38. G. W. Barnes to T. Freeman, Nov. 16, 1839, Slave Trade Papers, BPL; John W. Pittman to John B. Williamson, Feb. 13, 1837, Black History Collection, LOC; Armfield to Ballard, Jan. 26, 1832, Ballard Papers, SHC.

39. Philip Thomas to William Finney, Jan. 24, 1859, Finney Papers, DU.

40. Philip Thomas to William Finney, Jan. 19, 1860, ibid.

41. Michael Tadman wrote: "There were numerous auctioneers and agents (a prominent example being Alonzo J. White, whose detailed account book survives) who dealt in slaves purely or essentially on a commission basis and who, therefore, do not rank in our count of traders proper"; *Speculators and Slaves*, 55. Robert Gudmestad has also argued that "for the purposes of this study, a slave trader or speculator is a man who bought slaves in one state and sold them in another on a regular basis as the sole or

principal source of his income. . . . Obviously, others such as brokers, auctioneers, and commission merchants sold slaves, but were not primarily concerned with the interstate market"; "A Troublesome Commerce," 4n.

42. Gideon Pillow to Z. B. Oakes, Aug. 5, 1856, Oakes Papers, BPL; Joseph Weatherby to Z. B. Oakes, Sept. 6; 1856, ibid.; Tadman, *Speculators and Slaves*, 55–57; Drago and Melnick, "Old Slave Mart Museum," 147–52. For a good overview of Oakes's business dealings, see the 652 letters written to him in the Oakes Papers, BPL. The letters written by Oakes's agent A. J. McElveen have been reprinted in Drago, ed., *Broke by the War*.

43. Lexington *Kentucky Statesman*, Jan. 7, 1859, May 28, 1851; *Lexington Observer and Reporter*, May 26, 1849.

44. Lynch Broadside, MOHS; *Galveston News*, Nov. 20, 1860, quoted in Rozek, "Galveston Slavery," 83; *Liberator* (Boston), Apr. 13, 1838.

45. Nashville *Republican Banner*, Dec. 16, 1856; *Missouri Democrat*, July 28, 1854.

46. St. Louis *Missouri Republican*, Feb. 3, 1858; Lexington *Kentucky Statesman*, Jan. 7, 1859.

47. Tadman, *Speculators and Slaves*, 57–64.

48. *Richmond Whig*, Dec. 11, 1834, quoted in *Liberator*, Dec. 27, 1834.

49. "Extract from the Autobiography of Otis Bigelow," Bancroft Papers, CU; Corey, *History of the Richmond Theological Seminary*, 46–48, 75–76; Tait to R. C. Ballard, Aug. 2, 1836, Ballard Papers, SHC. Tait's Jail was located on the corner of 15th Street and Cary. Lumpkin's was on 15th Street between Franklin and Broad.

50. For examples of interregional traders who spent the entire season selling their slaves out of a New Orleans depot owned by one of these brokers, see the testimony of David T. Ross, Dec. 9, 1846, *Brinegar v. Griffin*, No. 302, 2 La. Ann. 154 (1847), UNO; and the testimony of Charles F. Hatcher, Mar. 1, 1854, *Person v. Rutherford*, No. 3585, 11 La. Ann. 527 (1856), UNO.

51. *Concordia Intelligencer* (Vidalia, LA), Dec. 10, 1853; Nashville *Republican Banner*, Oct. 1, 1859. A similar ad by Hatcher also appeared in the *Charleston Mercury*, Nov. 17, 1859.

52. New Orleans *Picayune*, Oct. 6, 1853, Dec. 16, 1856, Oct. 26, 1858, and Oct. 12, 1859.

53. *Mobile Advertiser*, Jan. 1, 1850; Ford & Lloyd broadside, USC; *Memphis Eagle and Enquirer*, Jan. 28, 1852. For a good example of the many services that southern auctioneers performed to help conduct a large-scale slave sale, see the letters between John D. Warren and the Charleston firm Capers & Heyward, Warren Papers, USC.

54. *Richmond Enquirer*, Apr. 18, 1861; Wade, *Slavery in the Cities*, 203.

55. Pulliam & Co. to "Dear Sir," Jan. 15, 1860, Negro Collection, DU.

56. Brown, *Narrative of William W. Brown*, 41.

57. Benjamin Kendig Scrapbook, NOPL; New Orleans *Picayune*, Dec. 6, 1859; New Orleans *Delta*, Dec. 22, 1857; William D. Ellis to Z. B. Oakes, Oct. 6, 1857, Ellis Papers, NYHS.

58. A. J. and D. W. Orr to John Springs III, Jan. 15, 1848, quoted in Tadman, "Hidden History of Slave Trading," 27; Articles of Agreement, June 24, 1843, Badgett Papers, NCSA.

59. Hadden, "Judging Slavery," 7–8.

60. Deposition of Seneca Bennett, Succession of Elihu Cresswell, No. 2423, 8 La. Ann. 122 (1853), UNO; testimony of Benjamin Thorn quoted in Northup, *Twelve Years a Slave*, 247.

61. *Liberator*, Sept. 6, 1850; Abdy, *Journal of a Residence*, 2:180; New Orleans *Picayune*, Oct. 7, 1846; Ingraham, *The South-west*, 2:245; Stephenson, *Isaac Franklin*, 93; Bancroft, *Slave Trading*, 263–64; Hurst, *Nathan Bedford Forrest*, 58; *Savannah Republican*, Jan. 20, 1857.

62. Reed and Matheson, *Narrative of the Visit*, 1:32; Alexandria *Phenix Gazette*, Apr. 11, 1832; *Cambridge* (MD) *Chronicle*, Feb. 1, 1834.

63. B. V. Liffey to John Hunt, Dec. 13, 1833, Liffey Letter, UVA. For other examples of potential agents writing directly to large Richmond traders for work, see John Rucker to Browning, Moore & Co., July 16, 1860, Chase Papers, LOC; J. O. Stanfield to E. Moore, Aug. 30, 1860, ibid.; and John Flum to Edward [Stokes], [n.m.] 13, 1860, ibid. For examples of potential auctioneers writing to large Richmond traders for work, see D. M. Pattie to Browning, Moore & Co., Apr. 21, 1860, ibid.; and J. R. Moss to Edward H. Stokes, Apr. 19, 1861, ibid.

64. A. Gunn to Joseph S. Totten, Jan. 14, 1835, Totten Papers, NCSA; Henry Tayloe to Benjamin Tayloe, Jan. 5, 1835, Tayloe Papers, UVA; B. R. Owen to William Campbell, Jan. 28, 1840, Campbell Papers, DU.

65. Isaac Franklin to R. C. Ballard, Dec. 8, 1832, Ballard Papers, SHC; J. R. Franklin to R. C. Ballard, Dec. 13, 1833, ibid.; Isaac Franklin to R. C. Ballard, Mar. 10, 1834, ibid.

66. John Frazier to Edward H. Stokes, Feb. 10, 1860, Chase Papers, LOC; Andrews, *Slavery and the Domestic Slave-Trade*, 145–46; Bancroft, *Slave Trading*, 277–78.

67. For more discussion of slaves running away from slave traders or committing violence against them, see chap. 8; *State v. Williams*, No. 4671, 7 Rob. 252 (1844), UNO; *Niles' Register* (Baltimore), May 22, 1841; Bancroft, *Slave Trading*, 274–75.

68. Tadman, *Speculators and Slaves*, 204–6; Freudenberger and Pritchett, "Domestic Slave Trade," 475–76; Tansey, "Bernard Kendig," 170–71.

69. Ford, "Tale of Two Entrepreneurs," 200; testimony of James R. Bosley, *Coote v. Cotton*, No. 2410, 5 La. 12 (1832), UNO. The wages for salaried employees working in the slave trade varied considerably depending upon the type of work an individual was expected to do. But, in general, according to the testimony of one Mississippi man familiar with this business, "the salaries given to such persons vary from $30 to $70 per month," while another expert from Tennessee believed that "the services of agents for negro traders are worth from 20 to 50 dollars." It was also possible to find individuals working for as little as $10 per month and others for more than $100 per month, however, they seem to have been the exceptions and not the rule. Testimony of Richard Ferril, ibid.; deposition of Joseph Meek, ibid. For a good discussion of this issue, see also the other testimony in this case.

70. Bancroft, *Slave Trading*, chap. 8; Tadman, "Hidden History of Slave Trading," 7; Drago, ed., *Broke by the War*, 8–9; Heisser, "Bishop Lynch's People," 244; Stephenson, *Isaac Franklin*, chap. 2; Hurst, *Nathan Bedford Forrest*, part 1; Howell, "John Armfield, Slave-trader," 4–5. This interpretation of slave trading as an avenue of opportunity for those of modest backgrounds to get ahead is contrary to that of Michael Tadman, who has argued that "most traders began their careers with a base of family wealth," and

"major traders, then, nearly always came from wealthy (usually planter) families"; *Speculators and Slaves*, 208–9; "Hidden History of Slave Trading," 16. While this was the case for some individuals, it definitely did not apply to all (most likely, not even a majority), and it was also not true for many of the most successful traders in the South, such as Isaac Franklin, John Armfield, and Nathan Bedford Forrest.

71. Tait to R. C. Ballard, Aug. 25, 1836, Ballard Papers, SHC; P. Pascal to B. Raux, Nov. 10, 1831, Pascal Papers, HU. Author's translation of "quon ne régardes plus nos negres, on donne la préferance au dernier arrive."

72. W. H. Betts to Edward [Stokes], Dec. 31, 1859, Slavery Collection, AAS; John W. Calhoun to William Finney, Jan. 12, 1860, Finney Papers, DU.

73. Peter Stokes to William H. Hatchett, Mar. 22, 1846, Hatchett Papers, DU; Meek to Logan, June 3, 1835, Meek Papers, VHS.

74. Glen to Isaac Jarratt, Nov. 22, 1832, Jarratt Papers, SHC; *New-Orleans Argus*, Nov. 21, 1828.

75. A. J. McElveen to Z. B. Oakes, Oct. 22, 1853, Oakes Papers, BPL; S. Mansfield to J. S. Sizer, July 14, 1856, Sizer Papers, MDAH; Woodroof to "Dick," Feb. 24, 1856, Chase Papers, LOC.

76. Isaac Franklin to R. C. Ballard, May 22, 1834, Ballard Papers, SHC; James R. Franklin to R. C. Ballard, Jan. 18, 1832, ibid.; John Armfield to R. C. Ballard, Dec. 21, 1832, ibid.

77. Isaac Franklin to R. C. Ballard, Dec. 8, 1832, June 11, 1833, June 8, 1832, ibid.; James R. Franklin to R. C. Ballard, Mar. 24, 1833, ibid.

78. Franklin to Ballard, Apr. 9, 1834, ibid.

79. Philip Thomas to William Finney, Jan. 20, 1859, Finney Papers, DU; James H. Bryan to Z. B. Oakes, Dec. 7, 1856, Oakes Papers, BPL; Peter Stokes to William H. Hatchett, Feb. 8, 1846, Hatchett Papers, DU.

80. Franklin to R. C. Ballard, May 7, 1833, Jan. 18, 1832, Ballard Papers, SHC. All of the members of Franklin & Armfield used the term "one-eyed man," usually to jokingly refer to themselves. In a recent article, Edward Baptist has made the argument that these men used this phrase not as a term of derision, but as a way of sexualizing themselves with a metaphor that "was plainly phallic." This argument seems extremely far-fetched, especially in relation to James Franklin's comments about finding some "one-eyed man" who would buy them out. According to Baptist's reading, this term was not used contemptuously but sexually, as in Franklin "counted on sexual desire to overcome economic reasoning." Clearly this was not the case: Franklin was hoping that some "fool" or "dick" would buy out all of the unmarketable men and women who were left over at the end of the season. All quotes from Baptist, "'Cuffy,' 'Fancy Maids,' and 'One-Eyed Men,'" 1640.

81. Isaac Franklin to R. C. Ballard, Feb. 10, 1832, Ballard Papers, SHC; J. R. Franklin to R. C. Ballard, Dec. 13, 1833, ibid.; entries for June 18, 1859, Feb. 2, 1860, and Dec. 24, 1859, Parker Diary, UGA.

82. Meek to Samuel Logan, Nov. 27, 1836, Meek Papers, VHS; John D. Glass to Henry Badgett, Jan. 12, 1848, Badgett Papers, NCSA.

83. J. K. White to Z. B. Oakes, Jan. 23, 1855, Oakes Papers, BPL; John M. Winstead to Charles Mason, Dec. 2, 1850, Winstead Letter, NCSA; Thomas W. Burton to William Long, Feb. 27, 1846, Long Papers, NCSA; Franklin to R. C. Ballard, Feb. 2, 1834, Ballard Papers, SHC.

84. John D. Badgett to Henry Badgett, Feb. 12, 1860, Badgett Papers, NCSA; Fields to Fields, Nov. 29, 1822, Fields Papers, DU.

85. Stephenson, *Isaac Franklin*, 18; Harriet Jarratt to Isaac Jarratt, Jan. 9, 1836, Oct. 29, 1835, Jarratt-Puryear Papers, DU; Isaac Jarratt to Harriet Jarratt, Nov. 9, 1835, ibid.

86. Richard C. Puryear to Jarratt, Feb. 17, 1832, ibid.; John D. Long to William Long, Mar. 9, 1846, Long Papers, NCSA; James Neal to "Dear Mother & Brother," Apr. 15, 1829, Neal Papers, SHC.

87. Testimony of Joseph Price, *Coote v. Cotton*, No. 2410, 5 La. 12 (1832), UNO.

88. Franklin to R. C. Ballard, Jan. 11, 1834, Ballard Papers, SHC; Richard C. Puryear to Isaac Jarratt, Feb. 17, 1832, Jarratt-Puryear Papers, DU; Baptist, "'Cuffy,' 'Fancy Maids,' and 'One-Eyed Men.'"

89. Franklin to R. C. Ballard, Sept. 27, 1834, Ballard Papers, SHC. After his marriage, Isaac Franklin and his new wife visited John Armfield and his wife on their honeymoon. Armfield also later served as one of Franklin's executors. Stephenson, *Isaac Franklin*, 19, 106. For an example of traders naming children after one another and spending Christmases together, see A. J. McElveen to Z. B. Oakes, Aug. 13, 1856, Oakes Papers, BPL; and William Wright to Z. B. Oakes, Dec. 18, 1853, ibid.

90. Schweninger, ed., *From Tennessee Slave to St. Louis Entrepreneur*, 112; testimony of J. W. Boazman, *Folger v. Kendig*, No. 5337, unreported (1858), UNO; William A. Creany to Betts & Gregory, Feb. 13, 1861, Chase Papers, LOC; Franklin to Ballard, Aug. 15, 1832, Ballard Papers, SHC.

91. John J. Toler to [Elias Ferguson], Jan. 22, 1858, Ferguson Papers, NCSA; Thomas Harrison to James Harrison, Jan. 6, 1836, Harrison Papers, SHC; A. J. McElveen to Z. B. Oakes, Nov. 1, 1856, Oakes Papers, BPL; entry for July 6, 1859, Parker Diary, UGA.

92. Tyre Glen to Thomas Glen, Jan. 9, 1836, Glen Papers, DU; Z. S. Finney to William Finney, Jan. 30, 1860, Finney Papers, DU.

93. Franklin to R. C. Ballard, May 30, 1831, and Nov. 5, 1833, Ballard Papers, SHC; Philip Thomas to William Finney, Dec. 3, 1859, Finney Papers, DU; Peter Stokes to William H. Hatchett, Feb. 8, 1846, Hatchett Papers, DU.

94. Entry for Jan. 2, 1860, Parker Diary, UGA; G. W. Eutsler to [Elias Ferguson], Aug. 16, 1856, Ferguson Papers, NCSA; Cohen, *A Calculating People*, 176. For a sampling of the various types of account books kept by southern slave traders (not all double-entry), see Sales Book (1818–1837), Rives Papers, DU; Account Book (1830–1833), Glen Papers, DU; Account Books (1831–1835), Ballard Papers, SHC; Account Book (1833–1835), Jarratt-Puryear Papers, DU; Account Books (1834–1835), Pascal Papers, HU; Account Book (1834–1835), Mitchell Papers, DU; Account Book (1836–1837), Whitehead Papers, DU; Dickinson, Hill & Co. Account Books (1846–1849 and 1855–1858), Slavery Collection, AAS; John R. White, Slave Record Book (1846–1860), Chinn Collection, MOHS; A. and A. T. Walker Account Book (1851–1861), SHC; Alonzo J. White Record Book (1853–1863), SCHS; Account Book (1856–1858), Bolton, Dickens & Co. Records, NYHS; Silas and R. F. Omohundro Sales Book (1857–1864), UVA; Hector Davis & Co. Record Books (1857–1864), CHS; L. C. Robards & Bro. Account Book (1863–1865), CHS; and A. Bryan Account Book (1864), Slavery Collection, CHS.

95. Joseph Meek to Samuel Logan, Oct. 9, 1836, Meek Papers, VHS; John Forsyth to Henderson Forsyth, Feb. 19, 1837, Forsyth Papers, DU; Franklin to R. C. Ballard, June 8, 1832, Ballard Papers, SHC; Tansey, "Bernard Kendig," 166–67; New Orleans *Picayune*,

Dec. 4, 1853. In his ad, Campbell noted that "the supply will be kept large and one and two years' credit given."

96. Joseph Meek to Samuel Logan, Mar. 19, 1835, Meek Papers, VHS; *Memphis Appeal*, Dec. 4, 1857.

97. Phillips, *American Negro Slavery*, 197; Newton Boley to William Crow, Dec. 3, 1841, Crow Letters, DU.

98. Life insurance policy, Nov. 21, 1850, *Person v. Rutherford*, No. 3585, 11 La. Ann. 527 (1856), UNO. For a copy of another such insurance policy taken out by Rutherford, see Nalle, Cox & Co. to C. M. Rutherford, Dec. 1, 1853, Ballard Papers, SHC.

99. Thomas to William Finney, Jan. 24, 1859, Finney Papers, DU; *Concordia Intelligencer*, Nov. 26, 1853; Franklin to Ballard, May 13, 1834, Ballard Papers, SHC; Thomas W. Collins to William Wright, Nov. 12, 1857, Slavery Collection, CHS.

100. D. M. Pulliam & Co., circular, Sept. 1, 1857, Bond Papers, NCSA; Betts & Gregory, circular, July 20, 1860, Negro Collection, DU; D. M. Pulliam & Co., circular, Apr. 3, 1858, Ferguson Papers, NCSA.

101. Entry for Dec. 10, 1859, Parker Diary, UGA; Alexander B. Puryear to James Dellet, Apr. 30, 1835, Dellet Papers, ADAH; Theophilus Freeman to Overly & Sanders, Sept. 21, 1839, Slave Trade Papers, BPL; J. J. Toler to Elias W. Ferguson, Dec. 24, 1858, Ferguson Papers, NCSA; John Hester to Joseph Dickinson, May 3, 1854, Joseph Dickinson Papers, DU; Franklin to R. C. Ballard, Mar. 4, 1832, Ballard Papers, SHC.

102. *Cambridge Chronicle*, Feb. 1, 1834; *Lexington Observer and Reporter*, Dec. 1, 1855; *Cambridge Chronicle*, May 23, 1833. For a discussion of the role that merchants advertising cash played in promoting consumerism in the North, see Ryan, *Cradle of the Middle Class*, 9; and Egerton, "Markets without a Market Revolution," 213.

103. *Centreville* (MD) *Times and Eastern-Shore Public Advertiser*, May 4, 1833, June 16, 1832.

104. Alexandria *Phenix Gazette*, June 2, 1829; *Missouri Democrat*, July 28, 1854; *Snow-Hill* (MD) *Messenger and Worcester County Advertiser*, Oct. 6, 1831; *Missouri Republican*, Jan. 23, 1852.

105. *Cambridge Chronicle*, May 25, 1833, and Dec. 19, 1835.

106. Paris (KY) *Western Citizen*, July 24, 1816; *Missouri Democrat*, July 28, 1854; Baltimore *Sun*, Jan. 8, 1851; Alexandria *Phenix Gazette*, Nov. 10, 1828, Apr. 9, 1830, Oct. 1, 1832, Jan. 15, 1833; Lexington *Kentucky Statesman*, Dec. 16, 1859.

107. *Missouri Republican*, June 6, 1860; *Lexington Observer and Reporter*, May 26, 1849; Columbia *Missouri Statesman*, Mar. 23, 1860, quoted in McGettigan, "Boone County Slaves," 191; Cumberland *Maryland Advocate*, Sept. 23, 1826.

108. Richard Smith to Axim Lewis, Mar. 25, 1825, Webb Papers, NCSA.

109. *National Intelligencer*, July 27, 1839; *Missouri Republican*, May 18, 1851; *Memphis Eagle and Enquirer*, Apr. 7, 1853. The historian most associated with claiming the "specialized" nature of the New Orleans market is Michael Tadman, who has argued that the nearby sugar planters desired slaves who were different from those wanted by other southerners and that this made the type of slaves purchased by traders who operated in that market somehow different as well; *Speculators and Slaves*, 22–25, 64–70; "Demographic Cost of Sugar," 1550–52. While it may be true that sugar planters purchased different types of slaves, there is little evidence that most slave traders selling in New Orleans actually skewed their purchases toward this clientele, especially

in comparison to the types of slaves they bought for other Deep South markets. For one thing, the vast majority of traders who purchased slaves to sell in New Orleans often sold the same or similar individuals in other markets as well. Moreover, the correspondence of Franklin & Armfield, the largest firm in the 1830s, indicates that it sold its slaves interchangeably between cotton and sugar planters. The only systematic study of the men and women the company sold out of its New Orleans office indicates that most of its sales, nearly three-eighths, went to residents of Orleans Parish, mostly within the city itself, and not to sugar planters, who made up the second largest group; Stephenson, *Isaac Franklin*, 86. Finally, most other major traders who operated out of that market, such as B. M. and W. L. Campbell, never specified "for the New Orleans market" in their notices, but used the much more common "for the Southern markets" instead; Baltimore *Sun*, May 12, 1849. Consequently, there seems little reason to believe that the designation "for the New Orleans market" meant anything unique or that the New Orleans market was as specialized as Tadman and others have made it appear.

110. Montgomery (AL) *Confederation*, Aug. 31, 1859; New Orleans *Picayune*, Oct. 12, 1859; Natchez *Mississippi Free Trader*, Feb. 1, 1859; New Orleans *Delta*, Jan. 18, 1857.

111. New Orleans *Picayune*, Dec. 6, 1859; Natchez *Mississippi Free Trader*, Nov. 4, 1857; Memphis *Morning Bulletin*, May 13, 1857; New Orleans *Picayune*, Oct. 5, 1860, Nov. 6, 1858; Montgomery *Confederation*, Jan. 15, 1859.

112. *Memphis Appeal*, June 11, 1856; *Memphis Eagle and Enquirer*, Mar. 20, 1857. For a good account of the colonial perception of various African groups, see Littlefield, *Rice and Slaves*, esp. chap. 1.

113. Ball, *Slavery in the United States*, 74; entry for Oct. 18, 1836, in Davis, ed., *Diary of Bennet H. Barrow*, 81–82.

114. New Orleans *Picayune*, Jan. 24, 1850, Oct. 11, 1860. As noted earlier, this arrangement also allowed Campbell to offer "Negroes for Sale all the Time," unlike most of his competitors; ibid., July 1, 1860.

115. Ibid., Sept. 19, 1860, July 30, 1853, Sept. 19, 1858, Jan. 14, 1857; Nashville *Republican Banner*, Dec. 24, 1856.

116. Joseph Bryan to Ellison S. Keitt, Apr. 20, 1860, Black History Collection, LOC; Ball, *Slavery in the United States*, 93; Douglass, "Speech of July 5, 1852," in Blassingame, ed., *Douglass Papers*, 2:374; Brown, *Narrative of William W. Brown*, 53.

117. Brown, *Slave Life in Georgia*, 99; Andrews, *Slavery and the Domestic Slave-Trade*, 150; James H. Taylor to Franklin H. Elmore, Jan. 30, 1836, Elmore Papers, LOC.

118. Elias W. Ferguson to [G. W. Eutsler], Aug. 13, 1856, Ferguson Papers, NCSA; John W. Walker to Chapley R. Wellborne, Sept. 20, 1818, Walker Papers, ADAH; Thomas Boudar to W. W. Hall, Jan. 26, 1848, Slavery Collection, OSMM.

119. *Memphis Avalanche*, Nov. 23, 1859; unknown New Orleans paper quoted in *Liberator*, Nov. 24, 1854; Moses handbill, Nov. 14, 1859, reproduced in Korn, *Jews and Negro Slavery*, 22; Alexandria *Louisiana Democrat*, Nov. 16, 1859; New Orleans *Picayune*, May 27, 1838.

120. Andrews, *Slavery and the Domestic Slave-Trade*, 136; Ingraham, *The South-west*, 2:245; Chambers, *Things as They Are in America*, 284–85; R. O. Harris to E. H. Stokes, Dec. 20, 1862, Chase Papers, LOC; testimony of James K. Blakeney, *Kock & McCall v. Slatter*, No. 1748, 5 La. Ann. 739 (1850), UNO.

121. Abdy, *Journal of a Residence*, 2:180; Andrews, *Slavery and the Domestic Slave-Trade*, 150, 80.

122. Ball, *Slavery in the United States*, 86–87.

123. This figure is based upon an average annual direct cost to traders of 13.5 percent of the price of slaves sold in the interregional trade; Freudenberger and Pritchett, "Domestic Slave Trade," 472–75. This estimate of 13.5 percent is lower than that provided in several other studies. In fact, in a later article, Jonathan Pritchett raised his estimate to 15 percent, a figure likewise used by Michael Tadman. Pritchett, "Interregional Slave Trade and the Selection of Slaves," 63–66; Tadman, *Speculators and Slaves*, 295. Therefore, it seems safe to assume that at least $1.5 million, if not more, was spent on this ancillary activity each year, and more than $2.1 million was spent on it each year in the 1850s.

124. The average value of the U.S. cotton crop is based upon New York prices for middling Uplands cotton between the years 1820 and 1860; Bruchey, ed., *Cotton and the Growth of the American Economy*, table 3-A. It averaged almost $84 million each year over that time period.

125. Dun & Co. report from the early 1850s, quoted in Tadman, "Hidden History of Slave Trading," 17.

126. Tadman, *Speculators and Slaves*, 192–99; Tansey, "Bernard Kendig," 168–69; receipt, July 24, 1855, Totten Papers, NCSA; Tadman, "Hidden History of Slave Trading"; Ford, "Tale of Two Entrepreneurs."

Chapter 5

1. The sale was advertised in newspapers as far away as Richmond and New Orleans, and while Butler's name was not listed in the advertisements, his ownership was well known. All but 20–30 of the 460 slaves advertised were sold at this auction (accounts disagree). Some were left on the plantation because of illness, and others were sold before the auction at private sale. The report by Mortimer Thomson first appeared in the *New-York Tribune*, Mar. 9, 1859, and was later reprinted, both by the *Tribune* and by the American Anti-Slavery Society, under the title *Great Auction Sale of Slaves*. *Savannah News* quoted in *Charleston Mercury*, Mar. 5, 1859; entry for Mar. 4, 1859, Parker Diary, UGA; Bancroft, *Slave Trading*, chap. 10; Bell, *Major Butler's Legacy*, 324–40.

2. Richter, "Slavery in Baton Rouge," 129; Capt. J. A. Wilson quoted in Trexler, *Slavery in Missouri*, 51.

3. Olmsted, *Journey in the Seaboard States*, 55.

4. *Memphis Eagle and Enquirer*, Sept. 28, 1855; *Kentucky Statesman*, Mar. 11, 1859; *Missouri Democrat*, Mar. 11, 1859; *Savannah Republican*, Jan. 20, 1857; Baton Rouge *Advocate*, Feb. 3, 1857; *New Orleans Bee*, Jan. 28, 1857.

5. Hall, *Travels in North America*, 3:197; W. H. Dennis to John E. Dennis, Feb. 14, 1847, Dennis Papers, DU; "Letters on Slavery" (1853), 15, Yarnall Papers, DU.

6. Even those historians who write about the domestic slave trade fail to examine in any depth the extent and significance of the local trade. While most mention the importance of this trade, they pass over it quickly and focus almost all of their attention on the interregional trade. See Bancroft, *Slave Trading*, 403–4; Tadman, *Speculators and Slaves*, 118–20, 136–40; and Johnson, *Soul by Soul*, 6–7.

7. *Baltimore Republican and Commercial Advertiser*, June 3, 1835; *National Intelligencer* (Washington, DC), June 10, 1834; *Virginia Northwestern Gazette* (Winchester), Aug. 15, 1818, quoted in Phillips, *American Negro Slavery*, 192.

8. Featherstonhaugh, *Excursion through the Slave States*, 1:119–23; interview of Lorenzo L. Ivy in Perdue et al., eds., *Weevils in the Wheat*, 153; interview of Catherine Beale in Blassingame, ed., *Slave Testimony*, 575.

9. John Kerrick (1921), quoted in Coleman, *Slavery Times in Kentucky*, 187–88; Olmsted, *Journey in the Back Country*, 152–53; Weld, *American Slavery As It Is*, 69.

10. Weld, *American Slavery As It Is*, 76; Owen, ed., *John Owen's Journal*, 9; testimony of Johnson McQueen, May 12, 1838, *Nelson v. Lillard et al.*, No. 800-1, 16 La. 336 (1840), UNO.

11. Dickey (1824) quoted in Rankin, *Letters on American Slavery*, 45–47n; *Western Luminary* (Lexington), June 5, 1833, quoted in McDougle, *Slavery in Kentucky*, 19; Rumple (1881) quoted in Conrad, ed., *In the Hands of Strangers*, 302.

12. Fearon, *Sketches of America*, 269–70; *New Orleans Mercantile Advertiser*, Jan. 21, 1830, quoted in Collins, *Domestic Slave Trade*, 46–47; Brown, *Narrative of William W. Brown*, 33–34.

13. For a good account of the export of slaves out of New Orleans, see the numerous records in the Outward Slave Manifests, NA.

14. Dickens, *American Notes*, 134; Lyman Abbott (1856) quoted in Bancroft, *Slave Trading*, 290; Russell, *North America*, 157; Olmsted, *Journey in the Seaboard States*, 308.

15. Thomas Morris to J. W. Latta, Sept. 14, 1857, Jones Papers, NCSA.

16. New Orleans *Picayune*, Aug. 11, 1857. Traders in the Upper South advertised in the smaller papers as well. In addition to its notice in the *Lexington Observer and Reporter*, Bolton, Dickens & Co. also ran this same ad in the *Mount Sterling Whig, Richmond Messenger, Frankfort Commonwealth, Paris Flag*, and *Lexington Observer and Reporter*, Jan. 10, 1857.

17. *Floridian and Journal*, Feb. 12, 1859; *Mississippi Free Trader*, Mar. 3, 1860; *New Orleans Bee*, Feb. 11, 1857.

18. Thomas W. Burton to William Long, Jan. 24, 1846, Long Papers, NCSA; Joseph Meek to Samuel Logan, Oct. 9, 1836, Meek Papers, VHS. By the late 1850s, roughly 7,500 out-of-state slaves were sold in New Orleans each year; Tadman, "Demographic Cost of Sugar," 1572–73. In his earlier work on the interregional trade, Michael Tadman argued that southern cities and towns accounted for only a small percentage of this traffic and that "the trade as a whole was dominated not by urban centers but by the rural grassroots." While Tadman did acknowledge that some cities, such as Richmond and Charleston, were important for the interregional trade, he argued that their primary function was as supply centers for the New Orleans trade. In addition, he noted that there were several urban markets in the importing states, although he did not elaborate. My point is that all southern cities and towns played an important role in the domestic trade and, also, that they benefited greatly from it. Tadman, *Speculators and Slaves*, 31, 42, 55–64, 94–97.

19. Baltimore *Republican* quoted in *Genius of Universal Emancipation* (Baltimore), Oct. 16, 1829; Donovan quoted in Bowditch, *Slavery and the Constitution*, 80; *Lynchburg Virginian*, Aug. 4, 1859; *Memphis Eagle and Enquirer*, June 13, 1852.

20. New Orleans *Picayune*, Oct. 5, 1859; Bancroft, *Slave Trading*, 54–58; John Montmollin to Z. B. Oakes, Feb. 3, 1857, letterhead, Oakes Papers, BPL; Talbott broadside,

July 2, 1853, reprinted in Coleman, *Slavery Times in Kentucky*, opp. 179; Montgomery *Confederation*, Aug. 31, 1859.

21. Lexington *Kentucky Statesman*, Dec. 16, 1859; Collier ad quoted in *Liberator* (Boston), May 18, 1833; New Orleans *Picayune*, Feb. 8, 1860; Baltimore *Sun*, Oct. 24, 1848; *Baltimore Republican and Commercial Advertiser*, July 2, 1834. For abolitionists who pointed out the irony of Purvis's ad, see Reed and Matheson, *Narrative of the Visit*, 1:208–9; and Andrews, *Slavery and the Domestic Slave-Trade*, 85.

22. St. Louis *Missouri Democrat*, July 28, 1854; letter to *New York Times*, Aug. 26, 1853, in McLaughlin, ed., *Olmsted Papers*, 2:205; Olmsted, *Journey through Texas*, 363.

23. Entry for Feb. 18, 1856, Reiff Journal, LSU; entry for Dec. 17, 1859, Marshall Diary, DU.

24. Bernhard, *Travels through North America*, 2:133–34; Emerson, *Journals*, 3:117.

25. *Lexington Observer and Reporter*, July 11, 1857; Bancroft, *Slave Trading*, 94–104, 165–78, 300–309; Drago and Melnick, "Old Slave Mart Museum"; James, *Antebellum Natchez*, 197; Barnett and Burkett, "Forks of the Road."

26. "Census of Merchants," NOPL; New Orleans *Picayune*, Aug. 11, 1857; Bancroft, *Slave Trading*, 312–20.

27. Schweninger, ed., *From Tennessee Slave to St. Louis Entrepreneur*, 112; Davies, *American Scenes*, 22–23.

28. Ball, *Ball's Splendid Tour*, 26–29; Buckingham, *Slave States of America*, 1:331–35; Russell, *North America*, 255–56; Bancroft, *Slave Trading*, 324–38; Kendall, "Shadow over the City," 147–50.

29. *Montgomery Directory* (1859–1860); *Natchez Courier*, Feb. 29 and Mar. 9, 1860; Bancroft, *Slave Trading*, 116–17, 177, 294, 315; U.S. Census, *Preliminary Report on the Census*, 243.

30. Levy ad in Richmond city directory (1852) in Bancroft Papers, CU; Redpath, *Roving Editor*, 247; New Orleans *Picayune*, Sept. 30, 1860.

31. George W. Barnes to Theophilus Freeman, Feb. 4, 1840, Slave Trade Papers, BPL; Nashville *Republican Banner*, Dec. 19, 1860.

32. J. J. Gurney quoted in Tadman, *Speculators and Slaves*, 54; Samuel M. Moore to James D. Davidson, Apr. 6, 1861, in Greenawalt, ed., "Unionists in Rockbridge County," 96; *New Orleans Crescent*, Jan. 9, 1860. For another indication of the large investment of southern banks in the slave trade, see the list of debts due to the Bank of Virginia and to the Farmers Bank of Virginia enclosed in Bacon Tait to R. C. Ballard, May 1, 1838, Ballard Papers, SHC.

33. John M. Bass quoted in Mooney, *Slavery in Tennessee*, 44; *Savannah Republican*, Mar. 6, 1860; entry for Mar. 7, 1860, Parker Diary, UGA.

34. Thomas W. Burton to William Long, Feb. 27, 1846, Long Papers, NCSA; *Savannah Republican*, Jan. 21, 1851; Woolfolk, "Taxes and Slavery," 187; Wade, *Slavery in the Cities*, 202–3.

35. For a discussion of the sources used in determining the number of slaves sold, the breakdown between local and interregional sales, and the historiography of local slave trading, see appendix B.

36. Goodstein, *Nashville, 1780–1860*, 75; interview of James Brown in Tyler and Murphy, eds., *Slave Narratives of Texas*, 25; Bill of Sale, July 20, 1838, Heartman Collection, XU.

37. M. B. Casey to William K. Oliver, Apr. 7, 1837, Oliver Papers, ADAH; *Charleston Courier*, Jan. 17, 1860; Thomas P. Copes to Joseph Copes, Oct. 31, 1846, Copes Papers, TUL; Samuel Steer to John Minor, Feb. 23, 1818, Minor Papers, LSU; A. Collins to J. D. Warren, Nov. 17, 1858, Warren Papers, USC.

38. Lexington *Kentucky Reporter*, Sept. 2, 1829; T. T. Wiatt to "Dear Friend," June 5, 1847, Norwood Collection, FSU; entry for Feb. 5, 1859, Pugh Diary, LSU; Halsey to Joseph Copes, Aug. 23, 1850, Copes Papers, TUL.

39. John R. Lyons to William W. Renwick, Apr. 4, 1854, quoted in Stampp, *Peculiar Institution*, 128–29; Craft, *Running a Thousand Miles for Freedom*, 10; *Charleston Mercury*, Oct. 2, 1838.

40. Rawick, ed., *American Slave*, 18:129; Drumgoold, *Slave Girl's Story*, 4; W. S. Mallicote to Betts & Gregory, Feb. 22, 1861, Chase Papers, LOC; *Lexington Observer and Reporter*, Apr. 18, 1857.

41. Huntsville *Alabama Republican*, June 22, 1821, quoted in Sellers, *Slavery in Alabama*, 120; *Floridian and Journal*, Sept. 19, 1857.

42. *Natchez Courier*, Dec. 3, 1853; *New-Orleans Argus*, July 14, 1826.

43. New Orleans *Picayune*, Sept. 7, 1858; *Vicksburg Whig*, Dec. 18, 1855; *New Orleans Crescent*, Mar. 23, 1859.

44. A. J. McElveen to Z. B. Oakes, Feb. 6, 1857, Oakes Papers, BPL; Clarke, *Narrative of Lewis Clarke*, 71; Philip Rainey to John Bennett, June 13, 1836, Rainey Papers, UVA.

45. For an example of a conditional purchase, see Bill of Sale, Oct. 13, 1855, where Henry Papin of St. Louis sold a thirty-year-old woman to Henry Chouteau for $1,000, and Papin promised to take the woman back and refund the money within six months if Chouteau was unhappy with her; Chouteau Collection, MOHS. For an example of a conditional sale, see Bill of Sale, Nov. 27, 1848, where James Hurley of Plaquemines Parish, Louisiana, sold a twelve-year-old boy to William Dougherty of New Orleans for $400, and Hurley had the option of buying the boy back before January 1, 1849, for the same price; Slavery Collection, MOHS.

46. James A. Poage to Samuel M. Williams, July 28, 1849, Williams Papers, RL; Alexander to John H. Bills, Apr. 9, 1861, Bills Papers, LSU; St. Louis *Missouri Republican*, Feb. 3, 1858.

47. Sale Notice, Jan. 10, 1855, reprinted in Coleman, *Slavery Times in Kentucky*, opp. 147; *Richmond Enquirer*, Dec. 13, 1814.

48. Thomas Culbreth to the Governor of Maryland, Feb. 21, 1824, in "Estimates of the Value of Slaves," 818; *Alexandria Gazette and Virginia Advertiser*, Jan. 4, 1859; *Cambridge* (MD) *Chronicle*, Dec. 10, 1836.

49. Haywood to Brickell, Apr. 25, 1815, and Woods to Haywood, Feb. 17, 1818, Haywood Collection, SHC.

50. John Callaway to Henry G. Callaway, Jan. 16, 1809, Pocket Plantation Papers, UVA.

51. For an example of a sheriff in Kentucky who was sued for a fraudulent sale, see Deposition of Walter Rodes, Fayette County Court, May 20, 1854, Frankel Papers, CHS; *A. Cecile, f.m.c., v. St. Denis, f.w.c.*, No. 709, 14 La. 184 (1839), UNO; Weems Bill of Sale, Feb. 18, 1860, Slavery Collection, LSU; Schafer, *Slavery and the Supreme Court of Louisiana*, chap. 5. For other good accounts of the prominent role that slave sales played in the southern courts, see Morris, *Southern Slavery and the Law*, chap. 5; Wahl, *Bondsman's*

Burden, chap. 2; and Gross, *Double Character*, chap. 1. According to Ariela Gross, "the road from the slave market in Southern towns inexorably led to the courthouse," *Double Character*, 45.

52. L. Atkison to F. Carter, Apr. 13, 1833, Carter Papers, SHC; Judge Porter quoted in Schafer, *Slavery and the Supreme Court of Louisiana*, 145; Fede, "Legal Protection for Slave Buyers."

53. James L. Petigru to Robert F. W. Allston, Apr. 15, 1837, in Easterby, ed., *South Carolina Rice Plantation*, 69.

54. "Mother" to Brodnax, Jan. 23, 1860, Brodnax Papers, DU; Campbell to Maria Campbell, Dec. 12, 1812, Campbell Papers, DU; Ellis to William D. Ellis, July 8, 1853, Ellis Papers, NYHS.

55. Carr to John B. Lucas, July 7, 1810, Lucas Collection, MOHS; Wallace to Andrew Grinnan, Apr. 18, 1855, Grinnan Papers, UVA; T. T. Wiatt to "Dear Friend," June 5, 1847, Norwood Papers, FSU.

56. *National Intelligencer*, Aug. 22, 1833; New Orleans *Picayune*, Dec. 25, 1855; *Louisville Public Advertiser*, Dec. 19, 1829, in Bancroft Papers, CU; *Wilmington Journal*, July 8, 1853.

57. *Richmond Whig and Public Advertiser*, Dec. 18, 1849; *National Intelligencer*, Dec. 22, 1836, Dec. 7, 1839; *New Orleans Bee*, Sept. 23, 1859; *Mobile Advertiser*, Jan. 7, 1860; Montgomery *Alabama Journal*, Nov. 28, 1828; New Orleans *Picayune*, Jan. 5, 1844.

58. Sale Notice, Oct. 28, 1859, Slavery Collection, CHS; Pelham broadside, USC; Frederick-Town *Herald*, Oct. 10, 1812; St. Francisville *Louisiana Chronicle*, Aug. 21, 1841.

59. Thomas B. Jackson to William Crow, Jan. 31, 1837, Crow Letters, DU; McDougle, *Slavery in Kentucky*, 22; James, *Antebellum Natchez*, 208.

60. Phillips, *American Negro Slavery*, 377–78; Bill of Sale, June 11, 1860, Kent Papers, LSU; Huntsville *Democrat*, Nov. 29, 1848.

61. Kilbourne, *Debt, Investment, Slaves*, 73; Russell, "Sale Day in South Carolina," chap. 1, quotations on 28. For a more in-depth discussion of court sales in South Carolina, see appendix B. In her study of New Orleans in 1850, Judith Schafer found that 68 percent of all the slave sales reported in the city's newspapers were the result of some legal action, and 78 percent of all slave auctions were occasioned by legal procedures. Of course, slave sales listed in newspapers do not include all of the slaves sold in the city, nor are they a representative sample, but these numbers do indicate the prominent role that court-ordered sales played in New Orleans; "New Orleans Slavery in 1850," 41. In addition, by the 1840s, court-ordered sales of slaves were frequent enough in Leon County, Florida, that the sheriff issued bills of sale on standardized forms, made specifically for this type of transaction; see Bill of Sale, Feb. 2, 1846, Carr Collection, UGA.

62. Campbell, *Empire for Slavery*, 94; Alexander W. Campbell to Robert F. W. Allston, Jan. 7, 1837, in Easterby, ed., *South Carolina Rice Plantation*, 384.

63. Sale Notice, Dec. 8, 1838, quoted in Coleman, *Slavery Times in Kentucky*, 119; Baton Rouge *Gazette and Comet*, Jan. 7, 1857.

64. *National Intelligencer*, Jan. 1, 1836; H. M. Somerville to Joseph J. Halsey, Aug. 26, 1859, Morton-Halsey Papers, UVA. For examples of various Charleston slave auctioneers conducting estate sales at the slave mart, see the numerous handbills in the Hutson-Lee Papers, SCHS.

65. For the best description of sale day, see Russell, "Sale Day in South Carolina," esp. chap. 2. See also Coleman, *Slavery Times in Kentucky*, 115–18.

66. Robert F. Kellam quoted in Taylor, *Slavery in Arkansas*, 72; *Jefferson City Examiner*, Dec. 5, 1858, quoted in St. Louis *Missouri Democrat*, Jan. 11, 1859; G. D. Gray to Angus Blakey, Dec. 31, 1860, Blakey Papers, DU; *Winnsboro Register*, quoted in *Charleston Mercury*, Dec. 8, 1859.

67. Ball, *Slavery in the United States*, 122–27.

68. John B. Lucas to William Lucas, May 8, 1836, Lucas Collection, MOHS; Dayton, Alabama, *Argus*, Jan. 5, 1849, quoted in Bowditch, *Slavery and the Constitution*, 86; Slave Sale Document, LSU.

69. A. S. Dillon to William Powell, Dec. 31, 1840, Powell Papers, DU.

70. Russell, "Sale Day in South Carolina," chap. 4; George Whitlock to George Carter, Jan. 18, 1805, Carter Papers, VHS.

71. *Richmond Enquirer*, Dec. 30, 1834. For examples of slave traders selling slaves at court sales in Virginia and Georgia, see Stephens & Taliafeno to Browning, Moore & Co., June 5, 1860, Chase Papers, LOC; and the entry for Aug. 2, 1859, Parker Diary, UGA.

72. Russell, "Sale Day in South Carolina," chap. 2; Benjamin Brand to Martin Dawson, Mar. 17, 1819, Brand Papers, VHS; A. J. McElveen to Z. B. Oakes, Mar. 5, 1855, Oakes Papers, BPL. For a discussion of local buyers and court sales in South Carolina, see appendix B. For an account of the predominance of local buyers at estate sales in Boone County, Missouri, see McGettigan, "Boone County Slaves," 193–95.

73. Jacobs, *Incidents in the Life*, 11–12; Hogan and Davis, eds., *William Johnson's Natchez*, 481; entry for Dec. 13, 1860, Pratt Diary, UK.

74. Estate inventory, June 18, 1828, Slavery Collection, MDAH; Carpenter, *Observations on American Slavery*, 28–29. For good accounts of the symbolic importance of slave auctions, see Oakes, *Slavery and Freedom*, 22–24; and Russell, "Sale Day in South Carolina," chap. 2.

75. It should be noted that the figure Gutman used to make this calculation, 2 million sales, is the same total that is offered in this text. For a full discussion of the total number of slaves sold, see appendix B. Gutman, *Slavery and the Numbers Game*, 124.

Chapter 6

1. *Liberator* (Boston), Jan. 1, 1831.

2. Ibid., Feb. 5, 1831.

3. Ibid., Apr. 23, 1831.

4. The first illustrated masthead ran for eight years until another replaced it. The new drawing featured scenes of both contemporary slavery and emancipation in the future. An auction sale once again represented slavery. The same announcement appeared on the auctioneer's stand, but this time a small child was on the block with his family watching from the side. In 1850, a third masthead appeared, which ran until the publication ceased printing in 1865. In addition to the scenes of slavery and emancipation, it also had a medallion portraying Jesus. The picture of slavery was once again an auction block with a small child upon it and an anguished black family looking on. But this time the announcement read: "SLAVES, HORSES, & OTHER CATTLE IN LOTS TO SUIT

PURCHASER," ibid., Mar. 2, 1838, May 31, 1850, Nov. 5, 1831; Garrison and Garrison, *William Lloyd Garrison*, 1:232.

5. For a good account of the shocking effect that slavery had on northern audiences, especially by the 1830s, see Huston, "Experiential Basis of Antislavery."

6. The term "middle ground" has taken on a number of meanings in recent years and is most often associated with encounters along the American frontier; see esp. White, *Middle Ground*. Yet, the concept has also been effectively used in describing parts of the Upper South and its unique version of slavery, most notably by Barbara J. Fields in her study of Maryland, *Slavery and Freedom on the Middle Ground*. For another account that looks at the Upper South as a borderland, where northern and southern values intermixed and abolitionists used that to their advantage, see Harrold, "On the Borders of Slavery and Race." I would like to thank James B. Stewart for pointing out the possibilities of viewing the Upper South as a middle ground and how that area shaped northern impressions of slavery.

7. For general works on the abolitionist movement, see Kraditor, *Means and Ends in American Abolitionism*; Sorin, *Abolitionism*; Dillon, *Abolitionists*; Stewart, *Holy Warriors*; and Goodman, *Of One Blood*.

8. "Germantown Friends' Protest against Slavery," in Bruns, ed., *Am I Not a Man*, 3–4. For a good account of the role that the Quakers played in the early antislavery movement, see Soderlund, *Quakers and Slavery*.

9. Zilversmit, *First Emancipation*, chaps. 6–8; Fladeland, *Men and Brothers*, chap. 3; McManus, *Black Bondage*, chaps. 10–11; MacLeod, *Slavery, Race and the American Revolution*, 40–47.

10. For examples of the many sermons and speeches in celebration of the African trade's abolition, see Jones, *A Thanksgiving Sermon, January 1, 1808*; Parrott, *Two Orations on the Abolition of the Slave Trade*; Gray, *A Sermon Delivered on 14th day of July, 1818*; and Gloucester, *An Oration, Delivered on January 1, 1823*.

11. For examples of the many tracts produced by the Society of Friends in reference to the African slave trade, see *View of the African Slave Trade*; *Extracts and Observations on the Foreign Slave Trade*; *Memorial on the African Slave Trade*; *Facts and Observations Relative to the African Slave Trade*; *Brief Statement of the Progress against the Slave Trade*; *Address to Our Fellow Members on the Slave-Trade*; and *Exposition of the African Slave Trade*.

12. Torrey, *Portraiture of Domestic Slavery*.

13. In its editorial against the domestic trade, *Freedom's Journal* (New York) argued, "It is high time that the citizens of the Union should arise as one man and put an end to a traffic which all civilized nations are at present endeavouring to abolish: we do not mean the foreign slave trade alone; we refer to our and their internal slave trade"; Oct. 17, 1828, quoted in Jacobs, ed., *Antebellum Black Newspapers*, 3–159. For good general accounts of the black abolitionists, see Quarles, *Black Abolitionists*; Pease and Pease, *They Who Would Be Free*; "Introduction to the American Series: Black Abolitionists in the United States, 1830–1865," in Ripley, ed., *Black Abolitionist Papers*, 3:3–69; and Goodman, *Of One Blood*, chap. 3.

14. *Genius of Universal Emancipation* (Baltimore), July 1821, Jan. and Nov. 1823. For a good account of Lundy's life, see Dillon, *Benjamin Lundy*.

15. *Genius of Universal Emancipation*, Nov. 1832.

16. Ibid., Nov. 1821, June 5, 1823. In part to help improve his understanding of how the domestic slave trade worked in the Deep South, Lundy planned a walking tour in 1828 from the Carolinas to Louisiana. This tour was permanently postponed, however, due to an unexpected trip to Haiti. Dillon, *Benjamin Lundy*, 141–42.

17. *Genius of Universal Emancipation*, Jan. 20, Feb. 24, Mar. 31, 1827.

18. Garrison to the editor of the *Boston Courier*, Aug. 12, 1828, in Merrill and Ruchames, eds., *Garrison Letters*, 1:66–68.

19. *Genius of Universal Emancipation*, Nov. 6, 20, 1829; Garrison to Francis Todd, May 13, 1830, in Merrill and Ruchames, eds., *Garrison Letters*, 1:93–94; Garrison and Garrison, *William Lloyd Garrison*, vol. 1, chaps. 4–7; Merrill, *Against Wind and Tide*, chap. 3; Thomas, *Liberator*, chaps. 4–5; Mayer, *All on Fire*, chap. 5.

20. For an indication of the admiration that Garrison had for Lundy and the influence that Lundy had on his life, see the lengthy obituary that Garrison wrote following Lundy's death; *Liberator*, Sept. 20, 1839.

21. American Anti-Slavery Society, *Declaration of Sentiments and Constitution*; *American Anti-Slavery Reporter* (New York), Jan. 1834; American Anti-Slavery Society, *First Annual Report*, 59.

22. Stanton to Brother Leavitt, *New York Evangelist*, Apr. 22, 1834.

23. When reprinted in the *Liberator*, the report was so long that Garrison felt a need to apologize for devoting so much space to it, claiming that "its ability and importance will abundantly atone for its great length." The document also later appeared in the *Reporter*, consuming almost fourteen of its sixteen pages. *Liberator*, May 31, June 7, 1834; *American Anti-Slavery Reporter*, July 1834.

24. *Liberator*, Oct. 5, 1833; Arfwedson, *United States and Canada*, 1:352.

25. "Are Slaveholders Man-Stealers?" *Anti-Slavery Record* (New York), Sept. 1837; Perry, *Radical Abolitionism*, 48–53.

26. Green, *Chattel Principle*, 4; Phelps, *Lectures on Slavery*, 30; "Letter of Smith to Smylie," 13.

27. Weld comments recorded by Henry Wright in November 1836, quoted in Perry, *Radical Abolitionism*, 51–52; Weld, *Bible against Slavery*, 6–9.

28. Weld, *American Slavery As It Is*, 110; Abzug, *Passionate Liberator*, 133–37. For an interesting reflection upon the connection between domestic animals and human slaves, see Jacoby, "Slaves by Nature?"

29. "The Gentlemen Farmers of Virginia Attending Their Cattle-Market," Leeds Anti-slavery Series, No. 48, in Armistead, *Five Hundred Thousand Strokes for Freedom*, 1; Garrison to Edward M. Davis, Jan. 8, 1838, in Merrill and Ruchames, eds., *Garrison Letters*, 2:334.

30. While the 120,000 figure was obviously too high, the abolitionists got this figure from an article in the *Virginia Times*; *Liberator*, Sept. 17, 1836; Harwood, "Abolitionist Image of Louisiana and Mississippi"; Richards, "Jacksonians and Slavery."

31. For a good example of the many pictorial illustrations used by the abolitionists, see Dumond, *Antislavery*, passim. For a reproduction of "Views of Slavery," see ibid., 251; *Anti-Slavery Record*, July 1836. This same illustration, which was used by southern newspapers for advertising slave sales, was previously criticized by Benjamin Lundy; see *Genius of Universal Emancipation*, Apr. 10, 1823.

32. Featherstonhaugh, *Excursion through the Slave States*, 1:120; Martineau, *Western Travel*, 1:235.

33. Mackay, *Life and Liberty*, 1:317; Bremer, *Homes of the New World*, 2:209; Berger, "American Slavery as Seen by Visitors"; Woods, "In the Eye of the Beholder."

34. *New York Evangelist*, Feb. 1, 1834. For another account of an abolitionist in the 1850s who traveled throughout the South visiting slave auctions and interviewing the people involved, see Redpath, *Roving Editor*.

35. Lerner, *Grimké Sisters*; Lumpkin, *Emancipation of Angelina Grimké*; Fladeland, *James Gillespie Birney*.

36. Weld, *American Slavery As It Is*, 7; Thomas, *Theodore Weld*, chap. 12. Two years later, Weld and James A. Thome published a similar work that focused entirely on the domestic trade; see *Slavery and the Internal Slave Trade*.

37. For accounts from former slaves in the 1830s describing their lives under slavery, including sale, before the New England Anti-Slavery Society and Massachusetts Anti-Slavery Society annual meetings, see *Liberator*, May 28, 1836, and Feb. 4, 1837. For slave narratives published as books during the 1830s, complete with accounts of sale, see Ball, *Slavery in the United States*; and Roper, *Narrative of Moses Roper*.

38. Weld to Gerrit Smith, Oct. 23, 1839, in Barnes and Dumond, eds., *Weld-Grimké Letters*, 2:811–12.

39. Kennicott, "Negro Antislavery Speakers in America"; Blassingame, ed., *Slave Testimony*; Foster, *Witnessing Slavery*; Starling, *Slave Narrative*.

40. Grandy, *Narrative of Moses Grandy*; Henson, *Life of Josiah Henson*; Brown, *Narrative of Henry Box Brown*; Pennington, *Fugitive Blacksmith*, iv–xiii.

41. Bibb, *Narrative of Henry Bibb*; Northup, *Twelve Years a Slave*; Brown, *Narrative of William W. Brown*; Lane, *Narrative of Lunsford Lane*, 18, 7–8.

42. Douglass had a number of masters while living in slavery, however, he was never actually sold. After his first owner's death, Douglass was given to that man's son, who later sent him to a "breaker" for a year. After a failed escape attempt, he was then sent back to Baltimore where he was rented out to several different masters. See speeches of Oct. 14, 1845, Mar. 10, 24, Sept. 11, 1846, and July 5, 1852, in Blassingame, ed., *Douglass Papers*, 1:40–42, 179–80, 196–97, 402–3; 2:371–76; Douglass, *Narrative of Frederick Douglass*; McFeely, *Frederick Douglass*, quotation on 173. For a more in-depth account of Douglass's experiences in slavery, see his later work, *My Bondage and My Freedom*.

43. A Former Resident of the Slave States, *Influence of Slavery upon the White Population*, 6; Walters, *Antislavery Appeal*, chap. 6.

44. *Anti-Slavery Record*, Mar. 1836; [Bourne], *Slavery Illustrated in Its Effects upon Woman*, vii. For a later argument that northern women were responsible for the continuation of slavery because they had not exerted their influence to abolish it, see Follen, *To Mothers in the Free States*.

45. Female Anti-Slavery Society, *Constitution and Address*, 8; Beecher, *Essay on Slavery and Abolitionism*, 109. For good accounts of the female abolitionists, see Lutz, *Crusade for Freedom*; Yellin, *Women and Sisters*; Ginzberg, *Women and the Work of Benevolence*; and Jeffrey, *Great Silent Army of Abolitionism*.

46. Grimké, *Appeal to the Women of the Nominally Free States*, 21; Grimké, "On the Condition of Women in the United States," in Ceplair, ed., *Grimké Writings*, 219–25.

47. Anthony Papers, LOC; Grimké, *Appeal to the Christian Women of the South.*

48. *Liberator,* June 4, 1831, Jan. 28, 1837, Jan. 7, 1832; *American Anti-Slavery Almanac* (1837), 41–44.

49. *Slave's Friend* (New York), vol. 2, nos. 5–12; Merrill, *Against Wind and Tide,* 134. For other works written especially for children in which stories, songs, and poems often centered on the domestic trade, see Collins, *Anti-Slavery Picknick; Child's Book on Slavery;* and *Child's Anti-Slavery Book.*

50. Stowe, *Uncle Tom's Cabin,* 623, 105.

51. Ibid., 51. In her follow-up work, Stowe argued that the domestic trade was "the vital force of the institution of slavery" and "the great trade of the country"; Stowe, *Key to Uncle Tom's Cabin,* 279, 291.

52. *Liberator,* May 23, 1835; Birney to Charles Hammond, Nov. 14, 1835, in Dumond, ed., *Birney Letters,* 1:268.

53. "Correspondence between Elmore and Birney," 29–30.

54. For a good account of the role that the domestic trade played in developing a political argument against slavery, see Lightner, "Door to the Slave Bastille"; Stanton speech, May 7, 1839, quoted in ibid., 244; Stewart, "Report of a Speech Delivered before a Joint Committee of the Legislature of Vermont" (Oct. 25–27, 1838), and "Address to the Abolitionists of the State of New York" (Oct. 1836), both in Marsh, ed., *Stewart Writings,* 175–79, 98–107.

55. Wiecek, *Sources of Antislavery Constitutionalism,* esp. chaps. 7–8.

56. Stewart, "Address to the Abolitionists of New York," 99.

57. Jay, *View of the Federal Government,* 88–89.

58. "Letter of Smith to Clay," 4–6.

59. Jay, *View of the Federal Government,* 185–86.

60. According to Harriet Martineau, an elderly James Madison also "believed that Congress has [the] power to prohibit the internal slavetrade"; *Western Travel,* 1:193. For good accounts of the founders' original intentions concerning Congress's ability to regulate the interstate slave trade and the conflicting interpretations that had developed by the time of the Missouri debates, see Berns, "Constitution and the Migration of Slaves"; and Lightner, "Founders and the Interstate Trade"; *Annals of Congress,* 16th Cong., 1st sess., 1199–1200, 291, 139; Lightner, "Door to the Slave Bastille," 236–37. See also the speeches of Representative Timothy Fuller (MA); Senators Walter Lowrie (PA), James Burrill (RI), and Benjamin Ruggles (OH); and Representatives John Taylor (NY), Clifton Claggett (NH), Daniel Cook (IL), William Plumer (NH), and Thomas Forrest (PA), *Annals of Congress,* 15th Cong., 2d sess., 1183–84; 16th Cong., 1st sess., 202–3, 210–18, 280–81, 959–60, 1038–39, 1093–98, 1432–34, 1560–61.

61. Jay, *View of the Federal Government,* 87.

62. All quotations from ibid., 80–83, 38. For earlier accounts in which Jay makes similar arguments, see *Inquiry into American Colonization;* and "Slavery and the Slave-Trade under the Authority of Congress," *Anti-Slavery Record,* Nov. 1837. For another important tract on this subject, see Weld, *Power of Congress.*

63. Child, *Appeal in Favor of Africans,* 30–34.

64. "Slavery and the Slave Trade in the District of Columbia," EI.

65. The story of the slave coffle passing the Capitol first appeared in Torrey, *Portraiture of Domestic Slavery,* 62; *Liberator,* Jan. 1, 1831; "Slave Market of America," LOC.

66. For a good example of this tactic, see *Northern Dealers in Slaves*, a tract that first appeared in the *Emancipator* (New York), Jan. 10, 1839, and was also reprinted by the American Anti-Slavery Society as a pamphlet.

67. Francis Jackson to Rep. Abbot Lawrence, Oct. 18, 1839, Anti-Slavery Letters, BPL; Grimkés to "Clarkson," Mar. 1837, in Ceplair, ed., *Grimké Writings*, 119; Jay, *View of the Federal Government*, 181–82.

68. It is impossible to know how many petitions were sent or how many people signed them. James Birney estimated that between January 1837 and March 1838 more than a half million people signed antislavery petitions, and the number of signatures was probably much higher and increased over the next few years. Henry B. Stanton put the figure at more than 2 million signatures in 1838 and 1839; "Correspondence between Elmore and Birney," 46, 65. For a discussion of these petitions, see Dumond, *Antislavery*, 245–48; and Miller, *Arguing about Slavery*, 305–11.

69. Anti-Slavery Convention of American Women, circular, BPL; Stewart, "Address to the Abolitionists of New York," 103.

70. New Hampshire Anti-Slavery Convention, *Proceedings*, 37; Dumond, *Antislavery*, 246. While these were the two most common petition topics in the third session of the Twenty-Fifth Congress (Dec. 1838–Mar. 1839), by the Twenty-Sixth Congress, the anti-Texas petitions numbered more than all other subjects combined.

71. Francis Jackson to Richard Fletcher, Oct. 30, 1838, Anti-Slavery Letters, BPL; Massachusetts General Court, *Report on the Powers of Congress and the Slave Trade*, 35; Lightner, "Door to the Slave Bastille," 246–47.

72. Slade, *Speech of Mr. Slade, December 23, 1835*; Morris, *Speech of Thomas Morris, February 9, 1839*; entry for Sept. 28, 1837, in Nevins, ed., *Diary of John Quincy Adams*, 484.

73. "The Influence of the Slave Power," 2. For another good pamphlet on this topic, see *Slavery and the Slave Trade at the Nation's Capital.* The best account of the role that the slave trade played in antislavery politics is Lightner, "Interstate Slave Trade in Antislavery Politics." For good accounts of the development of the Liberty party and later antislavery politics, see Sewell, *Ballots for Freedom*; and Kraut, ed., *Crusaders and Compromisers.*

74. William Goodell based his argument in part on the commerce clause, which he claimed gave Congress the power to determine what is and is not property; *Views of American Constitutional Law*, 43–47. During the 1850s Goodell served as editor of this group's main publication, *Radical Abolitionist* (New York). For his insistence that banning the interstate trade was not a "practical aim," see ibid., Sept. 1855. For another proponent of the view that Congress could abolish slavery in the states, see Spooner, *Unconstitutionality of Slavery.*

75. Free Soil party platforms of 1848 and 1852 quoted in Sewell, *Ballots for Freedom*, 198.

76. The best account of the ideology of the Republican party can be found in Foner, *Free Soil, Free Labor, Free Men.* For other views, see Trefousse, *Radical Republicans*; Holt, *Political Crisis of the 1850s*; and Gienapp, *Origins of the Republican Party.*

77. "Remarks of Mr. Giddings," Feb. 13, 1839, in *Liberator*, Mar. 22, 1839; *Congressional Globe*, 25th Cong., 3d sess., 181; Stewart, *Joshua R. Giddings*, chaps. 2–3.

78. Stewart, *Joshua R. Giddings*, chap. 4; *Congressional Globe*, 27th Cong., 2d sess., 342–49; Jones, "Peculiar Institution and National Honor." For later speeches in which

Giddings condemned the interstate trade, see Giddings, *Speeches*, 21–51, 289–318, 333–90, 467–87.

79. "An Address to the Anti-Slavery Christians of the United States" (June 1852) in Jay, *Miscellaneous Writings*, 624; Hamilton, *Prologue to Conflict*, 178.

80. Lexington *Kentucky Statesman*, Jan. 6, 1860.

81. Breckinridge's speech, Dec. 21, 1859, in ibid., Dec. 30, 1859; Edmund Ruffin, "Consequences of Abolition Agitation," *DeBow's Review* (New Orleans), June 1857, 588; ibid., Feb. 1861, 246. For other articles in *DeBow's Review* that also argued that one of the first actions of a Republican administration would be the prohibition of the interstate slave trade, see A. Roane, "The South, in the Union or Out of It," Oct. 1860, 453; and "Speech of Henry A. Wise," Jan. 1861, 117.

82. Second debate with Stephen A. Douglas at Freeport, Illinois, Aug. 27, 1858, in Basler, ed., *Lincoln Works*, 3:40; Lincoln to Mary Speed, Sept. 27, 1841, in ibid., 1:260; Lincoln to Joshua F. Speed, Aug. 24, 1855, in ibid., 2:320.

83. *New-York Tribune*, Mar. 2, 1865; Coffin, *Boys of '61*, 472–75; Drago, ed., *Broke by the War*, 1–5.

84. *Liberator*, Mar. 17, 1865; Garrison and Garrison, *William Lloyd Garrison*, 4:134–35. One indication of the importance of this event can be found in the poem written by Almira Seymour entitled "William Lloyd Garrison on the Auction-Block," *Liberator*, Apr. 7, 1865. The moving impact that this event had on Garrison can be seen in his letter to Jacob Horton, Mar. 17, 1865, in Merrill and Ruchames, eds., *Garrison Letters*, 5:262–63.

Chapter 7

1. Otey letter, Feb. 13, 1857, quoted in Howell, "John Armfield of Beersheba Springs," 56, passim; Nashville *Republican Banner*, Dec. 25, 1857; *Proceedings of a Convention of the Trustees*; Fairbanks, *History of the University of the South*, chaps. 3–4; Chitty, *Reconstruction at Sewanee*, 42–61. The seven states represented by official delegates at the Lookout Mountain convention were Alabama, Louisiana, Mississippi, North Carolina, South Carolina, Tennessee, and Texas.

2. Curran, *Bicentennial History of Georgetown University*, 116–21; Coppinger et al., *Beersheba Springs*, 14. Isaac Franklin also attempted to set up a school for poor children near his home in Sumner County, Tennessee. While the state legislature passed an act incorporating the "Isaac Franklin Institute," challenges to his will in Louisiana prevented the academy from materializing. Stephenson, *Isaac Franklin*, 118–20.

3. Among the many works on paternalism, the following have been influential in my thinking: Genovese, *World the Slaveholders Made* and *Roll, Jordan, Roll*; Rose, "Domestication of Domestic Slavery," in Rose, *Slavery and Freedom*, 18–36; Oakes, *Ruling Race*; Gallay, "Origins of Slaveholders' Paternalism"; Kolchin, *Unfree Labor*, part 1, and *American Slavery*, chap. 4; Parish, *Slavery*, chap. 4; Jones, *Born a Child of Freedom, Yet a Slave*; Bowman, *Masters and Lords*, chap. 5; Morgan, *Slave Counterpoint*, chap. 5; Morris, "Articulation of Two Worlds"; and Young, *Domesticating Slavery*.

4. *Annals of Congress*, 16th Cong., 1st sess., 1162, 1274. For a sampling of southern speeches on this topic, see the remarks of Senator John Elliott (GA), and Representatives

Alexander Smyth (VA), Benjamin Hardin (KY), Philip Barbour (VA), Charles Pinckney (SC), and Christopher Rankin (MS), ibid., 131, 996–97, 1079–80, 1239, 1317–18, 1343–44.

5. *Congressional Globe*, 25th Cong., 3d sess., 23.

6. Clay to Francis Brooke, Nov. 3, 1838, in Colton, ed., *Clay Works*, 5:431; Senate speech, Feb. 7, 1839, in ibid., 8:149.

7. Clay, *Remarks of Mr. Clay, on the Slavery Question*, 10.

8. *Congressional Globe*, 36th Cong., 2d sess., 83, 114. The clauses in the Confederate Constitution concerning commerce and slaves are Article 1, section 8; Article 4, section 2; and Article 4, section 3. Thomas, *Confederate Nation*, 311, 319–20.

9. Pollard, *Black Diamonds Gathered in the Darkey Homes of the South* (1859), in McKitrick, ed., *Slavery Defended*, 166–67; Holmes, "Review of *Uncle Tom's Cabin*" (1852), in ibid., 109.

10. Sturge, *Visit to the United States*, 31.

11. Olmsted, *Journey in the Seaboard States*, 555–56; entry for May 13, 1846, Fisher Diary, MDHS.

12. *DeBow's Review* (New Orleans), Mar. 1853, 271; Harper, *Memoir on Slavery* (1837), in Faust, ed., *Ideology of Slavery*, 110.

13. McIntosh, *Letters in Relation to Slavery* (1853), quoted in Moss, *Domestic Novelists*, 122; Thomas M. League to Thomas J. League, Aug. 21, 1850, League Papers, RL; Senate speech, July 22, 1850, in Colton, ed., *Clay Works*, 9:547.

14. Thornton, *Inquiry into Slavery*, 320, 336.

15. Wade quoted in Foner, *Free Soil, Free Labor, Free Men*, 146.

16. Some historians have argued that there was little difference between the paternalism of northern factory owners and that of southern planters. I disagree. While some early factory owners certainly acted paternalistically toward their workers, such actions noticeably declined over time. Moreover, there was a fundamental difference between hiring your laborers and owning them, especially in the power you had over their bodies and family life. Finally, never did northern factory owners use paternalism to defend industrial capitalism, unlike southern planters who used it to differentiate their way of life from the free-labor wage capitalism that was emerging in the North.

17. For two works that argue that the domestic slave trade undermined paternalism, see Tadman, *Speculators and Slaves*, chap. 8; and Jones, *Born a Child of Freedom, Yet a Slave*.

18. *Charleston Mercury*, May 16, 1838; *Genius of Liberty* (Leesburg, VA), Mar. 20, 1821; *Louisville Journal*, May 2, 1849; Tabb Catten to Richard Dickinson, Aug. 1, 1848, Slavery Collection, AAS.

19. Thomas Affleck's "Cotton Plantation Record and Account Book" (1846), Panther Burn Plantation Book, MDAH; plantation rules, 1840, Flynn Plantation Book, SHC; *New-York Tribune*, Jan. 12, 1859; entry for June 26, 1856, in Rosengarten, ed., *Tombee*, 669.

20. John Cheesborough to Elizabeth F. Blyth, Jan. 12, 1836, in Easterby, ed., *South Carolina Rice Plantation*, 66; C. C. Jones to Mary Jones, Dec. 10, 1856, in Myers, ed., *Children of Pride*, 270–71.

21. Diary entry for Jan. 22, 1850, Bills Papers, SHC; O. R. Smith to E. H. Stokes, July 13, 1863, Chase Papers, LOC; Alfred Moore to William A. Blount, Sept. 22, 1835, Blount Papers, NCSA.

22. R. D. Lunceford to David Lunceford, Nov. 25, 1860, Miscellaneous Letters, SHC; P. B. Barringer to David M. Barringer, Aug. 2, 1849, Barringer Papers, SHC.

23. Robert Thurston to James Baylor, Dec. 28, 1821, Heartman Collection, XU; L. J. Halsey to Joseph Copes, Apr. 2, 1850, Copes Papers, TUL; *Louisville Journal*, Sept. 3, 1845.

24. Schwartz, *Born in Bondage*, 162–63; D. Clayton to William S. Pettigrew, Dec. 11, 1852, Pettigrew Papers, SHC; Pettigrew to Clayton, Dec. 11, 1852, addendum, Feb. 7, 1853, ibid.

25. John W. Cotton to William H. Wills, Dec. 26, 1839, Wills Papers, SHC.

26. James Saul to Joseph S. Copes, Nov. 30, 1858, Copes Papers, TUL; William C. Lane to Mary Lane, July 29, 1853, Lane Collection, MOHS.

27. King, *Stolen Childhood*, 108; Blassingame, ed., *Slave Testimony*, 297; entry for Dec. 31, 1843, in Hogan and Davis, eds., *William Johnson's Natchez*, 470.

28. The historian who coined the term "key slaves" and developed it the furthest is Michael Tadman; see his essay "Key Slaves and the Poverty of Paternalism," which appears as the new introduction to the paperback edition of *Speculators and Slaves* (1996).

29. Alex C. Robertson to F. J. Robertson, July 28, 1853, Robertson Papers, TSL; Thomas Clemson to F. W. Pickens, Oct. 7, 1850, Pickens Papers, DU.

30. In 1860 the Census Bureau recorded 384,884 slaveholders: 46,282 (12 percent) owned twenty or more slaves; while 211,614 (55 percent) owned five slaves or fewer; U.S. Census, *Agriculture of the United States*, 247; Genovese, *Roll, Jordan, Roll*, 10; Kolchin, *American Slavery*, 111–12.

31. Leverich & Co. to John Hunt, Sept. 1, 1835, Negro Collection, DU; S. M. Scott to John J. Wherry, Apr. 29, 1858, Wherry Papers, DU; E. J. C. Wood to Z. B. Oakes, July 27, 1856, Oakes Papers, BPL.

32. *Richmond Whig and Public Advertiser*, Dec. 14, 1849; *Louisville Courier*, Dec. 5, 1859; Augusta *Chronicle and Sentinel*, Mar. 25, 1859; *Charleston Courier*, Dec. 14, 1857; Alexandria *Phenix Gazette*, Apr. 18, 1829.

33. Baltimore *Sun*, May 16, 1859; *Mississippi Free Trader and Natchez Gazette*, Nov. 4, 1836; Charleston *City Gazette and Daily Advertiser*, Mar. 1, 1796; *Cambridge Chronicle*, Oct. 18, 1834; notarized document signed by George Gibbs, Mar. 5, 1839, Gibbs Papers, UF.

34. Lewis Tutt to Richard Tutt, Feb. 4, 1839, Tutt Papers, DU; Warrenton (VA) *Palladium of Liberty*, Feb. 4, 1820, Bancroft Papers, CU; *National Intelligencer* (Washington, DC), Jan. 13, 1835, Dec. 13, 1836; A. Durnford to John McDonogh, June 9, 1835, McDonogh Papers, TUL; G. W. Eutsler to Elias Ferguson, Aug. 14, 1856, Ferguson Papers, NCSA.

35. Alexandria *Phenix Gazette*, Apr. 9, 1833; *National Intelligencer*, Mar. 8, 1834, July 26, 1833.

36. St. Louis *Missouri Democrat*, July 28, 1854; *National Intelligencer*, June 3, 1837.

37. William Bankhead to Dickinson, Hill & Co., Feb. 2, 1856, Chase Papers, LOC.

38. Baltimore *Sun*, Jan. 1, 1849; *Baltimore Republican and Commercial Advertiser*, Jan. 7, 1835; *Snow-Hill* (MD) *Messenger and Worcester County Advertiser*, Jan. 23, 1832, Nov. 2, 1830. For a good account of such deceptive sales tactics, see Bancroft, *Slave Trading*, 32–34.

39. *Niles' Register*, July 19, 1817; *Western Luminary*, Nov. 23, 1831.

40. The best account of the changing nature of the Upper South's views on the domestic trade is Gudmestad, "A Troublesome Commerce."

41. *Western Citizen*, Sept. 24, 1822; unknown Raleigh newspaper, Oct. 13, 1825, quoted in *Western Luminary*, Nov. 9, 1825; *Louisville Courier*, Nov. 12, 1849.

42. *Memphis Eagle*, Oct. 8, 1845.

43. The District of Columbia was originally composed of ten square miles of land ceded from the states of Maryland and Virginia. In 1846, Congress agreed to return the land ceded from Virginia back to that state. Hence, Alexandria, District of Columbia, then became Alexandria, Virginia, and subject to the laws of Virginia and not any possible laws that might restrict the slave trade within DC in the future. See the 1802 grand jury grievance contained within the 1827 Benevolent Society of Alexandria tract, Alexandria *Phenix Gazette*, June 22, 1827; petition of Mar. 24, 1828, quoted in *Liberator* (Boston), Mar. 14, 1835; petition of 1849, quoted in ibid., Feb. 9, 1849; Green, *Secret City*, 44.

44. Charleston City Council petition, Nov. 26, 1839, General Assembly Papers, SCSA; Committee Report (Judiciary) (1839), ibid.; Richland District, Mar. 4, 1846, Presentments to the Grand Jury, SCSA.

45. Amos, *Cotton City*, 85; Huntsville (AL) *Democrat*, May 16, 1833, quoted in *Western Luminary*, May 29, 1833; Gudmestad, "A Troublesome Commerce," 209–11.

46. J. P. Walworth to Douglas Walworth, Nov. 1850, Walworth Papers, LSU.

47. New Orleans Ordinances, Mar. 30, 1829, NOPL; *Courier*, Mar. 30, 1829, quoted in *Western Luminary*, June 3, 1829; Wade, *Slavery in the Cities*, 204–6; *Daily Orleanian*, Jan. 20, 1852, quoted in Johnson, *Soul by Soul*, 162.

48. Weld, *A Vacation Tour*, 284; Russell, *North America*, 277; Woodward, ed., *Mary Chesnut's Civil War*, 23.

49. Andrews, *Slavery and the Domestic Slave-Trade*, 80; Douglass quote, Dec. 4, 1879, in Blassingame, ed., *Douglass Papers*, 4:544; L. M. Mills narrative in Blassingame, ed., *Slave Testimony*, 504.

50. *New Orleans Price-Current, Commercial Intelligencer and Merchants Transcript*, June 25, 1842, Quitman Papers, SHC. See also other versions of this paper ranging from 1842 to 1858 in Ballard Papers, SHC; *Charleston Prices Current*, Apr. 2, 1856, W. S. Lawton & Co. Papers, UF; *St. Louis Exchange Reporter and Price-Current*, Mar. 5 and Apr. 15, 1857, Nov. 23, 1859, and Feb. 8, 1860, Ballard Papers; *American Anti-Slavery Reporter*, July 1834. Only rarely was the state of the slave market printed in a southern newspaper, such as when the *Richmond Enquirer* on July 29, 1859, reprinted one of the circulars released by that city's major traders.

51. *Natchez Courier*, Feb. 29, Mar. 6, 8, 9, 17, June 14, 28, 1860; *Mississippi Free Trader*, Mar. 3, 9, 10, 13, 16, 17, June 14, 28, 1860.

52. Fox-Genovese and Genovese, *Fruits of Merchant Capital*; Rogers, *Incidents of Travel*, 234.

53. *Savannah Republican*, Feb. 2, 1860.

54. Resolutions for Nov. 17, 1826, Jan. 16, 24, Feb. 9, Mar. 28, 1827, and Nov. 7, 1828, Lynchburg Common Council Ledger, UVA; Stampp, *Peculiar Institution*, 243–44.

55. Stampp, *Peculiar Institution*, 244; Bryan to Ellison S. Keitt, Apr. 14, 1860, Black History Collection, LOC.

56. Jefferson to Thomas M. Randolph, June 8, 1803, in Betts, ed., *Farm Book*, 19; John A. Warren to John D. Warren, Dec. 20, 1858, Warren Papers, USC; Asa Dickinson to William P. Dickinson, Oct. 21, 1859, Dickinson Papers, VHS.

57. *Maryland Journal and Baltimore Advertiser*, Mar. 23, 1792; testimony of J. B. Fanel, Apr. 13, 1852, *Coulter v. Cresswell et al.*, No. 2734, 7 La. Ann. 367 (1852), UNO; Account Book, Jan. 1, 1849, Leonard Papers, MOHS; A. W. DaCosta to Z. B. Oakes, Oct. 27, 1853, Oakes Papers, BPL; W. M. Beall to John Knight, Sept. 21, 1842, Beall Letter, MDHS.

58. John Cocke quoted in Miller, ed., *Dear Master*, 151; Wylly & Montmollin to Z. B. Oakes, Aug. 8, 1853, Oakes Papers, BPL; Robert Cartmell Diary, Dec. 16, 1859, quoted in Edwards, "Negroes . . . and All Other Animals," 32.

59. Jacobs, *Incidents in the Life*, 76; interview of Fannie Berry in Perdue et al., eds., *Weevils in the Wheat*, 48; Lenn to Memory, Nov. 30, 1857, Elliot Papers, FSU.

60. E. Crutchfield to R. C. Ballard, Feb. 23, 1856, Ballard Papers, SHC; James H. Taylor to Franklin H. Elmore, Mar. 24, 1836, Elmore Papers, LOC.

61. Entry for Jan. 6, 1858, in Racine, ed., *Piedmont Farmer*, 71; N. B. Powell to Farish Carter, Mar. 7, 1850, Carter Papers, SHC; John McDonogh to John H. Cocke, Nov. 20, 1845, McDonogh Papers, TUL.

62. Jones, *Born a Child of Freedom, Yet a Slave*, 3; interview of Isaiah Butler in Rawick, ed., *American Slave*, vol. 2, pt. 1, 158; Thomas Maskell to Samuel Plaisted, Aug. 8, 1838, Plaisted Correspondence, LSU.

63. Interview of Samuel Walter Chilton in Perdue et al., eds., *Weevils in the Wheat*, 71; Stroyer, *My Life in the South*, 42; Bruce, *The New Man*, 103; speech of Oct. 14, 1845, in Blassingame, ed., *Douglass Papers*, 1:42.

64. Manigault quoted in Jones, *Born a Child of Freedom*, 174–75.

65. Journal of Samuel Gaillard, Jan. 18, 1836, quoted in ibid., 199; J. G. Miller to "Gent," Apr. 16, 1860, Chase Papers, LOC; Robert R. W. Allston to Adele P. Allston, Apr. 10, 1863, in Easterby, ed., *South Carolina Rice Plantation*, 193–94.

66. Collins, *Memories of the Southern States*, 71.

67. Rufus Fairchild to Z. B. Oakes, Aug. 16, 1853, Oakes Papers, BPL; William Wright to Z. B. Oakes, Dec. 1, 1854, ibid.; William Portlock Bill of Sale, Mar. 1833, Pascal Papers, HU.

68. Tom Lighthouse to Z. B. Oakes, Oct. 14, 1853, Oakes Papers, BPL; John S. Campbell to Richard Dickinson, Aug. 5, 1848, Slavery Collection, AAS.

69. A. G. Porter to Z. B. Oakes, Jan. 17, 26, and Feb. 6, 1854, Oakes Papers, BPL.

70. James M. Sims to Theresa Sims, Dec. 29, 1859, quoted in Owens, *This Species of Property*, 185–86.

71. Blanchard and Rice, *Debate on Slavery*, 28–29.

72. For good accounts of using the slave trader as a scapegoat, see Tadman, *Speculators and Slaves*, chap. 7; and Gudmestad, "A Troublesome Commerce," 361–69.

73. *Democrat*, May 16, 1833, quoted in *Western Luminary*, May 29, 1833; Blanchard and Rice, *Debate on Slavery*, 55; Maryville (TN) *Millennial Trumpeter* quoted in *Western Luminary*, Dec. 3, 1834; Ingraham, *The South-west*, 2:245; *Niles' Register*, June 28, 1828.

74. Hundley, *Social Relations*, 139–45.

75. For an account of the more successful traders and their standing in their communities, see Tadman, *Speculators and Slaves*, 192–200.

76. Ingraham, *The South-west*, 2:245; New Hope Baptist Church (Buckingham Co., VA), Minute Book, May 7, 1836, Thornhill and Bocock Papers, UVA; B. F. Duvall to Martha Watkins, May 22, 1843, Tutt Papers, DU; Elizabeth B. Courts to R. J. B. L. Winn, Oct. 3, 1841, Winn Papers, MOHS; Weld, *American Slavery As It Is*, 173.

77. Martin narrative in Blassingame, ed., *Slave Testimony*, 704–6.

78. Thomas W. Burton to William Long, Feb. 20, 1845, Long Papers, NCSA; A. J. McElveen to Z. B. Oakes, Aug. 9, 1853, Oakes Papers, BPL; R. M. Owings & Co. to Z. B. Oakes, Dec. 1, 1856, ibid. For examples of slave traders purchasing husbands and wives from different owners in the Upper South and then selling them together as a married couple to a single owner in New Orleans, see William Christy, notary, Act 4, p. 103, Mar. 5, 1830, Certificates of Good Character, NONA; Christy, notary, Act 6, p. 292, Apr. 12, 1830, ibid.; Carlile Pollock, notary, Act 31, p. 243, Apr. 17, 1830, ibid. I would like to thank Jonathan Pritchett for drawing my attention to these documents.

79. Joseph Weatherby to Z. B. Oakes, Aug. 7, 1856, Oakes Papers, BPL; Corey, *History of the Richmond Theological Seminary*, 48–49; Drago, ed., *Broke by the War*, 12; Martineau, *Western Travel*, 1:270.

80. All but two were sent north: one individual was too ill to make the journey, and another was an orphaned infant who could not take care of herself. Succession of Cresswell, No. 2423, 8 La. Ann. 122 (1853), UNO; Schafer, *Slavery and the Supreme Court of Louisiana*, 178–79, 211.

81. Stowe, *Key to Uncle Tom's Cabin*, 325; Phelps, *Lectures on Slavery*, 51.

82. Stirling, *Letters from the Slave States*, 292–93.

83. Dennison, *Scandalize My Name*, chap. 3.

84. Featherstonhaugh, *Excursion through the Slave States*, 1:119–23.

Chapter 8

1. Toni Morrison, *Beloved*, 23.

2. Bill of Sale, Jan. 15, 1837, Baltimore County Court Records, MSA. For an example of a couple meeting in a coffle and marrying, see the interview of Wright Stapleton in Rawick, ed., *American Slave*, supp. 1, 10:2019–20.

3. Schweninger, *Black Property Owners*, 104–12; Koger, *Black Slaveowners*, 1–17, 80–101; Johnson and Roark, *Black Masters*, 129–34; *Niles' Register* (Baltimore), Oct. 10, 1818.

4. Tadman, *Speculators and Slaves*, 146–54; Stampp, *Peculiar Institution*, 199–200; Morris, *Southern Slavery and the Law*, 130.

5. Interview of Susan Hamlin in Rawick, ed., *American Slave*, vol. 2, pt. 2, 235; Ball, *Slavery in the United States*, 18; interview of Matilda Carter in Perdue et al., eds., *Weevils in the Wheat*, 68.

6. Northup, *Twelve Years a Slave*, 60; Gutman, *Black Family*, 290; testimony of Dr. David Devall, May 17, 1852, *Buhler v. McHatton*, No. 3448, 9 La. Ann. 192 (1854), UNO.

7. Jones, *Experience and Personal Narrative*, 24; Hayden narrative in Stowe, *Key to Uncle Tom's Cabin*, 305; interview of Gross and Smith in Blassingame, ed., *Slave Testimony*, 347.

8. Morrison, *Beloved*, 162; Tocqueville, *Journey to America*, 159. For a good account of the psychological costs that slavery (and the threat of sale) had on the enslaved, see Painter, "Soul Murder and Slavery."

9. Tadman, *Speculators and Slaves*, 45; Schwartz, *Born in Bondage*, 5; Hughes, *Thirty Years a Slave*.

10. Bill of Sale, Feb. 4, 1854, Newell Papers, TSL; *Federal Gazette and Baltimore Advertiser*, Sept. 17, 1796; Bill of Sale, July 31, 1815, Benoist-Charleville Papers, MOHS; *National Intelligencer* (Washington, DC), Nov. 28, 1837; Edward Stewart to John W. Gurley, Dec. 19, 1858, Gurley Papers, LSU.

11. Brown, *Slave Life in Georgia*, 15–16; interview of Ben Johnson in Mellon, ed., *Bullwhip Days*, 292.

12. Douglass, *Narrative of Frederick Douglass*, 90.

13. Watson, *Narrative of Henry Watson*, 7; interview of Charles Crawley in Perdue et al., eds., *Weevils in the Wheat*, 79; Blassingame, ed., *Slave Testimony*, 743–44.

14. Jones, *Experience and Personal Narrative*, 7–8; Brown, *Narrative of Henry Box Brown*, 15; Brown, *Slave Life in Georgia*, 9.

15. Gutman, *Black Family*, 219–20; interview of Delia Garlic in Rawick, ed., *American Slave*, 6:130–31; interview of Clark in ibid., 6:72–73.

16. Interview of White in Rawick, ed., *American Slave*, 6:413–14; interview of Eva Strayhorn in ibid., supp. 1, 12:300–301.

17. Interview of Sarah Ashley in Tyler and Murphy, eds., *Slave Narratives of Texas*, 7; Hall, *Travels in North America*, 3:34–40; Nathan Brown to Mary H., Jan. 13, 1838, Brown Letter Book, MOHS.

18. "John Parker Memoir," 5–6, Rankin-Parker Papers, DU.

19. Interview of Stephen Williams in Mellon, ed., *Bullwhip Days*, 290; Franklin to R. C. Ballard, Mar. 4, 1832, Ballard Papers, SHC.

20. McLaurin, *Celia, a Slave*; interview of Mollie Kinsey in Rawick, ed., *American Slave*, supp. 1, 4:373.

21. Hughes, *Thirty Years a Slave*, 10.

22. Ball, *Slavery in the United States*, 16–18; Brown, *Slave Life in Georgia*, 100; Clarke, *Narrative of Lewis Clarke*, 22; interview of Craig in Rawick, ed., *American Slave*, pt. 1, 2:230.

23. Interview of Moye in Mellon, ed., *Bullwhip Days*, 161.

24. Interview of Henry Lewis in Tyler and Murphy, eds., *Slave Narratives of Texas*, 29.

25. Chambers, *Things as They Are in America*, 274; Wiggins, "Play of Slave Children"; King, *Stolen Childhood*, 48; Schwartz, *Born in Bondage*, 129.

26. *Liberator* (Boston), Nov. 9, 1849; Montgomery *Alabama Journal*, Oct. 9, 1829.

27. Blane, *Excursion through the United States*, 226–27; *Louisville Journal*, Oct. 12, 1859, quoted in *New Orleans Bee*, Oct. 17, 1859; *St. Louis Republican*, June 2, 1858, quoted in New Orleans *Delta*, June 8, 1858; *Richmond Enquirer*, June 18, 1858.

28. Trial of Jesse, Feb. 18, 1856, Gov. Henry Wise Papers, Mar. 1856 folder, Virginia Executive Records, VSL. Not only was his wife carried away by the trader, but Jesse was found guilty and sold as a slave beyond the limits of the United States.

29. Charleston *City Gazette and Daily Advertiser*, Dec. 21, 1799; unknown Raleigh paper, Oct. 13, 1825, quoted in *Western Luminary* (Lexington, KY), Nov. 9, 1825; *Freedom's*

Journal (New York) Feb. 22 and Dec. 12, 1828; Lexington *Kentucky Reporter*, Sept. 9, 1829; *Niles' Register*, Sept. 5 and Dec. 26, 1829; *Richmond Enquirer*, Jan. 28, 1830.

30. Petition for Ned, May 22, 1836, quoted in Schwarz, *Slave Laws in Virginia*, 101; *Farmville* (VA) *Chronicle*, quoted in *Liberator*, May 10, 1834; *Savannah Republican*, Oct. 26, 1849.

31. For accounts of the *Creole* case, see *Niles' Register*, Jan. 22, 1842; and Jones, "Peculiar Institution and National Honor." For accounts of the *Decatur* case, see *Niles' Register*, May 20, 1826; and *Genius of Universal Emancipation* (Baltimore), Jan. 2, 1827. For accounts of the *Lafayette* case, see *Niles' Register*, Jan. 9, 1830; *Kentucky Reporter*, Jan. 20, 1830; and *Richmond Enquirer*, Jan. 28, 1830.

32. *Western Luminary*, Sept. 27, Oct. 4, and Nov. 1, 1826; Paris (KY) *Western Citizen*, Sept. 30, 1826; *Niles' Register*, Oct. 14 and Nov. 18, 1826.

33. *National Gazette*, Aug. 6, 1825, quoted in *Western Luminary*, Aug. 24, 1825; Kaye, "Neighbourhoods and Solidarity," 15; interview of Richard Macks in Rawick, ed., *American Slave*, 16:53. While it is not entirely certain that this woman was emancipated at the time of her release from jail, it is highly probable as U.S. troops were sent to protect her and "she was taken to Washington where she was set free," Macks interview.

34. Bremer, *Homes of the New World*, 2:533; *Glasgow Weekly Times*, Oct. 20, 1859, cited in Hurt, *Agriculture and Slavery*, 236.

35. *Niles' Register*, July 21, 1821; appeal, Feb. 14, 1860, *Walker v. Hays*, No. 6606, 15 La. Ann. 640 (1860), UNO; *Nashville Gazette* quoted in *Liberator*, Feb. 11, 1853; Catterall, ed., *Judicial Cases*, 3:216–17; Wahl, *Bondsman's Burden*, 42.

36. *Western Law Journal* (Cincinnati), 5 (1848), 528.

37. Interview of M. T. Judge, Feb. 23, 1913, Nixon Papers, ADAH; interview of William Johnson in Drew, ed., *North-Side View of Slavery*, 29; Franklin and Schweninger, *Runaway Slaves*, chap. 3. Of the sixty people in *North-Side View of Slavery* who gave a reason for flight, thirty-two (53 percent) listed sale as their primary motivation; of the remaining twenty-eight, nineteen (68 percent) had previously been sold or knew someone who had been sold.

38. *St. Louis Missouri Gazette & Public Advertiser*, Mar. 29, 1820, quoted in Strickland, "Aspects of Slavery in Missouri," 525; George Washington to B. A. Putnam, Apr. 27, 1853, *Walker v. Sanchez*, No. 4485, 13 La. Ann. 505 (1858), UNO.

39. New Orleans *Delta*, Feb. 25, 1856; *Memphis Eagle*, Nov. 4, 1845; New Orleans *Picayune*, Oct. 5, 1858, Oct. 9, 1859; deposition of Henry Bowman, June 7, 1856, Frankel Papers, CHS.

40. Walter Woodyard to "Dear Sir," Aug. 22, 1830, Kimball Papers, DU; unsigned letter to N. Elliot (sheriff of Howard Co.), n.d., Slavery Collection, MOHS; narrative of William Parker in Nichols, ed., *Black Men in Chains*, 287.

41. John N. Denning to L. W. Candler, Jan. 10, 1850, Peter Papers, UVA; William Wright to Z. B. Oakes, Oct. 25, 1853, Oakes Papers, BPL.

42. Walter Campbell to R. H. Dickinson, Aug. 15, 1848, and June 20, 1847, Slavery Collection, AAS; J. J. Price to Edward H. Stokes, Feb. 11, 1860, Chase Papers, LOC.

43. G. W. Eutsler to Elias W. Ferguson, Aug. 16, 1856, Ferguson Papers, NCSA; narrative of Levi Douglass and James Wright in Blassingame, ed., *Slave Testimony*, 303–4; manifests dated Feb. 8 and May 3, 1819, Inward Slave Manifests, NA; Jeremiah Smith to

Z. B. Oakes, Feb. 17, 1857, Oakes Papers, BPL; Thomas Lighthouse to Z. B. Oakes, Oct. 30, 1853, ibid.

44. *Hill v. White*, No. 4489, 11 La. Ann. 170 (1856), UNO; *New Orleans Crescent*, Jan. 9, 1860; *Fisk v. Bergerot*, No. 6814, 21 La. Ann. 111 (1869), UNO; *Richmond Enquirer*, May 29, 1853; *Memphis Eagle and Enquirer*, July 19, 1853.

45. *Richmond Whig and Daily Advertiser*, Sept. 18, 1849; *Louisville Courier*, July 25, 1859.

46. Huntsville (AL) *Southern Advocate*, Dec. 11, 1829; *Lexington Intelligencer*, July 7, 1838, quoted in *Liberator*, Sept. 11, 1846; Anna Lane to Sarah Glasgow (1851), Lane Collection, MOHS.

47. *Baton-Rouge Gazette*, Sept. 6, 1828; Bibb, *Narrative of Henry Bibb*, 99.

48. Unknown Pensacola paper, Aug. 10, 1829, quoted in *Genius of Universal Emancipation*, Oct. 16, 1829.

49. *Riggin v. Kendig*, No. 4718, 12 La. Ann. 451 (1857), UNO; *Fazende v. Hagan*, No. 4824, 9 Rob. 306 (1844), ibid.; entry for Aug. 3, 1860, in Chadwick, ed., "Diary of Samuel Edward Burges," 75.

50. Interview of Fannie Berry in Perdue et al., eds., *Weevils in the Wheat*, 42.

51. Grandy, *Narrative of Moses Grandy*, 5–6; narrative of Henry Stewart in Blassingame, ed., *Slave Testimony*, 414–15.

52. William Reynolds quoted in Eaton, *Growth of Southern Civilization*, 50–51; Randolph quoted in Genovese, *Roll, Jordan, Roll*, 456.

53. Virginia Boyd to R. C. Ballard, May 6, 1853, Ballard Papers, SHC; C. M. Rutherford to R. C. Ballard, Apr. 2 and Aug. 8, 1853, ibid.

54. C. Abner to E. Kingsland, Nov. 18, 1859, Abner Letter, VHS; Hamilton, *Men and Manners in America*, 2:216–18; interview of Edward Lycurgas in Rawick, ed., *American Slave*, 17:206.

55. Interview of Robert Williams in Perdue et al., eds., *Weevils in the Wheat*, 325–26; Weld, *A Vacation Tour*, 303; interview of Fannie Berry in Perdue et al., eds., *Weevils in the Wheat*, 49.

56. Marie Perkins to Richard Perkins, Oct. 8, 1852, in Blassingame, ed., *Slave Testimony*, 96–97; William Wright to Z. B. Oakes, Nov. 9, 1853, Oakes Papers, BPL; Susan and Ersey to "Dear Master" [Beverley Tucker], Oct. 24, 1842, in Blassingame, ed., *Slave Testimony*, 13.

57. Jane H. Criswell to Joseph Copes, Feb. 4, 1851, Copes Papers, TUL; Wise, *End of an Era*, 80–83; Abdy, *Journal of a Residence*, 3:350.

58. Brown, *Slave Life in Georgia*, 98; "John Parker Memoir," 31, Rankin-Parker Papers, DU. For a good account of the complex interaction among buyers, sellers, and the enslaved in the New Orleans slave pens, see Johnson, *Soul by Soul*, esp. chap. 6.

59. R. V. Tiffey to R. H. Dickinson, Feb. 7, 1847, Slavery Collection, AAS; A. J. McElveen to Z. B. Oakes, Oct. 21, 1856, Oakes Papers, BPL; Pleasant Howell to R. H. Dickinson, July 20, 1855, Dickinson Papers, CHS.

60. E. A. Gibbes to Z. B. Oakes, Jan. 29, 1857, Oakes Papers, BPL; Sales List, Feb. 11, 1828, Fields Papers, DU.

61. L. Wilkes to Dickinson, Hill & Co., July 11, 1855, Dickinson Papers, CHS; John S. Campbell to R. H. Dickinson, Aug. 5, 1848, Slavery Collection, AAS; Seth Woodroof to "Dick" [Richard Dickinson], Feb. 24, 1856, Chase Papers, LOC.

62. Testimony of T. Reddington, Jan. 10, 1854, *Nixon v. Bozeman & Bushy*, No. 3485, 11 La. Ann. 750 (1856), UNO; petition, Nov. 4, 1837, *Nelson v. Lillard et al.*, No. 800-1, 16 La. 336 (1840), ibid.; J. J. Toler to E. W. Ferguson, Dec. 27, 1858, Ferguson Papers, NCSA.

63. John W. Pittman to John B. Williamson, May 26, 1835, Black History Collection, LOC; "Traffic in Human Affections, with Reflections Thereon," Leeds Anti-slavery Series, No. 11, in Armistead, *Five Hundred Thousand Strokes for Freedom*; Rosalie S. Calvert to "Dear Parents," Aug. 12, 1803, in Callcott, ed., *Mistress of Riversdale*, 55; Alex Fitzhugh to R. H. Dickinson & Bro., Feb. 24, 1846, Slavery Collection, AAS.

64. Lewis to Lucy A. Gaulden, Oct. 28, 1860, Palmore Papers, UVA.

65. J. B. Dandridge to William B. Giles, Apr. 8, 1796, Dandridge Letter, VHS; entry for Jan. 6, 1858, in Racine, ed., *Piedmont Farmer*, 71.

66. Mrs. Barringer to "my daughter," May 15, 1863, Barringer Papers, SHC; Louis D. DeSaussure to Frederick [illegible], Feb. 11, 1854, DeSaussure Papers, USC; Romeo Young to "Dear Master," Dec. 3, 1860, Langdon, Young, and Meares Papers, SHC.

67. Tayler to Elizabeth F. Blyth, Sept. 2, 1838, in Easterby, ed., *South Carolina Rice Plantation*, 339.

68. Lester to Patsey Padison, Aug. 29, 1857, Allred Papers, DU.

69. For a full account of the William and Kate incident, see the many letters between Charles Jones and his parents, the Reverend Charles and Mary Jones, in Myers, ed., *Children of Pride*, 178, 186–87, 996–1028, 1310, 1338.

70. Hall quoted in Blassingame, *Slave Community*, 297–98.

71. Interview of Maggie Pinkard in Rawick, ed., *American Slave*, supp. 1, 12:257; interview of Stephen Williams in Mellon, ed., *Bullwhip Days*, 290; Bruce Grit [John Bruce], "Sketch of Childhood under Slavery," n.d., Bruce Collection, SC. For a good account of slave religion and the role it played in helping individuals to survive a sale, see Raboteau, *Slave Religion*, esp. chaps. 5–6.

72. Douglass, *My Bondage and My Freedom*, 99; Brown, *Narrative of William W. Brown*, 51; interview of Emma Howard quoted in Levine, *Black Culture and Black Consciousness*, 15. For a good account of slave songs and the role they played in helping individuals to survive a sale, see Levine, esp. chap. 1.

73. For a sampling of the literature on the slave family, see Blassingame, *Slave Community*, esp. chap. 4; Genovese, *Roll, Jordan, Roll*; Gutman, *Black Family*; White, *Ar'n't I a Woman?*; Malone, *Sweet Chariot*; Stevenson, *Life in Black and White*; and Schwartz, *Born in Bondage*.

74. Gutman, *Black Family*, 124–28, chap. 5; Holt, "Symbol, Memory, and Service," 197–99; Malone, *Sweet Chariot*, 240; Kemble, *Journal of a Residence*, 204–5.

75. Thomas W. Burton to William Long, Dec. 29, 1845, Long Papers, NCSA; Pheobia and Cash to Delions, Mar. 17, 1857, in Starobin, ed., *Blacks in Bondage*, 57.

76. Scriven to Dinah Jones, Sept. 19, 1858, in Starobin, ed., *Blacks in Bondage*, 58.

77. T. T. Bradley to A. Higgans, July 11, 1859, quoted in Cassity, "Slaves, Families, and 'Living Space,'" 209.

78. Ducket quoted in Gutman, *Black Family*, 144; Matilda Gurley to Jane Gurley, Sept. 9, 1830, Gurley Papers, SHC; owner of Old Nancy to Thomas Davis, Sept. 17, 1824, Davis Papers, UVA.

79. James M. Gilbert to Lewis Thompson, Mar. 14, 1860, Thompson Papers, SHC.

80. Blair to "My Dear Husband," Apr. 8, 1861, Pugh-Williams-Mayes Papers, LSU.

81. T. D. Jones to Eliza, Sept. 7, 1860, Butler Papers, LSU; Jane Dennis to "my dear daughter," Oct. 6, 1861, ibid.

82. Lenn to Memory, Nov. 30, 1857, Elliot Papers, FSU.

83. Douglass, *My Bondage and My Freedom*, 37–38.

84. E. A. Edwards to Z. B. Oakes, Apr. 14, 1857, Oakes Papers, BPL.

Epilogue

1. *New-York Tribune*, Apr. 4, 1865.

2. *Christian Record* (Philadelphia), Apr. 22, 1865; Litwack, *Been in the Storm So Long*, 169.

3. Josiah M. Perus to Phebe, Oct. 6, 1862, Barrett Papers, UVA. Bernard Lynch's slave pen in St. Louis was also used to house Confederate prisoners of war; see Trexler, *Slavery in Missouri*, 49.

4. Coleman, *Slavery Times in Kentucky*, 164; Foner, *Reconstruction*, 97; Corey, *History of the Richmond Theological Seminary*, 77.

5. Unknown agent quoted in Foner, *Reconstruction*, 82; Litwack, *Been in the Storm So Long*, 229–47.

6. Hawkins Wilson letters, both May 11, 1867, quoted in Berlin and Rowland, eds., *Families and Freedom*, 17–20.

7. J. H. Nichols to William Peacock, Jan. 31, 1892, Kelly Letter, MDAH; Johnson, "Looking for Lost Kin"; Foner, *Reconstruction*, 84.

8. Interview of William Hamilton in Tyler and Murphy, eds., *Slave Narratives of Texas*, 10; interview of Carol A. Randall in Perdue et al., eds., *Weevils in the Wheat*, 236; interview of Sylvia Cannon in Rawick, ed., *American Slave*, vol. 2, part 1, 188; interview of Lorenzo L. Ivy in Perdue et al., eds., *Weevils in the Wheat*, 153; interview of Patience M. Avery in ibid., 15.

9. Drew, ed., *North-Side View of Slavery*, 283–84; Swint, ed., *Dear Ones at Home*, 124; interview of Anna Harris in Perdue et al., eds., *Weevils in the Wheat*, 128.

10. Munford, *Virginia's Attitude toward Slavery and Secession*, 101–2; *Charleston Courier*, May 27, 1871; Charleston *News and Courier*, Feb. 4, 1899; Drago, ed., *Broke by the War*, 6, 11. See also Tadman, "Hidden History of Slave Trading," 20.

11. Coleman, *Slavery Times in Kentucky*, 164n. For early defenders of Forrest, see Wyeth, *That Devil Forrest*; and Henry, *"First with the Most" Forrest*.

12. Johnson, *Soul by Soul*, 55; Silas and R. F. Omohundro Sales Book, UVA; http://web.wm.edu/oieahc/spon.html; http://www.omohundros.com/lineagechart. In 1996, the Institute of Early American History & Culture added "Omohundro" to its name thanks to a generous donation by Mr. and Mrs. Malvern H. Omohundro, Jr. Mr. Omohundro's grandfather was John Burwell Omohundro, who was a younger brother of the slave traders Silas and Richard.

13. Drago and Melnick, "Old Slave Mart Museum."

14. The designation of "luxury boutique hotel" comes from the St. James Hotel Web page; see http://saintjameshotel.com.

15. Letter from Jim Barnett, director, Division of Historic Properties, Mississippi Department of Archives and History, Mar. 17, 2004.

Appendix A

1. Collins, *Domestic Slave Trade*, chap. 3.

2. Phillips, *Life and Labor in the Old South*, 158; Gray, *History of Agriculture*, chap. 28.

3. Most of Bancroft's calculations were for individual states, although he did estimate that 198,390 slaves were transported in the interstate trade during the 1850s. Using his rate of 70 percent, the total number of individuals forcibly removed during the decade would then equal 283,414. Bancroft, *Slave Trading*, chap. 18.

4. Stampp, *Peculiar Institution*, chap. 6; Elkins, *Slavery*, 236–37; Wade, *Slavery in the Cities*, 197–206; Genovese, *Political Economy of Slavery*, esp. 136–44.

5. Evans estimated the total interstate movement of slaves during the 1830s at 320,000; during the 1840s, 223,000; and during the 1850s, 279,500. Conrad and Meyer, "Economics of Slavery"; Evans, "Some Economic Aspects of the Slave Trade."

6. Calderhead, "Border State Slave Trade." For another account arguing against an extensive interstate trade, although not mentioning Bancroft by name and based on cursory evidence, see Miller, "Importance of the Slave Trade."

7. Fogel and Engerman broke down their estimate of the total slave movement as follows: 1820s, 121,000; 1830s, 223,000; 1840s, 149,000; and 1850s, 193,000. Fogel and Engerman, *Time on the Cross*, 1:44–58; 2:43–48, 53.

8. Gutman, *Slavery and the Numbers Game*, 102–11.

9. Herbert Gutman and Richard Sutch, "The Slave Family: Protected Agent of Capitalist Masters or Victim of the Slave Trade?" in David et al., *Reckoning with Slavery*, 94–133; Sutch, "Breeding of Slaves for Sale."

10. Sweig, "Reassessing the Interstate Slave Trade."

11. Russell, "Sale Day in South Carolina," 57–62; Calderhead, "Border State Slave Trade," 47.

12. It should also be noted that Freudenberger and Pritchett had records for more Deep South slave sales in one year from Kent County, Maryland (eighty-three), than Calderhead calculated for the entire decade (seventy-five). Freudenberger and Pritchett, "Domestic Slave Trade"; Calderhead, "Border State Slave Trade," 51.

13. In their study, Freudenberger and Pritchett found that more than 72 percent of the slaves imported into the Louisiana sugar parishes in 1830 were male. That same year, only 55 percent of the slaves imported into the state's cotton parishes were male. Tadman, *Speculators and Slaves*, 22–25; Freudenberger and Pritchett, "Domestic Slave Trade," 451–52.

14. Tadman, *Speculators and Slaves*, chap. 2.

15. Although Robert Fogel has recently revised some of his earlier findings, he has not significantly changed the figures in question here. His totals for the overall slave migration are identical to those cited in *Time on the Cross*, and while admitting in the main text that estimates vary for the magnitude of the interregional slave trade, his evidence and methods companion volume argues that the computations employed in the earlier work are still the most reliable. Fogel, *Without Consent or Contract*, 65–67; *Evidence and Methods*, 195–99.

16. According to Tadman, "Had my calculations made greater allowance for subregions within states (rather than generally taking whole states as net importing or net

exporting blocs), even higher totals would have been indicated"; *Speculators and Slaves*, 41–42.

Appendix B

1. Collins, *Domestic Slave Trade*; Bancroft, *Slave Trading*, 403–4; Phillips, *American Negro Slavery*, 190–92; Stampp, *Peculiar Institution*, 237.

2. According to Calderhead's data, in the eight counties studied, a total of 5,037 slaves were sold and 810 of them were sold south. Therefore, the ratio of local sales (4,227) to sales south was 5.2 to 1. Calderhead, "Border State Slave Trade," 51.

3. Fogel and Engerman, *Time on the Cross*, 1:53, 2:53.

4. In truth, an annual sales rate of 1.92 percent would average out to more than 52,500 sales per year for a total of more than 2.1 million sales over the forty-year period. This would equal, on average, a slave sale once every 3.4 minutes. Gutman, *Slavery and the Numbers Game*, 124–26.

5. Herbert Gutman and Richard Sutch, "The Slave Family: Protected Agent of Capitalist Masters or Victim of the Slave Trade?" in David et al., *Reckoning with Slavery*, 94–133.

6. Tadman, *Speculators and Slaves*, 112, 120. Interestingly, Tadman made no mention of the local trade in his chapter "The Scale of Negro Speculation."

7. Russell's work is extremely helpful for extrapolating information from Tadman's footnotes. Unfortunately, there are several mathematical errors in his text. Therefore, while I have followed his method for extracting Tadman's data, I have corrected his figures where appropriate and made some additional calculations of my own. Russell, "Sale Day in South Carolina," 65; Tadman, *Speculators and Slaves*, 120.

8. It appears that when calculating the number of local, noncourt sales, Russell figured 40 percent of the local court sales instead of 40 percent of the total local sales. This dropped his final estimates to 232,307 slave sales and an average sales rate of 1.70 percent. Russell, "Sale Day in South Carolina," 65–74.

9. For a good account of the problematic nature of slavery in Maryland, see Fields, *Slavery and Freedom on the Middle Ground*. Fields also argues that a brisk local trade predominated in Maryland, however, except for some minor revisions, she bases her argument on Calderhead's study.

10. The closest thing to quantitative evidence for slave sales in a slave-importing state can be found in McGettigan, "Boone County Slaves." Included in this study of a slave-importing county in Missouri is a sample of 1,078 bills of sale taken primarily from probate records. McGettigan argues that 98 percent of these sales went to local buyers. While he is probably correct that a majority of sales were local, his sample most likely suffers from the same problem of undercounting interstate sales that mars Calderhead's study. Nevertheless, these records do indicate that for the years 1830–1860, at least 0.82 percent of the county's slave population was sold each year. While this figure is not necessarily high in itself, it is derived from only a sample of the records, and the actual total was undoubtedly much greater. For another study, albeit without much quantitative evidence, which argues that an active slave trade,

NOTE TO PAGE 296

both local and interstate, was present in this part of Missouri, see Hurt, *Agriculture and Slavery*, 223–37.

For similar studies arguing that an active slave trade was present in the other slave-importing states, see Sydnor, *Slavery in Mississippi*, chap. 7; Sellers, *Slavery in Alabama*, chap. 5; Taylor, *Slavery in Arkansas*, chap. 5; Taylor, *Slavery in Louisiana*, chap. 2; Smith, *Slavery in Florida*, chap. 3; and Campbell, *Empire for Slavery*, chaps. 3–4. For similar studies arguing that an active slave trade was present in other slave-exporting and transitional states, see Flanders, *Slavery in Georgia*, chap. 8; Mooney, *Slavery in Tennessee*, chap. 2; and Coleman, *Slavery Times in Kentucky*, chaps. 5–7.

BIBLIOGRAPHY

Manuscript Collections

ALABAMA DEPARTMENT OF ARCHIVES AND HISTORY

James Dellet Papers
H. C. Nixon Papers
William K. Oliver Papers
Walker Family Papers

AMERICAN ANTIQUARIAN SOCIETY

William B. Banister Diary
Newton Family Papers
Slavery in the United States Collection

BOSTON PUBLIC LIBRARY

Anti-Slavery Convention of American Women. *Circular to the Societies of Anti-Slavery Women in the United States,* n.p., n.d.
Anti-Slavery Letters Written to W. L. Garrison and Others
Ziba B. Oakes Papers
Slave Trade Papers

CHICAGO HISTORICAL SOCIETY

Hector Davis & Co. Record Books
Richard H. Dickinson Papers
Julius Frankel Papers
L. C. Robards & Bro. Account Book
Slavery Collection

COLUMBIA UNIVERSITY

Frederic Bancroft Papers

DUKE UNIVERSITY

Joseph Allred Papers
Angus R. Blakey Papers
Archibald H. Boyd Papers
John G. Brodnax Papers
Campbell Family Papers
William Crow Letters
John E. Dennis Papers

Joseph Dickinson Papers
Joseph and Washington Dickinson Papers
Obadiah Fields Papers
William A. J. Finney Papers
John A. Forsyth Papers
Benjamin Franklin Papers
Tyre Glen Papers
Robert S. Gracey Papers
William H. Hatchett Papers
Edward Brodnax and Davis S. Hicks Papers
Jarratt-Puryear Family Papers
Franklin G. Kimball Papers
Eugene Marshall Diary
Jesse Mercer Papers
James A. Mitchell Papers
Negro Collection
Francis W. Pickens Papers
William C. Fitzhugh Powell Papers
Rankin-Parker Papers
David S. Reid Papers
Francis E. Rives Papers
Langhorne Scruggs Papers
James A. Tutt Papers
John J. Wherry Papers
Floyd L. Whitehead Papers
Samuel O. Wood Papers
Francis C. Yarnall Papers

ESSEX INSTITUTE LIBRARY

Joseph and Joshua Grafton Papers
"Slavery and the Slave Trade in the District of Columbia," broadside, n.p., n.d.
Ward Family Papers
Waters Family Papers

FLORIDA STATE UNIVERSITY

Elliot Family Papers
Olin Norwood Collection

HARVARD UNIVERSITY

Paul Pascal Papers

LIBRARY OF CONGRESS

Susan B. Anthony Papers
Black History Collection
Cornelius Chase Family Papers
Franklin H. Elmore Papers

"Slave Market of America," broadside, New York, 1836

LOUISIANA STATE UNIVERSITY

John H. Bills and Family Papers
Butler Family Papers
Lemuel P. Conner and Family Papers
Facsimile Collection
John W. Gurley Papers
Amos Kent Papers
William Minor Papers
Samuel Plaisted Correspondence
Alexander F. Pugh Papers
Pugh-Williams-Mayes Papers
Anton Reiff Journal
Slave Sale Document, court order, Nov. 5, 1849
Slavery Collection
Douglas Walworth Papers

MARYLAND HISTORICAL SOCIETY

W. M. Beall Letter
Sidney G. Fisher's Mount Harmon Diaries

MARYLAND STATE ARCHIVES

Maryland Governor and Council, Pardon Papers

MASSACHUSETTS HISTORICAL SOCIETY

Adams Family Papers

MISSISSIPPI DEPARTMENT OF ARCHIVES AND HISTORY

Peggie P. Kelly Letter
James T. Magruder Papers
Miscellaneous Manuscript Collection
Panther Burn Plantation Record Book
Henry E. Sizer Papers
Slavery Collection

MISSOURI HISTORICAL SOCIETY

Benoist-Charleville Papers
Nathan Brown Letterbook
Chinn Collection
Chouteau Collection
William C. Lane Collection
Abiel Leonard Papers
Lucas Collection
Lynch Broadside, Jan. 1, 1858
Slavery Collection

Dr. John F. Snyder Collection
Winn Family Papers

NATIONAL ARCHIVES

Inward Slave Manifests, New Orleans, Record Group 36, U.S. Customs Service
Outward Slave Manifests, New Orleans, Record Group 36, U.S. Customs Service

NEW ORLEANS NOTARIAL ARCHIVES

Certificates of Good Character

NEW ORLEANS PUBLIC LIBRARY

Benjamin Kendig Scrapbook
"Census of Merchants," New Orleans Treasurer's Office, 1854
New Orleans Conseil de Ville, Ordinances and Resolutions

NEW-YORK HISTORICAL SOCIETY

Bolton, Dickens & Co. Records
William D. Ellis Papers
New York Manumission Society, "Minutes"

NORTH CAROLINA STATE ARCHIVES

Badgett Family Papers
Asa Biggs Papers
John G. Blount Papers
John W. Bond Papers
Elias W. Ferguson Papers
A. Hopkins Letter
Southgate Jones Papers
William Long Papers
Archibald S. McMillan Collection
Mary J. Rogers Collection
Joseph S. Totten Papers
Randolph Webb Papers
John M. Winstead Letter

OLD SLAVE MART MUSEUM

Slavery Collection

ROSENBERG LIBRARY

Thomas M. League Papers
Samuel M. Williams Papers

SCHOMBURG CENTER FOR RESEARCH IN BLACK CULTURE

John E. Bruce Collection

South Carolina Historical Society

Hutson-Lee Papers
Alonzo J. White Record Book

South Carolina State Archives

General Assembly Papers
Presentments to the Grand Jury

Southern Historical Collection

Rice C. Ballard Papers
Daniel M. Barringer Papers
John H. Bills Papers
Farish Carter Papers
Andrew Flynn Plantation Book
Jane Gurley Papers
James T. Harrison Papers
Ernest Haywood Collection
E. V. Howell Papers
Isaac Jarratt Papers
Langdon, Young, and Meares Family Papers
Francis T. Leak Papers
Miscellaneous Letters
Neal Family Papers
Pettigrew Family Papers
Quitman Family Papers
Lewis Thompson Papers
A. and A. T. Walker Account Book
William H. Wills Papers

Tennessee State Library and Archives

Laura L. Robertson Papers
Small Collections: Newell Papers

Tulane University

Joseph S. Copes Papers
Kuntz Collection
John McDonogh Papers
William N. Mercer Papers
Ambert O. Remington Letters

University of Florida

Jimmy Gibbs Papers
W. S. Lawton & Co. Papers

UNIVERSITY OF GEORGIA
Carr Collection
William F. Parker Diary

UNIVERSITY OF KENTUCKY
William M. Pratt Diary

UNIVERSITY OF NEW ORLEANS
Supreme Court of Louisiana Collection

UNIVERSITY OF SOUTH CAROLINA
Sylvester Bleckley Papers
Louis D. DeSaussure Papers
Ford & Lloyd Broadside, Feb. 1, 1853
Joseph J. Norton Papers
Charles P. Pelham Broadside, Jan. 2, 1854
John D. Warren Papers
Thomas Waties Papers

UNIVERSITY OF VIRGINIA
Clifton W. Barrett Papers
Carter-Smith Papers
Isaac Davis Papers
Gilliam Family Papers
Gooch Family Papers
Grinnan Family Papers
B. V. Liffey Letter
Lynchburg Common Council Ledger
Morton-Halsey Family Papers
Silas and R. F. Omohundro Slave Sales Book
Palmore Family Papers
Peter Family Papers
Pocket Plantation Papers
Rainey Family Papers
Tayloe Family Papers
Thornhill Family and Thomas S. Bocock Papers
Floyd L. Whitehead Papers

VIRGINIA HISTORICAL SOCIETY
C. Abner Letter
Benjamin Brand Papers
Carter Family Papers
Holmes Conrad Papers
Julius B. Dandridge Letter

Asa D. Dickinson Papers
Harrison Family Papers
Holladay Family Papers
Joseph Meek Papers
Preston Family Papers

VIRGINIA STATE LIBRARY
Virginia County Records
Virginia Executive Letterbooks
Virginia Executive Records

XAVIER UNIVERSITY
Charles F. Heartman Collection

Government Documents

Annals of Congress
Congressional Globe
Massachusetts General Court, 1838 sess., Senate Doc. 87. *Report on the Powers and Duties of Congress upon the Subject of Slavery and the Slave Trade.*
South Carolina House of Representatives. *Report of the Minority of the Special Committee of Seven, to Whom Was Referred So Much of His Late Excellency's Message No. 1, as Relates to Slavery and the Slave Trade.* Columbia, SC, 1857.
———. *Report of the Special Committee of the House of Representatives, of South Carolina, on So Much of the Message of His Excellency Gov. Jas. H. Adams, as Relates to Slavery and the Slave Trade.* Columbia, SC, 1857.
U.S. Bureau of the Census. *Agriculture of the United States in 1860: Compiled from the Original Returns of the Eighth Census, under the Direction of the Secretary of the Interior.* Washington, DC, 1864.
———. *Historical Statistics of the United States: Colonial Times to 1957.* Washington, DC, 1960.
———. *Negro Population, 1790–1915.* 1918; reprint, New York, 1968.
———. *Preliminary Report on the Eighth Census, 1860.* Washington, DC, 1862.

Newspapers and Periodicals

ALABAMA
Huntsville *Democrat*
Huntsville *Southern Advocate*
Mobile Advertiser
Mobile Register
Montgomery *Alabama Journal*
Montgomery *Confederation*

DISTRICT OF COLUMBIA

Alexandria *Phenix Gazette*
National Intelligencer (Washington)
Washington *Globe*
Washington Union

FLORIDA

Tallahassee *Floridian and Journal*

GEORGIA

Augusta *Chronicle and Sentinel*
Gazette of the State of Georgia (Savannah)
Georgia Gazette (Savannah)
Milledgeville *Federal Union*
Savannah Republican

KENTUCKY

Lexington *Kentucky Reporter*
Lexington *Kentucky Statesman*
Lexington Observer and Reporter
Louisville Courier
Louisville Journal
Paris *Western Citizen*
Western Luminary (Lexington)

LOUISIANA

Alexandria *Louisiana Democrat*
Baton Rouge *Advocate*
Baton-Rouge Gazette
Baton Rouge *Gazette and Comet*
Concordia Intelligencer (Vidalia)
DeBow's Review (New Orleans)
New-Orleans Argus
New Orleans Bee
New Orleans Crescent
New Orleans *Delta*
New Orleans *Picayune*
St. Francisville *Louisiana Chronicle*

MARYLAND

Baltimore Republican
Baltimore Republican and Commercial Advertiser
Baltimore *Sun*
Cambridge Chronicle
Centreville Times and Eastern-Shore Public Advertiser

Cumberland *Maryland Advocate*
Federal Gazette and Baltimore Advertiser
Frederick-Town *Herald*
Genius of Universal Emancipation (Greeneville, TN, 1821–1824; Baltimore, 1824–1839)
Maryland Journal and Baltimore Advertiser
Niles' Register (Baltimore)
Snow-Hill Messenger and Worcester County Advertiser

MASSACHUSETTS

American Anti-Slavery Almanac (Boston and New York, NY)
Boston Gazette
Boston Whig
Liberator (Boston)

MISSISSIPPI

Aberdeen *Sunny South*
Jackson *Mississippian*
Mississippi Free Trader and Natchez Gazette
Natchez Courier
Natchez *Mississippi Free Trader*
Vicksburg Whig

MISSOURI

St. Louis *Missouri Democrat*
St. Louis *Missouri Republican*

NEW YORK

American Anti-Slavery Reporter
Anti-Slavery Record
Emancipator
Freedom's Journal
New York Evangelist
New-York Gazette; or, the Weekly Post-Boy
New York Herald
New York Times
New-York Tribune
Radical Abolitionist
Slave's Friend
United States Magazine and Democratic Review

NORTH CAROLINA

Wilmington Journal

OHIO

Western Law Journal (Cincinnati)

PENNSYLVANIA

Christian Recorder (Philadelphia)
Pennsylvania Gazette (Philadelphia)

SOUTH CAROLINA

Charleston *City Gazette and Daily Advertiser*
Charleston *Courier*
Charleston *Mercury*
Charleston *News and Courier*
South-Carolina Gazette and Country Journal (Charles-Town)

TENNESSEE

Memphis Appeal
Memphis Avalanche
Memphis Eagle
Memphis Eagle and Enquirer
Memphis *Morning Bulletin*
Nashville *Republican Banner*

TEXAS

Austin *State Gazette*
Palestine *Trinity Advocate*

VIRGINIA

Alexandria Gazette and Virginia Advertiser
Farmers' Register (Petersburg)
Leesburg *Genius of Liberty*
Lynchburg Virginian
Richmond *Dispatch*
Richmond *Enquirer*
Richmond *Examiner*
Richmond Whig and Public Advertiser
Virginia Gazette (Williamsburg)
Virginia Gazette and Weekly Advertiser (Richmond)
Virginia Independent Chronicle (Richmond)

Primary Sources, Published

Abdy, Edward S. *Journal of a Residence and Tour in the United States of North America, from April, 1833, to October, 1834.* 3 vols. London, 1835.
American Anti-Slavery Society. *Declaration of Sentiments and Constitution of the American Anti-Slavery Society.* New York, 1835.
———. *First Annual Report of the American Anti-Slavery Society.* New York, 1834.
———. *Fourth Annual Report of the American Anti-Slavery Society.* New York, 1837.

Andrews, Ethan A. *Slavery and the Domestic Slave-Trade in the United States.* Boston, 1836.

Anti-Slavery Convention of American Women. *Proceedings of the Third Anti-Slavery Convention of American Women, Held in Philadelphia, May 1st, 2d and 3d, 1839.* Philadelphia, 1839.

Arfwedson, Carl D. *The United States and Canada, in 1832, 1833, and 1834.* 2 vols. London, 1834.

Armistead, Wilson. *Five Hundred Thousand Strokes for Freedom: A Series of Anti-Slavery Tracts of Which Half a Million Are Now First Issued by the Friends of the Negro.* London, 1853.

Ball, Charles. *Slavery in the United States: A Narrative of the Life and Adventures of Charles Ball, a Black Man.* New York, 1837.

Ball, J. P. *Ball's Splendid Mammoth Pictorial Tour of the United States.* Cincinnati, OH, 1855.

Barnes, Gilbert H., and Dwight L. Dumond, eds. *Letters of Theodore Dwight Weld, Angelina Grimké Weld, and Sarah Grimké, 1822–1844.* 2 vols. New York, 1934.

Basler, Roy P., ed. *The Collected Works of Abraham Lincoln.* 8 vols. New Brunswick, NJ, 1953.

Bayard, Ferdinand M. *Voyage dans l'Intérieur des États-Unis, á Bath, Winchester, dans la Vallée de Shenandoah, etc., etc., pendant l'été de 1791.* 2d ed. Paris, 1798.

Beecher, Catharine E. *An Essay on Slavery and Abolitionism, with Reference to the Duty of American Females.* Philadelphia, 1837.

Berlin, Ira, and Leslie S. Rowland, eds. *Families and Freedom: A Documentary History of African-American Kinship in the Civil War.* New York, 1997.

Bernhard, Duke of Saxe-Weimar Eisenach. *Travels through North America, during the Years 1825 and 1826.* 2 vols. Philadelphia, 1828.

Betts, Edwin M., ed. *Thomas Jefferson's Farm Book.* Princeton, NJ, 1953.

Bibb, Henry. *Narrative of the Life and Adventures of Henry Bibb, an American Slave.* 3d ed. New York, 1850.

Birney, James G. *The American Churches, the Bulwarks of American Slavery.* 3d ed. 1840; reprint, Concord, NH, 1885.

Blanchard, Jonathan, and N. L. Rice. *A Debate on Slavery: Held in the City of Cincinnati, on the First, Second, Third, and Sixth Days of October, 1845.* Cincinnati, OH, 1846.

Blane, William N. *An Excursion through the United States and Canada during the Years 1822–23.* London, 1824.

Blassingame, John W., ed. *Frederick Douglass Papers.* 5 vols. New Haven, CT, 1979–1992.

———. *Slave Testimony: Two Centuries of Letters, Speeches, Interviews, and Autobiographies.* Baton Rouge, LA, 1977.

Bourne, George. *Picture of Slavery in the United States of America.* Middletown, CT, 1834.

[Bourne, George]. *Slavery Illustrated in Its Effects upon Woman and Domestic Society.* Boston, 1837.

Bowditch, William I. *Slavery and the Constitution.* Boston, 1849.

Bremer, Fredrika. *The Homes of the New World: Impressions of America.* 2 vols. New York, 1853.

Brown, Henry Box. *Narrative of Henry Box Brown.* Boston, 1849.

Brown, John. *Slave Life in Georgia: A Narrative of the Life, Sufferings, and Escape of John Brown, a Fugitive Slave.* Ed. F. N. Boney. 1855; reprint, Savannah, GA, 1972.

Brown, William Wells. *Narrative of William W. Brown, a Fugitive Slave.* Boston, 1847.

Bruce, H. C. *The New Man: Twenty-Nine Years a Slave, Twenty-Nine Years a Free Man.* 1895; reprint, New York, 1969.

Bruns, Roger, ed. *Am I Not a Man and a Brother: The Antislavery Crusade of Revolutionary America, 1688–1788.* New York, 1977.

Buckingham, James S. *The Slave States of America.* 2 vols. London, 1842.

Cairnes, John E. *The Slave Power: Its Character, Career, and Probable Designs.* New York, 1862.

Callcott, Margaret L., ed. *Mistress of Riversdale: The Plantation Letters of Rosalie Stier Calvert, 1795–1821.* Baltimore, MD, 1991.

Carey, Henry C. *The Slave Trade, Domestic and Foreign: Why It Exists, and How It May Be Extinguished.* Philadelphia, 1853.

Carpenter, Russell L. *Observations on American Slavery: After a Year's Tour in the United States.* London, 1852.

Catterall, Helen T., ed. *Judicial Cases Concerning American Slavery and the Negro.* 5 vols. Washington, DC, 1926–1937.

Ceplair, Larry, ed. *The Public Years of Sarah and Angelina Grimké: Selected Writings, 1835–1839.* New York, 1989.

Chadwick, Thomas W., ed. "The Diary of Samuel Edward Burges, 1860–1862." *South Carolina Historical and Genealogical Magazine* 48 (Apr., July, Aug. 1947): 63–75, 141–63, 206–18.

Chambers, William. *Things as They Are in America.* 1854; reprint, New York, 1968.

Child, Lydia Maria. *An Appeal in Favor of That Class of Americans Called Africans.* Boston, 1833.

Child, Lydia Maria, comp. *The Patriarchal Institution, as Described by Members of Its Own Family.* New York, 1860.

The Child's Anti-Slavery Book: Containing a Few Words about American Slave Children, and Stories of Slave-Life. New York, 1859.

The Child's Book on Slavery; or, Slavery Made Plain. Cincinnati, OH, 1857.

Clarke, Lewis. *Narrative of the Sufferings of Lewis Clarke, during a Captivity of More Than Twenty-Five Years, among the Algerines of Kentucky, One of the So-Called Christian States of North America.* Boston, 1845.

Clay, Henry. *Remarks of Mr. Clay, of Kentucky, on Introducing His Propositions to Compromise, on the Slavery Question.* Washington, DC, 1850.

Coffin, Charles C. *The Boys of '61; or, Four Years of Fighting.* 1866; reprint, Boston, 1881.

Collins, Elizabeth. *Memories of the Southern States.* Taunton, England, 1865.

Collins, John A. *The Anti-Slavery Picknick: A Collection of Speeches, Poems, Dialogues and Songs; Intended for Use in Schools and Anti-Slavery Meetings.* Boston, 1842.

Colton, Calvin, ed. *The Works of Henry Clay: Comprising His Life, Correspondence and Speeches.* 10 vols. New York, 1904.

Conrad, Robert E., ed. *In the Hands of Strangers: Readings on Foreign and Domestic Slave Trading and the Crisis of the Union.* University Park, PA, 2001.

Cooke, Jacob E., ed. *The Federalist.* Middletown, CT, 1961.

Corey, Charles H. *A History of the Richmond Theological Seminary, with Reminiscences of Thirty Years' Work among the Colored People of the South.* Richmond, VA, 1895.

"Correspondence, between the Hon. F. H. Elmore, One of the South Carolina Delegation in Congress, and James G. Birney, One of the Secretaries of the American Anti-Slavery Society." *Anti-Slavery Examiner,* No. 8. New York, 1838.

Craft, William. *Running a Thousand Miles for Freedom; or, The Escape of William and Ellen Craft from Slavery.* London, 1860.

Davies, Ebenezer. *American Scenes—and Christian Slavery.* London, 1849.

Davis, Edwin A., ed. *Plantation Life in the Florida Parishes of Louisiana, 1836–1846, as Reflected in the Diary of Bennet H. Barrow.* 1943; reprint, New York, 1967.

Davis, John. *Travels of John Davis in the United States of America, 1798 to 1802.* Ed. John V. Cheney. 2 vols. 1803; reprint, Boston, 1910.

Dew, Thomas R. *Review of the Debate in the Virginia Legislature of 1831 and 1832.* Richmond, VA, 1832.

Dickens, Charles. *American Notes.* 1842; reprint, London, 1966.

Douglass, Frederick. *My Bondage and My Freedom.* 1855; reprint, New York, 1969.

———. *Narrative of the Life of Frederick Douglass, an American Slave.* 1845; reprint, New York, 1968.

Drago, Edmund L., ed. *Broke by the War: Letters of a Slave Trader.* Columbia, SC, 1991.

Drew, Benjamin, ed. *A North-Side View of Slavery: The Refugee; or, The Narratives of Fugitive Slaves in Canada.* Boston, 1856.

Drumgoold, Kate. *A Slave Girl's Story.* Brooklyn, 1898. In *Six Women's Slave Narratives,* ed. William L. Andrews. New York, 1988.

Dumond, Dwight L., ed. *Letters of James Gillespie Birney, 1831–1857.* 2 vols. New York, 1938.

Easterby, J. H., ed. *The South Carolina Rice Plantation, as Revealed in the Papers of Robert F. W. Allston.* Chicago, IL, 1945.

Emerson, Ralph Waldo. *Journals and Miscellaneous Notebooks.* Ed. William H. Gilman et al. 16 vols. Cambridge, MA, 1960–1982.

"Estimates of the Value of Slaves, 1815." *American Historical Review* 19 (July 1914): 813–38.

Evans, Estwick. *A Pedestrious Tour, of Four Thousand Miles, through the Western States and Territories, during the Winter and Spring of 1818.* Concord, NH, 1819.

Farrand, Max, ed. *The Records of the Federal Convention of 1787.* Rev. ed., 4 vols. New Haven, CT, 1966.

Faust, Drew G., ed. *The Ideology of Slavery: Proslavery Thought in the Antebellum South, 1830–1860.* Baton Rouge, LA, 1981.

Fearon, Henry B. *Sketches of America.* London, 1818.

Featherstonhaugh, George W. *Excursion through the Slave States.* 2 vols. London, 1844.

Female Anti-Slavery Society. *Constitution and Address of the Female Anti-Slavery Society of Chatham-Street Chapel.* New York, 1834.

Fitzpatrick, John C., ed. *The Writings of George Washington.* 39 vols. Washington, DC, 1931–1944.

Follen, Eliza L. *To Mothers in the Free States.* Anti-Slavery Tracts, No. 8. New York, 1855.

Ford, Paul L., ed. *The Works of Thomas Jefferson.* 12 vols. New York, 1904–1905.

A Former Resident of the Slave States. *Influence of Slavery upon the White Population.* Anti-Slavery Tracts, No. 9. New York, 1855.

Garrison, Wendell P., and Francis J. Garrison. *William Lloyd Garrison, 1805–1879: The Story of His Life Told by His Children*. 4 vols. New York, 1885–1889.

Giddings, Joshua R. *Speeches in Congress*. Boston, 1853.

Gloucester, Jeremiah. *An Oration, Delivered on January 1, 1823*. Philadelphia, 1823.

Goodell, William. *Views of American Constitutional Law, in Its Bearing upon American Slavery*. Utica, NY, 1844.

Grandy, Moses. *Narrative of the Life of Moses Grandy, Late a Slave in the United States of America*. 2d ed. Boston, 1844.

Gray, Thomas. *A Sermon Delivered in Boston, before the African Society, on 14th day of July, 1818; the Anniversary of the Abolition of the Slave Trade*. Boston, 1818.

Green, Beriah. *Chattel Principle: The Abhorrence of Jesus Christ and the Apostles; or, No Refuge for American Slavery in the New Testament*. New York, 1839.

Greenawalt, Bruce S., ed. "Unionists in Rockbridge County: The Correspondence of James Dorman Davidson Concerning the Virginia Secession Convention of 1861." *Virginia Magazine of History and Biography* 73 (Jan. 1965): 78–102.

Greene, Jack P., ed. *The Diary of Colonel Landon Carter of Sabine Hall, 1752–1778*. 2 vols. Charlottesville, VA, 1965.

Grimes, William. *Life of William Grimes, the Runaway Slave*. New York, 1825.

Grimké, Angelina E. *Appeal to the Christian Women of the South*. New York, 1836.

———. *An Appeal to the Women of the Nominally Free States, Issued by an Anti-Slavery Convention of American Women*. 2d ed. Boston, 1838.

Hall, Basil. *Travels in North America, in the Years 1827 and 1828*. 3 vols. Edinburgh, 1829.

Hamer, Philip, ed. *The Papers of Henry Laurens*. 15 vols. Columbia, SC, 1968– .

Hamilton, Thomas. *Men and Manners in America*. 2 vols. Edinburgh, 1833.

Henson, Josiah. *The Life of Josiah Henson, Formerly a Slave, Now an Inhabitant of Canada, as Narrated by Himself*. Boston, 1849.

Hogan, William R., and Edwin A. Davis, eds. *William Johnson's Natchez: The Ante-Bellum Diary of a Free Negro*. Baton Rouge, LA, 1951.

Hughes, Louis. *Thirty Years a Slave: From Bondage to Freedom*. Milwaukee, WI, 1897.

Hundley, Daniel R. *Social Relations in Our Southern States*. New York, 1860.

Hunt, Gaillard, ed. *The Writings of James Madison*. 9 vols. New York, 1900–1910.

"The Influence of the Slave Power." *Emancipator Extra*, Tract No. 3. Boston, 1843.

Ingraham, Joseph H. *The South-west, by a Yankee*. 2 vols. 1835; reprint, New York, 1968.

Jacobs, Donald M., ed. *Antebellum Black Newspapers*. Westport, CT, 1976.

Jacobs, Harriet A. *Incidents in the Life of a Slave Girl: Written by Herself*. Ed. Jean F. Yellin. 1861; reprint, Cambridge, MA, 1987.

Janson, Charles W. *The Stranger in America, 1793–1806*. 1807; reprint, New York, 1935.

Jay, William. *An Inquiry into the Character and Tendency of the American Colonization, and American Anti-Slavery Societies*. New York, 1835.

———. *Miscellaneous Writings on Slavery*. Boston, 1853.

———. *A View of the Action of the Federal Government, in Behalf of Slavery*. New York, 1839.

Jones, Absalom. *A Thanksgiving Sermon, Preached January 1, 1808, in St. Thomas's, or the African Episcopal Church, Philadelphia: on Account of the Abolition of the African Slave Trade, on that Day, by the Congress of the United States*. Philadelphia, 1808.

Jones, Thomas H. *Experience and Personal Narrative of Uncle Tom Jones; Who Was for Forty Years a Slave. Also the Surprising Adventures of Wild Tom, of the Island Retreat, a Fugitive Negro from South Carolina.* Boston, 185?.

Kaminski, John P., ed. *A Necessary Evil? Slavery and the Debate over the Constitution.* Madison, WI, 1995.

Kemble, Frances A. *Journal of a Residence on a Georgian Plantation in 1838–1839.* New York, 1863.

Lambert, John. *Travels through Canada, and the United States of North America.* 3d ed., 2 vols. London, 1816.

Lane, Lunsford. *The Narrative of Lunsford Lane, Formerly of Raleigh, N.C.* Boston, 1842.

"Letter of Gerrit Smith to Hon. Henry Clay." *Anti-Slavery Examiner,* No. 9. New York, 1839.

"Letter of Gerrit Smith to Rev. James Smylie, of the State of Mississippi." *Anti-Slavery Examiner,* No. 3. New York, 1837.

Mackay, Charles. *Life and Liberty in America.* 2 vols. London, 1859.

Marsh, Luther R., ed. *Writings and Speeches of Alvan Stewart, on Slavery.* New York, 1860.

Martineau, Harriet. *Retrospect of Western Travel.* 2 vols. London, 1838.

McKitrick, Eric L., ed. *Slavery Defended: The Views of the Old South.* Englewood Cliffs, NJ, 1963.

McLaughlin, Charles C., ed. *The Papers of Frederick Law Olmsted.* 6 vols. Baltimore, MD, 1977–1992.

Meats, Stephen, and Edwin T. Arnold, eds. *The Writings of Benjamin F. Perry.* 3 vols. Spartanburg, SC, 1980.

Mellon, James, ed. *Bullwhip Days: The Slaves Remember.* New York, 1988.

Memphis City Directory and General Business Advertiser. Memphis, TN, 1855.

Merrill, Walter M., and Louis Ruchames, eds. *The Letters of William Lloyd Garrison.* 6 vols. Cambridge, MA, 1971–1981.

Miller, Randall M., ed. *"Dear Master": Letters of a Slave Family.* Ithaca, NY, 1978.

Montgomery Directory for 1859–60. Montgomery, AL, 1859.

Morris, Thomas. "Speech of Hon. Thomas Morris, of Ohio, in Reply to the Speech of the Hon. Henry Clay, in Senate, February 9, 1839." *Anti-Slavery Examiner,* No. 10. New York, 1839.

Myers, Robert M., ed. *The Children of Pride: A True Story of Georgia and the Civil War.* New Haven, CT, 1972.

Nevins, Allan, ed. *The Diary of John Quincy Adams, 1794–1845.* New York, 1951.

New Hampshire Anti-Slavery Convention. *Proceedings of the N.H. Anti-Slavery Convention, Held in Concord, on the 11th & 12th of November, 1834.* Concord, NH, 1834.

Nichols, Charles H., ed. *Black Men in Chains: Narratives by Escaped Slaves.* New York, 1972.

Northern Dealers in Slaves. New York, 1839.

Northup, Solomon. *Twelve Years a Slave.* Ed. Sue Eakin and Joseph Logsdon. Baton Rouge, LA, 1968.

Olmsted, Frederick Law. *A Journey in the Back Country.* New York, 1860.

———. *A Journey in the Seaboard Slave States.* New York, 1856.

————. *A Journey through Texas; or, a Saddle-Trip on the Southwestern Frontier*. New York, 1857.

Owen, Thomas M., ed. *John Owen's Journal of His Removal from Virginia to Alabama in 1818*. Baltimore, MD, 1897.

Palfrey, John G. *The Inter-State Slave Trade*. Anti-Slavery Tracts, No. 5. New York, 1855.

Parrott, Russell. *Two Orations on the Abolition of the Slave Trade Delivered in Philadelphia in 1812 and 1816*. Philadelphia, 1969.

Pennington, James W. C. *The Fugitive Blacksmith; or, Events in the History of James W. C. Pennington*. 2d ed. London, 1849.

Perdue, Charles L., Thomas E. Barden, and Robert K. Phillips, eds. *Weevils in the Wheat: Interviews with Virginia Ex-Slaves*. Charlottesville, VA, 1976.

Phelps, Amos A. *Lectures on Slavery and Its Remedy*. Boston, 1834.

Phillips, Ulrich B., ed. *Plantation and Frontier Documents: 1649–1863*. 2 vols. Cleveland, OH, 1909.

Plumer, William. *Memorandum of Proceedings in the United States Senate, 1803–1807*. Ed. Everett S. Brown. New York, 1923.

Proceedings of a Convention of the Trustees of a Proposed University for the Southern States. Atlanta, GA, 1857.

Racine, Philip N., ed. *Piedmont Farmer: The Journals of David Golightly Harris, 1855–1870*. Knoxville, TN, 1990.

Rankin, John. *Letters on American Slavery, Addressed to Mr. Thomas Rankin, Merchant at Middlebrook, Augusta Co., VA*. Boston, 1833.

Rawick, George P., ed. *The American Slave: A Composite Autobiography*. 19 vols. Westport, CT, 1972.

Redpath, James. *The Roving Editor*. New York, 1859.

Reed, Andrew, and James Matheson. *A Narrative of the Visit to the American Churches, by the Deputation from the Congregational Union of England and Wales*. New York, 1835.

Ripley, C. Peter, ed. *The Black Abolitionist Papers*. 5 vols. Chapel Hill, NC, 1985–1992.

Robin, C. C. *Voyages dans l'Intérieur de la Louisiane, de la Floride Occidentale, et dans les Isles de la Martinique et de Saint-Domingue, pendant les Années 1802, 1803, 1804, 1805 et 1806*. 3 vols. Paris, 1807.

Rogers, Charlton H. *Incidents of Travel in the Southern States and Cuba*. New York, 1862.

Roper, Moses. *A Narrative of the Adventures and Escape of Moses Roper, from American Slavery*. Philadelphia, 1838.

Rosengarten, Theodore, ed. *Tombee: Portrait of a Cotton Planter*. New York, 1986.

Russell, Robert. *North America: Its Agriculture and Climate*. Edinburgh, 1857.

Schweninger, Loren, ed. *From Tennessee Slave to St. Louis Entrepreneur: The Autobiography of James Thomas*. Columbia, MO, 1984.

Sedgwick, Theodore. *Thoughts on the Proposed Annexation of Texas to the United States*. New York, 1844.

Slade, William. *Speech of Mr. Slade, of Vermont, on the Subject of the Abolition of Slavery and the Slave Trade within the District of Columbia; Delivered in the House of Representatives, December 23, 1835*. Washington, DC, 1836.

Slavery and the Slave Trade at the Nation's Capital. Liberty Tract, No. 1. New York, 1846.

Society of Friends. *An Address to Our Fellow Members of the Religious Society of Friends on the Subject of Slavery and the Slave-Trade in the Western World*. Philadelphia, 1849.

————. *A Brief Statement of the Rise and Progress of the Testimony of the Religious Society of Friends, against Slavery and the Slave Trade.* Philadelphia, 1843.

————. *An Exposition of the African Slave Trade, from the Year 1840, to 1850, Inclusive.* Philadelphia, 1851.

————. *Extracts and Observations on the Foreign Slave Trade.* Philadelphia, 1839.

————. *Facts and Observations Relative to the Participation of American Citizens in the African Slave Trade.* Philadelphia, 1841.

————. *Memorial of the Society of Friends, in Pennsylvania, New Jersey and Delaware, on the African Slave Trade.* Philadelphia, 1840.

————. *Slavery and the Domestic Slave Trade, in the United States.* Philadelphia, 1841.

————. *A View of the Present State of the African Slave Trade.* Philadelphia, 1824.

Spooner, Lysander. *The Unconstitutionality of Slavery.* Boston, 1845.

Spratt, Leonidas W. *The Foreign Slave Trade.* Charleston, SC, 1858.

————. *Speech upon the Foreign Slave Trade, before the Legislature of South Carolina.* Columbia, SC, 1858.

Starobin, Robert S., ed. *Blacks in Bondage: Letters of American Slaves.* New York, 1974.

Stirling, James. *Letters from the Slave States.* 1857; reprint, New York, 1969.

Stowe, Harriet Beecher. *The Key to Uncle Tom's Cabin; Presenting the Original Facts and Documents upon Which the Story is Founded.* Boston, 1853.

————. *Uncle Tom's Cabin; or, Life among the Lowly.* Ed. Ann Douglas. 1852; reprint, New York, 1981.

Stroyer, Jacob. *My Life in the South.* 4th ed. Salem, MA, 1898.

Sturge, Joseph. *A Visit to the United States in 1841.* Boston, 1842.

Swint, Henry L., ed. *Dear Ones at Home: Letters from Contraband Camps.* Nashville, TN, 1966.

Thompson, John. *The Life of John Thompson, a Fugitive Slave.* 1856; reprint, New York, 1968.

Thomson, Mortimer N. *Great Auction Sale of Slaves, at Savannah, Georgia, March 2d and 3d, 1859.* New York, 1859.

Thornton, Thomas C. *An Inquiry into the History of Slavery: Its Introduction into the United States, Causes of Its Continuance, and Remarks upon the Abolition Tracts of William E. Channing.* Baltimore, MD, 1841.

Tinling, Marion, ed. *The Correspondence of the Three William Byrds of Westover, Virginia, 1684–1776.* 2 vols. Charlottesville, VA, 1977.

Tocqueville, Alexis de. *Journey to America.* Ed. J. P. Mayer. New Haven, CT, 1959.

Torrey, Jesse. *A Portraiture of Domestic Slavery, in the United States.* Philadelphia, 1817.

Townsend, John. *The Doom of Slavery in the Union: Its Safety Out of It.* Charleston, SC, 1860.

Tyler, Ronnie C., and Lawrence R. Murphy, eds. *The Slave Narratives of Texas.* Austin, TX, 1974.

Watson, Henry. *Narrative of Henry Watson, a Fugitive Slave.* Boston, 1848.

Weld, Charles R. *A Vacation Tour in the United States and Canada.* London, 1855.

Weld, Isaac. *Travels Through the States of North America.* 2d ed., 2 vols. London, 1799.

Weld, Theodore D. *American Slavery As It Is: Testimony of a Thousand Witnesses.* New York, 1839.

———. *The Bible against Slavery: An Inquiry into the Patriarchal and Mosaic Systems on the Subject of Human Rights.* New York, 1837.

———. *The Power of Congress over the District of Columbia.* New York, 1838.

Weld, Theodore D., and James A. Thome. *Slavery and the Internal Slave Trade in the United States of North America.* London, 1841.

Weston, George M. *The Progress of Slavery in the United States.* Washington, DC, 1857.

Windley, Lathan A., ed. *Runaway Slave Advertisements: A Documentary History from the 1730s to 1790.* 4 vols. Westport, CT, 1983.

Wise, John S. *The End of an Era.* Boston, 1899.

Woodward, C. Vann, ed. *Mary Chesnut's Civil War.* New Haven, CT, 1981.

Wright, Louis B., and Marion Tinling, eds. *The Secret Diary of William Byrd of Westover, 1709–1712.* Richmond, VA, 1941.

Secondary Sources, Books

Abzug, Robert H. *Passionate Liberator: Theodore Dwight Weld and the Dilemma of Reform.* New York, 1980.

Alvarez, Eugene. *Travel on Southern Antebellum Railroads, 1828–1860.* University, AL, 1974.

Amos, Harriet E. *Cotton City: Urban Development in Antebellum Mobile.* University, AL, 1985.

Atack, Jeremy, and Peter Passell. *A New Economic View of American History from Colonial Times to 1940.* 2d ed. New York, 1994.

Bailyn, Bernard. *The Ideological Origins of the American Revolution.* Cambridge, MA, 1967.

Bancroft, Frederic. *Slave Trading in the Old South.* 1931; reprint, New York, 1959.

Beeman, Richard R. *The Evolution of the Southern Backcountry: A Case Study of Lunenburg County, Virginia, 1746–1832.* Philadelphia, 1984.

———. *Patrick Henry: A Biography.* New York, 1974.

Bell, Malcolm. *Major Butler's Legacy: Five Generations of a Slaveholding Family.* Athens, GA, 1987.

Berkhofer, Robert F. *The White Man's Indian: Images of the American Indian from Columbus to the Present.* New York, 1978.

Berlin, Ira. *Many Thousands Gone: The First Two Centuries of Slavery in North America.* Cambridge, MA, 1998.

Berlin, Ira, and Ronald Hoffman, eds. *Slavery and Freedom in the Age of the American Revolution.* Charlottesville, VA, 1983.

Blassingame, John W. *The Slave Community: Plantation Life in the Antebellum South.* Rev. ed. New York, 1979.

Blight, David W. *Race and Reunion: The Civil War in American Memory.* Cambridge, MA, 2001.

Bogger, Tommy L. *Free Blacks in Norfolk, Virginia, 1790–1860: The Darker Side of Freedom.* Charlottesville, VA, 1997.

Bowman, Shearer D. *Masters and Lords: Mid-19th-Century U.S. Planters and Prussian Junkers.* New York, 1993.

Bruchey, Stuart, ed. *Cotton and the Growth of the American Economy, 1790–1860.* New York, 1967.

Campbell, Randolph B. *An Empire for Slavery: The Peculiar Institution in Texas, 1821–1865.* Baton Rouge, LA, 1989.

Chaplin, Joyce E. *An Anxious Pursuit: Agricultural Innovation and Modernity in the Lower South, 1730–1815.* Chapel Hill, NC, 1993.

Chitty, Arthur B. *Reconstruction at Sewanee: The Founding of the University of the South and Its First Administration, 1857–1872.* Sewanee, TN, 1954.

Clark, Christopher. *The Roots of Rural Capitalism: Western Massachusetts, 1780–1860.* Ithaca, NY, 1990.

Cohen, Patricia C. *A Calculating People: The Spread of Numeracy in Early America.* Chicago, IL, 1982.

Coleman, J. Winston. *Slavery Times in Kentucky.* Chapel Hill, NC, 1940.

Collins, Winfield H. *The Domestic Slave Trade of the Southern States.* New York, 1904.

Coppinger, Margaret B., et al. *Beersheba Springs, 150 Years, 1833–1983: A History and a Celebration.* Beersheba Springs, TN, 1983.

Coughtry, Jay. *The Notorious Triangle: Rhode Island and the African Slave Trade, 1700–1807.* Philadelphia, 1981.

Crofts, Daniel W. *Reluctant Confederates: Upper South Unionists in the Secession Crisis.* Chapel Hill, NC, 1989.

Curran, Robert E. *The Bicentennial History of Georgetown University: From Academy to University, 1789–1889.* Vol. 1. Washington, DC, 1993.

David, Paul A., et al. *Reckoning with Slavery: A Critical Study in the Quantitative History of American Negro Slavery.* New York, 1976.

Davis, David B. *The Problem of Slavery in the Age of Revolution, 1770–1823.* Ithaca, NY, 1975.

Dennison, Sam. *Scandalize My Name: Black Imagery in American Popular Music.* New York, 1982.

Dew, Charles B. *Apostles of Disunion: Southern Secession Commissioners and the Causes of the Civil War.* Charlottesville, VA, 2001.

Dillon, Merton L. *The Abolitionists: The Growth of a Dissenting Minority.* DeKalb, IL, 1974.

——. *Benjamin Lundy and the Struggle for Negro Freedom.* Urbana, IL, 1966.

Du Bois, W. E. B. *The Suppression of the African Slave-Trade to the United States of America, 1638–1870.* New York, 1896.

Dumond, Dwight L. *Antislavery: The Crusade for Freedom in America.* Ann Arbor, MI, 1961.

Dupre, Daniel S. *Transforming the Cotton Frontier: Madison County, Alabama, 1800–1840.* Baton Rouge, LA, 1997.

Eaton, Clement. *The Growth of Southern Civilization, 1790–1860.* New York, 1961.

Egerton, Douglas R. *Charles Fenton Mercer and the Trial of National Conservatism.* Jackson, MS, 1989.

Elkins, Stanley M. *Slavery: A Problem in American Institutional and Intellectual Life.* 3d ed. Chicago, IL, 1976.

Essah, Patience. *A House Divided: Slavery and Emancipation in Delaware, 1638–1865.* Charlottesville, VA, 1996.

Fairbanks, George R. *History of the University of the South, at Sewanee, Tennessee.* Jacksonville, FL, 1905.

Fehrenbacher, Don E. *Prelude to Greatness: Lincoln in the 1850s.* Stanford, CA, 1962.

———. *The Slaveholding Republic: An Account of the United States Government's Relations to Slavery.* Ed. Ward M. McAfee. New York, 2001.

Fields, Barbara J. *Slavery and Freedom on the Middle Ground: Maryland during the Nineteenth Century.* New Haven, CT, 1985.

Fladeland, Betty. *James Gillespie Birney: Slaveholder to Abolitionist.* Ithaca, NY, 1955.

———. *Men and Brothers: Anglo-American Antislavery Cooperation.* Urbana, IL, 1972.

Flanders, Ralph B. *Plantation Slavery in Georgia.* Chapel Hill, NC, 1933.

Fogel, Robert W. *Without Consent or Contract: The Rise and Fall of American Slavery.* New York, 1989.

Fogel, Robert W., and Stanley L. Engerman. *Time on the Cross: The Economics of American Negro Slavery.* 2 vols. Boston, 1974.

Fogel, Robert W., Ralph A. Galantine, and Richard L. Manning, eds. *Without Consent or Contract: The Rise and Fall of American Slavery: Evidence and Methods.* New York, 1992.

Foner, Eric. *Free Soil, Free Labor, Free Men: The Ideology of the Republican Party before the Civil War.* New York, 1970.

———. *Reconstruction: America's Unfinished Revolution, 1863–1877.* New York, 1988.

Ford, Lacy K. *Origins of Southern Radicalism: The South Carolina Upcountry, 1800–1860.* New York, 1988.

Foster, Frances S. *Witnessing Slavery: The Development of Ante-bellum Slave Narratives.* Westport, CT, 1979.

Fox-Genovese, Elizabeth, and Eugene D. Genovese. *Fruits of Merchant Capital: Slavery and Bourgeois Property in the Rise and Expansion of Capitalism.* New York, 1983.

Franklin, John H., and Loren Schweninger. *Runaway Slaves: Rebels on the Plantation.* New York, 1999.

Freehling, Alison G. *Drift toward Dissolution: The Virginia Slavery Debate of 1831–1832.* Baton Rouge, LA, 1982.

Freehling, William W. *The Road to Disunion: Secessionists at Bay, 1776–1854.* New York, 1990.

Frey, Sylvia R. *Water from the Rock: Black Resistance in a Revolutionary Age.* Princeton, NJ, 1991.

Genovese, Eugene D. *The Political Economy of Slavery: Studies in the Economy and Society of the Slave South.* New York, 1965.

———. *Roll, Jordan, Roll: The World the Slaves Made.* New York, 1974.

———. *The World the Slaveholders Made: Two Essays in Interpretation.* New York, 1969.

Gienapp, William E. *The Origins of the Republican Party, 1852–1856.* New York, 1987.

Ginzberg, Lori D. *Women and the Work of Benevolence: Morality, Politics, and Class in the Nineteenth-Century United States.* New Haven, CT, 1990.

Goodman, Paul. *Of One Blood: Abolitionism and the Origins of Racial Equality.* Berkeley, CA, 1998.

Goodstein, Anita S. *Nashville, 1780–1860: From Frontier to City.* Gainesville, FL, 1989.

Gray, Lewis C. *History of Agriculture in the Southern United States to 1860.* Washington, DC, 1933.

Green, Constance M. *The Secret City: A History of Race Relations in the Nation's Capital.* Princeton, NJ, 1967.

Greene, Evarts B., and Virginia D. Harrington. *American Population before the Federal Census of 1790.* 1932; reprint, Gloucester, MA, 1966.

Gross, Ariela J. *Double Character: Slavery and Mastery in the Antebellum Southern Courtroom.* Princeton, NJ, 2000.

Gutman, Herbert G. *The Black Family in Slavery and Freedom, 1750–1925.* New York, 1976.

———. *Slavery and the Numbers Game: A Critique of "Time on the Cross."* Urbana, IL, 1975.

Hahn, Steven. *The Roots of Southern Populism: Yeoman Farmers and the Transformation of the Georgia Upcountry, 1850–1890.* New York, 1983.

Hahn, Steven, and Jonathan Prude, eds. *The Countryside in the Age of Capitalist Transformation: Essays in the Social History of Rural America.* Chapel Hill, NC, 1985.

Hamilton, Holman. *Prologue to Conflict: The Crisis and Compromise of 1850.* Lexington, KY, 1964.

Henretta, James A. *The Origins of American Capitalism: Collected Essays.* Boston, 1991.

Henry, Robert S. *"First with the Most" Forrest.* Indianapolis, IN, 1944.

Hodges, Graham R. *Root and Branch: African Americans in New York and East Jersey, 1613–1836.* Chapel Hill, NC, 1999.

Holt, Michael F. *The Political Crisis of the 1850s.* New York, 1978.

Horsman, Reginald. *Expansion and American Indian Policy, 1783–1812.* East Lansing, MI, 1967.

Hoxie, Frederick E., Ronald Hoffman, and Peter J. Albert, eds. *Native Americans and the Early Republic.* Charlottesville, VA, 1999.

Hurst, Jack. *Nathan Bedford Forrest: A Biography.* New York, 1993.

Hurt, R. Douglas. *Agriculture and Slavery in Missouri's Little Dixie.* Columbia, MO, 1992.

Inscoe, John C. *Mountain Masters, Slavery, and the Sectional Crisis in Western North Carolina.* Knoxville, TN, 1989.

James, D. Clayton. *Antebellum Natchez.* Baton Rouge, LA, 1968.

Jeffrey, Julie R. *The Great Silent Army of Abolitionism: Ordinary Women in the Antislavery Movement.* Chapel Hill, NC, 1998.

Johnson, Michael P., and James. L. Roark. *Black Masters: A Free Family of Color in the Old South.* New York, 1984.

Johnson, Walter. *Soul by Soul: Life inside the Antebellum Slave Market.* Cambridge, MA, 1999.

Jones, Norrece T. *Born a Child of Freedom, Yet a Slave: Mechanisms of Control and Strategies of Resistance in Antebellum South Carolina.* Hanover, NH, 1990.

Jordan, Winthrop D. *Tumult and Silence at Second Creek: An Inquiry into a Civil War Slave Conspiracy.* Baton Rouge, LA, 1993.

———. *White over Black: American Attitudes toward the Negro, 1550–1812.* Chapel Hill, NC, 1968.

Kilbourne, Richard H. *Debt, Investment, Slaves: Credit Relations in East Feliciana Parish, Louisiana, 1825–1885.* Tuscaloosa, AL, 1995.

King, Wilma. *Stolen Childhood: Slave Youth in Nineteenth-Century America.* Bloomington, IN, 1995.

Klein, Rachel N. *Unification of a Slave State: The Rise of the Planter Class in the South Carolina Backcountry, 1760–1808*. Chapel Hill, NC, 1990.

Koger, Larry. *Black Slaveowners: Free Black Masters in South Carolina, 1790–1860*. Columbia, SC, 1985.

Kolchin, Peter. *American Slavery, 1619–1877*. New York, 1993.

———. *Unfree Labor: American Slavery and Russian Serfdom*. Cambridge, MA, 1987.

Korn, Bertram W. *Jews and Negro Slavery in the Old South, 1789–1865*. Elkins Park, PA, 1961.

Kraditor, Aileen S. *Means and Ends in American Abolitionism: Garrison and His Critics on Strategy and Tactics, 1834–1850*. New York, 1969.

Kraut, Alan M., ed. *Crusaders and Compromisers: Essays on the Relationship of the Antislavery Struggle to the Antebellum Party System*. Westport, CT, 1983.

Kulikoff, Allan. *The Agrarian Origins of American Capitalism*. Charlottesville, VA, 1992.

———. *Tobacco and Slaves: The Development of Southern Cultures in the Chesapeake, 1680–1800*. Chapel Hill, NC, 1986.

Lerner, Gerda. *The Grimké Sisters from South Carolina: Rebels against Slavery*. Boston, 1967.

Levine, Lawrence E. *Black Culture and Black Consciousness: Afro-American Folk Thought from Slavery to Freedom*. New York, 1977.

Littlefield, Daniel C. *Rice and Slaves: Ethnicity and the Slave Trade in Colonial South Carolina*. Baton Rouge, LA, 1981.

Litwack, Leon F. *Been in the Storm So Long: The Aftermath of Slavery*. New York, 1979.

Lumpkin, Katharine D. *The Emancipation of Angelina Grimké*. Chapel Hill, NC, 1974.

Lutz, Alma. *Crusade for Freedom: Women of the Antislavery Movement*. Boston, 1968.

MacLeod, Duncan J. *Slavery, Race and the American Revolution*. London, 1974.

Malone, Ann P. *Sweet Chariot: Slave Family and Household Structure in Nineteenth-Century Louisiana*. Chapel Hill, NC, 1992.

Mayer, Henry. *All on Fire: William Lloyd Garrison and the Abolition of Slavery*. New York, 1998.

McColley, Robert. *Slavery and Jeffersonian Virginia*. 2d ed. Urbana, IL, 1973.

McCoy, Drew R. *The Last of the Fathers: James Madison and the Republican Legacy*. New York, 1989.

McCusker, John J. *How Much Is That in Real Money? A Historical Price Index for Use as a Deflator of Money Values in the Economy of the United States*. Worcester, MA, 1992.

McDougle, Ivan E. *Slavery in Kentucky, 1792–1865*. 1918; reprint, Westport, CT, 1970.

McFeely, William S. *Frederick Douglass*. New York, 1991.

McLaurin, Melton A. *Celia, a Slave*. Athens, GA, 1991.

McManus, Edgar J. *Black Bondage in the North*. Syracuse, NY, 1973.

McPherson, James M. *Battle Cry of Freedom: The Civil War Era*. New York, 1988.

Merk, Frederick. *Fruits of Propaganda in the Tyler Administration*. Cambridge, MA, 1971.

Merrill, Walter M. *Against Wind and Tide: A Biography of William Lloyd Garrison*. Cambridge, MA, 1963.

Miller, John C. *The Wolf by the Ears: Thomas Jefferson and Slavery*. New York, 1977.

Miller, William L. *Arguing about Slavery: The Great Battle in the United States Congress*. New York, 1996.

Mooney, Chase C. *Slavery in Tennessee*. Bloomington, IN, 1937.

Morgan, Philip D. *Slave Counterpoint: Black Culture in the Eighteenth-Century Chesapeake and Lowcountry*. Chapel Hill, NC, 1998.

Morris, Thomas D. *Southern Slavery and the Law, 1619–1860*. Chapel Hill, NC, 1996.

Morrison, Michael A. *Slavery and the American West: The Eclipse of Manifest Destiny and the Coming of the Civil War*. Chapel Hill, NC, 1997.

Morrison, Toni. *Beloved*. New York, 1987.

Moss, Elizabeth. *Domestic Novelists in the Old South: Defenders of Southern Culture*. Baton Rouge, LA, 1992.

Munford, Beverly B. *Virginia's Attitude toward Slavery and Secession*. New York, 1909.

Nash, Gary B., and Jean R. Soderlund. *Freedom by Degrees: Emancipation in Pennsylvania and Its Aftermath*. New York, 1991.

Oakes, James. *The Ruling Race: A History of American Slaveholders*. New York, 1982.

———. *Slavery and Freedom: An Interpretation of the Old South*. New York, 1990.

Owens, Leslie H. *This Species of Property: Slave Life and Culture in the Old South*. New York, 1976.

Parish, Peter J. *Slavery: History and Historians*. New York, 1989.

Pease, Jane H., and William H. Pease. *They Who Would Be Free: Blacks' Search for Freedom, 1830–1861*. New York, 1974.

Perry, Lewis. *Radical Abolitionism: Anarchy and the Government of God in Antislavery Thought*. Ithaca, NY, 1973.

Phillips, Christopher. *Freedom's Port: The African American Community of Baltimore, 1790–1860*. Urbana, IL, 1997.

Phillips, Ulrich B. *American Negro Slavery*. 1918; reprint, Baton Rouge, LA, 1966.

———. *Life and Labor in the Old South*. Boston, 1929.

———. *The Slave Economy of the Old South: Selected Essays in Economic and Social History*. Ed. Eugene D. Genovese. Baton Rouge, LA, 1968.

Prucha, Francis P. *American Indian Policy in the Formative Years, 1790–1834*. Cambridge, MA, 1962.

Quarles, Benjamin. *Black Abolitionists*. New York, 1969.

———. *The Negro in the American Revolution*. Chapel Hill, NC, 1961.

Raboteau, Albert J. *Slave Religion: The "Invisible Institution" in the Antebellum South*. New York, 1978.

Ransom, Roger L. *Conflict and Compromise: The Political Economy of Slavery, Emancipation, and the American Civil War*. New York, 1989.

Rawick, George P. *From Sundown to Sunup: The Making of the Black Community*. Westport, CT, 1972.

Reidy, Joseph P. *From Slavery to Agrarian Capitalism in the Cotton Plantation South: Central Georgia, 1800–1880*. Chapel Hill, NC, 1992.

Reinier, Jacqueline S. *From Virtue to Character: American Childhood, 1775–1850*. New York, 1996.

Robinson, Donald L. *Slavery in the Structure of American Politics, 1765–1820*. New York, 1971.

Rose, Willie L. *Slavery and Freedom*. Ed. William W. Freehling. New York, 1982.

Rothenberg, Winifred B. *From Market-Places to a Market Economy: The Transformation of Rural Massachusetts, 1750–1850*. Chicago, IL, 1992.

Ryan, Mary P. *Cradle of the Middle Class: The Family in Oneida County, New York, 1790–1865*. New York, 1981.

Schafer, Judith K. *Slavery, the Civil Law, and the Supreme Court of Louisiana*. Baton Rouge, LA, 1994.

Schwartz, Marie J. *Born in Bondage: Growing Up Enslaved in the Antebellum South*. Cambridge, MA, 2000.

Schwarz, Philip J. *Slave Laws in Virginia*. Athens, GA, 1996.

———. *Twice Condemned: Slaves and the Criminal Laws of Virginia, 1705–1865*. Baton Rouge, LA, 1988.

Schweninger, Loren. *Black Property Owners in the South, 1790–1915*. Urbana, IL, 1990.

Sellers, Charles. *The Market Revolution: Jacksonian America, 1815–1846*. New York, 1991.

Sellers, James B. *Slavery in Alabama*. University, AL, 1950.

Sewell, Richard H. *Ballots for Freedom: Antislavery Politics in the United States, 1837–1860*. New York, 1976.

Shade, William G. *Democratizing the Old Dominion: Virginia and the Second Party System, 1824–1861*. Charlottesville, VA, 1996.

Sheehan, Bernard W. *Seeds of Extinction: Jeffersonian Philanthropy and the American Indian*. New York, 1973.

Shenton, James P. *Robert John Walker: A Politician from Jackson to Lincoln*. New York, 1961.

Siegel, Frederick F. *The Roots of Southern Distinctiveness: Tobacco and Society in Danville, Virginia, 1780–1865*. Chapel Hill, NC, 1987.

Silber, Nina. *The Romance of Reunion: Northerners and the South, 1865–1900*. Chapel Hill, NC, 1993.

Sinha, Manisha. *The Counterrevolution of Slavery: Politics and Ideology in Antebellum South Carolina*. Chapel Hill, NC, 2000.

Smith, Daniel B. *Inside the Great House: Planter Family Life in Eighteenth-Century Chesapeake Society*. Ithaca, NY, 1980.

Smith, Julia F. *Slavery and Plantation Growth in Antebellum Florida, 1821–1860*. Gainesville, FL, 1973.

Soderlund, Jean R. *Quakers and Slavery: A Divided Spirit*. Princeton, NJ, 1985.

Sorin, Gerald. *Abolitionism: A New Perspective*. New York, 1972.

Stampp, Kenneth M. *The Peculiar Institution: Slavery in the Ante-Bellum South*. New York, 1956.

Starling, Marion W. *The Slave Narrative: Its Place in American History*. 2d ed. Washington, DC, 1988.

Stephenson, Wendell H. *Isaac Franklin: Slave Trader and Planter of the Old South*. Baton Rouge, LA, 1938.

Stevenson, Brenda E. *Life in Black and White: Family and Community in the Slave South*. New York, 1996.

Stewart, James B. *Holy Warriors: The Abolitionists and American Slavery*. Rev. ed. New York, 1997.

———. *Joshua R. Giddings and the Tactics of Radical Politics*. Cleveland, OH, 1970.

Stokes, Melvyn, and Stephen Conway, eds. *The Market Revolution in America: Social, Political, and Religious Expressions, 1800–1880*. Charlottesville, VA, 1996.

Sydnor, Charles S. *Slavery in Mississippi*. 1933; reprint, Baton Rouge, LA, 1966.

Tadman, Michael. *Speculators and Slaves: Masters, Traders, and Slaves in the Old South*. Madison, WI, 1989.

Takaki, Ronald T. *A Pro-Slavery Crusade: The Agitation to Reopen the African Slave Trade*. New York, 1971.

Taylor, George R. *The Transportation Revolution, 1815–1860*. New York, 1951.

Taylor, Joe G. *Negro Slavery in Louisiana*. Baton Rouge, LA, 1963.

Taylor, Orville W. *Negro Slavery in Arkansas*. Durham, NC, 1958.

Thomas, Benjamin P. *Theodore Weld: Crusader for Freedom*. New Brunswick, NJ, 1950.

Thomas, Emory M. *The Confederate Nation, 1861–1865*. New York, 1979.

Thomas, John L. *The Liberator, William Lloyd Garrison: A Biography*. Boston, 1963.

Trefousse, Hans L. *The Radical Republicans: Lincoln's Vanguard for Racial Justice*. New York, 1969.

Trexler, Harrison A. *Slavery in Missouri, 1804–1865*. Baltimore, MD, 1914.

Wade, Richard C. *Slavery in the Cities: The South 1820–1860*. New York, 1964.

Wahl, Jenny B. *The Bondsman's Burden: An Economic Analysis of the Common Law of Southern Slavery*. New York, 1998.

Wallace, Anthony F. C. *Jefferson and the Indians: The Tragic Fate of the First Americans*. Cambridge, MA, 1999.

Walters, Ronald G. *The Antislavery Appeal: American Abolitionism after 1830*. Baltimore, MD, 1976.

Watson, Harry L. *Liberty and Power: The Politics of Jacksonian America*. New York, 1990.

Wayne, Michael. *Death of an Overseer: Reopening a Murder Investigation from the Plantation South*. New York, 2001.

Webber, Thomas L. *Deep Like the Rivers: Education in the Slave Quarter Community, 1831–1865*. New York, 1978.

White, Deborah G. *Ar'n't I a Woman? Female Slaves in the Plantation South*. New York, 1985.

White, Richard. *The Middle Ground: Indians, Empires, and Republics in the Great Lakes Region, 1650–1815*. New York, 1991.

White, Shane. *Somewhat More Independent: The End of Slavery in New York City, 1770–1810*. Athens, GA, 1991.

Whitman, T. Stephen. *The Price of Freedom: Slavery and Manumission in Baltimore and Early National Maryland*. Lexington, KY, 1997.

Wiecek, William M. *The Sources of Antislavery Constitutionalism in America, 1760–1848*. Ithaca, NY, 1977.

Woodman, Harold D., ed. *Slavery and the Southern Economy: Sources and Readings*. New York, 1966.

Wright, Gavin. *The Political Economy of the Cotton South: Households, Markets, and Wealth in the Nineteenth Century*. New York, 1978.

Wyeth, John A. *That Devil Forrest: Life of General Nathan Bedford Forrest*. 1899; reprint, New York, 1959.

Yellin, Jean F. *Women and Sisters: The Antislavery Feminists in American Culture*. New Haven, CT, 1989.

Young, Jeffrey R. *Domesticating Slavery: The Master Class in Georgia and South Carolina, 1670–1837.* Chapel Hill, NC, 1999.

Zilversmit, Arthur. *The First Emancipation: The Abolition of Slavery in the North.* Chicago, IL, 1967.

Secondary Sources, Articles and Dissertations

Abbott, Richard H. "Yankee Farmers in Northern Virginia, 1840–1860." *Virginia Magazine of History and Biography* 76 (Jan. 1968): 56–63.

Appleby, Joyce. "Commercial Farming and the 'Agrarian Myth' in the Early Republic." *Journal of American History* 68 (Mar. 1982): 833–49.

Baptist, Edward E. "'Cuffy,' 'Fancy Maids,' and 'One-Eyed Men': Rape, Commodification, and the Domestic Slave Trade in the United States." *American Historical Review* 106 (Dec. 2001): 1619–50.

Barnett, Jim, and H. Clark Burkett. "The Forks of the Road Slave Market at Natchez." *Journal of Mississippi History* 63 (Fall 2001): 169–87.

Berger, Max. "American Slavery as Seen by British Visitors, 1836–1860." *Journal of Negro History* 30 (Apr. 1945): 181–202.

Berns, Walter. "The Constitution and the Migration of Slaves." *Yale Law Journal* 78 (Dec. 1968): 198–228.

Bernstein, Barton J. "Southern Politics and Attempts to Reopen the African Slave Trade." *Journal of Negro History* 51 (Jan. 1966): 16–35.

Brady, Patrick S. "The Slave Trade and Sectionalism in South Carolina, 1787–1808." *Journal of Southern History* 38 (Nov. 1972): 601–20.

Bushman, Richard L. "Markets and Composite Farms in Early America." *William and Mary Quarterly* 55 (July 1998): 351–74.

Calderhead, William. "How Extensive Was the Border State Slave Trade? A New Look." *Civil War History* 18 (Mar. 1972): 42–55.

———. "The Role of the Professional Slave Trader in a Slave Economy: Austin Woolfolk: A Case Study." *Civil War History* 23 (Sept. 1977): 195–211.

"Capitalism in the Early Republic." Special issue of *Journal of the Early Republic*, ed. Paul A. Gilje 16 (Summer 1996): 159–308.

Cassity, Michael J. "Slaves, Families, and 'Living Space': A Note on Evidence and Historical Context." *Southern Studies* 17 (Summer 1978): 209–15.

Chaplin, Joyce E. "Creating a Cotton South in Georgia and South Carolina, 1760–1815." *Journal of Southern History* 57 (May 1991): 171–200.

Clark, Elizabeth B. "'The Sacred Rights of the Weak': Pain, Sympathy, and the Culture of Individual Rights in Antebellum America." *Journal of American History* 82 (Sept. 1995): 463–93.

Cohen, William. "Thomas Jefferson and the Problem of Slavery." *Journal of American History* 56 (Dec. 1969): 503–26.

Conrad, Alfred H., and John R. Meyer. "The Economics of Slavery in the Ante Bellum South." *Journal of Political Economy* 66 (Apr. 1958): 95–130.

Crofts, Daniel W. "Late Antebellum Virginia Reconsidered." *Virginia Magazine of History and Biography* 107 (Summer 1999): 253–86.

Davis, David B. "American Slavery and the American Revolution." In *Slavery and Freedom in the Age of the American Revolution*, ed. Ira Berlin and Ronald Hoffman, 262–80. Charlottesville, VA, 1983.

Deyle, Steven. "'By farr the most profitable trade': Slave Trading in British Colonial North America." *Slavery and Abolition* 10 (Sept. 1989): 107–25.

Drago, Edmund, and Ralph Melnick. "The Old Slave Mart Museum, Charleston, South Carolina: Rediscovering the Past." *Civil War History* 27 (June 1981): 138–54.

Dunn, Richard S. "Black Society in the Chesapeake, 1776–1810." In *Slavery and Freedom in the Age of the American Revolution*, ed. Ira Berlin and Ronald Hoffman, 49–82. Charlottesville, VA, 1983.

Edwards, Gary T. "'Negroes . . . and All Other Animals': Slaves and Masters in Antebellum Madison County." *Tennessee Historical Quarterly* 57 (Spring–Summer 1998): 24–35.

Egerton, Douglas R. "Markets without a Market Revolution: Southern Planters and Capitalism." *Journal of the Early Republic* 16 (Summer 1996): 207–21.

Escott, Paul D. "Yeoman Independence and the Market: Social Status and Economic Development in Antebellum North Carolina." *North Carolina Historical Review* 66 (July 1989): 275–300.

Eslinger, Ellen. "The Shape of Slavery on the Kentucky Frontier, 1775–1800." *Register of the Kentucky Historical Society* 92 (Winter 1994): 1–23.

Evans, Robert. "Some Economic Aspects of the Domestic Slave Trade, 1830–1860." *Southern Economic Journal* 27 (Apr. 1961): 329–37.

Fede, Andrew. "Legal Protection for Slave Buyers in the U.S. South: A Caveat Concerning *Caveat Emptor*." *American Journal of Legal History* 31 (Oct. 1987): 322–58.

Feller, Daniel. "The Market Revolution Ate My Homework." *Reviews in American History* 25 (Sept. 1997): 408–15.

Finkelman, Paul. "Jefferson and Slavery: 'Treason against the Hopes of the World.'" In *Jeffersonian Legacies*, ed. Peter S. Onuf, 181–221. Charlottesville, VA, 1993.

———. "Slavery and the Constitutional Convention: Making a Covenant with Death." In *Beyond Confederation: Origins of the Constitution and American National Identity*, ed. Richard Beeman et al., 188–225. Chapel Hill, NC, 1987.

Fogel, Robert W., and Stanley L. Engerman. "Philanthropy at Bargain Prices: Notes on the Economics of Gradual Emancipation." *Journal of Legal Studies* 3 (June 1974): 377–401.

Ford, Lacy K. "Making the 'White Man's Country' White: Race, Slavery, and State-Building in the Jacksonian South." *Journal of the Early Republic* 19 (Winter 1999): 713–37.

———. "The Tale of Two Entrepreneurs in the Old South: John Springs III and Hiram Hutchison of the South Carolina Upcountry." *South Carolina Historical Magazine* 95 (July 1994): 198–224.

Frederickson, George M. "The Skeleton in the Closet." *New York Review of Books*. Nov. 2, 2000, 61–66.

Freehling, William W. "The Complex Career of Slaveholder Expansionism." In *The Reintegration of American History*, 158–75. New York, 1994.

Freudenberger, Herman, and Jonathan B. Pritchett. "The Domestic United States Slave Trade: New Evidence." *Journal of Interdisciplinary History* 21 (Winter 1991): 447–77.

Frey, Sylvia R. "Between Slavery and Freedom: Virginia Blacks in the American Revolution." *Journal of Southern History* 49 (Aug. 1983): 375–98.

Gallay, Alan. "The Origins of Slaveholders' Paternalism: George Whitefield, the Bryan Family, and the Great Awakening in the South." *Journal of Southern History* 53 (Aug. 1987): 369–94.

Goldfarb, Stephen J. "An Inquiry into the Politics of the Prohibition of the International Slave Trade." *Agricultural History* 68 (Spring 1994): 20–34.

Goldin, Claudia D. "The Economics of Emancipation." *Journal of Economic History* 33 (Mar. 1973): 66–85.

Goodstein, Anita S. "Black History on the Nashville Frontier, 1780–1810." *Tennessee Historical Quarterly* 38 (Winter 1979): 401–20.

Greenwald, Bruce C., and Robert R. Glasspiegel. "Adverse Selection in the Market for Slaves: New Orleans, 1830–1860." *Quarterly Journal of Economics* 98 (Aug. 1983): 479–99.

Gudmestad, Robert H. "A Troublesome Commerce: The Interstate Slave Trade, 1808–1840." Ph.D. diss., Louisiana State University, 1999.

Gunderson, Gerald. "The Origin of the American Civil War." *Journal of Economic History* 34 (Dec. 1974): 915–50.

Hadden, Sally. "Judging Slavery: Thomas Ruffin and *State v. Mann*." In *Local Matters: Race, Crime, and Justice in the Nineteenth-Century South*, ed. Christopher Waldrep and Donald G. Nieman, 1–28. Athens, GA, 2001.

Harrold, Stanley. "On the Borders of Slavery and Race: Charles T. Torrey and the Underground Railroad." *Journal of the Early Republic* 20 (Summer 2000): 273–92.

Harwood, Thomas F. "The Abolitionist Image of Louisiana and Mississippi." *Louisiana History* 7 (Fall 1966): 281–308.

Heisser, David C. R. "Bishop Lynch's People: Slaveholding by a South Carolina Prelate." *South Carolina Historical Magazine* 102 (July 2001): 238–62.

Henretta, James A. "The 'Market' in the Early Republic." *Journal of the Early Republic* 18 (Spring 1998): 289–304.

Hickin, Patricia. "John C. Underwood and the Antislavery Movement in Virginia, 1847–1860." *Virginia Magazine of History and Biography* 73 (Apr. 1965): 156–68.

Holt, Sharon A. "Symbol, Memory, and Service: Resistance and Family Formation in Nineteenth-Century African America." In *Working toward Freedom: Slave Society and Domestic Economy in the American South*, ed. Larry E. Hudson, 193–210. Rochester, NY, 1994.

Howell, Isabel. "John Armfield of Beersheba Springs." *Tennessee Historical Quarterly* 3 (Mar. and June 1944): 46–64, 156–67.

———. "John Armfield, Slave-Trader." *Tennessee Historical Quarterly* 2 (Mar. 1943): 3–29.

Hughes, Sarah S. "Slaves for Hire: The Allocation of Black Labor in Elizabeth City County, Virginia, 1782 to 1810." *William and Mary Quarterly* 35 (Apr. 1978): 260–86.

Huston, James L. "The Experiential Basis of the Northern Antislavery Impulse." *Journal of Southern History* 56 (Nov. 1990): 609–40.

———. "Property Rights in Slavery and the Coming of the Civil War." *Journal of Southern History* 65 (May 1999): 249–86.

Jacoby, Karl. "Slaves by Nature? Domestic Animals and Human Slaves." *Slavery and Abolition* 15 (Apr. 1994): 89–99.

Johnson, Michael P. "Looking for Lost Kin: Efforts to Reunite Freed Families after Emancipation." In *Southern Families at War: Loyalty and Conflict in the Civil War South*, ed. Catherine Clinton, 15–34. New York, 2000.

Jones, Howard. "The Peculiar Institution and National Honor: The Case of the *Creole* Slave Revolt." *Civil War History* 21 (Mar. 1975): 28–50.

Kaye, Anthony E. "Neighbourhoods and Solidarity in the Natchez District of Mississippi: Rethinking the Antebellum Slave Community." *Slavery and Abolition* 23 (Apr. 2002): 1–24.

Keim, C. Ray. "Primogeniture and Entail in Colonial Virginia." *William and Mary Quarterly* 25 (Oct. 1968): 545–86.

Kendall, John S. "Shadow over the City." *Louisiana Historical Quarterly* 22 (Jan. 1939): 142–65.

Kennicott, Patrick C. "Negro Antislavery Speakers in America." Ph.D. diss., Florida State University, 1967.

Klein, Herbert S. "Slaves and Shipping in Eighteenth-Century Virginia." *Journal of Interdisciplinary History* 5 (Winter 1975): 383–412.

Komlos, John, and Bjorn Alecke. "The Economics of Antebellum Slave Heights Reconsidered." *Journal of Interdisciplinary History* 26 (Winter 1996): 437–57.

Kotlikoff, Laurence J. "The Structure of Slave Prices in New Orleans, 1804 to 1862." *Economic Inquiry* 17 (Oct. 1979): 496–518.

Kulikoff, Allan. "Uprooted Peoples: Black Migrants in the Age of the American Revolution, 1790–1820." In *Slavery and Freedom in the Age of the American Revolution*, ed. Ira Berlin and Ronald Hoffman, 143–71. Charlottesville, VA, 1983.

Lightner, David L. "The Door to the Slave Bastille: The Abolitionist Assault upon the Interstate Slave Trade, 1833–1839." *Civil War History* 34 (Sept. 1988): 235–52.

———. "The Founders and the Interstate Slave Trade." *Journal of the Early Republic* 22 (Spring 2002): 25–51.

———. "The Interstate Slave Trade in Antislavery Politics." *Civil War History* 36 (June 1990): 119–36.

Lydon, James G. "New York and the Slave Trade, 1700 to 1774." *William and Mary Quarterly* 35 (Apr. 1978): 375–94.

Mason, Matthew E. "Slavery Overshadowed: Congress Debates Prohibiting the Atlantic Slave Trade to the United States, 1806–1807." *Journal of the Early Republic* 20 (Spring 2000): 59–81.

McGettigan, James W. "Boone County Slaves: Sales, Estate Divisions and Families, 1820–1865." *Missouri Historical Review* 72 (Jan. and Apr. 1978): 176–97, 271–95.

Merrell, James H. "Declarations of Independence: Indian-White Relations in the New Nation." In *The American Revolution: Its Character and Limits*, ed. Jack P. Greene, 197–223. New York, 1987.

Merrill, Michael. "Putting 'Capitalism' in Its Place: A Review of Recent Literature." *William and Mary Quarterly* 52 (Apr. 1995): 315–26.

Miller, William L. "A Note on the Importance of the Interstate Slave Trade of the Ante-Bellum South." *Journal of Political Economy* 73 (Apr. 1965): 181–87.

Morgan, Philip D. "Black Society in the Lowcountry, 1760–1810." In *Slavery and Freedom in the Age of the American Revolution*, ed. Ira Berlin and Ronald Hoffman, 83–141. Charlottesville, VA, 1983.

Morgan, Philip D., and Michael L. Nicholls. "Slaves in Piedmont Virginia, 1720–1790." *William and Mary Quarterly* 46 (Apr. 1989): 211–51.

Morris, Christopher. "The Articulation of Two Worlds: The Master-Slave Relationship Reconsidered." *Journal of American History* 85 (Dec. 1998): 982–1007.

Newman, Richard S. "Prelude to the Gag Rule: Southern Reaction to Antislavery Petitions in the First Federal Congress." *Journal of the Early Republic* 16 (Winter 1996): 571–99.

Painter, Nell. "Soul Murder and Slavery: Toward a Fully Loaded Cost Accounting." In *U.S. History as Women's History: New Feminist Essays*, ed. Linda K. Kerber, Alice Kessler-Harris, and Kathryn K. Sklar, 125–46. Chapel Hill, NC, 1995.

Pritchett, Jonathan B. "The Interregional Slave Trade and the Selection of Slaves for the New Orleans Market." *Journal of Interdisciplinary History* 28 (Summer 1997): 57–85.

———. "Quantitative Estimates of the United States Interregional Slave Trade, 1820–1860." *Journal of Economic History* 61 (June 2001): 467–75.

Pritchett, Jonathan B., and Richard M. Chamberlain. "Selection in the Market for Slaves: New Orleans, 1830–1860." *Quarterly Journal of Economics* 108 (May 1993): 461–73.

Pritchett, Jonathan B., and Herman Freudenberger. "A Peculiar Sample: The Selection of Slaves for the New Orleans Market." *Journal of Economic History* 52 (Mar. 1992): 109–27.

Ransom, Roger, and Richard Sutch. "Capitalists without Capital: The Burden of Slavery and the Impact of Emancipation." *Agricultural History* 62 (Fall 1988): 133–60.

Richards, Leonard L. "The Jacksonians and Slavery." In *Antislavery Reconsidered: New Perspectives on the Abolitionists*, ed. Lewis Perry and Michael Fellman, 99–118. Baton Rouge, LA, 1979.

Richardson, David. "The British Slave Trade to Colonial South Carolina." *Slavery and Abolition* 12 (Dec. 1991): 125–72.

Richter, William L. "Slavery in Baton Rouge, 1820–1860." *Louisiana History* 10 (Spring 1969): 125–45.

Roeckell, Lelia M. "Bonds over Bondage: British Opposition to the Annexation of Texas." *Journal of the Early Republic* 19 (Summer 1999): 257–78.

Rothstein, Morton. "The Antebellum South as a Dual Economy: A Tentative Hypothesis." *Agricultural History* 41 (Oct. 1967): 373–82.

Rozek, Barbara J. "Galveston Slavery." *Houston Review* 15, no. 2 (1993): 67–101.

Russell, Thomas D. "Sale Day in Antebellum South Carolina: Slavery, Law, Economy, and Court-Supervised Sales." Ph.D. diss., Stanford University, 1993.

Scanlon, James E. "A Sudden Conceit: Jefferson and the Louisiana Government Bill of 1804." *Louisiana History* 9 (Spring 1968): 139–62.

Schafer, Judith K. "The Immediate Impact of Nat Turner's Insurrection on New Orleans." *Louisiana History* 21 (Fall 1980): 361–76.

———. "New Orleans Slavery in 1850 as Seen in Advertisements." *Journal of Southern History* 47 (Feb. 1981): 33–56.

Schlotterbeck, John T. "Plantation and Farm: Social and Economic Change in Orange and Greene Counties, Virginia, 1716–1860." Ph.D. diss., Johns Hopkins University, 1980.

Shugerman, Jed H. "The Louisiana Purchase and South Carolina's Reopening of the Slave Trade in 1803." *Journal of the Early Republic* 22 (Summer 2002): 263–90.

Strickland, Arvarh E. "Aspects of Slavery in Missouri." *Missouri Historical Review* 55 (July 1971): 505–26.

Sutch, Richard. "The Breeding of Slaves for Sale and the Westward Expansion of Slavery, 1850–1860." In *Race and Slavery in the Western Hemisphere: Quantitative Studies*, ed. Stanley L. Engerman and Eugene D. Genovese, 173–210. Princeton, NJ, 1975.

Sweig, Donald M. "Reassessing the Human Dimension of the Interstate Slave Trade." *Prologue* 12 (Spring 1980): 5–21.

"A Symposium on Charles Sellers' *The Market Revolution: Jacksonian America, 1815–1846*." *Journal of the Early Republic* 12 (Winter 1992): 445–76.

Tadman, Michael. "The Demographic Cost of Sugar: Debates on Slave Societies and Natural Increase in the Americas." *American Historical Review* 105 (Dec. 2000): 1534–75.

———. "The Hidden History of Slave Trading in Antebellum South Carolina: John Springs III and Other 'Gentlemen Dealing in Slaves.'" *South Carolina Historical Magazine* 97 (Jan. 1996): 6–29.

Tansey, Richard. "Bernard Kendig and the New Orleans Slave Trade." *Louisiana History* 23 (Spring 1982): 159–78.

Wallenstein, Peter. "Flawed Keepers of the Flame: The Interpreters of George Mason." *Virginia Magazine of History and Biography* 102 (Apr. 1994): 229–60.

Watson, Harry L. "'The Common Rights of Mankind': Subsistence, Shad, and Commerce in the Early Republican South." *Journal of American History* 83 (June 1996): 13–43.

———. "Slavery and Development in a Dual Economy: The South and the Market Revolution." In *The Market Revolution in America: Social, Political, and Religious Expressions, 1800–1880*, ed. Melvyn Stokes and Stephen Conway, 43–73. Charlottesville, VA, 1996.

Wax, Darold D. "Black Immigrants: The Slave Trade in Colonial Maryland." *Maryland Historical Magazine* 73 (Mar. 1978): 30–45.

———. "Negro Imports into Pennsylvania, 1720–1766." *Pennsylvania History* 32 (July 1965): 254–87.

Weiman, David F. "Farmers and the Market in Antebellum America: A View from the Georgia Upcountry." *Journal of Economic History* 47 (Sept. 1987): 627–47.

Westbury, Susan. "Slaves of Colonial Virginia: Where They Came From." *William and Mary Quarterly* 42 (Apr. 1985): 228–37.

Wiggins, David K. "The Play of Slave Children in the Plantation Communities of the Old South, 1820–1860." *Journal of Sport History* 7 (Summer 1980): 21–39.

Williams, Jack K. "The Southern Movement to Reopen the African Slave Trade, 1854–1860: A Factor in Secession." *South Carolina Historical Association Proceedings* (1960): 23–31.

Wood, Betty. "Some Aspects of Female Resistance to Chattel Slavery in Low Country Georgia, 1763–1815." *Historical Journal* 30 (Sept. 1987): 603–22.

Woods, James M. "In the Eye of the Beholder: Slavery in the Travel Accounts of the Old South, 1790–1860." *Southern Studies* 1 (Spring 1990): 33–59.

Woolfolk, George R. "Taxes and Slavery in the Ante Bellum South." *Journal of Southern History* 26 (May 1960): 180–200.

INDEX

Italicized page numbers refer to illustrations and tables.

347

58

6

economy, northern, 8, 140–41, 175
economy, southern, 6–10, 41–46
  abolitionism and, 179, 192
  African slave trade and, 79
  importing of slaves into, 53–54
  interregional slave trade and, 283
  slave migration and, 283
  slave prices and, 55–60, 59, 63–65, 70–73, 306n31, 307–8nn43–47
  slave traders and, 139, 140, 324nn123,124
  westward expansion and, 66–67, 309nn7,8
  white South and, 224, 229
economy, Virginian, 40–41, 46–48
Edwards, A. F., 246
Elam, R. H., 130, 136
Eleventh Ward Freedman's Aid Society, 205, 335n84
Elkins, Stanley, 12–13, 284
Ellis, G. L., 164
Ellison, William, 246
Emancipation, 11, 240, 243, 276–79
emancipation of slaves, 8, 26, 29, 76–77, 85, 91–92, 179, 225
Emerson, Ralph Waldo, 152
Engerman, Stanley, 13, 285–86, 288–89, 292–93, 296, 346n7
entail, 35
entrepreneurs, 6, 96, 100, 104, 106, 140, 280
escape from slavery. See runaway slaves
estate sales
  abolitionism and, 188
  children of slaves and, 249
  interregional slave trade and, 287
  local slave trade and, 167–71, 328n64, 329nn72,74
  slave traders and, 118
  white South and, 212, 218, 241
evangelicalism, 224
Evans, Estwick, 38
Evans, Robert, 284, 346n5
Evening Post (New York), 309n7
executors, 127, 167, 171, 321n89
exemption laws, 76–78
exiled convicts, 50–51, 305n19
exporting of slaves, 44–55, 284, 306n22. See also interregional slave trade
  abolitionism and, 184, 201, 331n30
  African slave trade and, 79–80, 84
  as part of everyday life, 145–46, 148
  secession and, 61–62
  slave prices and, 56–60, 65, 73–76, 311n25

slave traders and, 95, 97–105, 118
  white South and, 224–25
Express (Petersburg, VA), 73
extended families, 270

factory owners, 214, 336n16
Fame (brig), 129
families
  of slave owners, 164–65, 188–89, 213–15, 218–19
  of slaves
    abolitionism and, 8, 176, 184, 186–90
    African-American resistance and, 249–52, 257, 261–64, 269–74, 344nn69,73
    African slave trade and, 83
    domestic slave trade and, 12–13
    Emancipation and, 277–78
    exporting of slaves and, 52–53, 306n24
    interstate slave trade and, 17, 37, 39
    local slave trade and, 159, 161, 164–65, 171
    selling of as part of everyday life, 148
    slave sales and, 10, 27, 32–35
    white South and, 211–12, 215–22, 232–36, 239–40, 244, 340n78
  of slave traders, 125–27, 279, 321n89
Farmers' Register, 48, 305n12
Featherstonhaugh, George, 146, 185
Federalist, 25
Federal Union (Milledgeville, GA), 72
female abolitionists, 189, 332n45. See also names of female abolitionists
Ferguson, Elias, 108
fictive kin, 270
field hands, 219–21
Fields, Barbara J., 330n6, 347n9
Fields, Obadiah, 109, 125–26
financiers, 97, 113, 118–19
Finney, Sterling, 107–9
Finney, Zachary, 111
First Congregational Negro Church (Lexington, KY), 277
Fitzhugh, George, 312n55
Flag of the Union (Jackson, MS), 149
flatboats, 107, 147, 255
flight. See runaway slaves
flogging, 252, 263, 266
Florida Purchase, 23, 67
Floridian and Journal (Tallahassee, FL), 72, 83, 149, 159